THE CLOSED BOOK

The Closed Book

HOW THE RABBIS TAUGHT THE JEWS
(NOT) TO READ THE BIBLE

REBECCA SCHARBACH
WOLLENBERG

PRINCETON UNIVERSITY PRESS
PRINCETON & OXFORD

Copyright © 2023 by Princeton University Press

Princeton University Press is committed to the protection of copyright and the intellectual property our authors entrust to us. Copyright promotes the progress and integrity of knowledge created by humans. By engaging with an authorized copy of this work, you are supporting creators and the global exchange of ideas. As it is protected by copyright, any intentions to reproduce, distribute any part of the work in any form for any purpose require permission; permission requests should be sent to permissions@press.princeton.edu. Ingestion of any PUP IP for any AI purposes is strictly prohibited.

Published by Princeton University Press
41 William Street, Princeton, New Jersey 08540
99 Banbury Road, Oxford OX2 6JX

press.princeton.edu

GPSR Authorized Representative: Easy Access System Europe - Mustamäe tee 50, 10621 Tallinn, Estonia, gpsr.requests@easproject.com

All Rights Reserved

First paperback printing, 2025
Paperback ISBN 9780691243313

The Library of Congress has cataloged the cloth edition of this book as follows:

Names: Wollenberg, Rebecca Scharbach, author.
Title: The closed book : how the Rabbis taught the Jews (not) to read the Bible / Rebecca Scharbach Wollenberg.
Description: Princeton : Princeton University Press, [2023] | Includes bibliographical references and index.
Identifiers: LCCN 2022022474 (print) | LCCN 2022022475 (ebook) | ISBN 9780691243290 (hardback) | ISBN 9780691243306 (ebook)
Subjects: LCSH: Bible. Old Testament—Criticism, interpretation, etc., Jewish—History. | Rabbinical literature—History and criticism. | Bible. Pentateuch—Hermeneutics. | Bible—Canon.
Classification: LCC BS1186 .W65 2023 (print) | LCC BS1186 (ebook) | DDC 221.6—dc23/eng/20220912
LC record available at https://lccn.loc.gov/2022022474
LC ebook record available at https://lccn.loc.gov/2022022475

British Library Cataloging-in-Publication Data is available

Editorial: Fred Appel & James Collier
Production Editorial: Ali Parrington
Jacket/Cover Design: Katie Osborne
Production: Erin Suydam
Publicity: Kate Hensley & Charlotte Coyne
Copyeditor: Aviva Arad

Jacket/Cover image: Torah by Republica / Pixabay

This book has been composed in Arno

For the twins

CONTENTS

Acknowledgments ix

Abbreviations and Citation Practices xi

Rabbinic Literature: Editions Cited xiii

Introductory Remarks: The People of the Book before the Book 1

1 A Makeshift Scripture: Tales of Biblical Loss, Reconstruction, and Forgery 26

2 A Book That Kills: Rabbinic Stories about Lethal Encounters with Biblical Text 59

3 A Neglected Text: Mistaken Readings, Bible Avoidance, and the Dangers of Reading as We Know It 98

4 A Spoken Scripture: Unlinking the Written from the Oral in Rabbinic Practices of Bible Reading 119

5 A Third Torah: Oral Torah, Written Torah, and the Embrace of a Spoken Scripture 163

6 A Closed Book: The Torah Scroll as the Body of Revelation 193

Concluding Remarks: From the Third Torah to God's Monograph 221

Index 247

ACKNOWLEDGMENTS

THIS WORK would not have been possible without the assistance of several institutions. The National Endowment for the Humanities supported the completion of this book with a year-long fellowship. The American Academy of Religion and Medieval Academy of America provided support for the final chapter of the monograph. The Society of Biblical Literature offered both a unique opportunity for feedback from senior scholars and financial support through their De Gruyter Prize, David Noel Freedman Award, and A. R. Pete Diamond Award.

This work likewise benefitted from generous mentorship that went well above and beyond the call of duty. James T. Robinson made his advice constantly available on early drafts of this work—reading multiple drafts right down to the footnotes with unceasing generosity. As did Wendy Doniger, who took the time to read manuscripts in some quite unlikely places in the course of her travels. The Michigan Society of Fellows offered years of advice and financial support. Deborah Dash Moore helped usher this monograph through each stage of the completion and publishing process.

I sometimes wonder if we do enough to acknowledge the ways editors and reviewers shape our texts behind the scenes. This book owes much to Katie Van Heest, Kathryn Medill, Daniel Rosenberg, and Adrianne Spunaugle, who each offered vital editorial input at different stages of this manuscript—as well as Fred Appel, whose early involvement and advice crucially reshaped the direction of the manuscript. This monograph also received its final shape, perhaps even more than usual, thanks to the very helpful feedback of several anonymous readers at the press.

Writing is a collaborative practice. And this book could not have been completed without the feedback and support of several writing groups. My earliest readers were the members of Wendy Doniger's evening "problems seminar." I would like to especially acknowledge those whose participation overlapped with mine for multiple years—including Drew Durdin, Sam Hopkins, Alex

Hsu, Anne Mocko, Chaz Preston, and Alex Rocklin—this manuscript is a very different one because of them. A huge thank you is owed to the accountability group that kept me writing through the pandemic—Isabel Cranz, Alice Mandell, Malka Simkovich, and Chontel Syfox—and to Daniel Picus, who served a similar role through our shared file folders and chats. My daily writing partners have likewise given more real-time feedback than I can possibly name: Devi Mays and Bryan Roby, who sat and wrote together in my office for hours on end, and our broader daily writing group, particularly those who saw this book through its pandemic completion, Hoda Bandeh-Ahmadi, Daniel Birchok, Melissa Burch, Jessie DeGrado, Kristi Fehervary, Alicia Ventresca Miller, Yasmin Moll, Melissa Phruksachart, Renee Ragin Randall, Swapnil Rai, Holly Singh, Scott Stonington, and Anoush Suni. Finally, I would like to thank the senior colleagues who continued to reach out to me to share my work with various working groups and who were so understanding when circumstances did not always permit—the thoughtful inclusivity of scholars like Gabriele Boccaccini, Marc Hirshman, Chris Keith, and Liv Ingeborg Lied make the field a better place.

This book was, of course, also reshaped by the extensive feedback of many colleagues. In very rough chronological order: Simi Chavel generously commented on the entire manuscript as it began the transition from dissertation to book. Jay Crisostomo, Dan Birchok, Aileen Das, Kevin Ko, Eva Mroczek, Seth Sanders, and Devorah Schoenfeld all offered vital advice on how to (re)frame the project in these earlier stages. Jeffrey Veidlinger and Sarah Stroumsa offered important restructuring suggestions for the emerging monograph, Maya Barzilai sagely suggested that I take out much of the early Christianity, and R. R. Neis proposed the phrase "third Torah," which came so close to becoming the title of this book. Marc Brettler, Eva Mroczek, Hindy Najman, Ellen Muehlberger, and the members of the Frankel Institute Jews and Materiality group convened by R. R. Neis all offered crucial feedback on chapter 1. Ellen Muehlberger generously took on extra reading work during the lockdown to help me solve a problem with chapter 2. David Lambert and the members of the Cultures of Reading in the Ancient Mediterranean World colloquium convened by Chris Keith and William Johnson offered feedback on the first half of chapter 4. Megan Nutzman generously consulted when I was stuck on chapter 6.

Finally, this book could not have been finished without the support of my extended family, who read far more than their fair share of this manuscript and without whose support completing this book as a single parent during the pandemic would have been impossible.

ABBREVIATIONS AND CITATION PRACTICES

TALMUDIC LITERATURE is referenced using the following prefixes appended to the full name of the tractate:

m Mishnah
t Tosefta
y Palestinian Talmud
b Babylonian Talmud

All other rabbinic literature is cited using the full name of the work. The standard Vilna pagination is used when referencing the Babylonian Talmud.

Manuscript variations for the Mishnah, Tosefta, Palestinian Talmud, and Babylonian Talmud are taken from the digital images provided by the Jewish National and University Library, David and Fela Shapell Family Digitization Project, and the Friedberg Jewish Manuscript Society Digization Project, especially the Friedberg Genizah Project and the Friedberg Talmud Bavli Variants Project.

All translations are my own.

RABBINIC LITERATURE: EDITIONS CITED

Mishnah, Tosefta, Talmud, and the Minor Tractates

The Six Orders of the Mishnah. Explicated by Chanoch Albeck and pointed by Chanoch Yalon. 7th edition. Jerusalem: Mosad Bialik; Tel Aviv: Dvir, 1988.

Tosefta, According to Codex Vienna, with Variants from Codices Erfurt, London, Genizah Mss. and Editio Princeps (Venice 1521), together with References to Parallel Passages in Talmudic Literature, and a Brief Commentary by Saul Lieberman. New York: Jewish Theological Seminary, 1962.[1]

Tosephta, Based on the Erfurt and Vienna Codices, with Parallels and Variants. Edited by M. S. Zuckermandel, with "Supplement to the Tosephta," by Rabbi Saul Lieberman. New edition. Jerusalem: Wahrmann Books, 1970.

Talmud Yerushalmi, According to Ms. Or. 4720 (Scal. 3) of the Leiden University Library, with Restorations and Corrections. Introduction by Yaacov Sussmann. Jerusalem: The Academy of the Hebrew Language, 2001.

Avoth de-Rabbi Nathan Solomon Schechter Edition, with References to Parallels in the Two Versions and to the Addenda in the Schechter Edition. Prolegomenon by Menahem Kister. New York: Jewish Theological Seminary, 1997.

Masekhet Soferim, venilevu ʿaleha midrash masekhet Soferim. Edited by Michael Higger. New York, 1937.

Halakhic Midrash

Mekhilta d'Rabbi Ishmael, cum Variis Lectionibus et Adnotationibus. Edited by H. S. Horovitz completing the work of I. A. Rabin. 2nd edition. Jerusalem: Wahrmann Books, 1970.

Mekhilta d'Rabbi Simʿon b. Jochai. Fragmenta in Geniza Cairensi Reperta Digessit Apparatus Critic, Notis. Preface by J. N. Epstein, completing the work of E. Z. Melamed. Jerusalem: Shaʿarei Rachamim Yeshiva/Beit Hillel Press, n.d.

Sifra de-ve Rav hu Sefer Torat Kohanim: kolel midreshe ha-Tanaʾim . . . le-sefer Va-yikra ʿim perush. Edited by Isaac Weiss. Vienna, 1862.

Siphre d'be Rav, Fasciculus Primus: Siphre ad Numeros adjecto Siphre Zutta. Edited by H .S. Horovitz. Jerusalem, 1966.

Sifre ʿal sefer Devarim: ʿim hilufe girsaʾot veheʿarot. Edited by Eliezer Aryeh Finkelstein. New York, 1969.

---

1. I have used this edition for all the tractates for which it is available.

Midrash Rabbah

Midrash Bereshit Rabba. Critical Edition with Notes and Commentary. Edited by J. Theodor and Ch. Albeck. Second printing with additional corrections by Ch. Albeck. Jerusalem: Wahrmann Books, 1965.

Midrash Wayyikra Rabbah. A Critical Edition based on Manuscripts and Genizah Fragments with Variants and Notes. By Mordecai Margulies. Jerusalem: Wahrmann Books, 1972.

Midrasch Echa Rabbati. Sammlung agadischer Auslegungen der Klagelieder. Herausgegeben nach einer Handschrift aus der Bibliothek zu Rom cod. J. I. 4, und einer Handschrift des British Museum cod. 27089. Kritisch bearbeitet, kommentiert und mit einer Einleitung versehen. Edited by Salomon Buber. Hildesheim: Georg Olms, 1967.

Shir HaShirim Rabbah. Sefer Midrash Rabah: Midrash Rabah ʿal hamishah humshe torah ve-hamesh megilot. Vilna: Romm, 1887.

Later Midrash

Pesiqta Rabbati: A Synoptic Edition of Pesiqta Rabbbati Based on All Extant Manuscripts and the Editio Princeps. Edited by Rivka Ulmer. Atlanta: Scholars Press, 1997.

Pesikta de-Rav Kahana ʿal pi ketav yad ʾOksford, ve-shinuay nushaʾot mi-kol kitve ha-yad ve-seride ha-genizah. Edited by Dov Mandelbaum. New York, 1962.

Midrash Tanhuma: ʿal hamishah humshe Torah ʾim shene beʾuirim. Edited by Enoch Zondel ben Joseph. Warsaw, 1902.

THE CLOSED BOOK

INTRODUCTORY REMARKS

The People of the Book
before the Book

IF THE FIELD OF biblical studies has a foundation myth, it is the story of the great divide that separates modern critical analysis of the biblical text from the uncritical reading practices of the premodern religious thinkers who embraced the Bible as "an utterly consistent, seamless, perfect book" in which God speaks directly to his readers.[1] Seldom has a scholarly construct so thoroughly captured the public imagination. In debates about the appropriate role of the Bible in contemporary social life, both sides have been quick to embrace the notion that the academy's scientific analysis is opposed to the premodern reading practices of religious practitioners, who engage with the Bible in the modes of past centuries. In embracing this historicized inflection of contemporary fault lines,[2] both parties walk away with valuable spoils of war. The academy is assigned the values of innovation, scientific achievement, and intellectual progress. In exchange, certain types of religious Bible readers lay claim to the weight of nearly two thousand years of religious history.

1. James L. Kugel, *How to Read the Bible: A Guide to Scripture, Then and Now* (New York: Simon & Schuster, 2007), 15. For a recent review of scholarship on this issue, see Duncan MacCrae, *Legible Religion: Books, God, and Rituals in Roman Culture* (Cambridge: Harvard University Press, 2016), 143–47.

2. For more on the construction of these intellectual positions in early modernity, see Michael Legaspi, *The Death of Scripture and the Rise of Biblical Studies*, OSHT (Oxford: Oxford University Press, 2010), and the literature cited there. On the rise of similar patterns in Jewish communities, see Yaakov Elman, "The Rebirth of Omnisignificant Biblical Exegesis in the Nineteenth and Twentieth Centuries," *Jewish Studies Internet Journal* 2, no. 1 (2002): 1–42.

The early rabbinic relationship[3] with the Bible is often treated as the exemplar par excellence of this faithful reading practice. Yet an expansive survey of classical rabbinic traditions concerning biblical writings compels us to grapple with a much more complex picture of the premodern relationship to the Bible. While the late antique rabbinic authorities theoretically established the newly canonized Hebrew Bible as a central pillar of an emerging rabbinic Judaism, many early rabbinic statements about the nature of the biblical text and its status were ambivalent at best.

As we will see in the coming pages, many early rabbinic traditions did not valorize the Pentateuch as a perfect record of the divine will. Instead, they imagined the biblical text as a makeshift scripture—an echo of greater truths that had been cut off from the divine to be ravaged by history and repeatedly reconstructed by devoted human hands. In many early rabbinic traditions, indeed, the biblical text is identified not only as a dead form of sacred revelation pruned from an inexhaustible living branch of divine truth but also as a potentially deadly form of revelation. Drawing on the allegorical power of early rabbinic anxieties about the spiritual dangers posed by an uncontrolled female body, which was thought to carry immense power over men within a weakened vessel vulnerable to promiscuity and misdirection, classical rabbinic narratives often expressed concern about the tremendous supernatural power that written scripture contains within a limited material and linguistic vessel, which could be all too easily appropriated, misinterpreted, and corrupted.

---

3. I will use the designation "early rabbinic" and "classical rabbinic" interchangeably in this book to refer to the products of rabbinic Jewish culture from the period between roughly 200 CE and 650 CE. As such, this book cites materials gathered from all six major corpuses of late antique rabbinic literature: (1) the Mishnah, (2) the Tosefta, (3) early Palestinian "legal" midrash, (4) the Palestinian Talmud, (5) the early collections of "homiletic" midrash, (6) the Babylonian Talmud, as well as (7) later Palestinian midrash. Although it has become increasingly uncommon to analyze phenomena across the entire classical rabbinic period, basic practices of reading (particularly those associated with elementary education) are cultural phenomena that have proven slow to change over time and are often studied from a more longue durée perspective. (For a classic study along these lines, see Cavallo Guglielmo and Chartier Roger, *Histoire de la lecture dans le monde occidental* (Paris: Editions du Seuil, 1997). While I make no claim that early rabbinic practices of Bible reading remained unchanged over the entire course of late antiquity, the broad-strokes argument of this book proceeds on the premise that the classical rabbinic authorities cited here shared certain basic cultural assumptions concerning the nature of written text and its affordances that can be contrasted with the attitudes and practices of other periods.

Nor were these facets of the rabbinic imaginary purely theoretical. In a sacred reading culture[4] in which careful attention to written text was exoticized and even denigrated, liturgical performance of biblical lectionaries might continue unabated but direct informational reading of the biblical text was limited to the point where written scripture was effectively quarantined from communal life and the Hebrew Bible would largely cease to speak as a communicative document.

This does not mean, however, that the classical rabbinic authorities were forerunners of modern higher criticism—nor that the biblical tradition would be eliminated from early rabbinic religious life. Instead, we will explore how it came to be that communal authorities so deeply ambivalent about the biblical text nevertheless established the emerging canon of the Hebrew Bible as a fundamental pillar of late antique Jewish life and thought.

Early rabbinic doubts concerning biblical textuality did not destabilize the emergent rabbinic movement as a biblical religion in part because the recitation-heavy communal reading culture that had grown up around scripture in early rabbinic circles had already rendered the written text a secondary, even superfluous, witness to the biblical revelation in communal thought and practice. As memorized vocal iterations of the biblical tradition circulated independently from the written text in daily practice, this spoken tradition of the biblical revelation had become not only the dominant form of scripture in rabbinic quotidian life but would also come to have a profound impact on how many early rabbinic practitioners imagined the biblical heritage in more abstract terms. Indeed, these memorized spoken formulas of the biblical tradition came to be embraced in many early rabbinic circles as a pivotal third category of Torah, a living Spoken Scripture that linked the silent Written Torah of the parchment scrolls to the growing Oral Torah of the rabbinic legal tradition.

As these recited formulas of the scriptural tradition were increasingly embraced as the authentic soul of the biblical revelation, the written text could retreat into a less threatening role as a communicatively inert parchment

---

4. I take this concept from William A. Johnson, *Readers and Reading Cultures in the High Roman Empire: A Study of Elite Communities* (Oxford: Oxford University Press, 2010), as will be discussed in more depth in the ensuing pages. Readers in religious studies will likely be more familiar with David Brakke's (in many ways analogous) concept of varied communal "scriptural practices." David Brakke, "Scriptural Practices in Early Christianity: Towards a New History of the New Testament Canon," in *Early Christianity in the Context of Antiquity*, ed. David Brakke, Anders-Christian Jacobsen, and Joerg Ulrich (Bern: Peter Lang, 2012), 263–80.

vessel. This textual body, like its human counterpart, wielded sacred power most potently when it remained closed and covered so that its messy material and textual components were obscured and the physical vessel could become a dignified (and silent) conduit for a more intangible and otherworldly power.

This book thus demonstrates that even in the early days of the first millennium, when the Hebrew Bible was emerging as a distinct canon, biblical religion did not always work in the way that we have traditionally imagined it. Far from embracing this new textual transcript as a perfect blueprint for the religious life, many classical rabbinic inheritors of this sacred anthology were ambivalent about the very notion that knowledge of the divine will might ever be directly extracted from written text. These early rabbinic authorities thus constructed a scriptural universe[5] in which the written text of the Hebrew Bible was increasingly hemmed in with ritual honorifics that enhanced the normative power of the *idea* of a singular Sinaitic revelation that adhered to this written object while they simultaneously quarantined and silenced the biblical text as a written communication in practice.

In this system, the emerging textual canon came to function less as a written guide to God's will than as a ritual conduit for a very different iteration of the biblical tradition—a series of intangible spoken formulas of the scriptural tradition that would be embraced as the living soul to this fixed parchment body. For when these early rabbinic thinkers transferred the glamour of the new biblical canon to these recited biblical formulas passed from parent to child and teacher to student in different modes, the rabbinic Bible came to reside for all intents and purposes in spoken words. And while this Spoken Scripture would be ritually correlated to the biblical scrolls in occasional liturgical performances, it lived a qualitatively different kind of literary life—circulating primarily as decontextualized excerpts embedded in rabbinic teachings, conversation, and liturgy. The late antique traditions explored in this book thus thrived on a mélange of principles that modern thought treats as opposing categories: combining textual criticism of the biblical tradition with ritual perfectionism concerning material copies of the biblical text and uniting avoidance of the biblical text as a source of information with a communal culture thoroughly infused with biblical iterations in a different mode. The model of classical rabbinic biblicism explored in this book thus upends foundational categorizations concerning Bible reading that have structured so much popular thought about biblical religion.

---

5. I take this concept from Guy G. Stroumsa, *The Scriptural University of Ancient Christianity* (Cambridge, MA: Harvard University Press, 2016).

Detailed Discussion for the Specialist

This new portrait of a more complex early rabbinic scriptural universe may disrupt existing scholarly models of what the early rabbinic relationship with the Bible looked like, but, in doing so, it brings the classical rabbinic relationship with scripture into line with broader research trends that have emerged in the fields of biblical studies, comparative religion, and classics in the past twenty years. Building on early scholars such as Susan Niditch, who deconstructed the notion of a "great divide" between periods of orality and textuality in the development of the biblical tradition,[6] experts in Hebrew Bible such as David Carr, Bernard Levinson, and Raymond Person have made great strides in convincing the field of biblical studies that the texts found in the Hebrew Bible emerged in a reading culture distant from contemporary paradigms of "writing, book circulation, and silent reading." Biblical texts were generated instead in an environment characterized by a more complex interface "between writing, performance, memorization, and the aural dimension of literary texts."[7] In this complex literary ecology, a prophetic text was not conceptualized as a complete literary work represented by one authentic original but instead each version of a biblical text was "understood by the ancients as *one* instantiation of a traditional (oral and/or written) text."[8] Since a skilled scribe was "both thinker and religious visionary" in this system, "revelation is not prior to or external to the text" but rather each text produced was envisioned as an authentic reverberation of revelation.[9]

There has been a tendency among Hebrew Bible scholars to see this complex literary ecology dissolving with the emergence of the proto-Masoretic text into a more clear-cut culture of text and exegesis. But scholars of Second Temple Judaism such as Eva Mroczek, Hindy Najman, Judith Newman, and Molly Zahn have demonstrated that one still cannot "retroject notions of a fixed, stable text" onto sacred writing in the Second Temple period, when

6. Susan Niditch, *Oral and Written Word: Ancient Israelite Literature* (Louisville, KY: Westminster John Knox, 1996), 78.

7. David M. Carr, *The Formation of the Hebrew Bible: A New Construction* (Oxford: Oxford University Press, 2011), 5.

8. Raymond F. Person Jr., "Self-Referential Phrases in Deuteronomy: A Reassessment Based on Recent Studies concerning Scribal Performance and Memory," in *Collective Memory and Collective Identity: Deuteronomy and the Deuteronomistic History in Their Context*, ed. Johannes Unsok Ro and Diana Edelman (Berlin: de Gruyter, 2021), 219.

9. Bernard Levinson, *Legal Revision and Religious Renewal in Ancient Israel* (Cambridge: Cambridge University Press, 2008), 89.

written text remained in some sense "secondary to the oral transmission of these discourses as part of a larger and living tradition in the process of continuous renewal," so that considerable *mouvance* is still evident in the varied written forms of the biblical tradition from this period.[10] For sacred writing continued to be imagined as the product of an ongoing divine revelation only "partially instantiated in concrete scribal projects."[11] Thus, reworking an earlier text means updating "the content of that text in a way that one claims to be an authentic expression of the law already accepted as authoritatively Mosaic."[12] So long as any given copy of a text represented "only an incomplete (and potentially inaccurate) extract of the sum total of divine knowledge," scribes could envision the work of rewriting "as bringing the tradition more fully into conformity with the divine exemplar, or as reformulating or expanding it to include more of the divine knowledge believed to be accessible to humans"— so that they were "continuing to unfold a practically inexhaustible store of divine wisdom."[13]

This more open and participatory model of written revelation is generally imagined by all parties to have come to an end with the early rabbinic "embodiment of revelation in a limited written text, the Bible, once revealed to inspired prophets, but now completed and given into the hands of the sages."[14] Within the fields of Jewish studies and religious studies more broadly, the idea that the rise of rabbinic Judaism marks the natural end of previous scriptural models is intimately tied to the sense that 70 CE marks an evolutionary watershed in Jewish history. As Jonas Leipziger recently pointed out, our understandings of late antique Jewish reading practices are still inflected by a widely accepted narrative that "the 'old' sacrificial cult of the temple was substituted after 70

10. Judith H. Newman, *Before the Bible: The Liturgical Body and the Formation of Scriptures in Judaism* (Oxford: Oxford University Press, 2018), 5. For more on the development of the concept of textual fluidity borrowed from medieval studies in relation to New Philology, scribal versionism, and other related schools, see Liv Ingeborg Lied and Hugo Lundhaug, "Studying Snapshots: On Manuscript Culture, Textual Fluidity, and New Philology," in *Snapshots of Evolving Traditions: Jewish and Christian Manuscript Culture, Textual Fluidity, and New Philology*, ed. Liv Ingeborg Lied and Hugo Lundhaug (Berlin: de Gruyter, 2017), 1–19.

11. Eva Mroczek, *The Literary Imagination in Jewish Antiquity* (Oxford: Oxford University Press, 2016), 188.

12. Hindy Najman, *Seconding Sinai: The Development of Mosaic Discourse in Second Temple Judaism* (Leiden: Brill, 2003), 13.

13. Molly M. Zahn, *Genres of Rewriting in Second Temple Judaism: Scribal Composition and Transmission* (Cambridge: Cambridge University Press, 2020), 221.

14. Mroczek, *Literary Imagination*, 185.

CE by a 'literary cult' with the rabbinic emphasis on prayer and especially studying and reading Hebrew Scripture."[15] In recent years, of course, this model has been heavily nuanced by scholars such as Konrad Schmid, who argues that the "cult replacing functions of scripture and canon" did not take place in a single moment in 70 CE but instead represented a gradual sublimation taking place over the course of many centuries,[16] and Guy Stroumsa, who has framed the rabbinic turn to text as part of a broader Mediterranean movement from sacrifice to sacred textuality.[17] Yet we may need to further denaturalize the conceptual link that has been implicitly established between the fall of the cult and the rise of a particular attitude toward canonical reading.

Nor should the rising tide of scripturalism in this period be taken as the necessary death knoll of older attitudes toward revelation and authority. As Hindy Najman has observed, "within a family of approaches to the question of authorization, there could be both continuity and variation" so that more open Second Temple revelatory modes continued to thrive in communities such as Hellenistic Jewish Alexandria well into the new millennium.[18] Anne Kreps has similarly documented the ways in which late antique gnostic works such as the Gospel of Truth "endorsed a mode of open authority, recognizing ongoing oral and written revelation, instead of a closed canon of sacred books."[19] New Testament researchers such as Matthew Larsen and Yael Fisch have likewise argued that "discourses on textuality fluidity and growth" continued alongside the process of gospel textualization and proliferation[20] in ongoing oral metaprocesses of "intertextualization, decontextualization, and recontextualization."[21] If such echoes of Second Temple revelatory tropes did

---

15. Jonas Leipziger, "Ancient Jewish Greek Practices of Reading and Their Material Aspects," in *Material Aspects of Reading in Ancient and Medieval Cultures: Materiality, Prescence and Performance*, ed. Anna Krauss, Jonas Leipziger, and Friederike Schuecking-Jungblut (Berlin: de Gruyter, 2020), 149.

16. Konrad Schmid, "The Canon and the Cult: The Emergence of Book Religion in Ancient Israel and the Gradual Sublimation of the Temple Cult," *Journal of Biblical Literature* 131, no. 2 (2012): 304.

17. Guy G. Stroumsa, *La fin du sacrifice: Mutations religieuses de l'antiquité tardive* (Paris: Odile Jacob, 2005).

18. Najman, *Seconding Sinai*, 109.

19. Anne Kreps, *The Crucified Book: Sacred Writing in the Age of Valentinus* (Philadelphia: University of Pennsylvania Press: 2022), 2.

20. Matthew Larsen, *Gospels Before the Book* (Oxford: Oxford University Press: 2018), 5.

21. Yael Fisch, "The Origins of the Oral Torah: A New Pauline Perspective," *Journal for the Study of Judaism* 51, no. 1 (2020): 57.

indeed continue to permeate other Jewish and Jewish-adjacent corners of the changing scriptural landscape of late antiquity, then the claim that early rabbinic thinkers valorized a closed and all-containing written canon stands out against the streams of cognate religious movements of the era.

More importantly, perhaps, our understanding of how written canon functioned within the reading cultures of the Hellenistic and Roman Mediterranean more broadly has changed radically in recent years. As recently as the groundbreaking multi-author volume *Homer and the Bible in the Eyes of Ancient Interpreters*, one might still say that late antique Jewish readers of the Bible and Greco-Roman readers of Homer shared a common scholarly language of reading that "clearly distinguished between the canonical text and their own interpretation or commentary, taking seriously the author's intention and thus the literal meaning of the text."[22] While there is no question that many biblical reading cultures of the era would adapt scholarly apparatus and techne innovated by Greek- and Roman-speaking grammarians and rhetors,[23] even as the aforementioned volume was being published, changes were already afoot in the scholarly world that would subtly upend fundamental facets of this academic vision of how the relationship between canonical text and reader was conceived and practiced in the late antique Mediterranean milieu.

Drawing connections with biblical scholarship cited above, for instance, classicist Jonathan Ready has argued that the Homeric wild papyri represent a scribal ethos not unlike that attributed to biblical scribes, in which each "scribe produces a text that cleaves to his vision of what the traditional text should be . . . informed both by the text in front of him and by his previous encounters with written and oral texts."[24] This tendency toward textual *mouvance*, Ready thus demonstrates, had certainly not disappeared by the Ptolemaic period, even as the Homeric tradition was increasingly embraced as something approaching a canonical work.

Even as the formulas of the textual tradition congealed, scholars have demonstrated that late antique Mediterranean modes of reading these texts continued to generate other forms of wildness and multiplicity. C. M. Chin has

22. Maren R. Niehoff, "Why Compare Homer's Readers to Biblical Readers?," in *Homer and the Bible in the Eyes of Ancient Interpreters*, ed. Maren Niehoff (Leiden: Brill, 2012), 4.

23. See, for instance, Francesca Schironi, "Eusebius' *Gospel* Questions and Aristarchus on Homer—Similar Strategies to Save Different 'Sacred' Texts," in *The Rise of the Early Christian Intellectual*, ed. Lewis Ayres and H. Clifton Ward (Berlin: de Gruyter: 2020), 193–226.

24. Jonathan L. Ready, *Orality, Textuality, and the Homeric Epics: An Interdisciplinary Study of Oral Texts, Dictated Texts, and Wild Texts* (Oxford: Oxford University Press, 2020), 279.

pointed out, for instance, the ways in which the expansive late antique discipline of grammar rendered texts "susceptible to linguistic expansion via translation, transliteration, and etymologizing"[25] so that "Augustine's scripture is not strictly coterminous with the biblical canon"[26] and "intertexts from Virgil and Greek myth transforms the concrete Latin Heptateuch into a point of entry for a larger textual universe."[27] As Blossom Stefaniw portrays late antique Christian Bible reading: "The substructure is found in the Bible, and the object of study is the knowledge of the world inherited through it, an object tacitly elided with the world itself."[28] In such a context, the rise of fixed canon cannot be imagined to usher in an era of faithful reading so much as a period of intellectual exploration rooted in the expansive embrace of a canonical text. Thus, even if we imagine early rabbinic thinkers more as Roman provincials than as the inheritors of Second Temple Judaism, it remains difficult to maintain a historically informed vision of rabbinic reading in which a reader would approach the text of the Hebrew Bible as a closed and complete transcript of a divine monologue.

Nor did this state of affairs change radically after closed and canonized scriptural texts had become a mainstay of many religious communities across the globe. Religious studies scholars have increasingly come to understand typical modes of engaging with written scriptures across diverse communities in ways that are subtly at odds with the valorization of sacred informational reading that is ascribed to classical rabbinic authorities. While some historical reading cultures have certainly approached written scripture in scholastic modes similar to those that are ascribed to early rabbinic thinkers, many more have not. In the past thirty years, religious studies scholars have documented a widespread tendency across diverse communities to eschew the potential of written scriptures as communicative documents in their own right in favor of a bifurcation in which the social life of scriptures is lived out, on the one hand, as sounded, recited formulas and performances that function in many ways quite independently of the written text and, on the other hand, in literally or metaphorically closed texts qua cultic objects that serve as silent referents to the capacity of scripture as a conduit of sacred power.

25. C. M. Chin, *Grammar and Christianity in the Late Roman World* (Philadelphia: University of Pennsylvania Press, 2013), 74.

26. Ibid., 17.

27. Ibid., 107.

28. Blossom Stefaniw, *Christian Reading: Language, Ethics, and the Order of Things* (Berkeley: University of California Press, 2019), 215.

Since William Graham first gathered examples of oralized[29] scripture from a wide swath of global religious communities in *Beyond the Written Word*, researchers have analyzed the practical prominence of spoken scripture in virtually every type of religious community—from late antique Christians[30] and medieval Buddhists[31] to modern Korean *musogin*[32] and contemporary Christian communities.[33]

The function of oralized scriptures has sparked something approaching a subfield of its own, however, particularly in Qur'anic studies and in research on scriptural performance cultures in South Asia. Studies of variant traditions of the Ramayana, *katha* retellings of the Puranas and other sacred traditions from South Asia have copiously documented the ways in which these performed scriptural traditions do not capture folk orality in the imagined purity of a great divide narrative but emerge in creative spaces (much like the late antique parallels described above) in which oral performance and manuscript material have remained subtly, and apparently permanently, imbricated.[34] As McComas Taylor has described this dynamic in his ethnographic study of how Sanskrit verses are used in oral performance during Bhagavata Purana recita-

29. By which I mean to evoke not only scriptures that are preserved primarily in oral form but also "the specifically oral dimension of the written scriptural text"—that is, "the important, often primary, ways in which scripture has been a significantly vocal as well as visual fact: how individuals and groups have understood and dealt with their sacred scriptures not only as holy books to be calligraphed and illuminated, preserved and revered, paraded and displayed, but also as texts to be memorized, sung and chanted, read aloud, recited, retold and woven into the texture of their language, thought, and being as auditory facts." William Graham, *Beyond the Written Word: Oral Aspects of Scripture in the History of Religion* (Cambridge: Cambridge University Press, 1993), 7.

30. Carol Harrison, *The Art of Listening in the Early Church* (Oxford: Oxford University Press, 2013).

31. David Drewes, "Revisiting the Phrase 'sa pṛthivīpradeśaś caityabhūto bhavet' and the Mahāyāna Cult of the Book," *Indo-Iran Journal* 50, no. 2 (2007): 101–43.

32. Yohan Yoo, "Performing Scriptures: Ritualizing Written Texts in Seolwi-Seolgyeong, the Korean Shamanistic Recitation of Scriptures," *Postscripts* 10, no. 1–2 (2019): 9–25.

33. Brian Malley, *How the Bible Works: An Anthropological Study of Evangelical Biblicism* (Lanham, MD: AltaMira, 2004); *The Social Life of Scripture: Cross-Cultural Perspectives on Biblicism*, ed. James Bielo (Piscataway, NJ: Rutgers University Press, 2009); and Matthew Engelke, *A Problem of Presence: Beyond Scripture in an African Church* (Berkeley: University of California Press, 2007).

34. For a selection of now-classic work on this topic see Joyce Burkhalter Flueckiger and Laurie J. Sears, eds., *Boundaries of the Text: Epic Performances in South and Southeast Asia* (Ann Arbor: University of Michigan Press, 1991) and the works cited there.

tions, verses are *entextualized* "in the sense that the exponent draws on the authority of the Bhagavatapurana in the use of verses extracted from the text" while they are simultaneously *contextualized* "in the sense that the exponent adjusts or adapts his spoken discourse to a particular audience in a particular time and place."[35] Such bidirectionality is possible Ilona Wilczewska argues, because "internalizing the scripture can go to such a level that the text is not only memorized, but its language, themes, and images come to permeate the mental processes in various ways"[36] with the aim that "a qualified *katha* speaker is able to tell a story with passion and extract a moral from the story in a way that is applicable to anyone in the audience."[37] In studies of South Asian spoken scripture, we thus encounter a rich body of documentation on the ways in which spoken scripture continues to live out subtly different "textual lives" alongside written transcripts of those same tradition.

Research on Qur'anic recitation has brought a yet more subtle lesson to the table, demonstrating the ways in which even a spoken scripture that represents a word-for-word match for a written transcript may still take on a qualitatively different social life of its own in sounded and embodied circulation. Drawing on classic work, including Kristina Nelson's *The Art of Reciting the Qur'an* and Navid Kermani's *Gott ist schön*, researchers such as Anna M. Gade have revealed the ways in which even textually fixed recitation traditions may convey diverse "affective norms of beauty (including the use of melody), improvisation, and feeling"[38] while Michael Frishkopf has pointed to the ways in which these "sonic contrasts" between different styles of Qur'anic recitation "directly support theological interpretations."[39] Scholars such as Lauren Osborne, moreover, draw our attention to the ways in which recitation performances are contextually situated and multidimensional, so that these aural experiences of scripture include "the listener and listening cultures, rather than focusing

---

35. McComas Taylor, *Seven Days of Nectar: Contemporary Oral Performance of the Bhagavatapurana* (Oxford: Oxford University Press, 2016), 127 and 129.

36. Ilona Wilczewska, "'Live with the Text and Listen to Its Words': Bhagavata Recitation in Changing Times," in *The Bhāgavata Purāna: Sacred Text and Living Tradition*, ed. Ravi Gupta and Kenneth Valpey (New York: Columbia University Press, 2013), 214.

37. Ibid., 212.

38. Anna M. Gade, *Perfection Makes Practice: Learning, Emotion, and the Recited Qur'an in Indonesia* (Honolulu: University of Hawaii Press, 2004), 164.

39. Michael Frishkopf, "Mediated Qur'anic Recitation and the Contestation of Islam in Contemporary Egypt," in *Music and the Play of Power in the Middle East, North Africa and Central Asia*, ed. Lauden Noushin (Farnham: Ashgate, 2009), 100.

solely on the reciter and the moment of the recitation."[40] Rudolph Ware has advocated that we also take seriously the notion that one who has memorized the Qur'an is *hafiz* (in the sense that they embody scripture) since "this kind of embodiment goes beyond the metaphorical meanings of the term in English—as exemplar or practical application—and encompasses meanings closer to incarnation, instantiation, and manifestation."[41] Qura'nic studies has thus richly documented myriad ways in which a spoken scripture might technically duplicate its written transcript and yet simultaneously circulate in radically different exegetical and experiential modes.

Nor is the type of written text paired with these spoken scriptures most often a form of written communication that is read for information. Instead, these written texts are engaged not so much as a direct source of knowledge but as ritual artifacts—symbolic representations of revelation. As the classic work of Philip Lutgendorf on the interplay between spoken scripture and written scripture has captured the profound ritual silence of written scripture in such cases: a reader might recite from memory in front of a largely illegible manuscript because "if they glance at the text it is only to note the first word of a line or an approaching break for a dialogue" not to derive specific textual information[42] or a reader might even recite formulas from a closed book set before him without ever opening its petal-strewn cover.[43]

The ritual status of scriptural books as simultaneously relic and reliquary is beautifully captured in Jinah Kim's work on medieval Buddhist practices of ritual text in which a book might be opened to offer a simplified visual image of text at the conclusion of a ritual or rest closed on a stele for worship, so that the same book "is itself a relic as a sacred text and, at the same time it encases a true relic of the Buddha, his teachings written in beautiful letters."[44] As sacred

40. Lauren E. Osborne, "The Experience of the Recited Qur'an," *International Journal of Middle East Studies* 48, no. 1 (2016): 127.

41. Rudolph Ware, *The Walking Qur'an: Islamic Education, Embodied Knowledge, and History in West Africa* (Chapel Hill: University of North Carolina Press, 2014), 8.

42. Philip Lutgendorf, *The Life of a Text: Performing the Rāmcaritmānas of Tulsidas* (Berkeley: University of California Press, 1991), 306.

43. Phillip Lutegendorf, "Ram's Story in Shiva's City: Public Arenas and Private Patronage," in *Culture and Power in the Banaras: Community, Performance, and Environment*, ed. Sandra Freitag (Berkeley: University of California Press, 1989), 34. See, similarly, McComas Taylor, "Empowering the Sacred: The Function of the Sanskrit Text in a Contemporary Exposition of the Bhagavatapurana," in *Orality, Literacy and Performance in the Ancient World*, ed. Elizabeth Minchin (Leiden: Brill, 2011), 129–50.

44. Jinah Kim, *Receptacles of the Sacred: Illustrated Manuscripts and the Buddhist Book Culture in South Asia* (Berkeley: University of California Press, 2013), 40.

PEOPLE OF THE BOOK BEFORE THE BOOK   13

icons and relics, rather than sources of communication, these silent holy books thus manifest the powers ascribed to scriptures above and beyond their persuasive message.

Rabbinic studies has been largely inoculated against these trends in the study of how scriptures function, however, by a widespread tendency to attribute all *mouvance* in early rabbinic thought and practice to the development of the rabbinic tradition itself. When these broader trends in religious studies came to be applied within the field of rabbinics, therefore, they were directed toward studying the growth of the rabbinic tradition rather than scripture. As Steven Fraade has put it, scholars have almost universally seen midrash "an appropriate place to begin an examination of the complex interplay of oral and textual registers of tradition and its transmission, so much the focus of recent study of other traditional cultures and so much the character of Rabbinic culture from antiquity to the present."[45] In the wake of the association developed between trends in the study of scriptural practices and the growth of the rabbinic oral tradition, scholars such as Fraade, Elizabeth Shanks Alexander, Yaakov Elman, Richard Hidary, Catherine Hezser, Martin Jaffee, Shlomo Naeh, David Nelson, and Yaacov Sussmann,[46] fundamentally redefined our

45. Steven D. Fraade, "Literary Composition and Oral Performance in Early Midrashim," *Oral Tradition* 14, no. 1 (1999): 33.

46. For the role of orality in the formation of the body of work traditionally called the "Oral Torah," see, for instance, Elizabeth Shanks Alexander, *Transmitting Mishnah: The Shaping Influence of Oral Tradition* (Cambridge: Cambridge University Press, 2006); Yaakov Elman, "Orality and the Redaction of the Babylonian Talmud," *Oral Tradition* 14, no. 1 (1999): 52–99; Elman, "Orality and the Transmission of Tosefta Pisha in Talmudic Literature," in *Introducing Tosefta: Textual, Intratextual and Intertextual Studies*, ed. Harry Fox and Tirzah Meacham (Hoboken: Ktav, 1999), 117–74; Yaakov Elman and Israel Gershoni, eds., *Transmitting Jewish Tradition: Orality, Textuality, and Cultural Diffusion* (New Haven, CT: Yale University Press, 2000); Steven D. Fraade, *From Tradition to Commentary: Torah and Its Interpretation in Midrash Sifre to Deuteronomy* (Albany: SUNY Press, 1991); Catherine Hezser, *Jewish Literacy in Roman Palestine* (Tübingen: Mohr Siebeck, 2001); Richard Hidary, *Rabbis as Greco-Roman Rhetors: Oratory and Sophistic Education in the Talmud and Midrash* (Cambridge: Cambridge University Press, 2018); Martin Jaffee, *Torah in the Mouth: Writing and Oral Tradition in Palestinian Judaism, 200 BCE–400 CE* (Oxford: Oxford University Press, 2001); Shlomo Naeh "The Structure and Division of Midrash Torat Kohanim (Part 1)," *Tarbiz* 66 (1997): 483–515; Naeh, "The Art of Structures of Memory and the Organization of Texts in Rabbinic Literature," in *Mehqerei Talmud 3: Talmudic Studies in Memory of Professor Ephraim Urbach*, ed. Yaacov Sussmann and David Rosenthal (Jerusalem: Magnes, 2005), 543–89 (in Hebrew); David Nelson, "Textuality and Talmud Torah: Issues of Early Rabbinic Written and Oral Transmission of Tradition as Exemplified in Mekhilta of Rabbi Shimon b. Yohai"(*PhD* diss., Hebrew Union College, 1999); Nelson, "Oral Orthography: Early Rabbinic Oral and Written Transmission of Parallel Midrashic Tradition: In the

understanding of the way in which "rabbinic disciples encountered as oral tradition the performative embodiment of memorized rabbinic manuscripts"—by pushing us to recognized that (like scriptural traditions in other cultures) the rabbinic oral tradition functioned in a "continuous loop of manuscript and performance that had no 'ground zero.' "[47] It is thus the study of *rabbinic tradition* that has moved along with advancements in our understanding of how scripture and canon work within religious studies and cognate fields.

When the transformative force of these emerging insights was directed toward the study of the rabbinic tradition, however, they were simultaneously channeled away from the study of how *biblical* text functioned within the rabbinic community. I would argue that the tendency to bypass the rabbinic relationship with the Hebrew Bible in these investigations has its roots in foundational presuppositions regarding the forms of religious tradition available to early rabbinic communities. The diversion of emerging trends in scriptural studies away from the rabbinic relationship with the Hebrew Bible appears to derive ultimately from what Martin Jaffee has dubbed the "ontological" distinction ascribed to the fixed textuality of written scripture and the fluidity of the oral tradition in the early rabbinic system.[48] The fact that the classical rabbinic authorities primarily engaged with the Hebrew Bible as a series of memorized formulas in quotidian practice is one of those odd historical realities that is widely accepted on a nominal level and yet continues to go unacknowledged in the larger structures of scholarship[49]—a technical detail mentioned in foot-

---

Mekhilta of Rabbi Shimon B. Yoḥai and the Mekhilta of Rabbi Ishmael," *Association for Jewish Studies Review* 29, no. 1 (2005): 1–32; Nelson, "Orality and Mnemonics in Aggadic Midrash," in *Midrash and Context (Proceeds of the 2004 and 2005 SBL Consultation on Midrash)*, ed. Lieve M. Teugels and Rivka Ulmer (Piscataway, NJ: Gorgias, 2007), 123–38; and Yaakov Sussmann, "Torah shebeʿal peh," in *Mehqerei Talmud 3: Talmudic Studies in Memory of Professor Ephraim Urbach*, ed. Yaakov Sussmann and David Rosenthal (Jerusalem: Magnes, 2005), 209–384.

47. Jaffee, *Torah in the Mouth*, 124.

48. See Martin Jaffee's extended treatment of the "ontologically" textual nature of the Pentateuch even as it was orally incorporated in the rabbinic Oral Torah: "A Rabbinic Ontology of the Written and Spoken Word: On Discipleship, Transformative Knowledge, and Living Texts of Oral Torah," *Journal of the American Academy of Religion* 65, no. 3 (1997): especially 536 and 540–43. Indeed, Moshe Halbertal has argued that "[in rabbinic Judaism,] text is more than a shared matrix for a diverse tradition—it is one of the tradition's central operative concepts, like 'God' or 'Israel.' " Moshe Halbertal, *People of the Book: Canon, Meaning, and Authority* (Cambridge, MA: Harvard University Press, 1997), 2.

49. For a rich account of the practical circumstances that favored biblical memorization in early rabbinic circles, see Catherine Hezser, "Bookish Circles? The Use of Written Texts in Rab-

PEOPLE OF THE BOOK BEFORE THE BOOK 15

notes or brief asides that has yet to significantly influence our account of the way that early rabbinic culture engaged with its sacred scriptures.[50]

In some cases, this scholarly dichotomy is rooted in a binary reading of the emic rabbinic categories of Written and Oral Torah. In this imaginary, "the former consists of a fixed, closed text, the latter of a fluid oral transmission and expansion."[51] In other cases, this framing reflects deeply rooted narratives about the cessation of prophecy and the resulting calcification of revelation that took place in its wake. For with the cessation of prophecy, "the interpreter of scripture, not the prophet, would reveal God's will, and would do so not through inspiration or God's direct revelation but instead through the mastery of a skill."[52] With such accounts of the canonization and transmission process on the tips of so many tongues, it is not surprising that scholarly theories of scriptural *mouvance* were applied first to the fecund multiformity of rabbinic

---

binic Oral Culture," *Temas Medievales* 25 (2017): 63–82. The current book, however, seeks to garner increased recognition of this broader *implications* of this practice in the scholarly discussion by (1) demonstrating that this practice was ideologically as well as practically motivated, and (2) asking the reader to consider some of the resulting implications of early rabbinic reading practices for the study of the way that biblical religions relate to the written text of the Bible.

50. It is not uncommon in recent studies, for instance, to see qualifying statements such as this one: "By arguing that the rabbis acquired their knowledge of the Bible from hearing it read aloud ... I am not suggesting that the rabbis knew the text of the Torah *solely* as a heard document, or that the rabbis were in any way oblivious to the fact that the Torah was a written text. As I have explained, they were familiar with *every detail* in the Written Torah, and part of the rabbinic educational curriculum was learning to read and chant the Torah aloud from a scroll. Rabbis certainly consulted written texts of the Torah, some studied from written texts, and there are rabbinic stories that pivot on written copies of Scripture." David Stern, *Jewish Literary Cultures: The Ancient Period* (University Park: Pennsylvania State Press, 2015), 176.

51. Steven Fraade, "Concepts of Scripture in Rabbinic: Oral and Written Torah," in *Jewish Concepts of Scripture: A Comparative Introduction,* ed. Benjamin D. Sommer (New York: New York University Press, 2012), 31–32.

52. Michael L. Satlow, *How the Bible Became Holy* (New Haven, CT: Yale University Press, 2014), 267. For surveys of the classic scholarly literature on this question, as well qualifications to this account, see the classic surveys of Fredrik Greenspahn, "Why Prophecy Ceased," *Journal of Biblical Literature* 108, no. 1 (1989): 37–49; Thomas Overholt, "The End of Prophecy: No Players without a Program," *Journal for the Study of the Old Testament* 42, no. 3 (1988): 103–15; and Benjamin Sommer, "Did Prophecy Cease? Evaluating a Reevaluation," *Journal of Biblical Literature* 115, no. 1 (1996): 31–47. On the extent to which this developmental vision of Jewish textuality is reflected in the modern period, see S. Guzmen-Carmeli, "Texts as Places, Texts as Mirrors: Anthropology of Judaisms and Jewish Textuality," *Contemporary Jewry* 40 (2020): 471–92 and the literature cited there.

tradition and exegesis while the biblical text continues to be broadly portrayed as embodying all the limits and stability of textual fixity.

The scholarly vision of the rabbinic relationship with scripture has not remained static, however, as researchers in the parallel field of rabbinic exegesis have increasingly sought to define more precisely the hermeneutic modes of engaging with written scripture that held sway in different rabbinic schools and genres. The results have done much to nuance and complicate our vision of how early rabbinic authorities conceptualized and related to written scripture as researchers look beyond explicit rabbinic statements about nature of Torah and instead "make a conscious effort to reconstruct the *implicit* fore-understandings of Torah that determine the ancient readings."[53] As scholars such as Jonathan Kaplan, Tzvi Novick, Alexander Samely, and Azzan Yadin-Israel took these concerns to the study of the hermeneutic modes adopted in particular rabbinic corpora, novel facets of the rabbinic conceptualization of scripture emerged in stark relief.[54] While scholars such as Benjamin Sommer and Christine Hayes have recently begun to ask if we could use this research to paint a more explicit and abstract portrait of early rabbinic "conceptions of scripture" and revelation.[55]

These advances in the field of Jewish biblical interpretation have done little as yet, however, to shift the traditional academic portrayal of the role played by the Hebrew Bible in the rabbinic imagination and practice, which continues to hold sway within much of religious studies, rabbinic studies, and Jewish studies more broadly. This monograph seeks to work toward the goal of destabilizing this widely accepted portrait by uncovering the alternate structures that undergird broad swaths of early rabbinic thought and practice. Whether one understands the counter traditions analyzed in these pages to represent the dominant rabbinic stance toward written scripture or one underappreci-

53. Emphasis added. Azzan Yadin, *Scripture as Logos: Rabbi Ishmael and the Origins of Midrash* (Philadelphia: University of Pennsylvania Press, 2004), 9–10.

54. Jonathan Kaplan, *My Perfect One: Typology and Early Rabbinic Interpretation of Song of Songs* (Oxford: Oxford University Press, 2015), 184; Tzvi Novick, *What Is Good, and What God Demands,* Supplements to the Journal for the Study of Judaism (Leiden: Brill, 2010); Alexander Samely, *Rabbinic Interpretation of Scripture in the Mishnah* (Oxford: Oxford University Press, 2002); Azzan Yadin-Israel, *Scripture and Tradition: Rabbi Akiva and the Triumph of Midrash* (Philadelphia: University of Pennsylvania Press, 2015).

55. Benjamin Sommer, introduction to *Jewish Concepts of Scripture: A Comparative Introduction,* ed. Benjamin Sommer (New York: New York University Press, 2012); and Christine Hayes, *What's Divine about Divine Law? Early Perspectives* (Princeton, NJ: Princeton University Press, 2017), 166–270.

ated thread of early rabbinic tradition among many, these traditions call us to reconsider widely held presuppositions about the ways in which written scriptures were encountered and conceptualized in early rabbinic communities.

A Brief Outline of the Project

This book is divided into two parts. The chapters that make up part 1 argue that, rather than valorizing the Pentateuch and its prophetic echoes as perfect transcripts of the divine will, many early rabbinic practitioners experienced the Bible as a problem. In the first chapter, "A Makeshift Scripture," the reader is asked to reconsider the tenor of early rabbinic comments about the writtenness of scripture. The traditions analyzed in chapter 1 represent a stream of rabbinic thought in which the biblical text is theorized not as a perfect record of divine knowledge but as a treacherously limited and changeable vessel for preserving the divine will. The chapter begins by analyzing early rabbinic traditions about Ezra the Scribe and other scribal heroes who narrowly saved the biblical text from oblivion at repeated junctures in the history of Israel—even, at times, reconstructing the lost text from memory. In these narratives, the vulnerable material nature of each instantiation of the Bible text has rendered the biblical tradition susceptible to repeated erosion, loss, and change. The chapter continues by investigating early rabbinic traditions that contrast the first tablets of the law destroyed by Moses with the second tablets of the law ultimately bequeathed to the people of Israel. These two tablet traditions are treated as a form of narrative theorizing about the nature of written text and its limits as a vehicle for divine revelation. In such stories, the first (lost) tablets of the law come to represent the impossibility of authentically capturing the divine will in a material written text. While the second (received) tablets of the law become a locus for reflection on the inherently brittle and imperfect nature of the written revelation that was bequeathed to history.

In the second chapter, "A Book That Kills," the reader is asked to question the widespread presupposition that rabbinic practitioners embraced the biblical text as "a tree of life to all who grasp it" (Prov 3:18). In the early rabbinic traditions collected in chapter 2, the biblical text is imagined as a mortally dangerous artifact that can leave death and destruction in its wake. Unlike the first chapter, chapter 2 is not organized thematically but is instead divided into a rough chronology to highlight distinct developmental stages in rabbinic thinking about the perils of biblical texts and its affordances. The chapter opens by analyzing tannaitic traditions in which the mortal dangers of the

18 INTRODUCTORY REMARKS

biblical text emerge when it is read by *minim* (sectarians, heretics, or early Jesus followers). These traditions often use images of an adulterous wife to capture a notion that the biblical text was hazardous because the lures of its lyrical beauty and spiritual pleasures remained intact even as the text was corrupted and put into the service of the enemies of Israel—transforming the biblical text into a Trojan horse for heresy and spiritual poison. Later Palestinian sources transfigure the motif of textual promiscuity so that the danger posed by the biblical text lies not in its potential to be shared between communities but instead in the way the written text makes its unbounded spiritual forces available to anyone who approaches it. In these early amoraic sources, the tannaitic triangulation between biblical textuality, heresy, and physical death was now applied to actors *within* Israel. As a hypostasized font of divine power, the biblical text portrayed in these narratives produces a proliferation of uncontrollable spiritual modes, many of them deadly. In later Babylonian traditions, the imagery that emerged in previous traditions is further concretized and expanded until simple proximity with the biblical text can wipe out both individuals and populations without any transparent spiritual mechanism at work. In such traditions, the very existence of a material written revelation had become a source of a multiform and inchoate terror.[56]

Chapter 3, "Neglect of Text," argues that the dangers attributed to the biblical text in these mythologizing narratives were also reflected in more quotidian practical measures that restricted use of the biblical text as a source of religious information in many late antique rabbinic circles. Adopting a more expansive and nuanced definition of restriction and censorship, chapter 3 explores different modes through which late antique rabbinic authorities sidelined and restricted the written text of the Hebrew Bible as a source of communal information. The chapter opens by analyzing how practices of inaccurate citation both reflected and cultivated neglect of the written text of the Hebrew Bible by trivializing textual engagement as a potential source of knowledge. The chapter then looks at how diverse rabbinic injunctions deterred practitioners from deriving information directly from the written text of the Bible by discouraging informational reading in general, by placing restrictions on reading the Bible at certain times and on certain days, and by proscribing the circulation of vernacular copies of biblical texts. The third chapter thus completes

---

56. Similar to the phenomenon Matthew Engelke has called "terror of the text" (*Problem of Presence*, 7) following Johannes Fabian, "Text as Terror: Second Thoughts about Charisma," *Social Research: An International Quarterly* 46, no. 2 (1979): 166–203.

part 1 of the book, which explores different ways in which early rabbinic thinkers approached the biblical text as a problem.

Part 2 asks how a community so deeply ambivalent about the biblical text nevertheless elevated the Hebrew Bible as a central pillar of communal thought. The chapters in the second half of the book argue that this apparent paradox was possible because early rabbinic practitioners approached the practices of reading and engaging with written text very differently from modern informational readers. It argues that the memorization-heavy reading practices described in early rabbinic literature had already rendered the written text of the Hebrew Bible a secondary, even superfluous, witness to the biblical tradition in daily practice. So much so, in fact, that early rabbinic thinkers came to think of these recited oral formulas of the biblical traditions as a distinct revelation in their own right. Until Spoken Scripture came to be theorized as a third type of Torah that flourished in the liminal space between the consonantal transcripts of the Written Torah and the emerging rabbinic traditions of the Oral Torah—a more authentic echo of the scriptural revelation at Sinai than could be contained in a scroll's limited parchment.

Chapter 4, "Rabbinic Practices of (Bible) Reading," demonstrates that common early rabbinic modes of Bible reading bypassed the written text as a source of information—treating written words as nothing more than a ritual corollary to spoken language, in whose spoken formulas true meaning and communication were thought to reside. The chapter opens by exploring a widespread early rabbinic commitment to memorized ritual recitation as the primary mode of engaging with biblical text and argues that these practices of ritual reading served to marginalize written texts of the Hebrew Bible as a source of cultural transmission and knowledge. Since this mode of early rabbinic liturgical reading was rooted in recitation formulas passed directly from teacher to student and did not derive meaning directly from written words, both transmission and meaning in this reading practice were thought to reside primarily in the spoken words. The rest of the chapter seeks to illuminate this conceptual inversion of text and meaning by looking at early rabbinic literacy pedagogies as both representative and formative of a reading practice that treated written texts as secondary—and often temporary—props in the transmission of recited formulas from teacher to student.

Chapter 5, "The Third Torah," argues that this bifurcation of the biblical tradition into oral and written iterations was not merely an incidental development in rabbinic practice but was theorized by many early rabbinic thinkers as reflecting a more fundamental bifurcation of the scriptural revelation at

Sinai into two distinct historical echoes: a limited consonantal transcript preserved in the biblical text that was bequeathed to history and a more authentic spoken iteration of the biblical revelation transmitted through the living recitation of the tradition by human mouths. These traditions characterized the memorized spoken formulas of the biblical tradition as a discrete, qualitatively different, and ultimately superior witness to the biblical revelation—a distinct third form of Torah preserved at the interstices between the Oral and Written Torah. Chapter 5 opens by exploring how early rabbinic thinkers could conceive of two largely parallel formulas of the biblical tradition as distinct forms of revelation. This section first explores early rabbinic traditions in which the small divergences that foreshadowed the Masoretic *qere* and *ketiv* ("read thus, though it is written thus" traditions) were taken as signs of deeper metaphysical divergences between the spoken formulas of the biblical tradition and the consonantal transcript. The discussion then moves on to consider Babylonian rabbinic traditions in which *mikra* (the spoken formulas of the biblical tradition) and *masoret* (the written transcript of the biblical tradition) were imagined as distinct revelatory works, configured in a hierarchy of authenticity in which the spoken version of the biblical tradition was embraced as the primary witnesses to the biblical revelation. The chapter then examines in more detail the ways in which these memorized oral formulas of the biblical tradition were envisioned as a qualitatively superior echo of the biblical revelation that passed down almost material traces of a living revelatory divine speech through the corporeal mechanisms of breath, scent, and taste. The chapter closes by tracing traditions in which this third Torah of Spoken Scripture was imagined as the survival of its own distinct moment of biblical revelation: the first, more authentic, biblical revelation that was temporarily inscribed on the first tablets of the law and then released into its natural form as speech and sound with the smashing of the tablets.

Chapter 6, "The Closed Book," asks how practitioners imagined the status and character of the written consonantal transcript passed down on parchment scrolls once they no longer functioned as communicative witnesses to the biblical revelation. While many researchers have suggested that Torah scrolls functioned primarily as ritual objects, this chapter argues that we should go further and take seriously the many early rabbinic traditions in which the Torah scroll was envisioned as a form of corporeal avatar—an almost-living biological body that could act as an intermediary between the divine and the human. The chapter opens by analyzing the ways early rabbinic traditions treat the Torah scroll like the human body, as an entity that manifests sacred powers most strongly when it is closed, covered, and whole—so that the scroll's all-too-material textual facets are exposed to view only during the carefully regulated moments of intimacy allowed for liturgical recitation-reading. The chapter then explores the very biological bodily imagery utilized in traditions that imagine the Torah scroll being touched, moved, or physically manipulated in liturgical contexts—particularly in rituals in which the Torah scroll is treated as a member of the human community. The chapter closes by considering how the Torah scroll came to be imagined as a personified avatar of sacrality—a conduit between heaven and earth—in the absence of a sacrificial priesthood acting within the Temple cult. The chapters that make up the second part of the book thus argue that early rabbinic authorities were able to maintain the Pentateuch's central status in rabbinic thought and practice while retreating from the biblical text as a communicative document because the biblical text had come to be treated not as a written communication so much as a personification of revelation that housed a living recited soul within a powerful (if dangerous) parchment body.

The concluding chapter of the monograph asks how this portrait of the early rabbinic relationship with biblical text changes our perception of subsequent developments in the Jewish relationship with Bible. Contemporary Jewish approaches to the Bible are deeply rooted in the medieval tradition of systematic biblical commentary. Yet it has proven challenging to explain the sudden global rise of these new forms of commentary in the Middle Ages so long as medieval Jewish approaches to biblical textuality were projected back into the classical rabbinic period. With this new portrait of classical rabbinic approaches to the biblical text, stark contrasts begin to emerge between medieval Jewish conceptions of biblical textuality and those of the early rabbinic period. The conclusion thus suggests that the far-reaching transformations in Jewish modes of engaging with the biblical text that arose with the Middle Ages were not spurred by particular cultural or technological developments so as much as a sea change in Jewish conceptions of what *kind* of book the Bible was. That is, the conclusion theorizes that the all-important medieval shift in Jewish modes of engaging with the biblical text derived from a global transformation in the Jewish vision of the Bible's genre and affordances.

What This Book Is Not: Some Notes on Method

There are fields of research that intersect with various topics in this book that will not be extensively addressed as part of this work's scholarly genealogy.

Many of the themes analyzed in the first half of the book, for instance, also appear threaded through a series of groundbreaking contributions to academic theology generated on the Upper West Side of Manhattan over the course of the last fifty years by Abraham Joshua Heschel, David Weiss Halivni, and Benjamin Sommer.[57] However, this book is intended as a descriptive account of a particular reception history rather than a constructive project and it remains unclear to me, and others, how these two very different approaches might productively intersect.[58]

Scattered throughout this monograph, the reader will also find copious references to sectarians, Christians, and Romans of all walks of life—both within the primary source material produced by early rabbinic thinkers and in my own analysis of those late ancient materials. In order to maintain focus on rabbinic scriptural reading cultures, this book will not be theorized as an intervention in the field of Jewish-Christian relations or the study of late antique intercommunity relations more broadly. Instead, this project should be understood as loosely grounded in the following principles regarding intercommunity relations: First, this project is premised on the assumption that one can sometimes identify broader "antipodal" tendencies, as Shaye Cohen has put it, between certain early rabbinic and emerging Christian attitudes regarding the nature of scripture and its affordances—even if a direct textual genealogy between particular sources cannot be traced.[59] Yet the materials analyzed in the project are not limited to antipodal relations in which rival claims are configured as opposing positions. Instead, many of the materials cited here participated in similar, though not identical, ways in a broader Mediterranean vernacular emerging around the nature of canonical text and its function. When it came to reading, early rabbinic practices might be best categorized as what Seth Schwartz has called "accommodative"—in the sense that at the very "moment that the rabbis were striving to extricate themselves from the Roman

---

57. Abraham Joshua Heschel, *Heavenly Torah Refracted through the Generations,* vol. 1 (London: Soncino, 1962); vol. 2 (London: Soncino, 1965); and vol. 3 (New York: Jewish Theological Seminary of America, 1995); David Weiss Halivni, *Revelation Restored: Divine Writ and Critical Responses* (New York: Avalon, 1998); Benjamin D. Sommer, *Revelation and Authority: Sinai in Jewish Scripture and Tradition* (New Haven, CT: Yale University Press, 2015).

58. For an extended discussion of this challenge, see Sarah Wolf's review of *Revelation and Authority* in *Journal of Law and Religion* 33, no. 2 (2015): 322–25.

59. Shaye Cohen, "Antipodal Texts: B. Eruvin 21b–22a and Mark 7:1–23 on the Traditions of the Elder and the Commandment of God," in *Envisioning Judaism: Studies in Honor of Peter Schaefer on the Occasion of his Seventieth Birthday,* ed. Ra'anan S. Boustan (Tübingen: Mohr Siebeck, 2013), 108.

system . . . they were also demonstrating their commitments to some of its core values."[60]

The final way in which this book may deviate from expectations is one of bibliographic method. Both biblical studies and rabbinic studies participate with unusual robustness in a bibliographic practice that Anthony Grafton has famously attributed to the influence of German philology, whereby "footnotes often serve to prove the author's membership in a guild rather than to illuminate or support a particular point" as "citations are heaped up, without much regard to their origins or compatibility in order to make the text above them seem to rest on solid pilings."[61] Indeed, Anne Stevens and Jay Williams have argued that such notes are aimed less at "the traditional recognition of the work of like-minded scholars" than at establishing that the author possesses a proper "consciousness of their place in the field."[62] This is where the "Germanic footnote" becomes a problem, it seems to me. In the fields treated in this book, we do not currently have adequate bibliographic and technical apparatus available to comprehensively survey work on a particular passage or topic. Without a comprehensive apparatus in place, what we miss in our citations tends to systematically reproduce structures of inequity along networks of gender, ethnicity, class, geography, employment status, and institutional prestige. I am therefore wary of approaching footnotes as a ticket of admission to the guild when that technique has functioned so inefficiently to include and has proven so effective at excluding.

Within rabbinic studies, there is a particular manifestation of this practice about which I have strong reservations: the practice of citing and arguing against every previous author who has offered an analysis of a topic or passage that deviates from one's own. While *makhloket leshem shamayim* (dispute for the sake of heaven) may have sharpened the minds of the rabbinic thinkers we study, Jeffery Rubenstein has also painted a sobering picture of the social costs of such an intellectual milieu[63]—which we might do well to consider before adapting the discourse for modern studies of the subject. But the more

---

60. Seth Schwartz, *Were the Jews a Mediterranean Society? Reciprocity and Solidarity in Ancient Judaism* (Princeton, NJ: Princeton University Press, 2010), 165.

61. Anthony Grafton, *The Footnote: A Curious History* (Cambridge, MA: Harvard University Press, 1997), 43.

62. Anne H. Stevens and Jay Williams, "The Footnote, in Theory," *Critical Inquiry* 32, no. 2 (2006): 211.

63. Jeffery Rubenstein, *The Culture of the Babylonian Talmud* (Baltimore: Johns Hopkins University Press, 2005), 54–79.

pressing reason to eschew this practice, it seems to me, is that it tends to privilege those scholars who have had the most experience with this particular rhetoric from their time in elite, Ashkenazic, masculine yeshiva contexts. Those who trained exclusively in secular institutions and in women's, egalitarian, and non-Ashkenazic schools of advanced Talmud study were taught different modes of interacting with these texts, and with each other. This particular mode of relating to disagreement is only one of many native idioms.

The reader may take it as a given that this work is respectfully founded on the widely acknowledged pillars of the field. Although these works hover in the background, I have not attempted to cite each scholar's entire oeuvre to prove my familiarity with highly cited works in the field. Nor have I provided a bibliography, which would serve a similar purpose. Instead, I have tried to argue constructively in this book by citing primarily those authors whose thinking on a particular subject helped give shape to my argument. I will not as a rule include long lists of other readings of a passage, nor argue against other readings of a given text. Instead, I hold that alternate readings may successfully bring out different facets of these multivocal texts, without necessarily being in opposition to one another.

In the additional space created by abstaining from these widely embraced bibliographic practices, I have often sought out less acknowledged scholars and scholarly sources. I do this not in any attempt to diversify by checklist. (In fields that are so imbalanced ab initio, this seems an impossible and misguided task.[64]) Rather, I have often found the greatest delight and stimulation in works that seem to have fallen slightly by the wayside in the networks of convention—work by international academics, women and nonbinary scholars, researchers of color, and those working at less prestigious institutions. Those who have been marginalized by the field are also free of it in many ways. As a result, their work more often takes unexpected and winding paths of their own devising. As Sara Ahmed has put it in another context, "Work that has been too quickly . . . cast aside or left behind, work . . . created by not following the official paths laid out by disciplines" generates for us other paths which Ahmed

---

64. For the past decade, the Society of Biblical Literature membership has remained around or above 75 percent members who identify as men. According to the most recent Society of Biblical Literature's Member Data Survey, 24.22 percent of responders in the 2018 survey selected the identification "female," 75.68 percent selected the identification "male," and 0.10 percent selected the identification "transgender," Society of Biblical Literature, *Member Data Report*, January 2019, 8: https://www.sbl-site.org/assets/pdfs/sblMemberProfile2019.pdf.

has named "desire lines."[65] I hope that the resulting arguments of this book will, in turn, provide new food for thought to this alternate network—whether they make it at the center or not.

In a similar effort to put the thoughts of others before the task of garnering scholarly authority, I have done my best to seek out authorized English translations of modern quotations whenever I cite at any length from the foreign-language work of a contemporary scholar. All translations of premodern works from Hebrew, Aramaic, Greek, and Latin are, of course, my own—except in the rare cases where I have indicated. However, when a living author has authorized a particular translation into English, I am uncomfortable substituting my own linguistic judgment for theirs, in a misguided attempt to demonstrate that my many years in Israel were not wasted. So, while the translation of any passages quoted from modern works in Hebrew, German, French, or Italian are my own unless otherwise indicated, I will quote from English versions of each author's arguments wherever that is possible.

With all of this said, this book was completed amid a global pandemic. There were works which I wished to consult that I was not able to acquire for practical or budgetary reasons. I regret the insufficiencies this leaves in the final product. Nevertheless, as we so often say in acknowledgements, all errors and omissions are entirely my own.

65. Sara Ahmed, *Living a Feminist Life* (Durham, NC: Duke University Press, 2017), 15.

1

A Makeshift Scripture

TALES OF BIBLICAL LOSS, RECONSTRUCTION, AND FORGERY

CONSIDERING THEMSELVES uniquely skeptical about the compositional nature of biblical writings, modern readers often imagine that early Jewish thinkers embraced what Benjamin Sommer has called a "stenographic theory" of divine revelation, in which the Bible was imagined as a word perfect transcript of the divine will expressed at Sinai.[1] This modern scholarly vision does evocatively reproduce the historical imaginaries about antiquity that were constructed in the early modern debates that gave birth to biblical criticism as we know it.[2] But it does not accord with the many late antique Jewish traditions that described the biblical text as a contingent and historical document—a fractured echo of divine revelation rather than a pristine transcription of the divine will.[3]

1. Benjamin Sommer, *Revelation and Authority: Sinai in Jewish Scripture and Tradition* (New Haven, CT: Yale University Press, 2015), 2.

2. For more on the construction of these intellectual positions in early modernity, see Michael Legaspi, *The Death of Scripture and the Rise of Biblical Studies*, OSHT (Oxford: Oxford University Press, 2010) and the literature cited there.

3. In making this claim, I build upon the work of Benjamin Sommer and Yohanan Silman who argue that some rabbinic thinkers have imagined that the "Torah is received by human hands through the mediation of a process in which concealed facets are revealed gradually" in an ongoing process in which the Torah is "perfected." Yohanan Silman, *Kol gadol yelo yasaf: Torat Yisra'el ben shelemut lehishtalmut* (Jerusalem: Magnes 1999), 121, See also Sommer, *Revelation and Authority*. For more on how this developmental approach was manifest in early rabbinic sources, see Rebecca Scharbach Wollenberg, "A King and a Scribe Like Moses: The Reception of Deuteronomy 34:10 and a Rabbinic Theory of Collective Biblical Authorship," *Hebrew Union*

Rabbinic thinkers have already been acknowledged as sophisticated realists when it came to the developmental history of divine law. As Christine Hayes recently put it, "Even corrections that set aside or 'uproot' biblical law are disclosed with no indication that the nature of the law as divine and authoritative is thereby impugned."[4] In contrast to the models of revelation embraced in early modernity, immutability was simply not a criterion of sacredness for many rabbinic thinkers in late antiquity.

Rabbinic authorities are not generally recognized, however, as applying this stark recognition of revelatory change to the development of the biblical text—which is often imagined as a static counterpoint to the freedoms and growth of rabbinic tradition. Yet, as Chris Keith recently pointed out in a parallel context, this vision of how sacred textuality functioned in the ancient world subtly misidentifies late antique presuppositions about what ancient thinkers meant when they spoke of a sacred book by anachronistically imposing the modern "authority associated with the book-as-collection in the Miltonian sense"[5]—so that the notion of a sacred book evokes concepts such as "stable," "definitive," "finished," and "bound." Whereas for the late antique reader, the idea of a book often invoked instead "ancient conceptions of the *book-as-artifact*"[6] in which "writtenness enabled a realization of the tradition as a material artifact with an identifiable beginning and end" but made no claims concerning the complete, finished, or perfect nature of the book in question beyond "the simple fact that it was the manuscript in their hands."[7] In other words, to say that a revelation was a book in this context was to point to its contingent, material, and contextual nature.

This chapter explores a selection of early rabbinic traditions that evince a similar blunt realism concerning the historical contingency of the biblical text

---

College Annual 90 (2019): 207–24. However, the early rabbinic traditions analyzed in this chapter differ from those participatory theories of revelation, inasmuch as they approach the extant biblical text as somehow made lesser, even sometimes insufficient, through its interaction with human transmitters.

4. Although the passing of time did bring about "resistance to enactments that went so far as to contradict provisions of Torah law, as indicated by new strategies of concealment. See Christine Hayes, *What's Divine about Divine Law? Early Perspectives* (Princeton, NJ: Princeton University Press, 2017), 308.

5. Chris Keith, *Gospel as Manuscript: An Early History of the Jesus Tradition as Material Artifact* (Oxford: Oxford University Press, 2020), 46.

6. Ibid., 60.

7. Ibid.

itself, which is described as an imperfect document, ravaged by history, cut off from the divine, and reworked (perhaps even composed anew) by human hands. Rather than attempting to obscure the imperfect condition of the extant biblical text, these sources appear resigned to these misfortunes as the inevitable fate of even the most sacred written documents. In this chapter, such traditions are not read as mythicized accounts of a historical maculation of the scriptural text.[8] Instead, their constantly shifting referents (and very overabundance of examples) are interpreted as marking historicized myths of textual insufficiency intended not to make specific claims concerning the origins of the extant biblical text but to point to ground truths concerning the vulnerable and unreliable nature of written scripture.

The chapter opens with early rabbinic traditions that claim Ezra the Scribe altered, reconstructed, or composed the Pentateuch as we know it. These tales are read as a form of narrative theorizing about the historically contingent nature of the biblical text that was inherited by the early rabbinic authorities. These themes are amplified into a more abstract reflection on the inescapable vulnerabilities of written revelation in rabbinic accounts of other moments in the history of Israel in which the text of the Pentateuch was repeatedly lost and reconstructed.[9] The picture that emerges from these latter tales is unsettling: a failure in any link in this imagined chain of perpetual forgetting and reconstruction would have left the biblical revelation irretrievably corrupted. The possibility of such corruption, moreover, is one that the authors of these traditions did not entirely dismiss. On the contrary, the chapter closes by analyzing early rabbinic traditions about the altered revelation transmitted in the second tablets of the law (Exod 34). It argues that these traditions elevate and abstract the nagging sense of historical contingency treated above into a general principle that the form of biblical text which would enter history was always al-

---

8. In contrast to David Weiss Halivni, *Revelation Restored: Divine Writ and Critical Responses* (New York: Avalon, 1998), 16.

9. In doing this, I do not mean to deny the strength of the arguments made by Shlomo Naeh and Mark Leuchter, who read the Ezra sources analyzed here as rabbinic reflections on the Aramaic transition (Shlomo Naeh, "Script of the Torah in Rabbinic Thought (A): The Traditions concerning Ezra's Changing of the Script," *Leshonenu* [2008]: 125–43 [in Hebrew], and Mark Leuchter, "The Aramaic Transition and the Redaction of the Pentateuch," *Journal of Biblical Literature* 136, no. 2 [2017]: 249–68). Rather, I hope to bring out another facet of these texts that draws these motifs into broader historical and intercommunal trains of thought in which the particular paleographic changes grappled with here become part of a broader reflection on the mutable nature of written scripture.

ready a pale reflection of the divine will—a second edition made vulnerable to textual change by its inherent insufficiency.

The Book That Changed: Early Jewish Traditions about a Biblical Edition by Ezra the Scribe[10]

In some early rabbinic traditions, Ezra the Scribe was imagined to have altered, reconstructed, or composed the Pentateuch as we know it. This section argues that such traditions embraced the Ezra authorship postulate to articulate an instinct that the extant text of the Hebrew Bible was in some fundamental way a second edition—a textual tradition ravaged by history and time, which correlated only imperfectly with the original Sinaitic revelation.[11] With the exception of Mark Leuchter's and Shlomo Naeh's works that treat rabbinic descriptions of Ezra as a mode of grappling with the Aramaic transition and David Weiss Halivni's work in which he characterizes these traditions as memories of Ezra's historical role in restoring revelation in the Babylonian Talmud, 4 Ezra[12] has typically been the only early Jewish tradition on Ezran authorship treated in modern scholarship. This is probably because other late antique Jewish accounts of an Ezran edition of the Bible are not structured as

---

10. The materials in this subsection appear in a slightly different form in Rebecca Scharbach Wollenberg, "The Book That Changed: Tales of Ezran Authorship as a Form of Late Antique Biblical Criticism," *Journal of Biblical Literature* 138, no. 1 (2019): 143–60. It has been adapted here with the permission of the journal.

11. The textual cue for this narrative may emerge from a literary phenomenon called to our attention by Hindy Najman in which Ezra and Nehemiah attribute laws that do not occur in the Pentateuch to Moses (*Seconding Sinai: The Development of Mosaic Discourse in Second Temple Judaism* [Leiden: Brill, 2003], 112).

12. According to 4 Ezra, the text of the Hebrew Bible was lost during the Babylonian invasion of Jerusalem in 586 BCE and Ezra provided a replacement copy of the work. As Ezra laments after the destruction, "The Torah of our fathers has been made of no effect and the written covenants no longer exist" (4 Ezra 4:23) because "the law has been burned" (4 Ezra 14:21) in the destruction. (As translated by Michael Stone and Matthias Henze: "Therefore, Ezra relates: 'I opened my mouth and my heart poured forth understanding . . . so during the forty days, ninety-four books were written, and when the forty days were ended, the Most High spoke to me, saying, "Make public the twenty-four books that you wrote first and let the worthy and unworthy read them; but keep the seventy that were written last, in order to give them to the wise among your people. For in them are the springs of understanding, the fountains of wisdom and the river of knowledge." And I did so'" (4 Ezra 14:39–48). Michael Stone and Mattias Henze, *4Ezra and 2Baruch: Translations, Introductions, and Notes* (Minneapolis: Fortress, 2013), 81.

30 CHAPTER 1

independently comprehensible narratives but are instead preserved as analytic reflections cobbled together from secondary allusions to this popular narrative tradition. The thrust of these analytic musings is quickly clarified, however, by comparison with other late antique Mediterranean versions of this Ezra tradition, since early rabbinic traditions appear to refer to the same basic narrative outlines as early Christian accounts.

This is not the place to survey the full breadth of early Christian and philosophical traditions concerning an Ezran edition of the Hebrew Bible.[13] However, we can catch an instructive glimpse of the terrors of textual loss and forgery that would have echoed through this historical motif by looking at an anti-Christian account of Ezran authorship ascribed to Porphyry of Tyre, who is purported to have remarked in his (now lost) work *Against the Christians*:

> It appears to me to be replete with stupidity [to say]: "If you would believe Moses you would also believe me for he has written concerning me" (John 5:46). . . . Nothing Moses wrote has been preserved, for all his writings are said to have been burnt with the temple. All those written under his name afterwards were composed anew (συνεγράφη)[14] one thousand one hundred and eighty years after Moses' death by Ezra and his followers.[15]

---

13. For a fuller survey of early Christian traditions about Ezran editorial activity, see Wollenberg, "Book That Changed," 143–60. For a parallel study of Samaritan traditions about Ezra, see Lisbeth S. Fried, *Ezra and the Law in History and Tradition* (Columbia: University of South Carolina Press, 2014), 123–32. I have omitted a discussion of Samaritan traditions from this chapter because the origins of these medieval motifs remain unclear. On the difficulty of discerning whether "this negative attitude towards Ezra the Scribe could have entered Islam through Samaritan sources" or whether this motif should "be considered another example of the impact Islam had on Samaritan literature," see Hava Lazarus-Yafeh, *Intertwined Worlds: Medieval Islam and Bible Criticism* (Princeton, NJ: Princeton University Press, 1992), 60.

14. This phrase is quoted in an adaptation from the unique translation of Robert M. Berchman, *Porphyry against the Christians* (Leiden: Brill, 2005), 198. When Berchman translates συνεγράφη as "composed inaccurately," it seems to me that he first and foremost highlights the term's emphasis on composing from scratch, as in the phrase τοῖς τὰς ἱστορίας συγγράφειν, "those who would write histories" (Josephus, *Antiquities of the Jews* 1.1, ed. Ralph Marcus (Cambridge, MA: Harvard University Press, 1943), 2. But this translation also seems to draw on the sense of imperfect mimesis and representative replacement that permeates the term when it is used to describe the creation of art, as in the phrase εἰς εὐτέλειαν χηνὶ συγγεγραμμένῳ "[sparsely endowed with feathers] like a wild goose painted on the cheap" (Aristophanes, *Aristophanes Comoediae*, ed. F. W. Hall and W. M. Geldart, [Oxford: Clarendon, 1907], 2:801).

15. Frag. 465e as reproduced in Marcarius Magnes, *Apokritikos* 3.3. Greek taken from Makarios Magnus, *Apokritikos: Kritische Ausgabe mit deutscher Uebersetzung*, ed. Ulrich Volp (Berlin: de Gruyter, 2013), 108.

In this third-century account, the ever-present threat of textual loss and degradation is envisioned in its most extreme form—as a case of complete textual destruction. The Bible is envisioned here as the most vulnerably textual of texts. No supporting cultural apparatus preserves the contents of the textual tradition when the writing is lost—all meaning and memory conveyed by the text had been contained within the vessel of the written word. Porphyry's account also gives voice to anxiety concerning the unprovenanced nature of textual knowledge. For a skilled author is imagined to have produced a new written text ex nihilo that purported (falsely) to preserve an ancient tradition of revelation, yet only the most astute reader is able to discern the forgery. Even this brief story of Ezran authorship thus potently captures all that is potentially unreliable about textual modes of knowledge transmission, and projects these failures onto the extant biblical text.

Many early Christian thinkers would simultaneously defuse and domesticate these anxieties by treating the Ezran authorship tradition both as an intellectual space to explore the problem of textual vulnerability and as an answer to the problem of textual vulnerability as it related to biblical literature. Irenaeus, for instance, is remembered as suggesting:

> During the captivity of the people under Nebuchadnezzar the Scriptures had been ruined by corruption (διαφθαρεισῶν; corruptis). . . . But when seventy years later the Jews had returned to their own land in the times of Artaxerxes, king of Persia, Ezra the priest of the tribe of Levi was inspired (ἐνέπνευσεν; inspiravit) to order in his mind (ἀνατάξασθαι; rememorare) all the words of the former prophets and to reestablish (ἀποκαταστῆσαι; restituere) the Mosaic legislation (μωσέως νομοθεσίαν; legem quae data est per Moysem) for the people.[16]

For authors like Irenaeus, the problem of textual degradation and loss constituted a very real threat to sacred writings. Divine origins were no protection against the corrosion that historical forces exerted on textual traditions. More than simply acknowledging the theoretical dangers that textual corruption posed for the sacred writings, moreover, authors of this school maintained that such erosion had already taken its toll on the biblical revelation. The biblical text as they knew it was not imagined as a pristine copy of the revelation that had been conveyed to Moses at Sinai. Rather, the existing biblical text was

---

16. Irenaeus, *Against Heresies* 3.21.2. Translation my own. Greek and Latin are according to William Wigan Harvey, *Sancti Irenaei episcopi Lugdunensis Libros quinque adversus haereses* (Regiomonti: Typis Academicis, 1857), 2.114.

32   CHAPTER 1

imagined as a more approximate record of the Sinaitic revelation, which had been saved from oblivion by divinely inspired scribal maintenance and reconstruction.

Early rabbinic tales of Ezran authorship are threaded through with many of the same critical themes that characterized early Christian traditions concerning the possibility of Ezran authorship. The early rabbinic traditions that begin, "Ezra was worthy that the Torah should have been given at his hands," for instance, are sometimes interpreted as "extravagant expressions of admiration for Ezra."[17] I would argue, however, that the primary theme of these passages is the historical and changeable nature of the biblical text. Consider, for instance, the variations on the following passage preserved (and variously elaborated) in tSanhedrin 4:7; yMegillah 1:9 (71b); and bSanhedrin 21b–22a (cited here according to tSanhedrin 4:7):

> Ezra was worthy that the Torah should have been given at his hand, if it hadn't been that Moses preceded him . . . indeed the writing and language [as we have it] was given at [Ezra's] hand, as it is said, "The writing of the message was Aramaic script and its interpretation was Aramaic" (Ezra 4:7). What does mean, "Its interpretation was Aramaic?" That the writing was Aramaic. And it says, "They could not read the writing (ולא כהלין כתבא למקרא)" (Dan 5:8)—which teaches that [this new script] was only given on that very day, as it is written, "He shall write for himself this *mishneh hatorah* (משנה התורה)" (Deut 17:18). [*Mishneh hatorah* means] a Torah that is destined to change [its form] (לשתנות). Why is it called "Aramaic" (אשורי)? Because it came back with them from [the exile in] Babylon (אשור). Rabbi says: [This is not quite true.] The Torah was [originally] given to Israel in Aramaic writing but when they sinned its language changed for them. Then when they repented in the days of Ezra, it returned for them to Aramaic writing. As it is said, "Return to the stronghold, [prisoners of hope, lo today I tell you I will restore to you a double-change [משנה]" (Zech 9:12).

In formal terms, this passage is framed as an exegesis of the phrase "but they could not read the writing" in the story of the cryptic writing on the wall that appeared in the Babylonian court according to Daniel 5:8. The unreadable writing on the wall in Daniel 5:8 is exegeted here as a text of the Pentateuch, which had become indecipherable to the Jewish people by the time of the Babylonian exile. As the tale made its way through early rabbinic literature,

---

17. Lazarus-Yafeh, *Intertwined Worlds*, 59.

several alternative explanations were offered for how this state of incomprehensibility came about. But each of these tales cast doubts in its own way on the stability and reliability of the biblical text passed from generation to generation.

According to the first explanation offered in tSanhedrin 4:7, Ezra himself had rendered the biblical text temporarily indecipherable to the Jewish people during the Babylonian exile by reworking the biblical text to bring it into line with the spirit of the times—changing both the script (כתב) and (at least some of) the wording (לשון) of the biblical text to the imperial language of Aramaic. To support this surprising claim, the author of this tradition cites Ezra 4:7: וכתב הנשתון כתוב ארמית ומתרגם ארמית. In its original biblical context, this phrase simply means, "The text of the letter [that the government officials wrote to Artaxerxes to complain about Ezra] was in Aramaic script and Aramaic language."[18] However, the word for "letter" used in this passage is a rare Persian loan word that, transliterated into Aramaic, looks very much like the Hebrew word להשתנות (to be changed). TSanhedrin 4:7 thus reads the verse as stating: "The text [of the Bible] was changed to Aramaic writing and to Aramaic language." By leveraging a pattern of linguistic echoing in the concluding statement ("Why is [Aramaic square script] called 'Assyrian' [אשורי]? Because it came back with them from [the exile in] Babylon [אשור]"), this account thus suggests that the introduction of changes in the biblical text was associated with the cultural assimilation that arose under the shifting historical and linguistic circumstances of exile.[19] That is, this first tradition interprets the famous verse from Daniel as a statement that Ezra had composed a new edition of the Bible while the people were in exile—adapting both the writing and the language to their new home by bringing the ancient Hebrew tradition in line with the majority culture's imperial writing conventions.

Viewed from a vantage point after the composition of the early-medieval Aramaic targums (Bible translations), it is tempting to read this statement as a relatively limited etiology of those translations. By linking this tale to the

18. According to the use of "targum" to mean the spoken, comprehensible part of speech, as opposed to the script. For a selection of examples of this usage, see Marcus Jastrow, *A Dictionary of the Targumim, The Talmud Babli and Yerushalmi, and the Midrashic Literature* (New York: G. P. Putnam's Sons, 1903), 1695.

19. As Mark Leuchter has put it, describing the historical realities of the Aramaic transition: "The use of Aramaic script in the production of Hebrew-language texts subordinated the memory of Hebrew culture to the Aramaic culture promoted by the empire" ("Aramaic Transition," 254).

Aramaic portions of Daniel, however, tSanhedrin 4:7 implicitly associates Ezra's rewriting project with a more unsettling intersection of Hebrew and Aramaic in the biblical tradition: the jagged edges left in the biblical text by the inclusion of Aramaic passages in the books of Ezra, Daniel, and elsewhere. (And, indeed, the terminology *targum* is used elsewhere in tannaitic literature to refer to the Aramaic portions of Ezra and Daniel.)[20] In this reading of the story, which will be elaborated in the Babylonian Talmud's version of the tale, these suggestive editorial fractures in the biblical text are refigured as vestiges of an ancient scribal project in which Ezra produced a second version of the biblical text. According to this account, the shards of Ezra's revision project are visible today not in the rabbinic Aramaic translation tradition but in the imperial Aramaic square script used to transcribe the ancient Hebrew formulas and in the passages of Ezra's Aramaic-language edition that jut up here and there through the surface of the Hebrew text.

This critical strain is echoed (perhaps even amplified) in the next version of the story presented in tSanhedrin 4:7, according to which the alterations that Ezra introduced in the biblical text were aimed at returning the Torah to its original form after a sinful period in the history of Israel had caused the language of the Torah to change. Like the preceding version of the story, this tale leaves vague how serious the unintentional changes in question actually were. This ambiguity is accomplished by slipping back and forth between the claim that the "language" of the Pentateuch had changed (that is, the vital spoken meaning of the text, according the rabbinic vocabulary) and the idea that the "script" had changed (that is, the written signs used to record spoken meaning, according to the rabbinic lexicon).[21] In either case, however, this account imagines Ezra's editorial project as a form of scribal housekeeping— an attempt to restore the biblical text to its original state after a period of neglect and degradation. As tSanhedrin 4:7 puts it, this version of the story describes a "double change," in which the biblical text first moved away from its original form and was then later returned as faithfully as possible to its original state by an expert scribe. More importantly for our current purposes, perhaps, the changes that overtook the biblical text in this version of the story are not imagined as thoughtful adaptations implemented by a spiritual leader under challenging historical circumstances. Rather, they are presented as uncon-

20. See, for instance, Paul V. M. Flesher and Bruce Chilton's discussion of mYadayim 4:5: *The Targums: A Critical Introduction* (Waco: Baylor University Press, 2011), 317–18.

21. For more on the implications of these terms in the rabbinic vocabulary see, for instance, the discussion below on yMegillah 1:9 (71b).

trolled textual alterations that resulted from the neglect of a sinful people in the First Temple period. In this account of the changeable Torah, changes in the biblical text are attributed to corruption rather than redaction.

When First Temple waywardness is introduced as the historical context of Ezra's biblical restoration project, moreover, another story of serendipitous but suspicious textual restoration hovers ominously in the background. For this Tosefta account echoes a more famous moment of biblical textual restoration in 2 Kings 22:8–23:3, in which another priestly leader suddenly presents the people of Israel with a previously unknown "Book of the Torah" after the biblical tradition had been forgotten during a sinful period in the history of Israel. In that biblical account, substantial narrative space is given over to two themes of relevance to the Ezra story. 2 Kings emphasizes the apparent novelty of the biblical text in question and the unfamiliarity of its covenantal teachings to the people who received it. The 2 Kings narrative also draws attention to the fact that the communal leaders presented with this new-old version of the biblical text initially questioned the origins and authenticity of the work. When this 2 Kings story of textual restoration reverberates through a rabbinic passage constructed around the theme of a *mishneh torah*—a term that may mean either a changing Torah or a double Torah in the rabbinic lexicon—the disturbing notion that the biblical texts produced by these priestly leaders might represent *replacement* Torahs hangs heavy in the air. Whether we read this version of the Ezra story as an account of major textual changes or minor ones, this second version of the story is thus a tale shot through with multiform anxieties about the corruption and restoration to which the text of the Pentateuch has been subjected by the checkered history of Israel. As the Palestinian Talmud will sum up its own version of this passage, " 'He will write for himself this *mishneh hatorah* [lit.: copy of the Pentateuch]' (Deut 17:18). [This designation for the Pentateuch means:] a book of writing that is destined to change [להישתנות]" (yMegillah 1:9 (71b).

Like its early Christian parallels, this second Toseftan narrative leaves open to speculation how closely the newly restored text conformed to the Sinaitic original. While this account states that the Torah was returned to its original language by Ezra's restoration project, it does not offer assurances that the original text had been perfectly reconstructed, as medieval Jewish authors such as Yaʿqub al-Qirqisani would later do.[22] On the contrary, tSanhedrin 4:7 raises

22. See, for instance, Eve Krakowski's discussion of al-Qirqisani's treatment of this issue: "Many Days without the God of Truth": Loss and Recovery of Religious Knowledge in Early Karaite Thought," in *Pesher Nahum: Texts and Studies in Jewish Literature from Antiquity through*

36   CHAPTER 1

the possibility that Ezra was forced to undertake quite a significant amount of scribal reconstruction when it hints that Ezra worked not from a written document but from the strength of his own memory. In Rabbinic Hebrew, the terms *heart* and *memory* are often synonymous. So upon reading this early rabbinic statement that Ezra resembled Moses when he "prepared his heart" to "expound" the Torah and "make" the Law (Ezra 7:10), one cannot help but think of early Christian tales in which Ezra was forced to recreate the lost biblical text entirely from memory.[23] Indeed, since the phrase "familiar with the Torah as Ezra" was a popular early rabbinic idiom for someone who knew the entire biblical text by heart, it is even possible that this version of the story may have had a broader purchase in early rabbinic thought.[24]

Reading tSanhedrin 4:7 as a passage about textual change would seem to be affirmed by the nature of the additions that accrete to this tradition in the Palestinian and Babylonian Talmuds. Consider, for example, the way that the story of Ezra's textual restoration is colored by the following additions in the Palestinian Talmud. YMegillah 1:9 introduces the story that Ezra reworked the Pentateuch with the following remarks:

> They [ultimately] chose for themselves Assyrian [Aramaic] script and Hebrew language. And why is it called Assyrian (אשורי)? Because it is pleasant in its writing (מאושר בכתבו). R. Levi said that it is [called Assyrian] because they brought it back from Babylon (אשור).

The first sentence of this comment would appear to draw on the most radical visions of textual change latent in the earlier tradition. If Ezra's editorial project compelled the people to choose between two possible scripts and two possible languages, then it would seem that the people were faced with two complete parallel versions of the Pentateuch—one that transcribed an Aramaic version of the Bible in Aramaic square script and one that transcribed a Hebrew-language version of the Bible in Paleo-Hebrew script.

---

the *Middle Ages Presented to Norman Golb*, ed. Joel Kraemer and Michael Wechsler (Chicago: Oriental Institute of the University of Chicago Press, 2011), 122.

23. Indeed, Robert Kraft has drawn our attention to early Christian authors who count Ezra among the prophets for his extensive work of scriptural restoration ("Ezra Materials in Judaism and Christianity," in *Exploring the Scripturesque: Jewish Texts and Their Christian Contexts* (Leiden: Brill: 2009), 139–40.

24. See, for instance, the uses of this phrase in yMegillah 4:1 (74d) and Genesis Rabbah 36:26.

This opening frame also introduces an additional layer of source-critical realism to the account, in that it openly acknowledges that human transmitters made choices that affected the final shape of the biblical text. Moreover, these traditions imagine the textual choices in question as inflected by mundane, rather than spiritual, concerns. The first comment implies that Aramaic square script was preferred either for the ease with which it was written or for its pleasant aesthetic qualities,[25] while the second comment suggests that the biblical text had been transcribed in an Aramaic square script in order to bring it in line with the literary conventions of the dominant cultural milieu in exile. With the addition of this brief frame, yMegillah 1:9 thus transforms a story of textual restoration into a narrative about an intensive program of scribal editing and translation aimed to bring an ancient text in line with contemporary aesthetic and cultural values.

Nor does this opening frame represent the limits of the critical imagination that is given flight in this passage. In yMegillah 1:9 (71c), the Ezra story has also been juxtaposed to a narrative claim that evokes an even more radical possible reading of Ezra's editorial program:

> A certain watchman [*burgarius* or βουργάριος][26] falsified (בידא) an Aramaic [version] for them from a Greek [edition].

In later rabbinic literature, this remark is sometimes emended to "a watchman selected a Latin [translation] for them from the Greek [translation]"—and some modern scholars have supported this reading.[27] In the context of yMegillah 1:9, however, the standard text would seem to make more sense since all of the immediately adjacent traditions discuss Aramaic and Greek translations of the Pentateuch. The phrase "a certain watchman" is easily read as a veiled allusion to Ezra himself—a leader who oversaw a national revival built on the dual pillars of a restored Pentateuch and the military defense of a gradually rebuilt Jerusalem.[28] Even if we read this remark as an independent story, however, juxtaposing this tale of purposeful textual falsification with the story of an Ezran biblical edition raises new doubts concerning the nature of Ezra's

25. Depending on how one translates the phrase מאושר בכתבו.

26. On which terminology, see Christopher Furhmann, *Policing the Empire: Soldiers, Administrators, and Public Order* (Oxford: Oxford University Press, 2012), 225ff.

27. See, for instance, Arnaldo Momigliano, *Ottavo Contributo Alla Storia degli Studi Classici e del Mondo Antico* (Rome: Edizioni di Storia e Letteratura, 1987), 356–57 and the literature cited there.

28. On which see, for instance, Nehemiah 4.

Aramaic translation project because it demonstrates that a convincing but inauthentic Aramaic rendering of the Bible can be generated by linguistic reverse engineering, even without access to an original Semitic text. And this information takes on potentially alarming implications when considered in light of popular Mediterranean traditions like those described above, according to which Ezra was indeed faced with the challenge of reconstructing the biblical tradition without access to the original biblical text.

Based on the Ezra stories alone, it is difficult to say what precisely led the early rabbinic formulators of these traditions to imagine the text of the Hebrew Bible as unstable and historically contingent. However, in both the Palestinian (yMegillah 1:9 [71b]) and Babylonian Talmuds (bSanhedrin 21b–22a) an additional set of traditions have accreted to this passage that suggest some early rabbinic thinkers, at least, came to believe that the text of the Bible had undergone a certain amount of historical change because they saw evidence of these changes in the varied editions of biblical texts that surrounded them. BSanhedrin 21b, for instance, introduces the Ezra stories with the following statement:

> In the beginning, the Torah was given to Israel in Hebrew writing and the holy language, then it was given to them again in the days of Ezra in Assyrian script and Aramaic language. [In the end,] Israel chose for themselves Assyrian script and the holy language and they left the Hebrew writing (רועץ) and the Aramaic language for the lay folks. Who are the layfolks? Rav Hisda said: they are the Samaritans (כותאי). What is Hebrew script? Rav Hisda said it is "brick writing" (כתב ליבונאה) [i.e., the writing of the ostraca].[29]

This account of the historical relations that gave birth to various Hebrew and Aramaic iterations of the biblical text suggests that the authors of such traditions were aware that Semitic-language editions of the Bible similar but not identical to their own could be found throughout late antique Palestine and the Middle East—recorded in Paleo-Hebrew on ancient bits of clay and brick (כתב ליבונאה), transcribed in the neo-Paleo-Hebrew script (רועץ) of the Sa-

---

29. That is, the Middle Paleo-Hebrew found in archeological remains—judging by the shapes of the letters described in the parallel passage in the Palestinian Talmud. In yMegillah 1:9 (71b), for instance, the word ליבונאה is replaced with the word רעץ and the alphabet described includes a rounded ע (common to both Middle Paleo-Hebrew [i.e., 10th–5th c. BCE] and Samaritan script) and a bent ו (also common to both [and only] Middle Paleo-Hebrew and Samaritan script).

maritans (כותאי), and translated into a Samaritan Aramaic which was recorded in neo-Paleo-Hebrew script (כתב עברית ולשון ארמי).

YMegillah 1:9, similarly, records the (historically accurate) observation that "in the Torah of the ancients, neither the *mem* nor the *heh* was closed [as they are in the Aramaic square script]." And a related passage in bMegillah 3a proposes that "[the tradition of final forms for] *mem, nun, tzadi, peh,* and *kaf* were declared by the Seers [that is, the later prophets]" since "these [forms] existed [in ancient times] . . . but the [ancients] didn't know which [letter form] came in the middle of the word and which at the end of the word."[30] And from what we see in the extant works from Qumran, the medial and final forms were indeed often exchanged in those early writings.[31] It would seem, therefore, that the authors of these traditions imagined the biblical text as unstable and historically contingent because they saw paleographic and linguistic evidence of historical variation in the biblical writings around them.

The Game of Torah Telephone: Other Rabbinic Tales of Lost and Found Scriptures

Nor did early rabbinic thinkers consider Ezra's generation the only moment in the history of Israel when scripture had been subject to the exigencies of loss and reconstruction. From orthography to the cantillated punctuation tradition, diverse facets of the Pentateuch were imagined as textual features that had been forgotten and reconstituted at various points in Jewish history.[32] Many other traditions hint at the possibility that these moments of crisis involved more wholesale textual loss[33] and reconstruction.

---

30. For more on the interchange of medial letters in Paleo-Hebrew see Emmanuel Tov, *Textual Criticism of the Hebrew Bible,* expanded ed. (Minneapolis: Fortress, 2012), 197ff.

31. For representative examples, see the charts in Philip Alexander and Geza Vermes, eds., *Serekh Ha-Yaḥad and Two Related Texts,* Qumran Cave 4, 19 (Oxford: Clarendon, 1998), 20–23. For a possible explanation of this phenomenon see Tov, *Textual Criticism,* 378–86.

32. BMegillah 3a, for instance, lists the following facets of the biblical tradition as forgotten and reconstructed: various aspects of the written orthography; where verses ended; and the cantillation punctuation tradition. Nor was this exclusively a rabbinic motif. M. H. Segal argues, for instance, that 1 and 2 Maccabees also depict such a scenario ("The Promulgation of the Authoritative Text of the Hebrew Bible" *Journal of Biblical Literature* 72, no. 1 [1953]: 40–42).

33. Indeed, this motif of scriptural loss would survive outside of rabbinic circles well into the Middle Ages. Eva Mroczek, "Without Torah and Scripture: Biblical Absence and the History of Revelation," *Hebrew Studies* 61 (2020): 97–122.

40 CHAPTER 1

Not only did early rabbinic materials frequently elaborate, rather than efface, existing biblical accounts of the destruction and reconstruction of prophetic texts (such as Baruch's rewriting of Jeremiah's burnt prophecies),[34] but many early rabbinic traditions framed the loss of scriptural texts we see detailed in these biblical narratives as events that had continued to occur repeatedly in Jewish history, well into the rabbinic era. As Sifre Deuteronomy 48 puts it, for instance:

> It says, "*All* of you are standing today [in the presence of God (at Sinai)]" (Deut 29:9). If each one had not arisen and established the Torah in Israel (קיים תורה בישראל), would not Torah have been forgotten by Israel (תורה משתכחת מישראל)? [That is,] if Shaphan had not arisen in his era, and Ezra in his era, and R. Akiva in his era, would not Torah have been forgotten? As it is said, "How good is a word in its time" (Prov 15:23). "A word" that each one said [in his time] for there was a voice for all of them [at Sinai].

In such traditions, the account of lost and found Pentateuchal writings from the time of Shaphan (2 Kings 22:8–23:3) is imagined as reenacted not only in the time of Ezra but again in the time of R. Akiva. When scholars discuss these passages in relation to other questions in Jewish studies, they often read them as references to individual incidents in which a single Bible scroll was destroyed[35] or moments in which a portion of the rabbinic oral tradition was forgotten.[36] The notion that such statements might be taken literally as references to wide-scale textual loss or forgetting is never earnestly considered. Yet, in passages such as this one, two out of the three incidents cited in parallel were certainly remembered in the rabbinic tradition as eras of widespread textual loss or corruption. It seems most likely, therefore, that now-forgotten stories of textual loss and reconstruction were also attributed to R. Akiva in some early rabbinic traditions.

Read in light of parallel narratives in early rabbinic traditions, many similar passages are indeed shown to be stories about the problem of textual loss and recreation in the transmission of the biblical tradition. Consider, for instance, the following tradition from bSukkah 20a, which maintains that the Torah was lost and reestablished three times in the history of Israel:

34. See, for instance, Lamentations Rabbah 3:1 on Jeremiah 36:32.

35. That is, these statements are taken as referring to incidents resembling that described by Josephus in the *Jewish War* 2.12.229, ed. Martin Goodman (Oxford: Oxford University Press, 2017), 114.

36. In parallel to the scenarios such as that imagined in tEduyot 1:1.

In the beginning, when Torah was forgotten from Israel, Ezra came up from Babylon and established it (יסדה)). It happened again as before and it was forgotten (חזרה ונשתכחה). Hillel the Babylonian came up and established it. It happened again as before and it was forgotten. R. Hiyya and his sons came up and established it.

This passage is sometimes assumed to depict the process of reconstructing the rabbinic oral tradition. As we saw in the previous example, however, the first incident of forgetting and reconstruction listed in this passage (the Ezran Bible) was imagined elsewhere in early rabbinic tradition not as a moment in which the *oral* tradition was lost but as an instance of radical *textual* loss or corruption. BSukkah 20a presses us to read the other incidents in this list as parallel occurrences, in which precisely the same type of loss and restitution took place once again in later periods, since this short historical synopsis is punctuated by the repeating phrase "It happened again as before." In this case, the structure of the passage thus explicitly invites us to look for signs that the other moments of forgetting and reestablishment described were also instances in which the text of the Pentateuch had to be restored or recreated.

Although classical rabbinic literature does not preserve any narratives concerning a Hillelite edition of the Pentateuch that parallels the Ezra stories, this allusion to Hillel has sometimes been interpreted as an etiological remark about the origins of the biblical text—a story that seeks to explain the Babylonian forms introduced into biblical texts in Palestine in this period.[37] There are extant rabbinic traditions, moreover, that closely associate Hillel with both Moses and Ezra as a recipient of divine inspiration. TSotah 13:3, Song of Songs Rabbah 8:3, and bSanhedrin 11a,[38] for instance, report:

Once the later prophets Haggai, Zechariah, and Malachi died, *ruah hakodesh* (divine inspiration) departed from Israel, but even so they made use of the *bat kol* (divine echo, lit.: daughter of the voice). One time, they were sitting in the attic of Gadya's [bSanhedrin 11a: Gurya's] house in Jericho and a heavenly *bat kol* was produced and said to them, "There is one here who is worthy of *ruah hakodesh* (divine inspiration) [bSanhedrin 11a: worthy to receive the *shekhinah* (divine presence) like Moses our Teacher] only his generation isn't worthy of it." The sages looked at Hillel the Elder.

---

37. See, for instance, the classic treatment of Frank Moore Cross, *From Epic to Canon: History and Literature in Ancient Israel* (Baltimore: Johns Hopkins University Press, 2000), 217.

38. See also the rough parallel in bSotah 48b.

42   CHAPTER 1

And when he died, they said, "How pious and how humble, a [true] disciple of Ezra."

Whether or not this passage concerning Hillel's *worthiness* to receive divine revelation reflects a tradition that Hillel *did* receive divine revelation, it demonstrates that early rabbinic tradition was at least willing to consider the possibility that Hillel formed a link in this prophetic chain.

One does encounter explicit tales of textual loss and reconstruction, moreover, when one considers early rabbinic traditions about how R. Hiyya saved the Torah from oblivion. Like the story of Ezra, the tale of R. Hiyya is also a story in which the biblical text is lost and replaced. In the telling of bBava Metzia 85b and bKetubot 103b, for instance, R. Hiyya reconstructs sacred revelation virtually ex nihilo:

> Reish Lakish was making note of the graves of the rabbis. When he reached the grave of R. Hiyya it was concealed from him. He was discouraged and said: "Master of the Universe, did I not argue the Torah as he did?" A heavenly voice went out and said to him: "You argued the Torah like him, but you did not hold onto the Torah[39] as he did." When R. Hanina and R. Hiyya argued, R. Hanina said to R. Hiyya: "How can you argue with me? If, God forbid, Torah is forgotten from Israel, I could bring it back with my legal argument!" R. Hiyya said to R. Hanina: "How can you argue with *me*? Did I not actually make it so Torah was not forgotten in Israel?!"[40] What did I do? I went and sowed linen, and [from it] I raised up nets and caught deer, and I fed their meat to orphans, and I prepared scrolls, and I wrote out the Pentateuch, and I went up to the town and taught the correct reading of the Pentateuch to five children, and I taught the six orders of Mishnah to six children, and I said to them, teach each other the reading formula [for the

39. While רבץ is often translated as "spread" in this passage—reading the word as a metaphorical extension of the meaning "to sprinkle" or "to irrigate"—I would suggest that the content of the story that follows suggests instead a reading more in line with the Syriac use of the term, meaning "to hold onto" or "to keep within a space." See, for instance, the examples cited in J. Payne Smith, *A Compendious Syriac Dictionary* (Oxford: Clarendon, 1903), 527.

40. Although the tenses in this passage are ambiguous in both the printed and broader manuscript tradition, I read the incident as having occurred in the past (1) based on the parallel descriptions of this as a past incident in passages such as bSukkah 20a and yMegillah 4:1 (74d); (2) based on the comments that surround this narrative within the Talmudic texts themselves, and (3) in light of the fact that a conversation about current issues that took place in the past would now represent a historical story in any case.

Bible] and the Mishnah formula until I come back, and thus Torah was not forgotten in Israel."

This story is sometimes read as a story about the institution of elementary education in Israel—and certainly this is a narrative in which a particular educational tradition was established among the youth of Israel.[41] As we consider this tradition as a parallel to the Ezra stories, however, we would do well to appreciate that this is not only a story about the propagation of Torah but also the loss and recreation of the Pentateuch. Amram Tropper recently pointed out, for instance, that this passage draws on an earlier parallel to this story in yHagigah 1:7 (6b), in which R. Hiyya bar Abba is sent to the countryside to provide Bibles and encountered regions in which not a single Bible teacher or Mishnah tradition teacher can be found in the community.[42] As both yHagigah 1:7 and an earlier comment in the Babylonian Talmud put it, the Jewish people "had abandoned [God's] Torah." Read in light of this previous narrative, the passage paints yet another rabbinic portrait of biblical restoration in a time of crisis and loss.

Indeed, the formulas of the biblical tradition had been so thoroughly forgotten in this story that R. Hiyya was compelled to teach the formula of each book to a single recipient and to arrange for the reproduction of the tradition to spread out gradually from this original pupil. Moreover, the Pentateuch had not only been forgotten as a living tradition in this narrative but even the vestiges of the written text had disappeared so completely from the community that R. Hiyya was compelled to construct a new urtext from memory and arrange for its copying and dissemination. This tale emphasizes the novelty of R. Hiyya's edition of the Pentateuch when it claims that even the most basic structures that would make his literary efforts possible had disappeared from the community. R. Hiyya not only lacks parchment but must begin his literary efforts several steps earlier in the production process, laboriously growing flax to spin the nets necessary to catch the deer from whose skins he will make the parchment on which he will eventually inscribe the Pentateuch. While the formulator of this tradition lauds R. Hiyya's accomplishment, the narrative is

41. For a review of this scholarly trend, see Amram Tropper, *Rewriting Ancient Jewish History: The History of the Jews in Roman Times and the New Historical Method* (Abingdon: Routledge, 2016), 42–144. The role of the young students in this story is certainly striking. However, other versions of this tradition omit the educational aspects of the narrative entirely, focusing instead on Rabbi Hiyya's recreation of a Torah scroll ex nihilo (see, for instance, yMegillah 4:1 [74d]).

42. Tropper, *Rewriting*, 142–44.

simultaneously threaded through with anxieties concerning the historical fragility of the biblical text. In this tale, the forces of loss and forgetting nearly triumph and the biblical tradition is preserved by means of a treacherous bottleneck in which the entire tradition of the Pentateuch hangs on one man's memory.

If we read bSukkah 20a as a series of allusions to several such moments in the history of textual transmission, this telegraphic passage paints a vivid picture of the history of the biblical tradition as an alarming game of telephone, in which a series of losses and recreations transformed the Torah of Moses into the Torah of Ezra, then the Torah of Hillel, then the Torah of R. Hiyya. Whatever the practical result of this was understood to be, this passage paints a potentially disturbing picture of the vulnerability of the biblical text as a record of the divine will. Were any link in this chain of repeated forgetting and reconstruction to prove faulty, the text of the Pentateuch would be corrupted irretrievably for future generations—a historical possibility that was not entirely discounted by the authors of such traditions.

The Book That Unwrote Itself: Tales of the Second Tablets as a Poor Second Edition

Other classical rabbinic traditions suggest that it was not an accident of history that the inherited biblical text was a contingent and reworked product. As Sifre Deuteronomy elevates these occurrences to an abstract principle: "The Torah is destined to change" (Sifre Deuteronomy 160). Early rabbinic stories that unflatteringly contrast the first and second version of the tablets of the law (Exod 31–34), for instance, can be read as a form of narrative theorizing that elevates the contingent and secondary nature of the extant biblical text to a fundamental principle. This hermeneutic locates the roots of the historical vicissitudes of the biblical text in the deeper dictates of mythical time.

As the first instance of written revelation in the Hebrew Bible, the story of the two tablets (Exod 31–34) served as a natural locus for early rabbinic reflection on the nature of written revelation more generally. These biblical chapters took on even broader implications in a religious imaginary in which the tablets of the law were frequently treated as a metonymy for the Pentateuch as a whole.[43] Read in light of these traditions, Exodus 31–34 was often refigured in

---

43. See, for instance, tBerakhot 6:2, yShekalim 6:1 (49c), and ySotah 8:3 (22b), ySotah 8:3 (22b).

early rabbinic traditions as the story of two biblical revelations—a first, lost, revelation written by God in a moment of hope and a second, extant, revelation written by Moses during a period of human failing. From its inception, these traditions suggest, the text of the Torah that was ultimately given to the world was a second edition, which had already been shaped by human inadequacies and marked by the compromises inherent to written communication. This initial deficiency, in turn, would echo through the text's reception history. As bEruvin 54a puts it, "If the first tablets hadn't been broken, the Torah would never have been forgotten in Israel" (אלמלי לא נשתברו לוחות הראשונות לא נשתכחה תורה מישראל)."

Many traditions concerning the first tablets suggest that this more perfect version of the written revelation could never have entered historical time. Several traditions in this vein express doubts, for instance, that the materiality of the written medium was capable of capturing divine revelation. There was a widespread notion, for instance, that the first tablets represented a "miraculous product" (מעשה נסים) that defied the laws of nature. As Song of Songs Rabbah 5:14 variously pictures the impossible nature of the writing surface prepared for the first perfect form of the written revelation:

> Rabbi Yehoshua bar Nehemiah said, "They were made of [hard] blue gemstone but they could be rolled up [like a scroll]." While Rabbi Menahma said in the name of R. Abun, "They were carved out of the orb of the sun."

Since the original writing surface is identified with multiple (and irreconcilable) metaphorical vehicles, the particular substance of these images cannot be what interested the formulator of this tradition so much as their shared conceptual theme: the conviction that any material upon which the divine will was successfully inscribed must have been a substance that defied the laws of nature as we know them.

YShekalim 6:1 (49d) maintains that not only the writing surface but the writing materials for this first revelation took a dramatic and impossible form:

> The Torah that the Holy One, blessed be he, gave to Moses [the first time] was given to him as white fire carved on black fire. [The Torah] was fire. It was combined with fire. It was cut with fire. And it was given from fire. As it is written, "At his right hand the fire of knowledge" (Deut 33:2).[44]

---

44. See also the extensive list of parallel traditions cited in Barbara Holdrege, *The Veda and the Torah: Transcending the Textuality of Scripture* (Albany: SUNY Press, 1996), 473n92.

In traditions like this one, the gesture toward a more abstract principle is achieved through a repetition of the key image in different registers. Repeated variations on the claim that the first revelation consisted entirely of fire emphasize that the first (and fullest) attempt at a tangible revelation of the divine will was never captured or confined in the mundane materials of historical writing—stone and chisel, parchment and ink. Instead, it was manifest only in the most intangible and otherworldly of the material forces: fire.

The conviction that nothing short of a miracle could allow a fully divine revelation to be contained in the cold and limiting medium of written words on stone is given a more narrative form of expression in classical rabbinic traditions about the collection of sacred objects God established in the twilight before the first Sabbath—a period of paradox when the laws of nature were temporarily undetermined and when each of the instances when God would countermand the natural order and shake the created world were set for all of history. While the other objects in the list vary from one tradition to another,[45] both the writing on the first tablets and the writing materials that allowed that first inscription of divine revelation in writing are always counted among the miraculous and impossible objects. According to mAvot 5:6, for instance:

> Ten things were created in the interstitial hour [at twilight between the six days of creation and the first Sabbath]: the mouth of the earth [that miraculously swallowed Korach], the mouth of the well [that watered the Israelites in the desert], the mouth of the furnace [that failed to consume Abraham], the rainbow [after the flood], the manna [that sustained Israel in the desert], the staff [of Aaron and Moses that performed miracles in Egypt], the *shamir* [the worm that miraculously carved stones for the Temple without metal-cutting instruments], the writing [on the first tablets], the writing implements [with which the first tablets were written], and the [first] tablets (הכתב והמכתב והלוחות).

To the authors of such traditions, the notion that divine revelation could be successfully reduced to writing was just as uncanny and miraculous as a staff that could turn rivers of water into blood or a worm that cut through boulders of stone.

45. Alternate lists appear, for instance, in Sifre Deuteronomy 355 and bPesahim 54a and parallels. Consider, similarly, traditions that list the first tablets among the five miracles of God's hand, along with events such as Noah's ark and the plagues on Egypt (Pirke de Rabbi Eliezer 18:1).

A MAKESHIFT SCRIPTURE   47

Other traditions in this vein subtly remove the first tablets as a prototype for the extant biblical text by suggesting that this first more perfect form of the written revelation was never sustainable and could never have entered historical time. As bBava Kamma 55a conveys the sentiment:

> Why is "good" [the word that marks the completion of each act of creation in the biblical creation story] not written in regards to the commandments on the first tablets but is written in regards to the commandments on the second tablets? . . . Because they were destined to be broken [סופן להשתבר].

Per this tradition, the first tablets were not linguistically marked as finished because they were never meant to endure. From the very moment the first tablets were created, the formulators of this tradition argue, the first written revelation was distinguished as an innately ephemeral product.

A full and authentic written revelation could never be a permanent creation, proponents held, because a phenomenon as multifaceted and transcendent as the divine will naturally fights against the confinement and limitation of written transcription. One particularly popular rabbinic narrative explains that Moses broke the first tablets because the writing fled before it could be delivered to the Jewish people (yTa'anit 4:8 [68d]):[46]

> R. Yohanan said in the name of R. Yose bar Aviv, "The tablets were trying to fly away and flee and Moses caught hold of them, as it is written 'I took hold of the tablets' (Deut 9:17)." It was taught in the name of R. Nehemiah, "The writing itself flew off and fled." R. Ezra said in the name of R. Yehudah b. R. Rimon, "The tablets weighed forty *seah* and the writing was bearing their weight so that when the writing flew away they became heavy upon the hands of Moses and they fell and they broke."

Here again, the first written revelation is an impossible and paradoxical product. According to the laws that govern the natural world, the writing surface on which the first revelation was inscribed was hundreds of pounds heavier than a person could carry under normal circumstances. The first tablets were a gift that could not be given according to the laws of the natural world (at least not under the conditions described in the biblical narrative).

---

46. Compare Pirke de Rabbi Eliezer 45:8 and Targum Pseudo-Jonathan Exod 32:19. For a detailed discussion of this motif, see Pekka Lindqvist, "The Rewritten Broken Tablets," in *Rewritten Biblical Figures*, ed. Erkki Koskenniemi and Pekka Lindqvist (Winona Lake, WI: Eisenbrauns, 2010), 162–66.

48 CHAPTER 1

While the biblical text treats the destruction of the first tablets as a reaction to Israel's sinful idolatry, this passage suggests that the disintegration of the first tablets was inevitable—a coming apart that was inherent to their very composition. From the moment the first tablets were inscribed, the divine contents pulled in one direction, and the material medium in which they were inscribed pulled in the opposite direction. And before the revelation could even be presented to its intended recipients, the experiment had failed—the contents of the revelation were released back into the ether (as this passage puts it, "the writing flew away") and the tablets that had tried to anchor God's revelation to the material world lay shattered on the ground. What we learn from stories like these, I would argue, is that the early rabbinic thinkers who composed them saw the possibility of accurately preserving the unbounded divine will in letters etched on stone as a feat that an omnipotent divine being might successfully perform, but which even God himself could not sustain.

These claims of revelatory impossibility, in turn, raised doubts about what exactly the biblical text passed down through the generations represented. For if the fate of the first tablets illustrated that a full, authentic divine revelation could never be conveyed to its human recipients in writing, how were the second tablets—the symbolic representation of the extant written revelation—to be regarded? While a few medieval Jewish thinkers would come to valorize the second tablets,[47] classical rabbinic materials more often emphasized the limited and deficient nature of this recreated revelation. YMegillah 4:1 (74d), for instance, famously suggests that the first tablets had been a complete written revelation inscribed not only with the biblical text but also the expansive explanatory contents of Mishnah, Talmud, and midrash, while the second tablets contained only the extant biblical tradition, deemed meaningless without its oral counterpart.[48]

Early rabbinic thought on this matter is brought into sharper relief when read in tandem with analogous early Christian narrative motifs circulating in the broader late antique Mediterranean milieu.[49] Consider, for instance, two similar accounts drawn from early Christian and early rabbinic traditions that

47. See, for instance, Exodus Rabbah 46:1 and Ibn Ezra on Exodus 34:1.

48. The reader will also be familiar with more expansive versions of this tradition that imagined the first tablets inscribed not only with classical rabbinic literature and the novella of senior students but also practical rulings and late narrative traditions (Leviticus Rabbah 22:1 and Ecclesiastes Rabbah 1:8).

49. Although, again, I do not ascribe a direct genealogical relationship to any surviving early rabbinic and early Christian traditions on the topic.

A MAKESHIFT SCRIPTURE 49

each imagine the second tablets as a document that distances the recipient from authentic sacrality. Irenaeus contrasts the contents of the second tablets to those of the first tablets:

> First God gave them natural precepts . . . that is, the Decalogue (which one cannot be saved without observing) and demanded nothing more than these. As Moses affirmed in Deuteronomy in this way: "These are the words that God said . . . and added nothing . . . and wrote them on two tablets of stone" (Deut 5:22). . . . But when they turned back to make a calf and their souls reverted to Egypt longing to be enslaved instead of free, their desire was attained by their receiving slavery [through a new revelation] henceforth—which at least did not cut them off from God (*a Deo quidem non abscindentem*) although it enslaved them in a hard bondage (4.15.1). As the prophet Ezekiel said in explanation for the giving of such a law, "And their eyes followed the desires of their hearts, so I gave them precepts that were not good, and ritual formalities, in which they would not find life" (Ezra 20:25).[50]

In this early Christian rendering of the two-revelations narrative, the first revelation at Sinai was a life-giving revelation that would have bound the people of Israel to God with its simple natural precepts. The second tablets, in contrast, represented a revelation devoid of life-giving sacrality, which even the prophets of Israel recognized was "not good." Indeed, the nature of this second revelation was so problematic that the form of religious life it outlined was understood to represent a form of punishment—a ritualistic enslavement designed to control and chastise a community unprepared to be free. As we see in parallel sources that offer more detailed descriptions of this second revelation, the text in question was often understood to be the extant text of the Pentateuch—a document replete with purity laws, sacrifice, divorce, and other institutions that were understood to stand in contradiction to spiritual truth.[51] All that could really be said in favor of this document, this passage suggests, is that it was a compassionate compromise that served to distance a spiritually corrupt people from the divine rather than completely cutting them off from God.

---

50. Irenaeus, *Against Heresies* 4.15.1. Translation my own. Latin according to William Wigan Harvey, 2.187.

51. See, for instance, Justin Martyr, *Dialogue with Trypho* 19; Lactantius, *Divine Institutes* 4:10; Aphrahat, *Demonstrations* 15:18; *Apostolic Constitutions* 6.4.20; and *Didascalia* 26.

50 CHAPTER 1

A series of exegeses attributed to Rabban Yohanan b. Zakkai in tBava Kamma 7:3–5 similarly describes the second tablets in a way that associates them with the themes of divorce from God, slavery, and sacrifice:

Rabban Yohanan b. Zakkai used to say five things as a type of exegesis through parable[52] (כמן חומר):

Why were Israel exiled to Babylon of all places? Because it was the home of their father Abraham. He offered the following parable: This may be compared to a woman who has ruined herself (in relation to her husband) [by committing adultery] (שקלקלה על בעלה). Where does he send her [when he divorces her]? To the house of her father.

Concerning the first tablets it was said, "The tablets were the work of God [and the writing was the writing of God]" (Exod 32:16). But concerning the second tablets [it is said that] the tablets were the work of Moses (Exod 34:4, Exod 34:27–28) yet the writing was the writing of God (Exod 34:1). A[n explanatory] parable: What does the matter resemble? A king of flesh and blood who betrothed (קידש) a woman and brought his own scribe and quill and ink and the document (שטר) and the witnesses [to write the marriage bill]. [This is the first tablets.] Then she was ruined [by committing adultery] and she has to bring everything [with which to write the divorce document].[53] It is enough that the king writes his signature. [This is the second tablets.]

---

52. Reading this expression in keeping with its use in later classical rabbinic literature such as bKiddushin 22b.

53. In later iterations of this tradition, this story will sometimes be read as a story of two (unequal) marriage documents (Midrash Tanhuma Ki Tissa 17 and Exodus Rabbah 47:2). Indeed, Mordechai Friedman has argued that even the Tosefta's version of the tale could *conceivably* refer to two marriage bills, if we understand the second marriage bill to follow examples of medieval Egyptian marriage contracts in the "Palestinian formula," in which the groom might sign before the witnesses—a practice apparently described in yKiddushin 3:2 (63d), as well (Mordechai Akiva Friedman, "Khiyer yad vehatimat haluhot hasheniyim batosefta umidrash," *Te'udah* 7 [1991]: 179). Yet the only medieval midrash that spells out the procedure for a betrothal in relation to the Sinai event as a whole seems to imagine a process that mirrors most closely not the second document described in the Tosefta but the first: "And God said, 'carve yourself...' (Deut 10:1). [What is] the law when a Jewish man who betroths a woman, who needs to pay for the writing of the *ktav kiddushin* (marriage writ)? The sages transmitted the tradition that one does not write a betrothal writ or a marriage writ without the consent of both of them, but the groom pays the commission. And where do we learn that? From [the fact that] when God betrothed Israel at Sinai, as it is written 'God said to Moses, "Go to the people and

Indeed, [scripture] says: "When a prince sins" (Lev 4:22), happy is the generation whose prince brings a sin offering for his mistake. But it says: "His master will pierce his ear with an awl" (Exod 21:6). And why should the ear be distinguished for piercing above all the other organs? Because [the ear] heard [the words] at Mount Sinai: "For the Israelites are slaves to me" (Lev 25:55).[54] Yet it broke off the yoke of heaven, so a yoke of flesh and blood will rule over it. Therefore it is written in scripture that you will bring the ear and pierce it, since it didn't keep that which it heard.[55]

Another interpretation: He who didn't want to be enslaved to his master will come to be enslaved to his daughters.[56] But he said: "[Regarding] an altar of stones, do lift up iron on upon them" (Deut 27:5). And why did scripture choose to disqualify iron more than any other kind of metal? Because the sword is made from it and the sword is a symbol of punishment while the altar is a symbol of atonement—and one keeps a symbol of punishment away from a symbol of atonement. And if this is true concerning stones, which do not see and do not hear and do not speak when they bring atonement between the children of Israel and their father in heaven . . . isn't it all the more true concerning practitioners of Torah, who are an atonement for the world, that not one injurious thing should touch them? Indeed, it says, "You will build the altar of the Lord your God from whole stones (אבנים שלמות)" (Deut 27:6). [That is,] stones that bring peace (שלום). And if stones that do not see and do not hear and do not speak bring peace between the children of Israel and their father in heaven [so] God says they will be whole before me, how much more so [thanks to] practitioners of Torah, who are peace in the world, [will God say] they will be whole before me.

---

kiddashtam (sanctify or betroth them) today and tomorrow." ' And who wrote this document? Moses. As it is said 'Moses wrote this Torah' (Deut 31:9). And what payment did God provide Moses? The radiance of his face, as it is written, 'Moses did not know that it had rays of light' (Exod 34:29)" (Deuteronomy Rabbah 3:12).

54. YKiddushin 1:2 (11b) offers an alternative verse here: "You shall have no other gods before me" (Exod 20:3).

55. Reading this latter statement as a very loose paraphrase of the biblical tradition, in keeping with the rendering of this passage in yKiddushin 1:2 which omits the repetition of the phrase "as it is written" here.

56. Following the formulation in the Erfurt manuscript and the first printed edition of the Tosefta.

Read without reference to early Christian notions of the second tablets as an enslaving revelation and a decree divorcing Israel from God, this series of statements might not be immediately apparent as a continuous argument. When read against its broader intellectual context, however, this series of statements emerges as a subtle and surprising answer to the theory of the second tablets articulated by authors such as Irenaeus—simultaneously echoing this unflattering early Christian characterization of the Pentateuch and yet rehabilitating that portrait.

At a purely narrative level, of course, the opening parable in which the Northern Kingdom of Israel is imagined as a divorced wife sets the stage for the subsequent reading of the second tablets as a moment in which Israel is divorced from God, inasmuch as it introduces the principle that the relationship between God and the Jewish people is not static or eternal but that Israel may be "divorced" and "remarried" by God as her behavior merits. I would argue, however, that this allusion to the divorce allegory of Jeremiah 3:8–16 also sets the stage for the next parable in a darker way. The prophetic text can also be read as a statement about the imbrication of sacred writing, divine divorce, and spiritual alienation very similar to that proposed by tBava Kamma 7:4:

> As Israel committed adultery and was unfaithful at every opportunity, I sent her away and gave her a book of divorce (ספר כריתותיה). (Jer 3:8)

> Go and call out these words to the north and say, "Return, faithless Israel. God is merciful. I will not cause my anger to burn towards you, for I am generous. I, the Lord, am merciful and I will not stay angry forever." (Jer 3:12)

> In those days, God will be merciful and they will no longer speak of the Ark of the Covenant (ארון ברית) of the Lord. And it will not come to mind and they will not remember it. They will not be careful of it or perform it anymore. (Jer 3:16)

As an allegory of two lovers, this narrative sequence paints a poignant picture: a royal husband never forgets the faithless wife of his youth and remarries her in old age, when the memory of their rocky past together has faded and only the love remains.

A more unsettling meaning can be given to the vignette's terminology, however. The phrase "book of cutting off" is, of course, the standard lexicon for a divorce decree in the Hebrew Bible (Deut 24:1). When used to describe an estrangement between God and Israel, however, the phrase also evokes another, more ubiquitous, use of the word "cutting off" (כרת) in the Pentateuch: the spiritually loaded "cutting off" that will befall a sinner who has "broken [God's] covenant" (Gen 17:14) or "violated [God's] command" (Num 15:30). Further facets of meaning come to the fore when "book of cutting" is used in connection with allusions to the ark of the covenant, as it is in Jeremiah. The word "book" (ספר) is often used in the Hebrew Bible, of course, to refer to the Pentateuch in phrases such as the "book of Moses" (ספר משה) [57] or the "book of the covenant" (ספר הברית).[58] When imagined as a description of a sacred book, in turn, the word "cutting" (כריתות) evokes the phrase "to cut a covenant" (as in Exod 24:8, הברית אשר כרת עמכם and parallels). Originally, of course, the cutting associated with a biblical covenant was the literal act of cutting up the animal with which the covenant would be sealed (as in Gen 15:10). By late antiquity, however, the verb כרת has also begun to take on the meaning "to write" in some forms of Aramaic. To some late antique ears, therefore, the term ספר כריתות would be a phrase that brought to mind images of a book of covenantal sacred writing. When all of these associations were considered together, the third chapter of Jeremiah thus became (for some readers) a story that simultaneously evoked a divorce between God and Israel, the composition of the Pentateuch, and the notion that the receiver of the text in question was somehow being cut off from God.

Some early rabbinic traditions thus read these Jeremiah passages as suggesting that God had divorced Israel by handing them a covenant that represented a "book of cutting off" in the spiritual sense. Sifra Behukotai 1:2, for instance, understands the allegory of divorce and remarriage in Jeremiah to suggest God had given Israel a spiritually alienating covenant that would need to be annulled before God and Israel were spiritually reunited:

> "I will establish my covenant with you" (Lev 26:9). [This means:] It will not be like the first covenant, which you broke [לא כברית הראשונה שהפרתם אותה]. As it is said: "'Since they broke my covenant . . . though I was a husband to them,' declares God" (Jer 31:31). Rather it will be a new covenant that shall never be broken henceforth [ברית חדשה שלא תופר מעתה]. As it is said, "'Here the days are coming,' declares God, 'I will cut a new covenant with the house of Israel and the house of Judah'" (Jer 31:31).

57. Ezra 6:18, Nehemiah 13:1, 2 Chronicles 35:12, and parallels.
58. Exodus 24:7, 2 Kings 23:2, 2 Kings 23:21, 2 Chronicles 34:30, and parallels.

According to this interpretation, the book of divorce with which the allegorical husband sends his bride away in Jeremiah 3:8 can be imagined as a book containing a form of divine excommunication—he has divorced Israel not only physically but spiritually with a covenantal book of cutting off. As in Irenaeus, the covenant inherited from Sinai is imagined here as a form of covenant that divorces the people from God.

How such an image could be reconciled with a rabbinic theology that rejected supersessionism is explained by the next parable in the R. Yohanan b. Zakkai series. This passage represents a close allegorical reading of Exodus 31–34. For the purposes of this allegory, the pertinent elements of the biblical story are as follows: God wrote two tablets of the law with "the finger of God" and presented them to Moses (Exod 31:16–18). Before Moses could convey the tablets to the people, however, the Israelites committed the sin of the golden calf (Exod 32:1–14). Upon seeing this, Moses destroyed the divinely inscribed tablets he has just received (Exod 32:19). These lost tablets were then replaced with a second set of tablets that were engraved by Moses (Exod 34:27–28) but somehow also bore the writing of God (Exod 34:1).

Within the overarching narrative of Exodus 31–34, three exegetical cues were of particular concern to the formulators of tBava Kamma 7:4. First, they interrogate what it means to say that the first set of tablets were "written by the finger of God" (Exod 31:18). Second, they ask how the divinely composed tablets that were destroyed (Exod 31:16–18) differed from the final tablets written by Moses (Exod 34:27). Finally, they offer a solution to the puzzling claim that the second set of tablets were written both by Moses (Exod 34:4 and Exod 34:27–28) and by God (Exod 34:1). The Tosefta resolves the apparent contradiction by suggesting that Moses wrote this second text and God signed it.

Viewed from the point of view of the rabbinic marriage and divorce formulas standardized in the later Middle Ages, this statement is difficult to parse in relation to the themes of marriage and divorce alluded to in the Tosefta. In the formulas standardized in later halakhic literature, neither the *ketubah* (marriage contract) that had come to replace the *shtar kiddushin* (marriage writ) nor the *get* (divorce document) is signed by the husband. Read independently of these later developments, however, many early rabbinic references to the marriage writ or marriage contract seem to assume that the groom will either write the document himself or pay for a scribe to act as his agent.[59] While descriptions of divorce documents suggest that, in order to expedite divorces,

59. MKetubot 6:3, mBava Batra 10:3.

the divorce decree was often commissioned by the wife[60] and signed by the husband if not written in his autograph.[61] And, indeed, the earliest documentary examples of Jewish divorce decrees do indeed include the signature of the husband.[62]

Like the first tablets, then, a marriage writ was a document written (or commissioned) by a bridegroom in a time of hope as a necessary step toward acquiring the bride's loyalty and service. And like the first tablets, this document was written by the bridegroom or his agent but was not signed by the bridegroom. In parallel to the second tablets, on the other hand, an early rabbinic divorce writ was a document that could be composed on behalf of the bride to grant her freedom from a broken marriage—or even, in the wake of a misdeed, in order to release her from the obligations and punishments to which she was subject while under the marriage bond. This document was signed by the husband. The documents that marked the beginning and end of a rabbinic marriage were thus analogous in that both represented a document passed from husband to wife to define their relationship. The two documents were inversely related to one another inasmuch as one document established the relationship between the couple and the other dissolved it—just as the second tablet were thought to undo the newfound intimacy with the divine that had been offered by the first revelation.

With this allegory, the Tosefta has reconceived the narrative arc of Exodus 31–34 as follows: God first composes a written revelation that would function like a marriage writ, binding God and Israel together in holy intimacy. This is accomplished by the first tablets, composed directly by God. Before the marriage can be fully consummated, however, the bride Israel betrays her vows and fornicates with her golden calf lover in public. God is within his rights

60. BBava Batra 168a.

61. In keeping with this early position that the husband's signing of the divorce document was a distinct stage of divorce, some argue that witnesses (to the signing) could be waived if the husband wrote out the divorce document with its requisite names in his own recognizable handwriting, thereby signing his name within the document itself (mGittin 9:4), where others maintain that a divorce document could be written out generically as long as the signature was purpose written (bGittin 23a)—since it was the process of signing, not the process of writing, that was legally binding (mEduyot 2:3 and mGittin 2:5).

62. See, for instance, the Roman-era divorce document found at Wadi Murabba'at (Mur 19), which is signed by the divorcing husband al nafsha (for himself) before the signatures of the witnesses. (Transcription and images are available in Adah Yardeni, ed., 'Osef te'udot 'aramiyot, 'ivriyot venabatiyot miMidbar Yehudah vehomer karov (Jerusalem: Magnes, 2000), 1:131–33.

56   CHAPTER 1

to have his wayward bride executed (Deut 22:21). But the husband's agent destroys the marriage writ to protect her from punishment.[63] (As tBava Kamma 7:5 comments, "Happy is the generation whose prince [is willing] to incur a sin offering on her behalf.") The divine husband then agrees to a more merciful resolution of the problem. He will remove himself from the relationship and allow Israel's agent to compose a new divorce revelation that will free her from a level of intimacy that she has proven unable to withstand. In this allegory, the version of written revelation that was bequeathed to history was a "book of cutting" in all three of its possible meanings—(a) a version of the Pentateuch that (b) divorced the people of Israel from an angry God and (c) spiritually distanced them from divinity.

Thus far, the Tosefta concurs with cognate tales from early Christian authors that characterized the Pentateuch as a revelation that not only differed from the original ideal of divine revelation but actively distanced the people from God. In the next two parables, the Tosefta pushes the parallel still further when it identifies sacrifice and other ritual observances as the primary substance of this new revelation and, more surprisingly, accepts the identification of extant Pentateuchal law as a form of servitude akin to slavery. (As the Tosefta puts it, God declared "the Israelites are slaves to me" and "he who didn't want to become enslaved to his master" with dignity through the first revelation ended by becoming "enslaved to his daughters" in humiliation through the second revelation.) In other words, the authors of this series appear to have accepted the claim that the extant written revelation was a substitute revelation that temporarily abandoned the hope of an intimate divine-human relationship and instead enslaved the people to God with a more taxing and humbling observance.

This Tosefta tradition differed from parallel Mediterranean accounts of the second tablets only in the value that it ascribed to the servitude that the second version of revelation imposed. For unlike the early Christian authors cited

---

63. As Midrash Tanhuma Ekev 11:1 elaborates: "To what is the matter similar? To a king who betrothed a woman and said to her, 'Soon I will send you your *ketubah* (marriage contract) in the hands of a groomsman.' The king sent it after a while. But before [the groomsman] got there, he found that she had ruined herself with another man. What did the groomsman do? He tore up the *ketubah* (marriage contract). For he said, 'Better that she should be judged as a single woman and not as a married woman.'" (*Midrash Tanhuma 'im shene bi'urim*, ed. Enoch Zondel ben Joseph [Warsaw: D. Z. Zisberg, 1875], 105). As Avot de Rabbi Natan imagines the messenger's thought process, "If I give her a *ketubah* (marriage contract) now, she will be guilty of death" (Avot de Rabbi Natan B 1.2).

above, the Tosefta denies that these additional observances were imposed as a "punishment." Indeed, the final tradition in this series insists that these distancing observances were, on the contrary, the very antithesis of a punishment. They were a healing gift—an institution imposed for rehabilitation. The Tosefta argues that these observances would "bring atonement between the children of Israel and their father in heaven" and even serve as "an atonement for the world." Since Israel had proven unable to withstand spiritual intimacy with the divine in their current state, God held them apart from himself while they performed a program of rehabilitation that would slowly bring peace and understanding between God and Israel. In this account of the second tablets, written revelation is not associated with perfect understanding or divine truth; it is even described as a source of distance between humanity and the divine. But the revised revelation that was ultimately given to Israel is nevertheless identified not as a punishment but as a form of divine kindness—a secondary discipline that will prepare them to grow into the legacy of sacred truth that was promised to them as an inheritance.

Conclusion

The traditions gathered in this chapter do not disdain the form of written revelation that the rabbinic authorities had received. But neither do they valorize it as a perfect record of the divine will. The school of thought documented in this chapter maintains instead that the extant written revelation, both at its inception and throughout its transmission, was a makeshift scripture—an approximation of greater truths that had been repeatedly reshaped by human circumstances.

In an intellectual milieu that has been largely defined by early modern debates surrounding the rise of biblical criticism, such tropes might be expected to elicit shock or despair from premodern religious thinkers. And yet, if we were writing an affective history of the early Jewish relationship with the Bible, the traditions gathered in the first chapter of this book might be best characterized by a shared sense of resignation. The formulators of these traditions do not rail against the forces of cultural assimilation, aesthetic influences, and neglect that erode textual transmission and require written records to be continually reconstructed and repaired. The extant biblical text is accepted as unstable and historically contingent—leaving its inheritors with only a rough approximation of the Sinaitic revelation—because that is the inescapable nature of its medium, and written scripture is not immune.

The material and linguistic limitations of written text are treated in many of these traditions, indeed, as a priori rendering writing too circumscribed a vehicle to authentically represent the multifaceted will of an omniscient divine. For when tales of the second tablets trace the process of textual loss and recreation beyond history into the waters of mythical time, they suggest that the vicissitudes of the extant biblical text can be traced to its originary nature as always already a second edition. As an insufficient trace of a fuller revelatory instinct, the biblical text represented by the second tablets would always be vulnerable to the ravages of history and the human mind. According to this line of thought, written text as we know it simply could not adequately contain divine truth nor could the resulting sacred text ever be robust enough to be secured from the damage to which the medium of writing is inevitably subject in historical transmission.

2

A Book That Kills

RABBINIC STORIES ABOUT LETHAL
ENCOUNTERS WITH BIBLICAL TEXT

THE LAST CHAPTER ANALYZED early rabbinic traditions that imagine the biblical text had been lost, reconstructed, or reissued. These narratives grapple in different ways with the notion that the extant biblical text was a makeshift revelation that was by its very nature distanced from perfect truth. There are certainly good reasons to view this tendency to downgrade the biblical text with a certain cynicism. Early rabbinic authorities had a strong self-serving motive for circumscribing the revelatory authority of the written text in favor of their own interpretative traditions and authority.[1] And, indeed, many early rabbinic traditions on the theme of biblical insufficiency do contrast the limitations of the biblical text with the benefits of a living interpretive tradition.[2] Yet the concept of biblical insufficiency was certainly not invented for the promotion of the rabbinic authorities. The notion of an insufficient or incomplete scripture was a long-standing motif with roots in the Second Temple

---

1. As Martin Jaffee puts it more gently, "One can explain in a minimal sense why the fictionalization of rabbinic oral tradition as Torah in the Mouth proved so crucial to the developing social systems surrounding the rabbinic masters of the third century and beyond. The answer . . . has much to do with a larger struggle . . . over the relative primacy of the Sacred Book or its Expounders in the spiritual formation of literate intellectuals." Martin Jaffee, *Torah in the Mouth: Writing and Oral Tradition in Palestinian Judaism 200 BCE–400 CE* (Oxford: Oxford University Press, 2001), 7.

2. Consider, for instance, the classic parable contrasting the prophet with the sage in yAvodah Zarah 2:8 (41c) and the discussion of Steven Fraade, "Concepts of Scripture in Rabbinic: Oral and Written Torah," in *Jewish Concepts of Scripture: A Comparative Introduction,* ed. Benjamin D. Sommer (New York: New York University Press, 2012), 30–46.

period—gaining theological traction among scribal authors long before the rise of a self-consciously oral rabbinic cultural elite.[3]

In its prior Second Temple form, however, the insufficiency attributed to the biblical text was a fecund insufficiency—a limitation that pointed elsewhere and offered new avenues for creative productivity. In many early rabbinic iterations of this claim, the inherited motif seems to have taken a darker turn. Here the biblical text is not merely identified as a *dead* form of sacred truth pruned from an inexhaustible living branch of divine revelation but as potentially *deadly* form of revelation.

The present chapter limits its study to a selection of stories featuring one extreme example of this tendency: traditions in which engaging with the biblical text endangers the life of an individual or community.[4] Did the early rabbinic thinkers who formulated these stories believe that too close contact with the biblical text was literally lethal? Perhaps not.

Yet as we have learned from Ellen Muehlberger's recent work on imagined death in early Christian communities, late antique visions of death and dying can also be read as a rich "fund of thinking about the nature of humanity"[5]— particularly in the face of uncertainty. In the materials Muehlberger analyzes, the kind of death imagined for an individual formed part "a larger system of signals from which Christians drew certainty in the face of ambiguity" because assigning a famous person "a good death could be a signal of faithfulness that overrode evidence of promiscuity in life, while a bad death could be a signal of an essential failure that overrode evidence of political or social excellence in life."[6] This chapter adapts Muehlberger's model to analyze early rabbinic stories about lethal encounters with the biblical text—treating these stories as an analogous form of theoretical reflection on the ambiguous nature of the

---

3. See, for instance, Eva Mroczek, *The Literary Imagination in Jewish Antiquity* (Oxford: Oxford University Press, 2016); Hindy Najman, "Interpretation as Primordial Writing: Jubilees and Its Authority Conferring Strategies," *Jewish Studies Journal* 30 (1999): 379–410; Najman, *Seconding Sinai: The Development of Mosaic Discourse in Second Temple Judaism* (Leiden: Brill, 2003); and Benjamin Wright, "Jubilees, Sirach, and Sapiential Tradition," in *Enoch and the Mosaic Torah: The Evidence of Jubilees*, ed. Gabriele Boccaccini and Giovanni Ibba (Grand Rapids, MI: Eerdmans, 2009), 116–30.

4. Examples of milder consequences can be found in Rebecca Scharbach Wollenberg, "The Dangers of Reading as We Know It: Sight Reading as a Source of Heresy in Classical Rabbinic Literature," *Journal of the American Academy of Religion* 85, no. 3 (2017): 709–45.

5. Ellen Muehlberger, *Moment of Reckoning: Imagined Death and Its Consequence in Late Antique Christianity* (Oxford: Oxford University Press, 2019), 23.

6. Ibid., 31.

written revelation and its affordances. In the early rabbinic imaginary, the biblical text's penchant for triggering death and mortal danger offered supernatural evidence concerning the underlying perils of written revelation, which belied the famous rabbinic liturgical claim that the Hebrew Bible is universally "a tree of life for those who hold fast to it" (Prov 3:18).

Read as theoretical reflections on the nature of the biblical text, the passages in this chapter capture a growing instinct in some early rabbinic circles that very real spiritual and social dangers adhered to the possibility of inappropriately reifying written records of the biblical revelation as an extension of divinity when the written transcript of the biblical revelation was understood by many as something more like an echo of a divine voice congealed into written text. Such a misidentification of the nature of the biblical text, these stories suggest, could be dangerous to the point of death.

At first glance, the passages collected here appear to offer up an almost infinite diversity of ways in which the biblical text can endanger one's life. Below the surface, however, one may detect certain persistent threads of worry. In particular, the themes of textual promiscuity or infidelity are heavily woven into many of these stories.

In the age of mass printing and hypertext, we are accustomed to being warned against the promiscuity or infidelity of *readers*. For the proliferation of text in the print era soon brought about accusations concerning the "mischief of unconnected and promiscuous reading."[7] As a late nineteenth-century reviewer personified this imagery, "placed among the countless shelves of modern libraries . . . there are so many newcomers that a reader felt himself called upon to give up his best friend, to step across and chat with the smartly dressed crowd of strangers."[8] The subsequent arrival of a hypertext technology more literally allowed the reader to jump between texts or read several texts at once until this system evoked for many observers a sense that our new mediascape functioned under a "general rule of textual promiscuity."[9]

A few modern authors, however, have applied the concept of textual promiscuity not to readers who skip and skim unfaithfully from text to text but instead to the very texts themselves, which are imagined as betraying one reader with another. As Howard Bloch and Carla Hesse put it, "Electronic

---

7. Nineteenth-century author Samuel Taylor Coleridge as quoted in Karen Littau, *Theories of Reading: Books, Bodies, and Bibliomania* (Cambridge: Polity Press, 2006), 44.

8. Ibid., 45.

9. Stuart Moulthrop, "Informand and Rhetoric: A Hypertext Experiment," *Writing on the Edge* 4, no. 1 (1992): 118.

reading *necessarily* evokes images of uncontrollability, of promiscuity even, since, in the words of Grunberg and Giffard, 'the same work can be read simultaneously by as many readers as request it.'"[10] In this vision of the hypertext world, the ability to connect massive amounts of text indiscriminately across time and space cannot help but render "borderlines delimiting texts . . . porous and infinitely malleable," so that texts themselves become guilty of "textual promiscuity and miscegenation."[11]

While much of the modern discourse on textual promiscuity probably derives some of its vivid biological imagery from the confluence of early biological thought and text-critical models,[12] it nevertheless possesses an uncanny ahistorical resonance with the personified images of textual infidelity conjured by early rabbinic thinkers to imagine the perils of a written revelation. Each of these early rabbinic accounts explores in some way the dangers that can be posed by the creation of a sacred text-body—a tangible and independent material representation of divine truth that lives a literary social life independent of its author. For the rabbis were embedded in a broader epistemic culture in which the cosmos talked back. That is, late antique Mediterranean thinkers lived in a "cosmos that was both the subject and object of knowing; it was itself a rational organism."[13] In this epistemology, human beings could not only act on their environment "but can also be acted upon by the material, spiritual, social, and otherwise non-human elements of their world."[14] In this animated universe, the existence of an independent material manifestation of a sacred revelation posed very real challenges since the infidelities of a transformed and transforming sacred text could affect their human readers in modes similar to a faithless human partner or comrade.

In early rabbinic narrative, indeed, the biblical text is anthropomorphized as both an unfaithful partner and a traitorous comrade. In a few examples, rogue biblical texts are imagined as unfaithful in a strong sense. The biblical

10. Howard Bloch and Carla Hesse, introduction to in *Future Libraries,* ed. R. Howard Bloch and Carla Hesse (Berkeley: University of California Press, 2022), 4.

11. Carla Hess, "Humanities and the Library in the Digital Age," in *What's Happened to the Humanities,* ed. Alvin B. Kernan (Princeton, NJ: Princeton University Press, 2016), 112–13.

12. Yii-Jan Lin, *The Erotic Life of Manuscripts: New Testament Textual Criticism and the Biological Sciences* (Oxford: Oxford University Press, 2016).

13. This wording is attributed to C. M. Chin in C. M. Chin and Moulie Vidas, introduction to *Late Ancient Knowing: Explorations in Intellectual History,* ed. C. M. Chin and Moulie Vidas (Berkeley: University of California Press, 2015), 7.

14. Blossom Stefaniw, "Knowledge in Late Antiquity: What Is It Made of and What Does It Make?," *Studies in Late Antiquity* 2, no. 3 (2018): 270.

text is treated as actively betraying those to whom it owes its first loyalty, for instance, when a biblical text is envisioned as a sort of avatar of revelation that can be recruited to fight against the divine author's intended human recipients. In many cases, however, this embodied instantiation of revelation was not imagined as a strong subject—an actor whose body is true to its higher purpose.[15] Instead, the act of hypostasizing sacred truth into a limited material vessel was imagined to circumscribe the sacred power of that divine truth in a way that makes it vulnerable to abuse and corruption. This instinct is vividly captured, for instance, in the many early rabbinic traditions that imagine the biblical text as an adulterous woman. In doing so, the formulators of such rabbinic traditions leverage the allegorical power inherent to early rabbinic anxieties about the dangers posed by an independent female body, which was simultaneously thought to wield a passive power over men and yet simultaneously suffer from an incurable vulnerability to promiscuity and misdirection. In such cases, like an unfaithful rabbinic wife who brings great spiritual danger to her husband when she acquiesces to the caresses of another, the danger of the biblical tradition lies in the ease with which a written text quietly acquiesces to the interpretive desires of others.

The Warrior and the Wife: Stories of Dangerous Bibles in Tannaitic Tradition

In the earliest strata of rabbinic tradition, the nature of the mortal danger emanating from the biblical text is both subtly imagined and quite narrowly defined. Mishnah, Tosefta, and halakhic midrash bear witness to an emerging concern that the written text of the Hebrew Bible can be turned into a source of evil and death when it falls into the hands of the *minim* (sectarians or heretics).[16] As Sifre Numbers puts it, in the hands of the *minim*, written scripture is refigured into a font of "enmity, hatred, jealously, and accusers" that would be better "wiped out from the world" (Sifre Numbers 16).[17] While the

---

15. For more on the notion of a bifurcated subject and its connection to bodily or social weakness in late antiquity, see Mira Balberg and Ellen Muehlberger, "The Will of Others: Coercion, Captivity, and Choice in Late Antiquity," *Studies in Late Antiquity* 2, no. 3 (2018): 294–315.

16. For more on the complexities of this term, see the book-length treatment of Adiel Schremer, *Brothers Estranged: Heresy, Christianity and Jewish Identity in Late Antiquity* (Oxford: Oxford University Press, 2010).

17. See also bShabbat 116b.

64 CHAPTER 2

Sifre Numbers version of the tradition does not elaborate on the precise nature of the "enmity" and "accusations" that emerge from sectarian biblical texts, this vocabulary is closely associated in other early rabbinic traditions with threats of mortal danger to the Jewish community.[18]

While other tannaitic versions of this tradition will associate the dangers of sectarian biblical texts with communities in which the Hebrew Bible is being used in conjunction with Gospel texts,[19] Sifre Numbers 16 does not consider the question of new books being attached to the biblical text. Rather, the midrash is concerned with the notion that the text of the Hebrew Bible *itself* can be weaponized in a way that transforms its functional character:

> [In the ritual of the wife accused of adultery, the priest will write the verses] "in a book (ספר) and wipe it out in water" (Num 5:23). Because of this [use of the term "book" specifically associated with biblical scrolls], they said that one may not write the verses on a tablet nor on a papyrus sheet nor on a hide prepared for documents[20] but only in a ritual scroll (מגילה), as it is said, "in a book" (Num 5:23). Similarly, one may not write with gum resin, nor with iron-gall, but only with ink [ritually appropriate for writing biblical scrolls]. As it is said, "and wipe it out into bitter water," which means [that one must use ink] that can be dissolved.[21] And [from here we learn] that if God said to wipe out in water a book written in holiness in order to bring peace between a man and his wife, all the more so must one wipe out from the world the biblical books of the *minim* which produce enmity, hatred, jealously, and accusers (מטילים איבה ושנאה וקנאה ובעלי דבבות). Rabbi Yishmael says, "How does one treat the biblical books of the *minim*? One cuts out the mentions [of the name of God] and burns the rest." Rabbi Akiva says, "One burns the whole thing in its entirety because it was not written in holiness [as an authentic biblical scroll is]."

The pressing issue here is not the emerging differences between rabbinic Bibles and sectarian ones but their similarities. The passage is concerned that there are editions of the Bible in circulation that are linguistically and materi-

---

18. See, for instance, mAvot 2:11; bYoma 9b; Avot de Rabbi Natan A 16:4; bShabbat 32b.

19. See the treatment of tShabbat 13:5 below.

20. For more on these terms and their evolving meaning, see Menachem Haran, "Book-Scrolls at the Beginning of the Second Temple Period: The Transition from Papyrus to Skins," *Hebrew Union College Annual* 54 (1983): 111–22.

21. Since carbon ink can be wiped out by water but iron gall ink must be scraped by hand. For more on these processes, see Ron Hendel, *Steps to a New Edition of the Hebrew Bible* (Atlanta: Society of Biblical Literature Press, 2016), 170–72 and the literature cited there.

ally identical with the biblical books of the rabbinic Jewish community but nevertheless function in opposing modes to the rabbinic Bibles that they so closely resemble.[22] By introducing the problem of sectarian biblical books in the midst of a passage focused on the ritual minutiae through which biblical books are produced, the passage emphasizes the extent to which the textual bodies of these two sets of biblical texts are superficially similar, even identical. As Rabbi Akiva implicitly frames the problem, these two sets of biblical books might be indistinguishable except for the intangible distinction that one text was written "in holiness" and the other transcribed with improper intentions. But where rabbinic copies of these biblical books produce spiritual health, sectarian copies of these same texts give birth to its opposite. In this reading of biblical textuality, the nature of the biblical text is not fundamentally static in its sacrality. Even where the words remain the same, biblical texts can be transformed into a source of poison so potent that they must be "wiped out from the world."

More importantly for our purpose, this passage and others like it linguistically mark the biblical books themselves as the malicious actors in the scenario. A parallel version of this tradition in tShabbat 13:5, for instance, elaborates on the notion that sectarian biblical books themselves somehow pose a mortal danger to the Jewish community.

---

22. Whether this resemblance was entirely a figment of the rabbinic imagination or reflected some form of historical reality remains unclear. The identity of the *minim* cited itself remains unclear (for more on this problematic, see Schremer, *Brothers*). The adoption of codices has often been cited as the distinguishing media feature of early Christianity. See, for instance, Larry Hurtado, *The Earliest Christian Artifacts: Manuscripts and Christian Origins* (Grand Rapids, MI: Eerdmans, 2006), 43–94, and David Stern, *The Jewish Bible: A Material History* (Seattle: University of Washington Press, 2019), 58–61 and 66–68 and the literature cited there. But Eva Mroczek and others have argued that the construction of this dichotomy is itself more a scholarly echo of Christian supersessionism than a reflection of a historical reality. Eva Mroczek, "Scribes, Scrolls and Supersessionism: Insidious Tales of Material Texts in Antiquity" (lecture at Borns Jewish Studies Program, Indiana University, Bloomington, IN, December 2, 2011). Scholars have also increasingly taken up the study of Eastern Christian liturgical scrolls and other types of religious scrolls in early Christian communities. (See, for instance, the program of the Symposium on Eastern Christian Scrolls at Catholic University of America on February 22, 2019.) While Robert Bagnall's recent empirical study of early Christian books from Egypt offers the mixed conclusion that the "Christians may not have used the codex for other types of written material significantly earlier or to a much greater degree than other people" but "they did apparently adopt it from as early as date as we have evidence as the standard formation for professional copies of the Bible." Robert S. Bagnall, *Early Christian Books in Egypt* (Princeton, NJ: Princeton University Press, 2009), 79.

66   CHAPTER 2

One doesn't save either the empty writings of the Christian Bible[23] [reading *gilyonim* as a pun on the rabbinic word for blank sections on a biblical scroll, discussed in the preceding section, and the Christian word *euangelion*][24] nor the Pentateuchs [lit.: books][25] of the *minim* from burning [on Shabbat]. Rather they are allowed to burn in their place together with the mentions [of the name of God] (הזכרותיהן) that are in them. Rabbi Yose the Galilean says, "On weekdays, one cuts out the mentions of [the name of God] that are in them and puts those in *genizah* but burns the rest." Rabbi Tarfon said, "May I bury my sons, if these [biblical texts] come into my hands, I will burn them and the mentions [of the name of God] that are in them. For even if a man were running after me to kill me (הרודף רודף אחרי), I might enter a house of idol worship, but I would not enter their houses. For idolators don't recognize Him when they deny Him but these recognize Him and yet deny Him. About them scripture says, 'You put your [adulterous] sign (זכרונך)[26] behind the door and the mezuzah [and went away from me to reveal your nakedness and raised up and widened your bed and made a covenant with those whose bed pleasures you loved and whose nakedness you gazed on]' (Isa 57:8)." Rabbi Yishmael said, "If God said that we should wipe out with water a biblical text that was written in holiness in order to bring peace between a man and his wife [in the *sotah* ritual],[27] how much more so should we wipe out the biblical texts of the sectarians and their mentions of the name of God (הזכרותיהן) since they cause enmity between Israel and their father in heaven. For scripture says of them 'Will I not hate those who hate you, God, and fight those who rise up against you?' (Ps 139:21)."

As in Sifre Numbers, Tosefta Shabbat identifies "the biblical books of the sectarians" rather than their owners as the agents that "cause enmity between

23. While this reading of tShabbat 13:5 was at one time debated due to the ambiguity of the term *gilyonim* and the category of *minim* more broadly, it has increasingly been accepted as a reference to the Gospels in recent years. See, for instance, Steven T. Katz, "The Rabbinic Response to Christianity," in *Cambridge History of Judaism*, vol. 4, *The Rabbinic Period*, ed. Steven T. Katz (Cambridge: Cambridge University Press, 2006), 278–79 and the literature cited there.

24. Reading a pun here something like those described in bShabbat 116a–b: "R. Meir used to call it [that is, the Christian Bible] *'aven gilyon* (a wicked empty scroll). R. Yohanan used to call it *'avon gilyon* (a sin scroll)."

25. Reading the unmodified description biblical "books" as referring to *sifre Torah* (Torah scrolls) or their equivalent.

26. Which echoes the term הזכרותיהן (divine names) elsewhere in the passage.

27. Numbers 5:12–31.

Israel and their Father in Heaven." But Tosefta Shabbat also goes further and personifies these rogue biblical books as "those who hate you" and "those who rise up against you." Indeed, this passage advocates a direct campaign against these corrupt Bibles in which sectarian biblical books are not only passively destroyed but actively sought out and burned. However superficially similar they might appear to sacred biblical texts, these sectarian biblical books are not to be treated as blameless and inert captives that can be redeemed from a malicious enemy and rehabilitated through proper use—nor even as ambiguous manifestations of sacrality to be removed to a dignified if ambivalent burial.[28] Made physically independent of the revelation they represent, sectarian editions of the biblical text can become guilty actors in their own right.

In the Tosefta version of this tradition, the mortal dangers associated with sectarian biblical books are also brought out in sharper relief. In the mythical history of Israel, of course, alienation between God and Israel frequently produces literal dangers that mirror that supernatural conflict. The very nature of the disturbance in that relationship introduced by sectarian books in this passage thus implicitly evokes the possibility of more literal dangers to follow. Heightening this impending sense of threat are statements like Rabbi Tarfon's, which introduce the language of physical death into the discourse about sectarian biblical texts. The very phrasing of R. Tarfon's vow, "may I bury my sons," suggests that the death of one's children is somehow equivalent to the dangers carried by sectarian biblical texts. This imbrication of sectarian biblical texts and mortal danger is even more clearly marked in R. Tarfon's insistence that the mortal danger posed by a *rodef*, a killer chasing a victim to kill, is less severe than the dangers attached to entering sectarian houses of worship. Once the paradigmatic *rodef* killer has been introduced into the problematic, the mortal danger inherent to other motifs in this passage are suddenly brought into starker relief. War is, after all, a mortal struggle. The public adultery imagined in this passage left a woman vulnerable to the death penalty. And drinking the biblical writing dissolved in the *sotah* ritual brought the guilty party to a mystical death at the hands of heaven. It is this last motif, in which biblical text is transformed into a bitter mystical poison, that seems to capture best the inchoate sense of dread expressed throughout this passage. Just as the biblical scroll in the *sotah* ritual is transformed into a powerful but mysterious

---

28. On the equation of Torah disposal and human burial already in the tannaitic period, see Adiel Kadari, " 'This One Fulfilled What Is Written in That One': On an Early Burial Practice in Its Literary and Artistic Contexts," *Journal for the Study of Judaism in the Persian, Hellenistic, and Roman Period* 41, no. 2 (2010): 191–213.

supernatural poison, so sectarian Bibles transform the biblical revelation into a mystical threat—a spiritual source of literal dangers all the more terrifying since its mechanism is not transparent.

The mechanism at work in this analogy is clarified, however, if one considers the images of adultery threaded through the passage. Particularly in the Tosefta version of this tradition, the terror of uncontrolled biblical texts is evoked by referencing the terrors that early rabbinic thought attributed to the independent female body. Indeed, this passage is threaded through with multiform allusions to this parallel, as sectarian biblical texts are simultaneously compared to the illicit messages that an adulterous woman sends to her lover, to the biblical writing that must be destroyed in the *sotah* ritual in order to restore peace between a husband and his wayward wife, and to the adulterous wife herself. Just as (in the rabbinic imaginary) an act of adultery could refigure the apparently unchanging body of a living woman from beloved to hateful and from productive to mortally dangerous, so the text body of the Sinaitic revelation can be intangibly corrupted by entering into adulterous "covenants" with outsiders. For when sectarians recognize the existence of the God of Israel but deny the exclusivity of his covenant, these outsider readers metaphysically transform the inscriptions of God's name (הזכרות) in the biblical text into the traitorous signs (זכרונות) that the allegorical adulteress leaves for her lover in Isaiah 57:8. While the physical letters of the text body remain the same, the spirit of the biblical text is invisibly perverted so that sectarian texts of the Hebrew Bible no longer tie the Jewish people to God in holy marriage but instead invoke a supernatural "enmity between Israel and their Father in Heaven."

Where the sources above evoke images of marital infidelity without firmly establishing their metaphorical vehicle, traditions such as Sifre Deuteronomy 345 explicitly apply the metaphor of fidelity in marriage to a bond between the Torah and Israel. For according to Sifre Deuteronomy:

> The Torah is betrothed to Israel (מאורשה היא לישראל) and is like a married woman to the nations of the world (אשת איש לאומות העולם). And this is why it said, "Does a man bring fire into his lap without burning up his garments? Can a man walk on burning coals without his feet getting scorched?" (Prov 6:27–28). So it is with "one who approaches the wife of his fellow, no one who touches her will be clean" (Prov 6:29 inverted).

At the simplest level, this passage warns that "the nations are prohibited from 'touching' the Torah, just as a man is prohibited from touching another's wife."[29] Yet the line "no one who touches her will be clean" simultaneously evokes the dual prohibition that early rabbinic practice placed on an adulterous wife. A rabbinic adulteress was forbidden not only to her lover but also to her husband. As the adulterous wife is often imagined confessing her promiscuity to her husband, "I am defiled to you" (mSotah 1:3). This passage thus suggests that a biblical text that has been in the hands of an outsider should be treated as irreparably defiled in some way, just as an unfaithful rabbinic wife was imagined to poison or impurify her marital bed through infidelity.

In narrative traditions in this vein, moreover, sectarian engagement with the biblical text transmogrifies the biblical text into a toxin that is *literally* deadly to one who imbibes it. Consider, for instance, the famous pair of stories about early rabbinic interactions with the followers of Jesus[30] in tHullin 2:22–24.[31] The passage opens with the tale of Elazar b. Dama and the snake:

> A story about Elazar Ben Dama, who was bitten by a snake and came to Jacob, a man of Sama village, to heal him in the name of Jesus b. Pantera.[32] R. Yishmael would not allow him [to be healed]. They said to him "you are not permitted [to do this], Ben Dama!" He said to them, "I will bring you a proof text (ראיה)[33] that he may heal me." But he didn't have time to bring the proof text before he died. R. Yishmael said, "Happy are you, Ben Dama, that you went out in peace and did not violate the rabbinic decree of the sages since anyone who breaks through the sage's fence, in the end suffering comes to him, as it is written, 'He who breaks through a fence, a snake will bite him'" (Eccl 10:8).

Many fascinating and puzzling aspects of this story have been analyzed both often and well in recent years. It seems to me that there is nevertheless one

---

29. Steven D. Fraade, *From Tradition to Commentary: Torah and Its Interpretation in Midrash Sifre to Deuteronomy* (Albany: SUNY Press, 1991), 58.

30. This passage has been one of the least controversial identifications of an early Jesus follower in rabbinic literature (Schremer, *Brothers*, 93).

31. Compare yShabbat 14:4 (14d), Ecclesiastes Rabbah 1:8, and bAvodah Zarah 27b.

32. Widely understood to be a rabbinic name for Jesus.

33. Reading ראיה here according to its usage in tannaitic passages such as mShabbat 8:7 (R. Yose said to him, "Here is my proof [text]: 'to scoop water from a cistern' [Isa 30:14]).") Certainly, both the Palestinian and Babylonian Talmuds appears to understand the use of the term in this passage in that way since both of those reworking of the story (yAvodah Zarah 2:2 [21a] and bAvodah Zarah 27b) interpolate a possible biblical prooftext (Lev 18:5) and an explicit mention of a biblical verse respectively into the story at this juncture.

aspect of this passage that has not received the attention it deserves: the tension concerning the status and use of scripture.

It is tempting to assume that the life-threatening sin that Elazar b. Dama so narrowly (if ironically) avoided by dying was the act of being healed in the name of Jesus—after all, sectarian healing is the last item named in the list of prohibitions that immediately precedes this narrative in Tosefta Hullin. However, neither the items nor the order in this particular list appears to have been fixed.[34] And the second narrative paired with this one in Tosefta Hullin has nothing to do with healing but instead shares a thematic interest in the status of sectarian biblical interpretation. Nor, it seems to me, does the structure of this first narrative support a reading of the passage as a story about the question of sectarian healing. Much of the drama of this narrative emerges from the notion that Elazar b. Dama was narrowly saved from a worse fate by his abrupt death. R. Yishmael, for instance, clearly rejoices at Elazar b. Dama's narrow escape, and yet Ben Dama was not actually on the verge of being healed when he died—he was cut off in the middle of his argument with R. Yishmael *about* being healed. Indeed, if the length of rabbinic arguments in other sources from this period are any guide, it seems safe to say that Elazar b. Dama was in no danger of receiving medical attention at the moment when he began his discussion with R. Yishmael.

There was, however, another action from which Elazar b. Dama *was* saved only by the skin of his teeth. Indeed, the passage emphasizes, "There was not enough time for him to bring a proof text before died." Since Ben Dama had just said that he was about to quote his proof text, it seems that he was (quite miraculously) cut off in midsentence before he could actually quote the biblical verse in question.[35] From the perspective of narrative structure, the horrible danger from which Ben Dama narrowly escaped through his death was: citing a biblical proof text.

This reading is further supported by a dialogue that focuses on the relative authority of the biblical text as measured against rabbinic decree. From R.

---

34. Compare, for instance, bHullin 13a.

35. As Richard Kalmin has interpreted this: "The story implies that cure by a follower of Jesus is such a sensitive issue that Elazar ben Dama must be prevented forcibly from revealing his scriptural proof. Rabbis (and Jews in general) may be swayed by Elazar ben Dama's words, and had he been cured in Jesus' name many might have been drawn from rabbinic piety. Elazar ben Dama's death just before revealing his scriptural proof shows the hand of God, who intervenes at precisely the proper moment to ensure removal of the temptation to follow heresy." *The Sage in Jewish Society of Late Antiquity* (Cambridge: Routledge, 2002), 69.

Yishmael's (and the narrator's) point of view, there is no legal doubt that Elazar b. Dama is forbidden to perform the illicit healing that he proposes. All the weight of rabbinic authority is against him. Within the context of the chapter, the sages have already issued a general prohibition on heretical healing (tHullin 2:21). In the context of the story, R. Yishmael has issued a specific ruling forbidding Ben Dama to be healed ("R. Yishmael would not allow him."). More importantly, perhaps, R. Yishmael is supported in this decision by a group of rabbinic scholars.[36] At this point, according to most scholarly renderings of early rabbinic legal methodology, there is nothing that Elazar b. Dama could do to change his legal standing vis-à-vis the rabbinic authorities.

In the other camp sits Ben Dama, who is willing to face down this heavy weight of rabbinic authorities on the strength of a single biblical proof text. At first glance, this would seem like a very unequal struggle with a virtually predetermined outcome. After all, a single, dying dissenter is pitted against the entire rabbinic establishment (whether they are present in body or only in spirit). Yet, there is something triumphant in R. Yishmael's ironic quotation of his own biblical proof text after Ben Dama has been supernaturally prevented from citing a biblical quotation in support of his position—R. Yishmael seems to speak as if some dramatic struggle has been won.

The solution to this conundrum, it seems to me, is that Ben Dama does not merely represent an individual spiritual idiosyncrasy. Daniel Boyarin has suggested that this narrative ends with R. Yishmael's seemingly pointless and ironic warning that anyone who rebels against the rabbinic authorities will be bitten by a snake because it was intended to mark this snake-bite victim as an intimate of the Palestinian Christians—that is, someone who had already rebelled against the rabbinic authorities.[37] Others have objected to this reading on the grounds that no one would care if an obscure figure such as the relatively unknown Elazar b. Dama were an intimate of the Palestinian Christians.[38] From a historical point of view, this is certainly true. However, Elazar b. Dama is marked as an intimate of the early Jesus followers in this passage not as a historical memorandum but as a narrative foil.[39] In Elazar b. Dama, we encounter a proxy representative of a new community that, as the

36. The text reports that "*they* said to him, 'Ben Dama, you are not permitted!'"

37. Daniel Boyarin, *Dying for God: Martyrdom and the Making of Christianity* (Stanford, CA: Stanford University Press, 1999), 35.

38. Schremer, *Brothers*, 89.

39. I do not mean to suggest that Elazar b. Dama is himself supposed to be a Jesus follower—merely that he has been attracted to that community and its approach to the biblical

formulator of this passage understands it, holds up the biblical text as the preeminent font of spiritual authority and, in doing so, remakes the biblical tradition into a font of spiritual danger.[40]

If the struggle portrayed here is not about healing practices but rather about the dangers of overreliance on the Hebrew Bible, there is a certain satisfying irony in the fact that R. Yishmael celebrates the rabbinic victory over a misused biblical text by himself citing a biblical verse—but a biblical verse that most often appears in early Palestinian traditions as a proof text for the supremacy of rabbinic authority in arguments about whether the biblical text or the rabbinic tradition has more sacred force. As Ecclesiastes 10:8 is used, for instance, in ySanhedrin 11:4 (30a):[41]

> The members of the association said in the name of R. Yohanan, "The words of the scribes are more beloved than the words of the Torah and as pleasant as words of Torah. [As it is written], 'because your kisses are more beloved than wine' (Song 1:2)." R. Ba bar Kohen said in the name of R. Yehudah bar Pazi, "You should know that the words of the scribes are more pleasant than words of Torah. For, indeed, regarding R. Tarfon, if he had not recited [Shema] he would not have violated anything but a positive Torah commandment. But since he violated the words of the house of Hillel, he became liable to the death penalty inasmuch as 'if one breaks a fence, a snake will bite him' (Eccl 10:8)."

In such passages, the verse cited by R. Yishmael is brought as the ultimate demonstration of the authority of the oral tradition over the biblical text—as proof that to think otherwise is a crime worthy of death. In the context of this narrative, the verse thus functions as an assertion that Elazar b. Dama was

---

text. In the end, he is narrowly saved from cementing his allegiance to this alternative religious mode by dying before he can refigure a biblical quotation as a source of religious authority.

40. I also do not mean to suggest that this is an accurate portrayal of the early Christian value system. It is simply one of the characterizations of that community that classical rabbinic literature consistently reproduces, as we will see in upcoming pages. For an analogous study of caricatures of Jews in early Christian polemic literature, see Judith Lieu, *Image and Reality: The Jews in the World of Christians in the Second Century* (London: T&T Clark, 2003).

41. Although I would not usually cite the Palestinian Talmud as context for the Tosefta, in this case, the Palestinian Talmud collects several parallel but not identical versions of this particular tradition (see, in addition to the above, yBerakhot 1:4 [3b], yAvodah Zarah 2:2 [40d–41a], and yShabbat 14:4 [14d]), which leads me to believe that this particular tradition predates the Palestinian Talmud since it has had time to spread and insinuate itself into a variety of contextual frames.

A BOOK THAT KILLS   73

sentenced to death by heaven for being too enamored with the biblical text as a source of spiritual authority.

The story of Ben Dama is thus revealed as an early rabbinic reflection on the new dangers that had come to adhere to the text of the Bible with the emergence of sectarian Bible readers who would hold up the biblical text as a source of spiritual power directly accessible to any reader. The association between the biblical text and mortal danger that will become so prominent in later sources was beginning. If R. Yishmael is to be believed, Ben Dama lost his life so that he might be prevented from using the biblical text in an inappropriate way. As in tShabbat 13:5, the mystical mechanism at work in this linkage between sectarian engagement with the biblical text and literal death is not explicated—and yet the connection is vividly and explicitly marked.

The deadly mystical calculus that is purported to be at work in connection with sectarian Bible reading represents an even more prominent motif in the next story of the pair, on R. Eliezer's arrest (tHullin 2:24):[42]

A case concerning R. Eliezer, who was arrested for words of heresy (דברי מינות). They took him up to the platform to judge him and the *hegemon* said to him, "An old man like you would get involved with things like this?" He said to him, "The Judge is trustworthy over me." Since the *hegemon* thought that he was speaking about him, while what was actually meant was his Father in Heaven, he said to him, "Since you have trusted in me, so I will do likewise. I said to myself, 'Is it possible that this gray head would err with such things?' Dismissed! Behold, you are exempt." But when he had been released from the platform, he was troubled that he had been arrested for words of heresy. His students came to comfort him but he would not accept [comfort]. R. Akiva came and he said to him, "Master, may I say a word before you that you might not be troubled?" He said to him, "Speak." He said to him, "Perhaps one of the heretics said a word of heresy to you and you enjoyed it?" (שמא אחד מן המינין אמר לך דבר של מינות והנאך). He said, "Heavens, you have reminded me! One time I was walking in the marketplace of Tzipori and I encountered Jacob of Sikhnin village and he said a word of heresy in the name of Yeshua b. Pantiri and I enjoyed it and I was arrested for words of heresy because I had violated the words of the Torah, 'Distance yourself from her ways and do not draw near to the opening of her house' (Prov 5:8). For 'many have fallen dead at her hands [and many strong men have been killed by her]' (Prov 7:26)." As

42. Compare bAvodah Zarah 16b–17a and Ecclesiastes Rabbah 1:8.

74   CHAPTER 2

R. Eliezer said, "A man should always flee from ugliness and from anything resembling ugliness."

If the heretics (*minim*) in this story are indeed early Christians, as others have
already argued so convincingly,[43] the "words of heresy" that R. Eliezer heard
from Jacob of Sikhnin village must have been an exegesis of the Bible.[44] For
what other sort of sectarian teaching might a prominent rabbi listen to without
any uneasiness to mark the event in his memory?[45] Here again, it is the apparent independence and self-evident authority of written scripture that allows
the biblical text to become a shared mistress between communities.

While the biblical tradition might still appear beautiful or pleasant (נאה) in
the hands of heretics, this passage argues, it will be tainted with the same sort
of subterranean ugliness that results from female sexual immorality in the rabbinic imagination. As in tShabbat 13:5, the shared biblical tradition is cast here
as a physically beautiful but adulterous woman—physically unchanged but
metaphysically corrupted by the experience of being intimate with multiple
partners. While the body text might remain the same, and its literary beauty
might still elicit superficial pleasure, the very act of being shared somehow
transforms that beautiful and physically unchanged text-body from a source
of legitimate joy into a font of evil and danger. As in tShabbat 13:5 and tHullin
2:22–23, the biblical text is allegorized here as a woman dangerous to the point
of death—a source of spiritual taint so strong that even "strong men are killed"
at its hand. In this narrative, as elsewhere in the early tannaitic tradition, that
lethal threat is understood to translate into the most literal terms. R. Eliezer

43. This argument was first advanced in detail by Robert Travers Herford, *Christianity in
the Talmud and Midrash* (London: William & Horgate, 1903), 138–45, with a much-quoted
elaboration of this reading provided by Saul Lieberman, "Roman Legal Institutions in Early
Rabbinics and the Acta Martyrum," *Jewish Quarterly Review* 35 (1944): 1–57, especially 19–24.

44. As Marc Hirschman points out, this is certainly how the Babylonian Talmud understands the story—since the adaptation of this tradition in bAvodah Zarah 16b–17a interpolates
an account of the biblical exegesis that so impressed R. Eliezer. Marc Hirschman, *A Rivalry of
Genius: Jewish and Christian Biblical Interpretation in Late Antiquity* (Albany: SUNY Press,
2012), 6–7.

45. As Adiel Schremer has put it, this story emphasizes "the need to distance oneself from
the *minim* in general, and from Christians in particular, and not to be entrapped by the seeming
similarity between 'them' and 'us.'" And "the need to distinguish between a 'legitimate' teaching
and an 'illegitimate' one is intensified in the parallel version of this story, as found in the Babylonian Talmud" since "there we are fully informed concerning the 'teaching' which Rabbi
Eliezer heard from that Jacob in the name of Jesus, and that 'word of Torah' bears no mark of
heresy whatsoever" but is a "perfectly normal 'rabbinic' midrash" (*Brothers,* 93).

A BOOK THAT KILLS   75

might have strayed too near the door of an allegorical adulteress but he was in very literal danger of receiving the death penalty for his folly. As in the other traditions explored in this section, the biblical tradition has been corrupted here into a source of spiritual danger so potent that it physically endangers Israel.

Killer Bibles: Literalizing the Dangers of the Bible in Later Palestinian Tradition

Later Palestinian sources reproduce the triangulation of scripture, heresy, and death that one encounters in tannaitic accounts of lethal biblical text. In the later Palestinian sources, however, these themes are no longer associated with outside forces. The dangers of scripture do not derive from sectarian misuse in these traditions but are inherent in scripture itself.

This cautionary logic emerges, for instance, in narratives from this period in which martyrs are wrapped in Torah scrolls and burned. Gruesome death is associated with physical proximity to the Bible[46] and these narratives are threaded through with warnings about the dangers inherent to engaging too closely with the biblical text. Various versions of R. Hanina b. Teradion's martyrdom, for example, each emphasize in their own way the unusual importance of written scripture to the rabbi and his family—and the connection of

---

46. That is to say, the conjunction of human burning and book burning appears to be a purpose-made imaginative motif rather than a historical reality. As Joseph Howley, "Book-Burning and the Uses of Writing in Ancient Rome: Destructive Practice between Literature and Document," *The Journal of Roman Studies* 107 (2017), puts it, "From time to time, the ancient Roman burned books" (213). But even in the "realm of imagination" (216) (for these incidents are "*remembered* far more than they are *documented*" [225], such conflagrations did not include the death of the author—although one might occasionally imagine books burned before an execution-murder as an added humiliation [225] or documents burned before a suicide [231]). But in many cases, burning books might serve instead as a *protection* from execution (see for instance, Dirk Rohmann, *Christianity, Book-Burning, and Censorship in Late Antiquity: Studies in Text Transmission* (Berlin: de Gruyter, 2016,) 35 and 68, and even when "book offences" came to be punished "more harshly" in later centuries, "execution was still not the norm" (Rohmann, *Book-Burning*, 106). In keeping with these observations, Herbert Basser has argued convincingly that the R. Hananiah martyrdom tradition was originally constructed around the burning of the sage alone and only later expanded to include the burning of the Torah as a major parallel motif in the amoraic period. Herbert W. Basser, *In the Margins of the Midrash: Sifre Ha'azinu Texts, Commentaries, and Reflections* (Atlanta: Scholars Press, 1990), 49–63.

76 CHAPTER 2

this family idiosyncrasy with their subsequent deaths. Consider the way that tractate Semahot frames R. Hanina's martyrdom in Semahot 8:9–12:

When R. Akiva was killed in Caesarea, the news came to R. Yehudah b. Baba and R. Hanina b. Teradion and they girded themselves in sackcloth and said . . . "R. Akiva was not killed except as a sign. . . . Soon there will not be a single place in the Land of Israel is not strewn with corpses" . . .

R. Akiva said [a different interpretation regarding these cases]: "The king has four sons. One is smitten and is silent, one is smitten and rebels, one is smitten and pleads, and one is smitten and says to his father, 'Smite me [until I am chastised].' Abraham was smitten and was silent . . . Job was smitten and rebelled . . . Hezekiah was smitten and pleaded . . . though some say he also rebelled . . . David said to his father, '[Continue to] smite me.' As it is said [in Psalms], 'Thoroughly wash me of my sin and purify me from my misdeed' (Ps 51:4). [R. Hanina was like the fourth son.]"

When Rabbi Hanina b. Teradion was arrested for heresy (למינות), they designated him for burning, and his wife for execution by decapitation, and his daughter to sit in a brothel. He said to them, "What did you decree on this poor soul [my wife]?" They said, "Execution by decapitation." Regarding her fate, he recited the verses, "God is righteous in all his ways and merciful in all of his deeds" (Ps 145:17). "His actions are like an unblemished rock because all of his ways are justice, he is a God of faithfulness with no unrighteousness, he is just and straight dealing" (Deut 32:4). She said to them, "What did you decree for him?" They said to her, "Burning." On his fate, she recited the verse, "Great in advice and mighty in action, your eyes are open to all the ways of human beings, to give to each man according to his ways, the [correct] fruit of his actions" (Jer 32:19).

And when they burned him, they wrapped him in a Torah scroll and burned him together with the Torah scroll, upon which his daughter screamed and threw herself at his feet and said, "This is Torah and this is its reward?"

He said to his daughter, "If you are crying over me and it is regarding me that you are prostrating yourself, it is better that a fanned flame should consume me than the unfanned flame [reserved for the wicked in the afterlife]. As it is said [in Job], 'An unfanned flame will consume [the wicked one slowly]' (Job 20:26). But if you are crying over the Torah scroll, behold that this is a Torah of fire and fire cannot consume fire and behold that the writings are fleeing up in the air and the fire does not consume them but only the parchment alone (הרי אותיות פורחות ואין האש אוכלת אלא על הנייר)."

For regarding all the servants of the king, the great ones are punished for small things [as it says in the Prophets], "Therefore I have slain the prophets, killing them with my word (באמרי פי)" (Hos 6:5).

Semahot carefully frames the tortured execution of R. Hanina as an educational and expiating chastisement for a sin that might not at first seem to merit such a harsh punishment. Unlike many other cases in the rabbinic canon,[47] however, Semahot constructs this divine extremism not as an inexplicable form of mystical fastidiousness but as an act of mercy. For like the fourth son in the Rabbi Akiva model, R. Hanina welcomes this radical chastisement because it will "wash him of his sin" and "purify him of his sinful mistake." In the adapted words of Job, the "fanned flame" of this Roman fire has saved R. Hanina from the "unfanned flame" reserved for the wicked in the afterlife.

What then was the sin that R. Hanina (and his family) were required to expiate with their death and suffering? As in many of the tannaitic cases discussed above, this narrative is constructed around a triangulation of biblical text, heresy, and death. Like R. Elazar b. Dama, both R. Hanina and his wife are (too) quick with a proof text—the biblical text is apparently the primary thread from which their spiritual imagination is woven. Indeed, this quickness will become a subject of comment in the Babylonian Talmud's iteration of the narrative, which marvels that a "biblical proof text came to hand for them in the ... hour of judgment" (שנזדמנו להן ... מקראות ... בשעת ... הדין). Like the Toseftan R. Eliezer, moreover, this unmediated engagement with the biblical text ends with R. Hanina "arrested for heresy." And R. Hanina will die for his closeness with the biblical text—a symbolism made literal in this case when R. Hanina is physically wrapped in the text at his execution. As either the narrator or R. Hanina characterizes his final moments, God literally "killed" the sage "with [his] word."

The underlying logic of this fatal triangulation of scripture, heresy, and death is explored in more detail in this passage. The story closes with an account of R. Hanina's daughter, a character who has misidentified the nature of scripture (and needs to be re-educated concerning its true nature). The shocking, even perverse, extent to which she has elevated written scripture in her religious imaginary becomes apparent when R. Hanina is ready to believe that

---

47. As Ra'anan Boustan has put it regarding early rabbinic martyrologies more generally, these "martyrological accounts employ the motif of the 'martyr's peccadillo' ... within the martyrological genre, the more punctilious one's behavior, the more disastrous every sin proves to be." Ra'anan S. Boustan, *From Martyr to Mystic: Rabbinic Martyrology and the Making of Merkavah Mysticism* (Tübingen: Mohr Siebeck, 2005), 65.

his daughter might mourn the destruction of a single copy of the biblical text more than his own death. The reason she might do so is quickly revealed, however, by the contents of his reproof. For in this version of the narrative, R. Hanina's daughter appears be burdened with a theological misapprehension ascribed to R. Hanina's executioners in earlier versions of this tale. As the executioners are admonished in Sifre Deuteronomy 307, "Don't go thinking too highly of yourselves because you [believe you] have burned the Torah—[for the Torah is not contained in a scroll, rather] the moment you released it, it returned to its Father in heaven." Here, however, R. Hanina must explain to his own daughter what he has come to see through the process of his execution: divine revelation is not contained in the book being destroyed ("the fire consumes . . . the parchment alone"); rather, the true revelation resides beyond the material text as living fire and words ("the words fly upwards in the air and the fire does not consume them"). Herbert Basser has vividly captured this sense of Rabbi Hanina's statement with a surprising translation of the key proof text in this narrative, "I engraved the prophets, I killed them with the lamb parchments of my word" (Hos 5:6).[48] In this rendering of the text, R. Hanina has come to understand that the limited and material "lamb parchments of God's word" can kill and be killed but the true revelation will always escape this burning of its biological counterpart. When R. Hanina uses his last breath to persuade his daughter away from a perspective that he himself has presumably instilled in her,[49] R. Hanina provides a glimpse of the misapprehension from which he himself needed to be purified through this brutal form of execution: to imagine that the written text can successfully contain divine revelation is to invite a heresy dangerous to the point of death.

We find variations on this theme refracting through other late antique Palestinian traditions in which practitioners are burned together with their Torah scrolls. In accounts of the fall of Beitar from this period, for instance, the burning of Torah scrolls together with their scribes forms part of a larger imaginative matrix in which religiously outré behavior resulted in the dramatic conflagration of an unusual Jewish city. As the tale is told in yTaʿanit 4:5 (24a),[50] for instance, the downfall of Beitar is simultaneously tragic and yet not entirely undeserved:

48. Basser even argues that these words should be attributed to R. Hanina as his parting statement (*In the Margins*, 56).

49. This is how I read his preemptive lecture on a position she has not expressed: he knows she may worry about this because he has taught her to do so and now regrets it.

50. See, similarly, Lamentations Rabbah 2:2.

A BOOK THAT KILLS   79

According to R. Shimon bar Yohai, R. Akiva used to gloss the lemma "a star (*kokhav*) of Jacob" (Num 24:17) as "the false one of Jacob" [to refer to Bar Kokhba]. When R. Akiva used to see Bar [Kokhba], he would say "Ah, he is the King Messiah!" R. Yohanan b. [Torta] would say to him, "Akiva, grass will grow up through your cheeks and still the son of David will not come."

R. Yohanan said, "The voice [command] of [Hadrianus] Caeser killed [eighty thousand] myriad at Beitar. . . . Bar Kozeba was there and he had two hundred thousand soldiers who had severed a finger. The sages sent to [Bar Kokhba] and said to him, 'How long will you make Israel into men with ritually invalidating injuries?' He replied, 'How else can I test them?' They said to him, '[How about] anyone who cannot ride his horse and uproot a cedar of Lebanon will not be inscribed in your marching list.' There were two hundred thousand [tested] in one way and two hundred thousand [tested] in the other way."

And when [Bar Kokhba] went out to battle, he used to say, "Master of the Universe, don't strengthen [us] and don't weaken [us]! 'For have you not cast us off, Lord, so that God does not go out with our armies?' (Ps 60:12)."

For three and a half years, Hadrian lay siege to Beitar. And R. Elazar the Modai used to sit in sackcloth and ashes and pray every day saying, "Master of the Universe, do not sit in judgment today! Do not sit in judgment today!" . . . [But someone convinced Bar Kokhba that R. Elazar had betrayed the cause so Bar Kokhba] gave him a kick that killed him. Immediately a heavenly voice called out, " 'Behold the worthless shepherd who abandons his flock! A [heavenly] sword upon his right hand and upon his right eye. His right hand will wither and dry up and his right eye will go dark!' (Zech 11:17). You have killed R. Elazar the Modai, the right hand of Israel, and their right eye. Therefore, the right arm of this man will wither and his right eye will go dark."

Immediately, Beitar was surrounded and Bar Kozeba was killed . . . and they went on killing until the horses sunk in the blood up to their bridles and the blood rolled boulders weighing forty *seah* four miles out to the sea. And if you say it was close to the sea, was it not forty miles from the seashore?

They said three hundred small children's brains were found on a single rock. And they found three [Lamentations Rabbah adds: hundred] baskets [filled] with pericopes of tefillin, each nine times nine *seah*. And some said they found nine baskets, each weighing three times three *seah*. It is said that

Rabban Shimon ben Gamliel said, "There were five hundred writing schools (בתי סופרים) in Beitar, each with five hundred small children. And they used to say, 'If the hated ones come upon us, we will go out with these writing utensils and put out their eyes!' But sins caused them to wrap each and every one in his Torah scroll and burn him. And there wasn't a single one left but me."

The story of the martyred scribal students of Beitar is sometimes read as a parallel to the "four hundred and eighty synagogues in Jerusalem, each with a lower school (בית ספר) and an upper school (בית תלמוד)" that were destroyed by Vespasian at the end of the First Jewish Revolt (yMegillah 3:1 [73d]). But the differences between these two models is marked. Despite the similarity in terminology, the lower schools (בתי ספר) destroyed in Jerusalem were not dedicated to learning to write scripture but rather to the memorization of scripture as a preliminary step toward mastery of rabbinic literature. Where each "Bible school" (בית ספר) in Jerusalem is paired with a "house of rabbinic learning" (בית תלמוד) that shares its space (suggesting that both schools were dedicated to a continuous endeavor), for instance, the schools for scribes (בתי סופרים) in Beitar are described as standalone institutions. And where the lower school in Jerusalem is described as being dedicated "to [learning the memorized oral formula of] Bible recitation (מקרא)" in a mode parallel to the way the "upper school [was] for [learning the memorized oral formula of] the Mishnah," the scribal schools in Beitar are depicted as filled with students writing. With the unusual abundance of writing implements, phylactery texts, and Bible scrolls in the hands of the Beitar students, yTaʿanit suggests that the institutions destroyed in Beitar were not rabbinic elementary schools for the memorization of scriptural tradition but schools dedicated to the sacred scribal arts.

Although the intense cultivation of sacred scribal arts among the young of Beitar is not explicitly condemned, it is placed in continuity with a series of other innovative practices in Beitar that are treated as dangerously sinful by the standards of the rabbinic establishment. Throughout this iteration of the tale, Beitar is a portrayed as a city that has recklessly taken the fate of Israel into its own hands and in doing so has invited a looming judgment upon itself, staved off temporarily by the desperate protective prayers of Elazar the Modai. In this passage describing the temporary rule of the "False One," for instance, elite Jewish soldiers are produced by ritually maiming them in a way that leaves them invalid for Temple service. According to this rendering of the history,

A BOOK THAT KILLS 81

moreover, Bar Kokhba has raised a Jewish army that goes into battle actively rejecting the protecting hand of God. Just as the adult men of the city have forged a collective Jewish identity separate from God's intervention and worship, it is implied, so the children of the city are taught to produce divine scripture and holy texts independent of the supporting systems of rabbinic learning. Read in this context, the scribal endeavors of Beitar's schoolchildren emerge as one attempt among many to access (sacred) power directly and mechanically.

The link between biblical textuality and death in this passage, however, does not depend on the guilt of the practitioner. While the schoolchildren of Beitar have absorbed an ethos of sacred textuality to such an extent that they vividly imagine their writing implements as weapons in the fight against Israel's enemies, these scribal schools were nevertheless filled with legal innocents, children too young to be responsible for their own fate. As the passage emphasizes with great pathos, it was the brains of three hundred "small children" that were dashed on the rocks alongside the baskets of biblical passages they were writing for tefillin and burned together with the Torah scrolls they were writing. Without a guilty party to blame, there remains only a morbid association between gruesome death and the biblical texts that shared the children's fate, whether discarded on the rocks or burned together in a pyre. As we have seen in many other tales in this chapter, the specific mystical calculus that renders the biblical text a lethally dangerous companion remains elusive. But like an elite Jewish army without the God of Israel, biblical texts without a broader tradition to anchor and contain them are subtly coded here as dangerous to the point of death.

Many traditions further literalize this sense that a danger is inherent to biblical text when individuals die from simple physical proximity with copies of the biblical text. Of all the primordial artifacts preserved from the days of Moses, for example, only the ark of the covenant (which contained the physical remains of the biblical revelation at Sinai) was imagined to kill those who encountered it. YShekalim 6:1 (49c) expands on the Mishnah's discussion of this phenomenon:

> The sages used to say that the ark [of the covenant] was hidden away [נגנז] in the wood storage chamber [of the Temple]. Once a certain priest, who [was relegated to serve in the wood storage chamber because he] had a disqualifying injury, was standing and splitting logs in the wood storage chamber when he saw that the floor there was different than the rest. He

came over to tell his fellow [priest], "Come and look at this floor which is different from the rest." But he didn't manage to finish his sentence before his soul left his body [and he died]. So they knew by that sign that the ark was hidden away in that place. . . . [There was some debate about what the ark actually contained. Some said there were two arks.] One with the full Torah (התורה נתונה בתוכו) deposited in it and one with the fragments of the first tablets (שברי הלוחות נתונין בתוכו) deposited in it. . . . [Others maintained there was one ark with] four tablets in it, two whole tablets and two broken tablets . . . and a Torah scroll.

Like Elazar b. Dama sentenced to death by heaven, the priest in this story dies before he can finish a sentence concerning the biblical text. In contrast to that earlier narrative, however, the priest in this story is unequivocally killed by supernatural forces—there is no snake bite or preexisting political threat to obscure the nature of his death. The protagonist in this story is struck down suddenly by the mystical equivalent of a lightning bolt. And yet the priest is unambiguously blameless in a way that the protagonists of previous narratives were not. There is no possibility that the victim's own mode of engaging with the Bible misused the text and or that he himself had transformed the text into a source of danger through his own incorrect actions. The priest in question does not even know that the biblical artifacts which will endanger him are sitting under the floor.

Instead, this narrative ascribes danger to the physical text itself—without regard to its contents or how one interprets them. Some of the supernatural drama of this encounter, of course, must be attributed to the uniquely powerful nature of the artifacts involved. The biblical texts in question are not quotidian ritual copies but scriptural prototypes, the very tablets brought down from Mount Sinai and an authorized first edition of the extant scriptural tradition. And yet, this is not a generic tale of powerful, and thus dangerous, sacred objects. We do not find such lethal encounters associated with any of the other miraculous artifacts preserved from the Mosaic period. Rather the deadly nature of these textual objects is particular to their relationship with sacred textuality. The yShekalim narrative thus appears to capture something closer to the phenomenon that anthropologists Johannes Fabian and Matthew Engelke have dubbed "terror of the text," by which physical instantiations of the revelatory tradition "produce terror in a cosmological sense"[51] because they come

51. Matthew Engelke, "Text and Performance in the African Church: The Book 'Live and Direct,'" *American Ethnologist* 31, no. 1 (2004): 79.

A BOOK THAT KILLS   83

to represent all of the dangers that some communities impute to the stagnation and corruption of revelatory experience in a fixed tradition. The implications are not purely metaphysical. According to the anthropological evidence, participants actively avoid contact with material Bibles—withdrawing them from circulation or even destroying them.[52]

Read in light of these modern parallels, the statement that this ancient biblical material was "hidden away" (גנז) evokes a diverse collection of early rabbinic traditions in which the language of *genizah* describes sacred writings removed from circulation (or very nearly removed) in order to protect the reading public from the dangers they pose.[53] In bHagigah 13a, for instance, the text of Ezekiel is almost withdrawn from circulation (נגנז) because it unleashed lightning bolts not metaphorically but literally:

> The rabbis taught the case of a child who was reading the book of Ezekiel in his teacher's house. And [the child] understood the matter of the *hashmal* and a fire went out from the *hashmal* and burned him up. So they sought to hide (לגנוז) the book of Ezekiel.

As in the Yerushalmi passage, the biblical text described by bHagigah is fatally dangerous in and of itself. Unleashing its hazards does not require a malicious, or even a purposeful, reader—even a young child may unwittingly activate these forces. Such narrative parallels thus allow us to see yShekalim 6:1 as an account in which the written artifacts of Sinai were hidden away not to protect them from human beings but to protect human beings from the darker powers of this sacred writing. Indeed, the need for caution would seem to be reaffirmed by the deadly reach of these texts even after they have been hidden away.

Universalizing the Dangers of the Biblical Text: Tales of Lethal Bibles from Babylon

Early rabbinic traditions from Babylonia echo many of the same themes that permeated both strata of Palestinian reflections on the dangers of biblical text: heresy, the dangers posed by outsider readers, allegories of adulterous

---

52. Consider, for instance, the Bible burnings described Ibid., 77.

53. See, for instance, mPesahim 4:9 and bBerakhot 10b on Hezekiah's withdrawal of the Book of Healing, the near withdrawals of biblical books on bMenahot 45a, or the archiving of the ark of the covenant in bYoma 54a and its source in mShekalim 6:1, tShekalim 2:18, yShekalim 6:1 [49c], and tSotah 13:1.

84 CHAPTER 2

eroticism, the threat of gruesome death attached to physical proximity with biblical text, and mystical dangers emerging from biblical texts when they are unmoored from the anchoring context of the rabbinic tradition. In many Babylonian iterations, however, these dangers have been further abstracted and generalized. Some Babylonian traditions continue the process initiated in the Jerusalem Talmud in which the dangers of the biblical text are literalized and tied to physical manifestations of that tradition. In other cases, it is simply the scale of the damage wreaked by the biblical text that has grown, as entire populations fall in its wake. In still other instances, the dangers posed by the biblical text are no longer imagined to apply only to the Jewish people but have been universalized so that they may strike down Jew and non-Jew alike.

As the R. Hanina martyrdom tradition refracts through the Babylonian Talmud, for instance, the dangers posed by the biblical text in the narrative have been identified even more literally with the material text of the Hebrew Bible, so that they are completely disconnected from individual guilt or wrong thinking about that document. As in Palestinian iterations of the tradition, R. Hanina is arrested for cultivating an unusually close relationship with the biblical text. Whereas his colleague R. Elazar b. Perata is accused and exonerated of "teaching rabbinic tradition" (תנית), R. Hanina is charged and convicted for "occupying himself with the biblical text" (עסקת באורייתא) (Avodah Zarah 17b). In these later traditions, however, R. Hanina's own *conceptual* relationship with the biblical tradition is now largely exonerated for causing his troubles. Instead, in the bAvodah Zarah 18a version of this tale,[54] it is his unusually intimate relationship with the physical text of the Bible that ultimately leads him to a violent end:

> Our rabbis taught: When R. Yose b. Kisma became sick, R. Hanina b. Teradion when to visit him. [R. Yose b. Kisma] said to him, "Hanina, my brother, don't[55] you know that it was appointed by heaven that this nation should rule, and destroy God's house, and burn his Temple, and execute his beloved ones and kill his saints and still survive? But I have heard a rumor about you that a Torah scroll rests in your lap while you sit and gather crowds to expound[56] the Bible in public (שספר תורה מונח בחיקך ואתה יושב

54. For more on the complicated textual history of what I am calling this "version" of the tale, see Richard Kalmin, *Jewish Babylonia between Persia and Roman Palestine* (Oxford: Oxford University Press, 2006), 23–29.

55. Reading אין here with Munich 95 and Schocken-Jerusalem 3654.

56. Following MS Schocken-Jerusalem 3654 use of דוריש.

A BOOK THAT KILLS 85

(ומקהיל קהילות ודורש ברבים)."[57] [R. Hanina] said to him: "Heaven will have mercy on me."[58] [R. Yose b. Kisma] said to him, "I say sensible things (דברים של טעם) to you and you say to me that heaven will have mercy. I would be surprised if they don't burn you and a Torah scroll up in a fire." [R. Hanina] said to him, "My Master, what [waits for] me in the next world?" [R. Yose b. Kisma] said to him, "Does no incident come to mind for you?" [R. Hanina] said to him, "[There was] some Purim money that was exchanged for charity money in my possession and I distributed it to the poor." [R. Yose b. Kisma] said to him, "[If that is all you've got on your conscience], may your portion be my portion and your fate my fate."

They said: It was not many days before R. Yose b. Kisma died and the great ones of Rome traveled to bury him and they eulogized him with a great eulogy. And on their return, they found R. Hanina b. Teradion with a Torah scroll in his lap while he was sat and gathered crowds to expound the Bible in public (שהיה יושב ועוסק בתורה ומקהיל קהלות ברבים וס״ת מונח לו בחיקו).[59] And they wrapped him in the Torah scroll and they surrounded him with bundles of [slow-burning green] prunings and lit the fire with them. Then they brought woolen sponges and expanded them with water and rested them on his heart so that he would not die quickly. His daughter said to him, "Father, that I should see you like this!" He said to her, "My daughter,[60] if I were being burned alone this would be a hard thing for me. But now that I am burned and the Torah scroll is with me, the One who requires [punishment] for the humiliation of the Torah scroll will require [punishment] for me [as well]. His students said to him, "Rabbi, what do you see?" He said to them, "Blank parchments are burning but the letters are flying away (גוילין נשרפין ואותיות פורחות)." [They said], "[Then] you should also open your mouth so that the fire enters you [and your soul flies away]." [R. Hanina] said, "It is better that he who gave [the soul] should take it away so [a person] should not injure himself."

The passage then goes on to narrate the now-famous story of R. Hanina's executioner, who jumped into the fire to share the rabbi's fate and his portion in

---

57. Following MS Schocken-Jerusalem 3654 here, though the sense of the majority tradition (which simply parallels the repetition several lines later) is the same.

58. Again, following MS Schocken-Jerusalem 3654, where other manuscripts reduplicate R. Yose's use of the phrase without "on me" in the next line.

59. Following MS Schocken-Jerusalem 3654.

60. Following MSS Schocken-Jerusalem 3654, Paris 1337, and Hebrew 10/51.

the world-to-come. On the most literal level, the Babylonian Talmud frames its version of R. Hanina's execution as a case of natural consequences for the sage's unnecessary insistence on associating himself with a material instantiation of the biblical text. For when R. Hanina cradles the Torah scroll in his lap, he does not appear to be reading the text but rather using the Torah scroll as a symbolic referent, as rabbinic tradition imagined the high priest to do on the Day of Atonement when he was said to have rolled up the scroll of the Law, placed it on his lap, and recited from the biblical text by heart (mYoma 7:1).[61] Like his colleagues, R. Hanina teaches the biblical text from memory. Unlike his colleagues, R. Hanina insists on doing so while physically cradling a tangible instantiation of the text he teaches—whether as an expression of the unusually prominent place of the biblical text in his own piety, a symbolic recreation of past glories, or to add a note of visual defiance.

More importantly for our purposes, perhaps, R. Yose b. Kisma responds to this apparently pious practice with considerable impatience. He argues that R. Hanina is behaving irrationally (or, as the text puts it, acting in opposition to logical reason [דברים של טעם]) when he superfluously draws the attention of the authorities by publicly flaunting a material artifact of the revelation where none is needed.[62] Indeed, when R. Yose b. Kisma snaps at R. Hanina that he will be "surprised if they don't burn you and a Torah scroll up in the fire," the subtext seems to be that R. Hanina is asking for such torture and that, on some level, he would have it coming to him for his insistence on centering a physical copy of the biblical text in this way. Certainly, bAvodah Zarah 18a does not question R. Hanina's elevated piety or treat his execution as a necessary expiation for his misuse of the biblical text, as earlier versions of the story such as Semahot 8:9–12 would do. Where Semahot only implies Hanina would receive life in the world-to-come, Avodah Zarah makes R. Hanina's happy acceptance into the next world an explicit and dramatic portion of the narrative.

61. See also yYoma 7:1 (44a), ySotah 7:6 (21b), bYoma 70a, bSotah 41a. For more on this reading practice, see Rebecca Scharbach Wollenberg, "The People of the Book Before the Book" (PhD diss., University of Chicago, 2015), 75ff.

62. Like Mira Wasserman, I take the motif of the Torah scroll to be the guiding image in this passage. Mira Wasserman, *Jews, Gentiles, and Other Animals: The Talmud after the Humanities* (Philadelphia: University of Pennsylvania Press, 2017), 54. The notion that this visual icon will draw dangerous attention to R. Hanina is played out when the prominent citizens occupied with returning from R. Yose b. Kisma's funeral have their attention drawn to the spectacle of R. Hanina's teaching.

A BOOK THAT KILLS   87

Nevertheless, the Babylonian text does ultimately echo and affirm R. Yose
b. Kisma's frustrated suggestion that it is R. Hanina's intimate interaction with
a material artifact of the biblical revelation that has brought down worldly, if
not spiritual, dangers upon him. At the most basic level, there is a parallelism
that suggests a *midah keneged midah* (measure for measure) punishment in the
way the physical stance with which R. Hanina embraces the Torah scroll during teaching is echoed and reversed when the Torah scroll wraps him in its
own deadly embrace during his execution. As Mira Wasserman puts it:

> The image of the rabbi nestling the [closed] scroll conveys a sense of inti-
> macy and emphasizes the materiality of the scroll, depicting the Torah as
> an object to be cherished rather than as an abstract set of laws or teachings.
> During the execution, this image is reversed: the rabbi who had the scroll
> in his embrace is now wrapped up within the scroll.[63]

Cling too closely to the skins and sinews of the physical Torah scroll, this story
seems to suggest, and your own skins and sinews will be destroyed along with
this material-biological object you have elevated beyond its true place.

On a more subtle level, it becomes apparent just how much narrative traction is given to R. Yose b. Kisma's critiques of R. Hanina's behavior when one
contrasts the outlines of this story with parallel examples elsewhere in the
Babylonian Talmud. For unlike other Babylonian martyrological narratives in
this series,[64] R. Yose b. Kisma's criticisms of R. Hanina's behavior are ultimately upheld by means of repeated thematic reminders woven throughout.
In contrast to the R. Akiva martyrdom narrative, for instance, R. Hanina's fate
is treated with considerable ambivalence:

> The sages taught: One time, the Evil Kingdom decreed that Israel should
> not study Torah (שלא יעסקו ישראל בתורה). R. Pappos b. Yehudah came upon
> R. Akiva who was gathering crowds in public and studying Torah with them
> (שהיה מקהיל קהלות ברבים ועוסק בתורה). [R. Pappos b. Yehudah] said to him,
> "Aren't you afraid of the government?" [R. Akiva] said to him, "I will tell

---

63. Wasserman, *Jews, Gentiles, and Other Animals*, 54.

64. R. Akiva's martyrdom in Berakhot 61b, for instance, parallels R. Hanina's martyrdom
not only in that the two stories are often paired in the rabbinic tradition but also inasmuch as
the narratives are tied together with subtle linguistic connections throughout. For a list of literary parallels between these two narratives, see Kalmin, *Jewish Babylonia*, 27. Indeed, similarities
are so striking that MS Paris 671 interpolates phrases from the Hanina tale into the Akiva
narrative.

you a parable: To what is the matter similar? To a fox who was walking along the river and saw fish going in schools from place to place. He said to them, 'What are you fleeing from?' They said to him, '[We're fleeing] from the nets that people bring.' [The fox] said to them, 'Would you like to come up here on land and we can live together, me and you, just as my forefathers and yours lived together?' They said to him, 'You who are called the brightest of animals are not bright, but rather foolish. If we are afraid in the place that gives us life how much more so in a place of death for us.' And so too for us right now, we sit and engage in Torah [study], as it is written in it: 'Since it is your life and the length of your days' (Deut 30:20) so if we leave and abandon it how much more [danger would we be in].' [And the sages] said, it wasn't many days before they arrested R. Akiva and chained him up in the prison and they arrested R. Pappos b. Yehudah and chained him up next to him. [R. Akiva] said to him, "Pappos, who brought you here?" [R. Pappos] said to him, "Happy are you, R. Akiva, that you were arrested for words of Torah and woe is me to Pappos that they arrested him for worthless words [or unimportant things]."

The two stories use virtually identical language to describe the fatal crime of teaching in public ("he was gathering crowds and teaching Torah in public" [שהיה מקהיל קהלות ברבים ועוסק בתורה])—except that the R. Hanina story adds the phrase "with a Torah scroll sitting on his lap." By introducing this small contrast in the midst of similarities, the ostentatious presence of a Torah scroll becomes the focal difference refracting through these two parallel narratives.

In parsing this difference, the structural similarities and motifs shared between these two narratives similarly serve to call attention to the stories' thematic inversions. To begin with, the role of rabbinic accuser and accused in these two stories represents a nearly perfect inverse. The very format of question and answer is inverted in the two narratives. Where R. Pappos b. Yehudah merely asks Akiva briefly and almost deferentially whether he fears the government will punish him for teaching Torah in public, R. Yose b. Kisma is given space to state definitively (and at some length) his conviction that the Roman rule R. Hanina is flaunting has been ordained by heaven. And where R. Akiva's defense of his actions takes the form of a lengthy and compelling parable, R. Hanina answers the lengthy and impassioned charge against him so very briefly and unpersuasively that R. Yose b. Kisma accuses him of whimsicality. Even the small details of the story reflect a similar inversion. In bBerakhot 61b, for instance, the righteousness of Akiva's superior moral position is given voice

A BOOK THAT KILLS   89

on a formal level when he addresses his (mild) critic without honorific—and
R. Pappos repeats the minor slight by calling himself Pappos while addressing
R. Akiva with his title in the same breath. Conversely, in bAvodah Zarah 18a,
it is Hanina himself who loses status for the ideological stance he espouses
when R. Yose b. Kisma addresses him without honorific as simply "Hanina."

The narrative action in each of these cases likewise clearly upholds either
the martyr's position or that of his questioner. In bBerakhot 61a, it is R. Pappos
who is punished for his fearful lack of faith, by being imprisoned alongside the
man whom he had implied was behaving recklessly in relation to the authorities. Moreover, R. Pappos's final words explicitly confirm that this ironic fate
is a punishment for his foolish question to Akiva, when he exclaims in a som-
ber pun "woe is me to Pappos who was imprisoned for דברים בטלים," which
may be translated both "unimportant things" and "worthless words."

By contrast, the words of R. Hanina's accuser are ultimately mirrored (and
thereby confirmed) in the details of R. Hanina's fate. While R. Hanina never
seems to regret dying in the embrace of the Torah scroll, his end is almost
identical to the scenario predicted by R. Yose b. Kisma at the beginning of the
narrative. In the end, the letters of the biblical text (its holy soul, according to
the analogy of his students) are quick to flee, and R. Hanina is left to die en-
veloped in the empty parchment scroll that he held so close in life. Whether
the rabbi's ill-fated intimacy with this textual body was worth the fatal sacrifice
remains unclear.

The extent to which the contrasts in these two narratives can be traced to
the presence of a Torah scroll rather than the scholar in question becomes evident when one contrasts the stories of R. Akiva's martyrdom in bBerakhot 61a
and bMenahot 29b. While the R. Akiva of bBerakhot 61a is unequivocally
painted as a daring saint who has sacrificed himself righteously for the sake of
Israel, the R. Akiva of bMenahot 29b is a more ambiguous figure who is now
burdened with something closer to the fraught relationship with the written
text ascribed to R. Hanina, with whom he has traveled through the rabbinic
tradition so closely paired:

> In the hour when Moses went up to the heavens, he discovered the Holy
> One, blessed be he, sitting and attaching crowns to the letters (קושר כתרים
> לאותיות). He said to him, "Master of the Universe, who is delaying you?"
> [God] said to him, "There is one man who will exist in the future, after
> many generations, who will at that future time learn out from each and
> every stroke [of the written text] mounds and mounds of laws (לדרוש על כל

קוץ וקוץ תילין תילין של הלכות). His name is Akiva b. Yosef." Moses said to him, "Master of the Universe, show him to me." [God] said to him, "Turn around." He did so and found himself sitting at the end of the eighth row [in Rabbi Akiva's lesson] and he didn't have any idea what they were talking about. He became weak. When they arrived at a certain matter, Rabbi Akiva's students said to him, "Rabbi, from whence did you derive this?" He said to them, "It is a law [transmitted] to Moses at Sinai." Then Moses's mind was at ease.

[Moses] returned [to the heavens] and came before the Holy One, blessed be he. [Moses] said to him, "Master of the Universe, you have a man such as this and you give the Torah at my hand?" [God] said, "Silence! This is how it arose in my mind." [Moses] said to him, "Master of the Universe, you have shown me his Torah, show me his reward." [God] said to him, "Turn around." And he turned around. He saw that they were weighing [Rabbi Akiva's] flesh in the meat stands. [Moses] said to him, "Master of the Universe, this is Torah and this is its reward?!" [God] said to him, "Silence! This is how it arose in my mind."

As Azzan Yadin-Israel has argued so convincingly in various forums, bMenahot 29b represents a novel "scripturalization of divine revelation . . . as it is associated with the figure of R. Akiva."[65] For in this passage, R. Akiva's "greatness is explicitly textual," so radically imbricated with the material written instantiation of the revelation that Akiva is credited with "interpreting textual elements that are meaningless and thus uninterpretable" since "these non-semantic elements, crowns or jots, are textual in a way that words are not . . . they cannot be expressed vocally, which is to say, they cannot be transmitted orally."[66] In a break with the previous image of R. Akiva, this passage credits the sage with an interpretative model so thoroughly textual that it leaves no space for rabbinic tradition as an independent (extrascriptural) source.

65. Azzan Yadin-Israel, "Rabbi Aqiva and the Site of Revelation," in *Revelation, Literature, and Community in Late Antiquity,* ed. Moulie Vidas and Philippa Townsend (Tübingen: Mohr Siebeck, 2011), 177.

66. Ibid., 204. Although a similar observation could be made about the reading practices attributed to this passage in the alternative interpretations of Shlomo Naeh, "The Script of the Torah in Rabbinic Thought (B): Transcriptions and Thorns," *Leshonenu: A Journal for the Study of the Hebrew Language and Cognate Subjects* 72, nos. 1–2 (2010): 89–123 (in Hebrew), and Yakir Paz, "Binding Crowns to the Letters: A Divine Scribal Practice in Its Historical Context," *Tarbiz* 86, nos. 2–3 (2019): 233–68 (in Hebrew).

A BOOK THAT KILLS   91

Departing slightly from Yadin-Israel, however, I would submit that this new image of Akiva is not treated as entirely positive in the bMenahot narrative.[67] As in the Babylonian Talmud's version of R. Hanina's martyrdom above, Akiva is not explicitly accused of theological wrongdoing in relation to the biblical text. On the contrary, God himself facilitates R. Akiva's unusual feats of textual prowess by attaching the very textual elements R. Akiva will interpret. Yet it is not at all clear that this narrative either normalizes or valorizes R. Akiva's unique mode of engaging with the biblical text. To begin with, the opening lines of this passage suggest that engaging with a physical copy of the biblical text at this level of detail represents a deviation from the basic nature of the biblical revelation. According to this narrative, the original recipient of the biblical revelation (Moses) perceives any attention lavished on the nonsemantic or material aspects of the written transcript to be a waste of time—an unnecessary distraction that is "delaying" God from the primary task at hand. As it is characterized in bMenahot 29b, the written consonantal transcript was not a significant facet of the biblical revelation in its most essential form, since the man most intimately familiar with the fundamental iteration of the biblical revelation cannot imagine any use for a carefully constructed and embellished consonantal text. This theme is amplified by the discussion between God and Moses that follows the classroom incident. For neither the description of Akiva's small cohort of students[68] nor Moses's reaction to the scene suggests that Akiva's exegetical methods are the product of a broader historical movement or school of thought. Instead, Akiva is treated as a unique individual paralleling Moses himself. As Moses asks (twice) in the singular, "You have *a*

67. Indeed, Akiva's interest in sacred textuality in general is often approached with considerable ambivalence in early rabbinic tradition (Wollenberg, "People of the Book," 148–57).

68. Even within the embedded narratives themselves (that is the classroom incident and the death scene), moreover, the possibility that Akiva might be the founder of a mainstream school of thought is never raised, even by implication. While Akiva is portrayed as sitting at the front of a standard eight-row classroom of disciples, like many individual rabbinic figures in classical rabbinic stories, there is no reference to the multitudes of students that are typically attributed to the leader of a school or generation in classical rabbinic traditions. Akiva is pictured neither with the 24,000 students that he is imagined to have taught elsewhere in the Babylonian Talmud (bYevamot 62b) nor with the multitudes attributed to a sage such as Rav Huna, for instance, whose students were said to block out the light of the sun with the dust they shook from their clothes as they rose from their massive study sessions (bKetubot 106a). Even surrounded by his students, therefore, Akiva is portrayed in this passage in keeping with the classical rabbinic vision described in the previous paragraphs—that is, as a relatively isolated genius whose methods defy easy understanding or widespread imitation.

man such as this, and yet you give the Torah at *my* hand?" Just as Moses is imagined as unique among the prophets, who will never be able to match or reproduce his exceptional perceptions, the parallelism of this passage suggests that Akiva is likewise unique among the rabbis.

Moses's own hesitancy concerning R. Akiva's methods might, of course, be put down to the ancient motif of a prophet's blindness to the secret key concerning his own revelation.[69] In this case, however, God himself endorses the perception that a material written transcript of scripture is, and will continue to be, largely superfluous in mainstream Jewish engagement with the biblical revelation. When the prophet encounters God engrossed in embellishing the technical aspects of the written transcript of the biblical revelation, he does not ask *what* is causing God to delay the revelation but instead offers the strangely worded question, "Master of the Universe, *who* is delaying you?" Formulating his question around the assumption that only a single individual in the entire scope of Jewish history (that is, a very small minority of the Jewish people) could ever be interested in a carefully constructed consonantal text, Moses implicitly submits to divine judgment his skepticism that the written transcript could ever be an essential witness to the revelation.

At which point, God can either answer Moses's question according to its peculiar formulation—thereby sanctioning the prophet's underlying assumption—or he can grammatically reject the assumption upon which Moses's question is based by formulating his answer along more rhetorically (and grammatically) conventional lines. In his response, God not only accepts Moses's unusual formulation of the matter but even amplifies the themes implicit to the prophet's question. By using the odd phraseology "there is *one* man" who will learn from this transcript (and underscoring his singularity by giving Moses the name of this unique individual), God not only affirms but emphasizes that he is only paying close attention to the written transcript of the biblical revelation for the benefit of a single individual. Like Moses, God dissociates this unusual individual's embrace of the consonantal text from the original (which is to say, essential) nature of the biblical revelation by underscoring three times that this development will not come to pass until a great

---

69. The negative valence of this tale would seem to distinguish the implicit argument of bMenahot 29b from rabbinic theories of progressive revelation in which legitimate new facets of the Sinaitic revelation are uncoiled in future generations. See Rebecca Scharbach Wollenberg, "A King and a Scribe Like Moses: The Reception of Deuteronomy 34:10 and a Rabbinic Theory of Collective Biblical Authorship," *Hebrew Union College Annual* 90 (2019): 207–24.

distance has been put between the Jewish people and the original revelation. As he says, "There is one man who will exist *in the future*, only after *many generations*, who will *at that future time* learn out" lessons from the strokes of the letters.

As in the bAvodah Zarah 17b version of R. Hanina's martyrdom, moreover, there is a price attached to R. Akiva's unusual level of engagement with the material text of the Bible in bMenahot 29b. In both cases, the price of death is not portrayed as a punishment so much as an inevitability. These men must die because, for reasons that remain unclear to their prophetic and rabbinic onlookers, they feel compelled to engage closely with the physical manifestation of the biblical text. Indeed, in the story of R. Akiva the two phenomena (textuality and martyrdom) are equal in their sheer incomprehensibility to the onlooker. Like the sufferings of the biblical Job, both R. Akiva's unusual style of engaging with the biblical text and his horrific death are marked in this passage as mysteries that only God can fathom—phenomena that human beings must simply contemplate in awed silence. More importantly for our purposes, perhaps, the two mysteries of Akiva's life are connected with one another by God's parallel rebukes to Moses to stand in "silence" in contemplation of these two phenomena. In other words, the mysteries of theodicy are not deeper than the mysteries surrounding engagement with the textuality of the biblical revelation. In this version of R. Akiva's martyrdom, bMenahot 29b paints a picture of close engagement with the physical written text of the biblical revelation as a novel, rare, mysterious, and dangerous enterprise that leaves its champion ambiguously marked as a unique genius who must suffer the worst of worldly punishments.

Another version of this move toward locating the dangers of the biblical text within the text itself appears in a brief but famous passage from bSanhedrin 59a in which the biblical text has become lethally dangerous not only for Jews but also for outsiders. As in earlier tannaitic treatments, bSanhedrin 59a harbors concerns that outsiders can actually change the nature of the biblical text by interacting with it, and this passage continues the tradition of expressing that sentiment in sexualized tropes relating to the uncontrollability of the female body. In this later treatment, however, the danger of appropriation is identified as an inherent quality of the text itself. As bSanhedrin 59a puts it, the Bible is like a teenage daughter who is betrothed but not yet safely married off—an entity whose very beauty and charm make her a dangerous temptation to the outsiders who encounter her and a burden for her guardians:

Rabbi Yohanan said, "A gentile who studies the Torah (עוסק בתורה) deserves the death penalty, as it is said, 'The Torah that Moses commanded us, an inheritance' (Deut 33:4)—an inheritance for us and not for them." [If this is so, this severe prohibition] should have been counted among the seven Noahide commandments [which were commanded to all of humankind].[70] [But it is included,] according to one who says that [the Torah is called a] *morashah* [(an inheritance) in this verse], it is stolen—he steals from him [which is forbidden, according to the seven Noahide laws]. According to one who says that [the Torah is called a] a *me'urasah* [in this verse (that is, a betrothed woman)], then his punishment is like that for a betrothed maiden—which is stoning. They responded, "But Rabbi Meir used to say, 'From where do we learn that even a gentile who studies the Torah is like a high priest? From the verse, "that a human being might do them and live by them" (Lev 18:5).' [For] it does not say priests, Levites, and Israelites [will gain life through them] but rather the human being, from which we learn that even a gentile who studies Torah is equal to a high priest [in this regard]." [Yes, but that statement] there only applies to the [study of the] seven commandments [which were commanded to all humankind, not to the rest of the Torah].

While Rabbi Meir's universalizing declaration in this passage is sometimes cited as evidence that the early rabbinic sages saw the Bible as a universal possession, the statement serves precisely the opposite rhetorical purpose in the context of the passage as a whole. By raising the possibility that gentiles might derive benefit from engaging with the transcendent message of the Bible only to limit that benefit to the study of a handful of commandments, the author of this passage uses Rabbi Meir's statement as a form of inoculation[71] against the temptation to see the biblical message as fruitfully available to any reader.

The Bible has been refigured in this passage from a deed to Israel's inheritance[72] into the very inheritance itself—such that Israel's enjoyment of the covenant is marred and reduced if an outsider so much as steals a look at the

70. That is, the seven Noahide laws.

71. As this phenomenon is defined, for instance, in the classic article of W. J. McGuire and D. Papageorgis, "The Relative Efficacy of Various Types of Prior Belief-Defense in Producing Immunity against Persuasion," *Journal of Abnormal and Social Psychology* 62 (1961): 327–37.

72. For more on this motif, see Rebecca Scharbach Wollenberg, "Outside Bible Readers as an Author Character in Rabbinic Literature: Using Attribution to Preserve and Contain Subversive Positions" (forthcoming).

biblical text. According to this more sensitive vision of the biblical revelation, the Bible is an exquisitely vulnerable communal asset: a temptingly enticing inheritance, easily violated by the slightest encroachment, and with potentially devastating consequences for the rights of its legitimate possessors. In this, the formulators of this passage observe, the Bible is less like a *morashah* (מורשה) (a landed inheritance that is difficult to alienate from the heirs) and more like a *me'urasah* (מאורסה-מאורשה) (an engaged girl) who is imagined in rabbinic tradition as so terribly vulnerable that she is less a joy than a burden to her keepers. As bSanhedrin 100b reflects in the words of Ben Sira:

> A daughter is a false treasure. For fear of her, he won't sleep at night. In her childhood, lest she be tricked into promiscuity; in her youth, lest she run around being promiscuous.

In this comparison, the Bible might seem to be a treasure but it is a prize from which its possessor will derive little pleasure, thanks to the vulnerability and tendency to be promiscuous inherent to written text. Just as (according to this mindset) a virgin daughter must be constantly guarded from her own worst instincts lest she be irretrievably violated, so written scripture must be guarded against its own availability to every reader and defenselessness in the face of misinterpretation. For the formulators of this passage, the responsibility of safeguarding the biblical text was apparently experienced as a high-stakes game. As the passage intimates, a *betrothed* daughter is a particularly terrible burden to her guardian since she will be stoned to death for the adultery if she succeeds in consummating the promiscuous relations toward which she is naturally prone.

In the forgoing narratives, the dangers of biblical textuality are universalized inasmuch as they are literalized and treated as adhering to the biblical text itself rather than the behavior of those who approach it. In other narratives from this stratum, the themes remain similar to those found in earlier reflections on the danger of the biblical text, but the *scope* of the damage that can be wreaked by the biblical text is broadened and universalized. In the story of King Yannai and Elazar b. Po'irah (bKiddushin 66a), for instance, the mystical dangers ascribed to the biblical text are virtually indistinguishable from those imagined in the tannaitic sources at the beginning of this chapter. Yet the scale of the destruction attributed to this dangerous force has expanded exponentially. The story begins when King Yannai is instructed by the Pharisees not to demand his priestly rights since there was a rumor that his mother had been taken

96   CHAPTER 2

captive in her youth[73] and had thus been forbidden to her priestly husband.[74] At which point:

> Elazar b. Poʾirah said to King Yannai, "King Yannai, any ordinary man in Israel, this is the judgment for him but you are a king and a high priest, is this your judgment?" [King Yannai asked,] "Then what shall I do?" [Elazar replied,] "If you to listen to my advice, destroy [the sages who instructed you to not demand your priestly rights]. [Yannai asked,] "And the Torah, what will happen to it?" [Elazar replied,] "Look, it is bound and sitting in the corner (כרוכה ומונחת בקרן זוית). Anyone who wants to learn may come and learn!" R. Nahman bar Yitzhak said, "Immediately, heresy (מינות) was thrust into [Yannai], for he ought to have said 'This is sufficient for the Written Torah but what of the Oral Torah?'" Immediately, the evil broke out at the hands of Elazar b. Poʾirah and all of the sages of Israel were killed[75] and the world was simpleminded until Shimon ben Shetah restored the Torah as of old.

As in the story of Elazar b. Dama's attempt to bring a proof text, here even the speech act of identifying the biblical text as a sufficient and universally accessible record of revelation immediately produces the twin forces of heresy and death. For we are told that as soon as Elazar b. Poʾirah uttered his statement that the Torah was contained in the document in the corner, heresy was "*immediately*" thrust into Yannai and "evil *immediately* broke out at the hands of Elazar b. Poʾirah, so that all the sages of Israel were killed." Although it is suggested in other Babylonian traditions that Yannai himself killed the rabbis (bBerakhot 48a), the mechanism that caused their death remains unspecified in this narrative. Recalling the ill-fated priest in the ark of the covenant tradition, we simply learn that all the sages of Israel "immediately" died when the destructive power of the biblical text has been unleashed. But where the ark of the covenant story (and others like it) described the death of individuals, Elazar b. Poʾirah is imagined here as wiping out an entire generation of rabbinic teachers with one dangerous speech act. Independent of any particular

73. Since the kidnapping had threatened her presumptive legal standing as a virgin.

74. An individual who was required to marry a virgin in order to maintain his family's priestly standing.

75. In many Talmudic stories, King Yannai stands in as a powerful, if somewhat generic, enemy of rabbinic authority who is accused of executing nearly all the (proto-)rabbinic authorities of his generation. See, for instance, bBerakhot 48a and the allusion to King Yannai's execution of the sages in the passage about Jesus and R. Yehoshua censored from bSanhedrin 107a.

mode of engaging with written scripture, the biblical text has now become coded as a source of mortal danger to the entire community.

Some Concluding Remarks

Threaded through as these traditions are with the themes of heresy, covenantal adultery, communal rivalry, and sectarian biblical exegesis, it is tempting to construct these developments as a story about rabbinic reactions to early Christian claims on shared scriptures. Yet here, as in the first chapter, early Christian engagement with biblical text appears to have functioned less as a distinct rival interlocutor than as sand in the oyster of early rabbinic thought. Evidently shaken by the vulnerabilities that sectarian engagement had revealed in the written scriptures of Israel, many early rabbinic thinkers would nevertheless proceed to articulate broader and more fundamental concerns about the dangers posed by a material representation of divine truth.

Just as the human soul was subtly betrayed by the body that allowed it to enter the world—diminished by containment and made vulnerable to forces of temptation, physical coercion, and destruction—so sacred truth was subtly distorted by its reduction to a tangible form and thereby made vulnerable to misuse and misdirection. Even when misappropriated or perverted, however, the text-body of revelation retained a tempting aura of beauty and a very real supernatural power that made its accessibility a source of considerable danger. The traditions in this chapter capture the anxiety inherent to this tension by vividly narrativizing the dangers that emerge from misidentifying the nature of written scripture and failing to appreciate the true character of its capacities. At the most basic level, these are stories about resisting a temptation to see the biblical text as a form of communication fruitfully available to any reader. But they also function as a warning against more subtle perils, such as the way written communication can be bifurcated to serve two masters or the craving to fetishize a material instantiation of sacred truth.

3

A Neglected Text

MISTAKEN READINGS, BIBLE AVOIDANCE, AND THE DANGERS OF READING AS WE KNOW IT

THIS CHAPTER EXPLORES EVIDENCE that the strains of early rabbinic thought documented in the previous chapters were not purely abstract reflections. We see a similar ambivalence toward the biblical text manifest in rabbinic discussions of the daily activities through which one might engage with scriptural text in practice. Many early rabbinic authorities appear to have cultivated quotidian relationships with biblical text that ranged from benign neglect to active avoidance—and even censorship—of written scripture as a source of religious information.

To appreciate these practical restrictions, we need to rethink how we conceptualize what restriction and quarantine of sacred texts looks like. Early rabbinic modes of quarantining the biblical text have become increasingly legible in recent years as we have come to understand better the subtle nature of the limitations placed on Bible reading in other contexts—particularly the medieval Catholic examples that form the imaginative paradigm for so much scholarly thinking about censorship of biblical texts. In the decade since Andrew C. Gow revived the push against imagining a European Middle Ages in which the laity had no access to biblical texts,[1] numerous scholars have worked to nuance the notion that Bibles were simply forbidden to medieval

---

1. Andrew Colin Gow, "Challenging the Protestant Paradigm: Bible Reading in Lay and Urban Contexts of the Later Middle Ages," in *Scripture and Pluralism: Reading the Bible in the Religiously Plural Worlds of the Middle Ages and the Renaissance*, ed. Thomas Heffernan and Thomas E. Burman, Studies in the History of Christian Thought 123 (Leiden: Brill, 2006), 161–91.

believers.[2] Yet the circulation and consumption of biblical text in that period was also not completely unrestricted. In the process of demonstrating that "there was no outright ban" on vernacular Bible reading in the Catholic world,[3] these researchers have simultaneously nuanced the portrait of what restriction or censorship of Bible reading looks like. As in early rabbinic circles, medieval authorities often approached the practice of Bible reading by the laity with ambivalence and suspicion, but the measures taken to regulate communal engagement with scriptural texts were varied and partial—producing a "complex 'dynamic' between Bible reading and censorship."[4] This growing recognition that the dynamics of scriptural circulation and limitation are more complex than previously imagined, in turn, presses us to consider a much broader variety of practices as we analyze dynamics of scriptural quarantine in the early rabbinic context.

This chapter will therefore analyze a series of early rabbinic practices that limited quotidian engagement with biblical text. How often any individual limitation was put into practice is unclear. Indeed, some of the scenes analyzed in this chapter border on the fantastic to the eye of the modern reader. But I would maintain that it does not matter. We may still analyze these early rabbinic accounts of restrictions placed on Bible reading using a method originally advocated by Daniel Boyarin in which studying fictional "scenes of reading" can produce an "ethnography of reading."[5] As Annette Yoshiko Reed recently argued, the success of this method "is not predicated on the historical accuracy of the events described, inasmuch as it culls the verisimilitude of the narratives themselves, also with an eye to semantic fields of the specific terms therein used."[6] Verisimilitude is, of course, in the eyes of the beholder. But working with Second Temple texts, Reed applies the terminology "scenes of reading" to scenarios as fanciful as angelic dictation.[7] I propose that the threat of sudden mystical injury and other supernatural punishments were to the

2. Sabrina Corbellini, Mart van Duijn, Suzan Folkerts, and Margriet Hoogvliet, "Challenging the Paradigms: Holy Writ and Lay Readers in Late Medieval Europe," *Church History and Religious Culture* 93, no. 2 (2013): 174.

3. François Wim, "Vernacular Bible Reading in Late Medieval and Early Modern Europe: The 'Catholic' Position Revisited," *The Catholic Historical Review* 104, no. 1 (Winter 2018): 24.

4. Ibid., 27–28.

5. Daniel Boyarin, "Placing Reading: Ancient Israel and Medieval Europe," in *The Ethnography of Reading*, ed. Jonathan Boyarin (Berkeley: University of California Press, 1993), 12.

6. Annette Yoshiko Reed, *Demons, Angels, and Writing in Ancient Judaism* (Cambridge: Cambridge University Press, 2020), 110.

7. Ibid., 265.

rabbinic imagination what angelic messengers were to Second Temple practitioners: a simple "fact of life" that has since been pushed outside the boundaries of what we identify as quotidian experience. In other words, the very fact that early rabbinic sources imagined daily scenes of reading in which the use and circulation of biblical texts was limited or dangerous in itself paints a picture of a reading culture that was inclined to curtail direct engagement with biblical textuality—even without evaluating the historical accuracy of these scenarios.

This chapter will focus on three very different types of practices that limited the influence of biblical text: hermeneutic practices that trivialized and ignored the tenets of textual literacy, cultural norms that discouraged informational reading of sacred texts, and normative bans placed on Bible reading and the circulation of biblical translations. Though largely obscured from view until now by a scholarly focus on the superficially similar early rabbinic practice of creative philology,[8] a significant thread of the early rabbinic exegetical tradition featured ostentatiously mistaken renderings of the biblical text that attest to a biblical reading culture in which careful attention to written textual cues was exoticized and even denigrated. While such lack of interest in the technicalities of scriptural textuality might be read as a neutral amplification of the imagined gulf cultivated between some intellectuals and their scribes in the late antique Mediterranean,[9] this disinterest blossomed into something approaching real fear in early rabbinic traditions that identified the act of decoding written text for information as both mystically and literally danger-

---

8. To use the much-repeated language of Isaac Heinemann, *The Paths of Aggadah* (Jerusalem: Magnes, 1970), 96. In recent years, however, Heinemann's construction of creative philology has been overshadowed by Michael Fishbane's similar claim that "the creative elements of midrashic interpretation" are *"chiefly concerned with the creation of meaning*—not with exegesis" since "midrash not only creates exegetical information, as Heinemann asserts, but also the spheres of meaning in which new halakhic and theological norms are established and realized." Michael Fishbane, *The Midrashic Imagination: Jewish Exegesis, Though and History* (Albany: SUNY Press, 2012), 9.

9. For an extensive treatment of this dynamic in Second Temple and Greco-Roman circles, see Catherine Hezser, "Jewish Scribes in the Late Second Temple Period: Differences between the Composition, Writing, and Interpretation of Texts," in *Scriptures in the Making: Texts and Their Transmission in Late Second Temple Judaism*, ed. Raimo Hakola, Jessi Orpana, and Paavo Hakola (Leuven: Peeters, 2019), 149–72. For echoes of this dynamic in rabbinic circles, see Catherine Hezser, *The Social Structure of the Rabbinic Movement in Roman Palestine* (Tübingen: Mohr Siebeck, 1997), 467–75.

ous.[10] This oblique rejection of the practices associated with extracting information directly from sacred text were intensified in some circles, moreover, by normative rulings that actively sought to limit communal engagement with written records of the scriptural text in daily practice. Rather than fostering forms of rabbinic learning that closely engaged with the written text of scripture, as we have been led to expect by modern scholarship, these combined practices effectively quarantined the biblical text within daily religious life so that its power as a communicative document was highly curtailed.

They Were Experts, We Are Not Experts:
The Phenomenon of Mistaken Readings

If it is difficult to assimilate the picture painted in the first two chapters concerning rabbinic ambivalence toward the biblical text, this is due at least in part to the fact that the early rabbinic authorities are so often characterized in the contemporary scholarly literature as careful readers of scriptural minutiae. Certainly, a significant body of recent work on midrash as a literary genre has drawn our attention to the parallels between oral stylistic patterns in rabbinic traditions and those cultivated in Greek and Roman rhetorical academies,[11] and it has been extensively argued that the early rabbinic authorities consciously eschewed practices of informational reading and writing in the transmission of *rabbinic* traditions.[12] But acknowledging that many early rabbinic authorities eschewed independent forms of textual communication for transmitting the rabbinic tradition has done little to unseat the notion that early rabbinic thinkers engaged closely with the written text when it came to the Bible.[13] As Natalie Dohrmann recently put it, early rabbinic thought may have

10. While the previous chapter analyzed rabbinic traditions in which the biblical text itself was a lethally dangerous object, a separate set of early rabbinic traditions marked the *process* of informational reading (that is, the act of decoding sacred text to derive information) as dangerous. Additional examples of this phenomenon can be found in Rebecca Scharbach Wollenberg, "The Dangers of Reading as We Know It: Sight Reading as a Source of Heresy in Classical Rabbinic Literature," *Journal of the American Academy of Religion* 85, no. 3 (2017): 709–45.

11. For an analysis of this literature, see Richard Hidary, *Rabbis and Classical Rhetoric: Sophistic Education and Oratory in the Talmud and Midrash* (Cambridge: Cambridge University Press, 2017).

12. See the introduction to this monograph, note 59.

13. As Shlomo Naeh has famously summed up this dichotomy: "Professor Yaakov Sussmann has shown in his extended article on the Oral Torah that in the world of the rabbinic sages, the

witnessed "quiescence of other sites of reading and writing" but there was simultaneously an "amplification of the written bookishness of Scripture"[14] so that "the rabbis are rather bookish in a classical mode—even as their particular canon-making project (rather unlike those of their pagan neighbors) aims to end or drastically curtail the authority and cultural importance of books" in general.[15] As a field, we thus acknowledge that the mode of scholasticism constructed around the rabbinic tradition itself frequently resembled the self-consciously oral systems of their contemporaries in the rhetorical academies while simultaneously imagining that early rabbinic engagement with the Hebrew Bible was conducted in a different scholarly mode—something closer to the intensely text-oriented approach often attributed to the Alexandrian grammarians and their peers, who sought to preserve Homer's prestige in Greek-speaking circles by establishing a definitive text of his aging works and producing an exacting commentary tradition on that carefully edited text.[16]

The modern scholarly portrait of early rabbinic authorities as careful readers of the biblical text takes its shape in large part from the rhetorical form of early rabbinic midrash, which is imbued with a rhetoric of textual minutiae. Without doubt, many classic midrashic traditions give the impression of exquisite attention to textual detail. Midrashic interpretations often hang on the strength of a single *et* or a punning play on the spelling of a particular word. A closer look at these wordplays, however, reveals a strange challenge to our vi-

---

only book that was 'written and published' was the Bible; the rabbinic sages transmitted their own [Oral] Torah through oral memorization. The letters of the Holy Book were, therefore, the only text that the rabbinic sages encountered which was fixed not only in its wording but also in the form of its written text and its letters down to the minutiae of the textual details." Shlomo Naeh, "Script of the Torah in Rabbinic Thought (A): The Traditions concerning Ezra's Changing of the Script," *Leshonenu* [2008]: 125 (in Hebrew).

14. Natalie Dohrmann, "Jewish Books and Roman Readers: Censorship, Authorship, and the Rabbinic Library," in *Reconsidering Roman Power: Roman, Greek, Jewish, and Christian Perceptions and Reactions,* ed. Katell Berthelot (Rome: Publications de l'Ecole Française de Rome, 2020), 424.

15. Ibid., 429.

16. Although the best-known exposition of this theory is undoubtedly Saul Lieberman's classic essay on the topic (Saul Lieberman, *Hellenism in Jewish Palestine: Studies in the Literary Transmission, Beliefs, and Manners of Palestine in the I Century B.C.E.—IV Century C.E.* [New York: Jewish Theological Seminary of America, 1950], 20–82), this theory continues to be propounded by a wide variety of authors. Consider, for instance, the variations on this theory appearing in the collected volume, Maren Niehoff, ed., *Homer and the Bible in the Eyes of Ancient Interpreters* (Leiden: Brill, 2012).

sion of rabbinic attentiveness to sacred textuality. When one examines closely early rabbinic interpretative traditions that appear most ostentatiously engaged with various categories of textual minutiae, they are often revealed as purely performative rhetorical exercises. In many of these passages, scriptural exegesis that mimics close reading of a biblical text does not actually correspond to any written version of the biblical passage supposedly being studied—and frequently fails to adhere to even the basic linguistic conventions of textual meaning-making. Indeed, some of these exegeses are so disconnected from the formulas of the written text that they might best be characterized as mistaken readings. In other words, many rabbinic exegetical traditions that appear at first to engage closely with the written text do not in fact engage the biblical text as we know it, at all. Nor can these mistaken readings be dismissed as problems of manuscript transmission, since it is not uncommon for such passages to remark explicitly on a tradition's blatant textual misreadings without correcting them. So marked, these pseudotextual exegetical traditions stand as ambivalent and ironic explorations of early rabbinic *disinterest* in the workings of textual meaning-making.

A great deal has been written about examples of this phenomenon that might conceivably be attributed to variants in the manuscript traditions of the biblical text. BBava Batra 9a, for instance, constructs its entire exegesis around written orthography but bases its reading on the claim that the word פרס in Isaiah 58:7 is spelled פרש. Similarly, bBerakhot 7b fashions an elaborative philological comparison around the suggestion that 1 Chronicles 17:9 reads לכלותו rather than the extant (and linguistically preferably) wording לבלתו.[17]

There are many other types of mistaken readings, however, for which historical-critical explanations could not account. BSukkah 6b, for instance, specifically claims to produce a close textual reading based on the Pentateuch's consonantal transcript—within a passage explicitly debating the relative importance of the consonantal text and the oral "read-formulas" of biblical passages.[18] This passage does excerpt phrases from the extant biblical text as we

17. Even since the publication of Victor Aptowitzer's *Das Schriftwort in der rabbinischen Literatur* (Vienna: A. Hoelder, 1906), the notion that rabbinic literature can be leveraged for text criticism of the Hebrew Bible has remained widespread. For a recent brief history of this school of thought, see Dagmar Boerner-Klein, "The Variant Reading ולו/ולא of Psalm 139:16 in Rabbinic Literature," in *Ancient Readers and Their Scriptures: Engaging the Hebrew Bible in Early Judaism and Christianity,* ed. Garrik Allen and John Anthony Dunne (Leiden: Brill, 2018), 209–13.

18. For more on this rabbinic practice, see chapter 5 of this monograph.

104   CHAPTER 3

know it. Yet the textual reconstruction produced from these excerpts contradicts the written text's most basic semantic cues—and, indeed, all possible grammatical readings of these written words. Which is to say, this tradition leverages the biblical text as we know it to offer a close textual reading that only functions if we are willing to ignore the actual textual and linguistic details and imagine the biblical excerpt in question *as if* it were worded slightly differently:

> The sages taught: [A ritual tabernacle (sukkah) has] two full walls and a third that is at least a handbreadth. R. Shimon says: [A ritual tabernacle has] three full walls and a fourth that is at least a handbreadth. What was their disagreement based on? The sages maintained *yesh em lamasoret* (the written text has primacy) but R. Shimon maintains *yesh em lamikra* (the read-formula has primacy[19]). The sages maintained the written text has primacy: [So they read according to the written text:] "in a tabernacle (בסכת) ... in a tabernacle (בסכת) ... in tabernacles (בסכות)" (Lev 23:42–43). Behold there are four [tabernacles] here. Subtract one [instance] as the original [commandment to build a tabernacle] and three remain for you [to count toward the number of walls to be used in the sukkah]. . . . But R. Shimon maintained [that we should render the verse according to the read-formula]: "in tabernacles (בסכות) ... in tabernacles (בסכות) ... in tabernacles (בסכות)." Behold there are six here. Subtract one [double instance] as the original [commandment to build a tabernacle] and four remain for you [to count toward the number of walls to be used in the tabernacle].

This grammatically transgressive reading is evocative of the scholarly concept of creative philology to the extent that "the ultimate subject of that joke is the dissonance between the religion of the Rabbis and the Book from which it is supposed to be derived."[20] For this passage makes much of its engagement with the written transcript of the biblical text as an independent communicative document. And yet, the purportedly textual interpretation offered here works only if the biblical phrases בסכת . . . בסכת . . . בסכות (with ת) are read as if they say "in the sukkah (בסכה) ... in the sukkah (בסכה) ... in the sukkot (בסכות)" (so that the first two instances end with the letter ה). That is, the defective (ו-less) spelling of בסכת cannot actually be read as a standalone sin-

---

19. Alternately, some classical rabbinic traditions suggest that the two transcripts each taught necessary (but different) rulings: יש אם למקרא ולמסורת (bKiddushin 18b). See, similarly, bPesahim 86a, bSanhedrin 4a, bMakkot 7b, bBekhorot 34a, and bKeritot 17a.

20. James Kugel, "Two Introductions to Midrash," *Prooftexts* 3, no. 2 (1983): 133–34.

gular form but only as a series of incomplete construct forms: "in the sukkah of (בסכת) . . . in the sukkah of (בסכת) . . . in the sukkot (בסכות)"—which renders even the excerpted form of the passage nonsensical. While claiming to grant primacy to the written text of the Bible as the most authentic communication of the biblical tradition, the formulators of this passage have produced something like a parody of close textual reading. They assert primacy for the rules of independent literary communication while mangling the practice of textual engagement to such an extent that the resulting interpretation is nonsensical by the standards of basic literacy.

Classical rabbinic sources themselves, moreover, frequently acknowledge such readings as inaccurate or inattentive readings of the biblical text. In some passages this is done explicitly, such as when an exegesis based on a reading mistake is followed by a statement noting the mistake. In the Mekhilta (Vayassa 1), for instance, we encounter the following tradition:

> "There he tested him (נסהו)" (Exod 15:25) [means] there he raised him up (נשא) to greatness. These are the words of R. Yehoshua. For it says [in scripture], "Evil-Merodach elevated (נשא) . . . the head of Yehoachin King of Judah" (2 Kgs 25:27) and "he elevated (נשא) the head of the sons of Gershon" (Num 4:22). Rabbi Elazar ha-Modai said, "And yet doesn't 'greatness' only appear with the letter *shin*? But here it is written with the letter *samekh*. Rather we might say 'there נסהו' comes to teach 'there he tested them' that is, there God tested [the people of] Israel."

Rabbi Yehoshua's faulty reading is quoted here in full. Like many other mistaken readings, it is preserved as part of the rabbinic tradition. But unlike some other cases, its mistake is marked here for posterity in no uncertain terms. From the standpoint of a modern reader, there is something slightly shocking—something almost incomprehensible—about the nonchalance with which the Mekhilta simultaneously notes and dismisses this egregious case of textual misreading.

Yet such cases are naturalized by early rabbinic traditions to the point where these habits of misreading and misspelling are characterized as something bordering on a formal principle of rabbinic engagement with the biblical text. YShabbat 7:2 (9b), for instance, elevates these indiscriminate orthographic substitutions to something approaching a rabbinic norm:

> "These (אלה) are the things [that God commanded you to do: Labor on six days and the seventh day will be a holy Sabbath for you" (Exod 35:1–2). The

rabbis of Keisrin said . . . "[We derive the number of thirty-nine forbidden labors from the gematria of the word 'these' (אלה)]: *Aleph* (א) is one, *lamed* (ל) is thirty, and *het* (ח) is eight, [which adds up to thirty-nine]." For the sages did not refrain from explicating a verse [to distinguish] between *heh* (ה) and *het* (ח) (לא מתמנעין רבנן דרשין בין ח״א לח״ת).

In this statement, incorrect readings are characterized as a lack of finickiness. The sages did not let textual details get in the way of a good reading.

Other statements in this vein evince a similar lack of negative judgement about failure to attend to textual minutiae in quotidian reading life. BShabbat 103b, for instance, repeats the early rabbinic tradition that the phrase "you shall write them" in Deuteronomy 6:9 represents a directive that a mezuzah must be written with "perfect writing" (כתיבה תמה). It then offers the explanation that this phrase means that a mezuzah is ritually required to be written such that, for *this* object, one must not write *aleph*s as *ayin*s . . . or *beit*s as *kaf*s . . . or *gimel*s as *tzadi*s . . . or *resh*s as *dalet*s . . . or *het*s and *heh*s . . ." and so forth. No surprise is expressed that one might *otherwise* expect to write the letter *het* as *heh* or *gimel* as *tzadi*. In a similar spirit, the passage goes on to lump together what we would consider significant changes in spelling with nonsemantic scribal practices (such as open and closed letter forms) to claim that these textual rules evolved over the course of Jewish history—and were not always part of sacred orthography.[21] In other words, bShabbat 103b simultaneously avers that, as ritual objects, mezuzot must be written in exact correspondence to an official orthographic tradition and makes such a requirement sound almost outlandishly exacting.

Another passage on bKiddushin 30a similarly casts such orthographic cares away into the mythical past. This passage evaluates the normative tradition that a scholar should divide his studies in equal parts between Bible, Mishnah, and Talmud. Before this rabbinic practice was introduced, the passage maintains, "the ancient ones" devoted themselves entirely to Bible and were such experts in the textual minutiae that they were called "scribes (*sofrim*) because they [would go so far as] to count (*sofrim*) the letters in the Torah." The passage then goes on to offer a mild parody of this expertise by claiming that these counting scribes had identified the middle letter, word, and verse of the Pentateuch and the book of Psalms, respectively. But rather than identifying a

---

21. Thus, bShabbat 104a debates whether "the Seers," or prophets, established the difference between medial and final letters or whether the people "forgot these" distinctions and the prophets "reestablished" them.

technically plausible letter in the middle of Pentateuch as this purported middle letter, the passage simply identifies a vivid symbolic placeholder for this midpoint in the large scribal *vav* in Leviticus 11:42.[22] Nor does it seem that the formulators of this passage were unaware of the picturesque, if ironic, lack of exactitude. For this statement is followed by two successive cases in which a rabbinic authority suggested that they check the scribes' unlikely identification by "bringing a Torah scroll and counting in it" (ניתי ספר תורה ונימנינהו), only to be informed that the checking was futile since the scribes of old "were experts in full and defective spelling and we are not experts" (אינהו בקיאי בחסירות ויתרות אנן לא בקיאינן). Indeed, the entire passage appears to be framed as a narrative vehicle for this very principle. According to this reading, bKiddushin 30a represents a dramatized admission that some early rabbinic sages were both aware of and resigned to their own atrophying expertise in the textual particulars of the written tradition of the Hebrew Bible.

Far from depicting highly competent scholastic consumers of biblical text, such traditions represent their rabbinic protagonists as textual bumblers—literary antiheroes who appear at first to engage with the written text only to reveal themselves as almost comically uninterested in the technical conventions of written communication. In passages like these, early rabbinic thinkers are not presented as oral tradents in a solely oral community nor as illiterates unfamiliar with the norms of textual communication. In each of these cases, the quality of biblical literariness is recognized and used as a foil to paint a portrait of early rabbinic literary culture as a scholastic tradition with a mind above written text.

Bad Things Come to Those Who Read: The Dangers of (Bible) Reading

Some early rabbinic traditions not only express disinterest in the mechanics of sacred textuality but articulate a distinct anxiety concerning the practice of extracting information directly from the biblical text. Consider, for instance, the following pair of traditions from yShabbat 16:1 (15c). One tradition in the pair serves as an anchor model, which grounds its aversion to informational reading (that is, reading practices in which novel information is extracted

---

22. A letter which Adin Steinsaltz calculates is three full chapters after the middle letter in the Masoretic Pentateuch (*Steinsaltz Talmud Bavli: Kiddushin,* ed. Adin Steinsaltz (Hatfield: Koren, 2010), Kiddushin 30a.

directly from written text)[23] in a well-established rabbinic normative principle that rabbinic oral traditions should not be transmitted through writing. In this passage, practitioners are warned against sight-reading from written iterations of rabbinic texts and this problematic mode of engaging with written text is identified as a source of supernatural danger. Once the first tradition has anchored this principle in the already well-established arena of rabbinic oral tradition, the second tradition of the pair then applies this norm to a more counterintuitive case: reading unfamiliar biblical texts. In this second narrative, the act of acquiring information directly from the biblical text is similarly imagined to bring the unwary reader injury at the hands of heaven.

By informational reading, I mean the now-common mode of decoding a text to acquire new information. As will be discussed in greater detail in chapter 4, this mode of engaging with written text was sufficiently alien to the self-consciously oral scholasticism of early rabbinic culture that it did not merit its own conceptual category or even a consistent terminology in the rabbinic vocabulary. Instead, the act of sight-reading for new information is vividly described using a variety of contingent descriptions of the physical postures associated with the act: "he eyed the book" (עיין בספרא), "he observed the book" (אסתכל בספרא), "pulling from within the book" (מושט מן סיפרא), or "gazing on a book" (חזא ספר).[24] In other cases, the act of reading for information is not given its own descriptive terminology but is instead contrasted with other forms of rabbinic reading in order to sketch its outlines through comparison.

Like the dangers ascribed to physical manuscripts of the biblical text in the previous chapter, the narratives in yShabbat 16:1 do not specify the precise mechanism through which supernatural danger is activated by the act of informational reading—nor even whether the dangers in question are at core spiritual, social, or physical phenomena. As if to amplify the ambiguity, yShab-

23. For more rabbinic descriptions of this category of reading see Wollenberg, "Dangers."

24. As Yaakov Sussmann has pointed out, the classical rabbinic authorities do occasionally use this vocabulary to refer to insider practices, such as the act of looking at a Bible scroll. See Yaakov Sussmann, "Torah shebeʿal peh," in *Mehqerei Talmud 3: Talmudic Studies in Memory of Professor Ephraim Urbach*, ed. Yaakov Sussmann and David Rosenthal (Jerusalem: Magnes, 2005), 280n79 for a short but comprehensive list of such references. I would note, however, that many of the passages cited by Sussmann do not necessarily describe reading for information but rather depict the act of skimming a written text for other purposes, such as searching for a particular word or obtaining a word count (see, for instance, yShabbat 7:2 [9b] and bShabbat 49a).

A NEGLECTED TEXT 109

bat 16:1 (15c)[25] gruesomely illustrates the unpleasant consequences of gathering new knowledge about the rabbinic tradition by means of sight-reading with an uncanny mélange of supernatural and physical dangers:

> R. Yehoshua b. Levi said, "The one who writes down the legendary material has no portion [in the world-to-come]. . . . I have never in all my days read by sight (איסתכלית בספרא) [lit.: looked at] a book of legendary material— except for one time. It happened that I read [lit.: saw] that it was written, 'One hundred and seventy-five portions are written in the Torah corresponding to the years of our father Abraham . . . and one hundred and forty-seven songs are written in Psalms corresponding to the years of our father Jacob . . . and Israel answers *halleluyah* one hundred and twenty-three times, corresponding to the years of Aaron.' But even though [I learned something], I am troubled [lit.: sought after] in the nights."

> R. Hiyya b. Ba[26] once sight read from (חמא) [lit.: looked at] a certain book of legend and said, "If what is written is [conveyed] correct[ly], let the hand of the one who wrote it be severed." Someone said, "It was the father of that very man [R. Hiyya] who wrote it!" [R. Hiyya b. Ba] said, "As I said, let the hand of he who wrote it be cut off." And so it came to pass," like the fulfillment of "an error[oneous command] that has [already] gone out from before the ruler [and must therefore be fulfilled]" (Eccl 10:5).

This passage acknowledges the tempting possibility that one might acquire knowledge that is otherwise unavailable by utilizing the form of reading that is called "looking at a book." But as R. Yehoshua b. Levi learns from his brief foray into the land of informational reading, knowledge attained by book study comes at a price. For while R. Yehoshua b. Levi learned a new religious lesson from what he read (a thoroughly laudable use of this unusual literacy technique), he was nevertheless "sought after in the nights" (מתבעית בליליא) as a result of his action—a phrase that conjures up traditions of night demons and other forms of supernatural persecution.[27] Put another way, the mode by which R. Yehoshua b. Levi acquired his information was sufficiently disruptive

---

25. Compare also bGittin 60a, bTemurah 14b, and bBerakhot 23a.

26. Frequently known elsewhere in the Jerusalem Talmud as בר ווא and in the Babylonian Talmud as רבי חייא בר אבא,

27. As Leviticus Rabbah 6:6 puts it using this same vocabulary: "It is always the way of the dead to seek (לתובען) among the living."

that the acquisition of new sacred learning was not enough to wipe out the spiritual taint.

R. Hiyya b. Ba's brief consideration of another transcription of rabbinic tradition had even more severe consequences. Even a passing perusal would lead him to unintentionally cause very real physical harm when he blurted out his unrelenting outrage that a document had ever been created that made the rabbinic tradition available for informational reading. Like an "erroneous [command] that has gone out from before the king [and must therefore be fulfilled]," this case of mistaken mystical revenge was an error committed in a moment of emotional distraction[28]—a mistake that occurred because the great sage was agitated and disturbed by the consequences of his own questionable behavior (that is, the act of sight-reading the contents of this written communication in the first place).

These cautionary tales about the dangers of approaching the rabbinic tradition through informational reading are then paralleled to a corresponding narrative about the perils of reading unfamiliar biblical texts. The second narrative in this pairing leverages the vivid dangers of the previous tales to hint at the more subtle dangers inherent to reading practices in which religious information is derived by deciphering unfamiliar portions of the biblical text. This passage describes a situation in which the amount of time in which reading unfamiliar biblical texts was allowed had already been severely circumscribed by rabbinic decree,[29] but three sages sought to bend the rule by reading a single biblical verse outside of those limiting parameters:[30]

> While they ruled that one may not read from the holy writings except [for a very limited period of the day] from the [time of the] afternoon offering onward [until nightfall],[31] one may recite [the text] from memory and expound on it. And if one needs [to check] a [single] word, he may take [the text] and check [that word]. An illustration of this principle: Rabbi and R. Hiyya the Great and R. Yishmael b. R. Yose were sitting before an open text of the scroll of Lamentations on the day before the Ninth of Av (which fell on the Sabbath) reading the text for meaning (יושבין ופושטין)[32] from the

28. For other examples of this terminology see, for instance, yShabbat 14:4 (14d), yKetubot 2:6 (26c) and yAvodah Zarah 2:2 (40d), mAvodah Zara 20:4, bKetubot 23b, bKetubot 62b.

29. On which ruling, see the following subsection of this chapter.

30. For more on this reading, see the parallel narratives in Leviticus Rabbah 15:4 and Lamentations Rabbah 4:23.

31. That is, from 9.5 halakhic hours after sunrise.

32. Reading *poshtin* here as something of a pun evoking both the meaning of the term as

A NEGLECTED TEXT   111

time of the afternoon offering onward [until nightfall]. [But when the allotted period for Bible reading was over,] they had one acrostic [line] left to
finish in the book. They said, "Let us come and finish it tomorrow [morning
before the reading]." But when [Rabbi] took leave to go to his house, he fell
and injured his finger and he recited the following verse concerning what
caused [his accident]: "Many are the pains of the wicked" (Ps 32:10). R. Hiyya
said to him, "You fell on account of our sins, as it is written, 'The Spirit of
the Lord, the Lord's Anointed, was caught in their pits [here a pun on "their
murmurings"]'[33] (Lam 4:2)." R. Yishmael b. R. Yose said, "[Even] if we
hadn't been examining this text [just now] we still should have said this.
And all the more so since we were examining this text." And he went to his
house and attached a dry sponge on [his hurt finger] and tied it with reeds.
R. Yishmael b. R. Yose said, "From this incident we learn three things: a
sponge is not a medical treatment [which would be forbidden to use on the
Sabbath] but rather a protective covering. Reeds are considered among the
things that are [always] ready prepared [for use on the Sabbath]. And one
must not read from the holy writings except from the time of the afternoon
offering onward [until nightfall].

In this passage, three sages are (re)reading the text of Lamentations, a rare and
lengthy lectionary that was going to be read to the congregation during the
memorial fast the following day. Although the sages were undoubtedly accustomed to hear the biblical text in question read at least once annually, the
text is apparently not one that they know well. (As the framing statement of
the passage puts it, this is not a text that they can "recite from memory and
expound upon.") Rather, they are described as (re)acquiring a basic familiarity

---

"stretched out" to indicate the scroll is opened and "literal meaning" to indicate that they are
(re)learning the correct wording and simple meaning of the text before them. That is, they were
reviewing this once-yearly liturgical reading in preparation for read-reciting the text the following day. This interpolation is speculative since it is never clarified whether they were reading so
that they could more fluently read-recite the book to the congregation or for their own information in preparation for the holiday.

33. That is, I would agree with A. K. Gavrilov that the practices of silent reading and reading
a text aloud "are always closely connected, even intertwined with each other, and it is quite
wrong to think of them as exclusive alternatives." "Techniques of Reading in Classical Antiquity,"
Classical Quarterly 47, no. 1 (2009): 59, *whenever we are speaking about two different modes of
reading for information.* For a recent review of this debate, see Chris Keith, *Gospel as Manuscript:
An Early History of the Jesus Tradition as Material Artifact* (Oxford: Oxford University Press,
2020), 18–19.

with the text in question in preparation for the holiday—sitting down with the text stretched out before them and (re)learning its literary contours and formulas.

Before they can finish working their way through the book, however, the limited period during which reading unfamiliar biblical texts had been allowed comes to a close. Rabbi proposes that they bend the rule to finish the small portion of the book that they failed to cover during their licit session at a morning meeting the next day. When they have agreed, Rabbi then rises to go and, in the process, injures his finger severely enough that it requires bandaging. Each of the sages then offers a biblical quotation describing the injury as a punishment for their bad behavior and identifying the problematic behavior in question as the fact they had agreed to continue reading outside the appointed hour. While the injury doled out for thinking about reading one extra line from a biblical book is a minor one (perhaps in keeping with the very limited extent of the reading in question), the dramatic proof texts cited serve to portray this minor hurt as continuous with the more significant mental and physical injuries that other sages incurred from sight-reading rabbinic texts. According to this pair of narratives, the dangers of reading as we know it (which are detailed with great vividness in relation to written rabbinic traditions) also adhere to the biblical text.

Quarantining Scripture: Limiting Bible Reading in Daily Life

Nor do such traditions appear to represent a purely theoretical lack of interest—or fear—regarding practices of reading biblical text for information. Instead, it seems that early rabbinic practitioners actively sought to limit practices of close textual engagement with the biblical tradition as a written document in daily communal life.

In tShabbat 13:1, for instance, the practice of engaging directly with the written text of the Hebrew Bible as a source of information is a highly circumscribed:

> While they ruled that one may not read from the holy writings (קורין בכתבי הקדש) except [for a very limited period of the day] from the [time of the] afternoon offering onward [until nightfall], one may recite [the text] from memory (שונין) and expound on it (דורשין). And if one needs [to check] a [single] word, he may take [the text] and check (נוטל ובודק) [that word].

A NEGLECTED TEXT   113

Here we are told that there are at least two (legally distinct) modes of engaging with the biblical text. On the one hand, one might recite and expound on already familiar passages from memory. And while the Tosefta acknowledges that one engaging with the biblical tradition in this way might occasionally feel compelled to check a word here and there, the assumption is that the text as a whole is otherwise well preserved in the reciter's mind. To emphasize the role of memory and oral recitation in this mode of reading, the passage borrows terminology more often used to designate the process of orally reviewing memorized rabbinic traditions. This mode of engaging with the biblical tradition is permitted in all times and places, according to our excerpt. On the other hand, one might read a less familiar biblical text in a way that engaged closely with the written text itself—looking into a written biblical text to acquire new (or at least less familiar) information. In this passage, the general rabbinic word for Bible "reading" is used to identify this process rather than one of the more unusual phrases sometimes adopted to describe the act of sitting before a written text to decode the written signs. However, the passage then explains that the form of reading described with this term is similar to but more extensive than the act of taking out a text and checking a word. Deriving a single word from a written text is permitted at all times. To read a larger section of a biblical text directly from the biblical text falls into a second category of engagement (that is, informational reading), which the passage suggests should be severely limited when it comes to the biblical text.

Precisely how much this ruling was understood to limit reading directly from the biblical text is not entirely clear. In some iterations of the tradition, the restriction appears to apply to all forms of scripture but is understood to apply only on the Sabbath. In tShabbat 13:1, for instance, R. Nehemiah glosses the limitation as follows:

> For what reason did they say one may not read in the holy writings? Because of secular documents. So that [practitioners] will say "If one may not read from holy writings [on the Sabbath], how much more so may one not read from secular documents."

R. Nehemiah's gloss of the prohibition suggests that the ban on reading unfamiliar biblical texts was applied only on the Sabbath—a day when reading everyday documents was forbidden (tShabbat 8:12).

Read in this way, this time limit imposed on daytime Bible reading would simply represent an expansion on the limitations placed on Sabbath Bible reading elsewhere in the Tosefta, such as tShabbat 1:11–12:

One may read from the holy writings when twilight is falling but one may not read them on the Sabbath evening when a light is required, even if [the light] is above him or even if [the light is] in a separate house or even if it is ten houses away.... [However,] Rabban Shimon b. Gamliel said small children may review their [prepared] Torah portions by lamp light.

While the time limits imposed on Bible reading are relatively circumscribed in an interpretation in which this prohibition applies only on Shabbat, the biblical texts falling under proscription are extensive. For just as tShabbat 13:1 implies that any form of informational reading from a biblical text could lead to secular reading, so tShabbat 1:11–12 includes all categories of biblical texts (Torah portions, Prophets, and Writings) in the ban on "holy writings" that must not be read on Friday nights. Thus, even if such an expansive restriction on informational Bible reading applied only on the Sabbath, it would have significantly limited the practice of reading unfamiliar biblical texts—since many practitioners would only have leisure to engage in religious study on the Sabbath.

In other iterations of the tradition, the ban on reading directly from the biblical text appears to have been interpreted as a daily restriction. Consider, for instance, the elaboration of this tradition in yShabbat 16:1 (15c):

Why don't they read them? Because [they want to prevent] neglect of the study house. (mShabbat 16:1).... They ruled that one may not read from the holy writings except from the afternoon offering onward [until the end of the day at nightfall].... From [the time of the afternoon offering] on, in a place where there is a house of study, one does not read them. But in a place where there is no house of study, one may read them. Yet you do not have [support for such a daily ban, since you do not have any explanation of the restriction] except that offered by R. Nehemiah that "it is [to discourage the reading of] secular document [which implies this is a merely Sabbath restriction].... Yet it is taught: Mishnah always takes precedent over Bible (מקרא). This [ruling thus] supports that which R. Shimon b. Yohai taught. For R. Shimon b. Yohai taught regarding one who engages with Bible, it is a [good] measure that is no [good] measure (העוסק במקרא מידה שאינה מידה). But one who occupies himself with Mishnah, it is a [good] measure for which one receives a reward.

In this interpretation of the tradition, Bible reading should be limited to the short period of the afternoon between the time of the (mid)afternoon offering and when the day ends at nightfall. In places where even this short time allotted for Bible reading could be better spent at the house of study, moreover, engaging with the written text of the Hebrew Bible is forbidden at all times. Moreover, it is implied here that this restriction applies to all portions of the Hebrew Bible since it is treated as applying even to Pentateuch (מקרא). For the Mishnah is ultimately understood here to suggest that studying the text of the Bible is prohibited whenever one might occupy oneself with other forms of religious learning. Indeed, the passage elevates this restriction to a general principle that rabbinic learning is always preferred to study of the biblical text, and Bible study is not a practice from which one receives a spiritual reward at all.

We see a similarly restrictive attitude in early rabbinic traditions that forbid the circulation of written targums (vernacular translations) of the biblical text. The prohibition on reading from written Bible translations has generally been interpreted in contemporary scholarship as part and parcel of the prohibition on transmitting rabbinic traditions in writing.[34] Yet the source most frequently cited in support of this position does not refer to written targum at all. Rather, yMegillah 4:1 (74d) relates:

> Rabbi Shmuel bar Rav Yitzhak once entered the synagogue and saw a certain schoolteacher pull his translation from the body of the [Torah] scroll [מן גו סיפרא]. He said to [the schoolteacher], "This is forbidden to you! [We keep] things that were said orally oral and things that were transmitted in writing in writing (דברים שנאמרו בפה בפה ודברים שנאמרו בכתב בכתב)."[35]

Here the schoolteacher is not reading from a written translation but instead cueing his oral translation by sight-reading from the Hebrew text of the Bible open in front of him, thus blurring the performative boundary between written text and oral interpretation. As Tanhuma Ha'azinu 5 will explicate the problem:

> This is what our teachers taught: It is forbidden for the one who translates [the lectionary for the congregation] to look at the Torah scroll and translate, so that [the congregants] should not say that the translation is written

34. As Willem Smelik puts it: "The status of Targum as part and parcel of the Oral Tora has always been taken for granted." *Rabbis, Language and Translation in Late Antiquity* (Cambridge: Cambridge University Press, 2013), 225.

35. On this phrase, compare bGittin 60b and bTemurah 14b. For more on the special function of the targum in a liturgical context, see chapter 5 of this monograph.

116 CHAPTER 3

in the Torah. And one who reads [the lectionary for the congregation] is forbidden to remove his eyes from the Torah [scroll], since [it must be clear] that the Torah [he reads] was [the one] given in writing, as it is written: "I wrote on the words on the tablets" (Exod 34:1).

From traditions such as these, perhaps the most important insight to be gained concerning biblical translation in this period is that liturgical translation of the Pentateuch remained a largely ad hoc and oral affair well into the classical rabbinic period—so that biblical translations circulating in writing likely had a different function.

As Willem Smelik recently articulated this instinct, there appears to have been a second mode of biblical translation addressed in early rabbinic tradition: "To the mode of *targum* as Oral Tora there is an obverse mode of *targum* as Holy Writ."[36] I would argue that the early rabbinic sources that follow sought to ban this second type of biblical translation as a way to restrict the practice of reading the biblical text as a source of religious education and edification. In the Tosefta with which we began this section, for instance, the prohibition on reading biblical texts before the time of the afternoon offering is followed immediately by the following statement concerning the circulation of biblical translations (tShabbat 13:2):

> If [scriptures] were written down in translation in any language, one may save them [from fire on the Sabbath] but one removes them from circulation (גונזין אותן). R. Yose told an illustrative story: R. Halafta went to Rabban Gamliel in Tiberias and found that he was sitting at the table of R. Yohanan ben Nazif and in his hand was a book of Job in translation (שהיה יושב על שולחנו של ר יוחנן בן נזיף ובידו ספר איוב תרגום) and he was reading from it (קורא בו). R. Halafta said to him, "I am reminded of Rabban Gamliel the Elder, your grandfather, who was sitting upon the upper ascent on Temple Mount and they brought before him a book of Job in translation and he said to his sons,[37] "Hide this away (גנזו) under the rubble wall." In that very hour, they went and hid it away.

This passage begins by establishing the legal category of written Bible translations. Like Hebrew scripture, and unlike written forms of rabbinic literature, one may desecrate the Sabbath to save biblical translations from destruction.

36. Smelik, *Translation*, 226.
37. YShabbat 16:1 (15c) and bShabbat 115a read he told a *builder* who archived *it* under the rubble wall (אמר לבנאי וגנזו תחת הנדבך).

In this passage, then, biblical translations are treated as a form of biblical literature rather than a facet of the rabbinic tradition.

These written translations of the biblical text are imagined, moreover, as
resembling a very specific type of biblical literature: the less frequently read
portions of Hebrew scripture described in the previous paragraph of the
Tosefta. Like portions of the Hebrew Bible that do not form part of a practitioner's memorized biblical archive, translations are imagined as a type of biblical text that particularly invites informational reading. While tShabbat 13:2
uses the generic term for Bible reading in the rabbinic lexicon (קוֹרֵא), the extended description that follows depicts postures particularly associated with
the practice of deriving information directly from written text in rabbinic traditions. For when Rabban Gamliel sits at R. Yohanan b. Nazif's table with the
book open in his hand, he is certainly not reciting and expounding upon a
familiar passage from memory. On the contrary, he has been surprised in a
posture all too familiar to the modern reader: he became so absorbed in reading a novel text that he sat right down in the place where he first encountered
it (someone else's table) and began to read in earnest. When the biblical tradition was transcribed as a vernacular text, rather than in the traditional Hebrew
formulas, it exposed the biblical tradition to being consumed as a book of
information.

When traditions like this one argue that biblical translations require *genizah*
(passive destruction through permanent archive), they are not suggesting
merely that this form of biblical text requires respectful disposal but actively
command practitioners to dispose of such texts as soon as possible. The reason
for this instinct is drawn out in the passage that follows. Not only is this passage positioned as following naturally from the restriction on reading unfamiliar biblical texts, but the narrative used to advocate for the *genizah* of such texts
describes an elite sage tempted into an illicit act of reading by this unusual
form of biblical text. Rabban Gamliel is quickly rescued from temptation by a
rebuke from his illustrious grandfather serendipitously delivered across the
generations. But the dangerous pull of these illicit biblical texts is amply illustrated by the very fact that such a sage should have become absorbed in a
practice that his own famous grandfather had ruled against in the sacred space
of the Temple Mount. For a layperson with practical literacy in Aramaic or
Greek, the narrative implies, such temptation might not be so easy to resist.
Therefore, translations that transform the biblical tradition into a form of reading text must be promptly removed from circulation, lest the biblical text be
laid open to informational reading.

Traditions like those gathered in this section thus sought to restrict practices that encouraged practitioners to approach the biblical text as a form of written communication from which they might derive knowledge directly through textual decoding. This was achieved both by placing limits on the times and places in which practitioners might approach the biblical text and by restricting the circulation of the biblical text in forms (such as written translation) that invited modes of informational reading.

Concluding Remarks

The traditions gathered in this chapter paint a portrait of an early rabbinic community in which the biblical text as a written document might be given an important place in the rabbinic imaginary but was not assigned an equivalent role in communal practice. Exegetical traditions suggest that the written details of the biblical text could safely be ignored by its scholarly interpreters, and its textual cues could be misrepresented with impunity. Some early rabbinic traditions even characterized the practice of reading the biblical text for information as positively dangerous. Other passages preserve practical rulings that would have significantly limited a rabbinic practitioner's direct access to the biblical text—whether by regulating the practitioner's own relationship to the biblical text or by cultivating a communal environment that discouraged informational Bible reading in general. Biblical traditions would continue to form a vital part of the rabbinic discourse, and liturgical performances of biblical lectionaries continued unabated. But for those who adopted these norms, informational reading was discouraged as a mode of engaging with the biblical text to the point where the written text itself would largely cease to speak as a communicative document. In such traditions, the biblical text *as a text* was effectively quarantined from communal life and practice.

4

A Spoken Scripture

UNLINKING THE WRITTEN FROM THE ORAL IN RABBINIC PRACTICES OF BIBLE READING

EARLY RABBINIC DOUBTS concerning biblical textuality did not destabilize the emergent rabbinic movement as a form of biblical religion in part because late antique rabbinic practitioners engaged with written text very differently than we do. Doubts regarding the written transcript of the biblical tradition were rendered less urgent in many early rabbinic circles because the communal reading culture[1] that had grown up around scripture had already rendered the written text a secondary, even superfluous, witness to the biblical revelation. In a reading culture in which most practitioners "read" a scriptural text by memorizing an oral formula that roughly corresponded to that text and then reciting it from memory sometimes (but not always) in ritual conjunction with a written copy, a memorized spoken tradition might frequently be *correlated* with written signs but words and meaning were not actually *drawn from* written text. In this ritual reading practice, which we will we call "recitation-reading," a reader only approached scriptural text if he already knew what it was going to say. For all intents and purposes, the biblical text had thus already ceased to function for these practitioners as a "speaking text" (an independent communicative document in its own right).

To be clear, this chapter is not an argument about rabbinic literacy, as such. That is, this is not an analysis of whether rabbinic practitioners could decode written text, and to what extent. Instead, I would invite the reader to rethink

1. For more on the concept of a "reading culture" see the account of William Johnson, *Readers and Reading Cultures in the High Roman Empire: A Study of Elite Communities* (Oxford: Oxford University Press, 2007).

more fundamental presuppositions about the *directionality* of reading—from whence meaning is derived in the engagement between reader and text. I would propose that most historical literacy practices can be divided into roughly three categories.[2] I would identify the first category as informational reading practices—literacy practices in which new information is derived by deciphering written text. This category would include both silent forms of sight reading and sounded forms of phonetic reading in which written signs are first translated into spoken words and then comprehended as new information. A second category might be described as ritual reading. This category would include a variety of practices in which a more or less fixed oral formula is recited from memory while the reader may (or may not) makes ritual reference to a written text. While this practice can sometimes resemble informational reading, ritual reading is done without extracting the formulas in question from the text during the reading. In other words, the defining feature of ritual reading practices is that the reader already knows what the written text in question is supposed to say. A third and final category of reading would encompass various forms of practical literacy. Practical literacy includes formulaic literacy tasks such as making or deciphering written memoranda of a business transaction, reading a menu, or deciphering a brief stylized missive from a correspondent. This chapter argues that many rabbinic practitioners were neutral on questions of practical literary, opposed informational reading practices (at least in relation to sacred text), and embraced the ritual reading practice that rabbinic traditions call *keriʾah* (קריאה) and we will call recitation-reading.

Early rabbinic reading practices so radically inverted the relationship that is ascribed to the human mind and written text in modern practices of comprehension literacy that it is tempting to acknowledge the existence of recitation-reading in early rabbinic practice but then proceed to analyze early rabbinic exegesis as if it were produced in a largely familiar system of scholarly engagement with a canonical text. To help destabilize this tendency, this chapter will consider early rabbinic literacy pedagogies as more vivid encapsulations of early rabbinic attitudes toward engaging with sacred text. Early rabbinic literacy pedagogies will be treated both as the foundational moments of a rabbinic reader's textual enculturation but also as literalized miniature portraits of the broader cultural logic of early rabbinic reading. Unlike many

2. For more on this issue see Rebecca Scharbach Wollenberg, "The Dangers of Reading as We Know It: Sight Reading as a Source of Heresy in Classical Rabbinic Literature," *Journal of the American Academy of Religion* 85, no. 3 (2017): 709–45.

A SPOKEN SCRIPTURE 121

Greek-, Latin-, and Syriac-reading intellectuals from the period, early rabbinic practitioners often left off their literacy education at these early stages, taking late antique elementary pedagogies of textual engagement with them into rabbinic contexts of higher learning. In many rabbinic contexts, these foundational techniques of interacting with written signs thus came to define the *fundamental* mode of engaging with written text.

To be perfectly clear, this chapter does not seek to analyze early rabbinic reading and literacy practices as benchmarks for communal literacy rates or societal tendencies toward orality versus textuality, as others have done. Instead, this analysis will treat the techne of early rabbinic reading practices and literacy pedagogies as an illustrative lens that provides insight into more abstract questions about how early rabbinic thinkers engaged with and conceptualized sacred text. For just as scriptural text was not used as a repository for meaning preservation or communicative transmission in quotidian engagements with sacred writing, so the broader rabbinic imaginary would correspondingly cease to conceptualize the biblical text as a repository for the preservation and transmission of the biblical revelation.

To Read as a Rabbi: When Meaning Is Applied to Written Text, Not Derived from It[3]

While it is widely acknowledged that many of the quotations from the biblical text in rabbinic discussions were likely produced from memory given the social contexts of rabbinic study and the scarcity of Torah scrolls,[4] the vital importance of this observation is seldom brought to bear more generally in studies of early rabbinic reading and the community's conceptual relationship to the biblical text.[5] A survey of classical rabbinic descriptions of keri'ah (the

---

3. The materials in this subsection appear in a slightly different form in Wollenberg, "Dangers of Reading." It has been adapted here with the permission of the journal.

4. See, for instance, Marc Hirshman, *Stabilization of Rabbinic Culture, 100 CE–350 CE: Texts on Education and Their Late Antique Contexts* (Oxford: Oxford University Press, 2009), 21–22, 30, 104. As Catherine Hezser sums it up: "Few rabbis would have been wealthy enough to own Torah scrolls, and even if they did, they would hardly have bothered to unroll them to search for particular verses or passages in a text that lacked page numbers, chapter headings and punctuation." Catherine Hezser, "From Oral Conversation to Written Texts: Randomness in the Transmission of Rabbinic Literature," in *The Interface of Orality and Writing: Speaking, Seeing, Writing in the Shaping of New Genres*, ed. Annette Weissenrieder and Robert B. Coote (Tübingen: Mohr Siebeck, 2010), 40.

5. Instead, studies of early rabbinic reading more often note that recitation-reading of the

most common terminology used to describe early rabbinic engagement with scriptural text), however, quickly reveals that the rabbinic tendency to quote from memory was not a product of happenstance but a fundamental facet of the sanctioned rabbinic mode of engaging with biblical text.

Appropriate interactions with the biblical text in the early rabbinic practice of *keri'ah* always began first and foremost with the memory of the practitioner. This early rabbinic practice, which scholars frequently translate as "reading," consisted of reciting a precise oral formula from memory with (or more often without) ritualized reference to a written text. When a late antique rabbinic Jew "read" the Bible according to this practice, he did not extract words or meaning from written signs but rather pulled words and formulas from memory which could then be brought into ritual association with a written text. In other words, the defining feature of this reading practice was the fact that a reader would only approach an important text if he *already knew what the written text in question was supposed to say.*[6]

Many early rabbinic rulings thus describe acts of recitation-reading that are starkly incompatible with contemporary understandings of literacy as a generic ability to derive information from written signs. Classical rabbinic references to read-reciting biblical text, for instance, do not treat the ability to read as a transferable skill that could be applied to any passage once it was acquired.

Bible in early rabbinic circles—like the act of reading in many communities from late antiquity—differed from most modern Western literacies in being voiced rather than silent. As David Stern puts it, following Daniel Boyarin, while in "medieval and modern Hebrew, the root q-r-' primarily denotes silent reading," the early rabbinic "word *mikra* [Bible] is best translated as 'that which is read aloud.'" (This last phrase is from Daniel Boyarin, "Placing Reading," 12, as quoted and contextualized in David Stern, "The First Jewish Books and the Early History of Jewish Reading," *Jewish Quarterly Review* 98, no. 2 [2008]: 177.) So that "the most important implication of the fact that the Bible was read aloud is that it strongly suggests that the Bible, despite being written, was known in practice . . . not as a text that had been (silently) read by individuals but as one that had been heard while read aloud (even if the person hearing was also the person reading it aloud)" (Stern, "Jewish Books," 178).

6. Or at the very least, a ritual reader approaches written text with a firm sense of the possible formulas in mind. In this sense, the category of ritual reading might include practices like those that Maarman Tshehla has described as "Bible literacy": "Although both my parents are nonliterate, it is incredible that they spell-read the Sesotho Bible in a manner not too dissimilar from mine. (After many years of neglect, I cannot read in Sesotho as well as I can in English.) They combine their knowledge of biblical tradition, collected over the years from sermons and/ or public readings of the Bible, with a patient identification of each letter and syllable until each word, phrase, or sentence rings familiar." Maarman Tshehla, "Translation and the Vernacular Bible in the Debate between my 'Traditional' and Academic Worldviews," in *Orality, Literacy and Colonialism in South Africa,* ed. Jonathan A. Draper (Leiden: Brill, 2004), 84.

A SPOKEN SCRIPTURE   123

In one passage concerning the number of people who should be invited to read-recite from the biblical text in the synagogue on the Sabbath, for instance, we learn that one person who "read-recites" might "know how to read" only "three verses," while another who "read-recites" might know how to read "seven verses"; still another might know how to read an entire "Torah portion" (yMegillah 4:3 [36a]). Similarly, in the classical rabbinic idiom, one might make statements such as "the one who taught you how to read-recite Ecclesiastes did not teach you how to read-recite Proverbs [דאקרייך קהלת לא אקרייך משלי]" (bShabbat 152b) or "the one who taught you how to read-recite the Prophets did not teach you how to read-recite the Writings" (bKetubot 106b). For the formulators of such statements, there is no presumption that a person who knows how to read-recite three verses will be able to decipher other passages and that a person who knows how to read-recite Ecclesiastes will necessarily be able to read-recite Proverbs.

Recitation-reading a biblical text is treated, inversely, as a skill that one might acquire in a single afternoon. BMegillah 4b, for instance, explains that one does not celebrate the holiday of Purim (the Feast of Esther) on the Sabbath because everyone is obligated in the "recitation-reading of the book of Esther" (קריאת מגילה) on the holiday—but not everyone knows how to do so. If Purim fell on the Sabbath, the author reasons, one who did not know how to read-recite the text might violate the Sabbath prohibition of carrying objects in the public domain by "taking [the scroll] in his hand and going to an expert to learn [how to read it]." Clearly, the recitation-reading imagined in this tradition could not represent even the most basic ability to decode a written text— much less to sight-read a complex literary offering written without vowels, as ancient Hebrew was, since decoding written text is hardly a skill learned in a day. Instead, the author of this tradition appears to envision a situation in which an individual who is experienced in read-reciting other biblical texts goes to an expert to learn the particular vocalized tradition of the book of Esther.[7] Although this early rabbinic vision of Bible recitation-reading was associated with the fixed formulas of written text, such passages suggest that it did not refer to a generic ability to decipher the written text of the Bible to acquire information.

Many classical rabbinic references to recitation-reading of the Bible depict a practice not essentially dependent upon text at all—at least not in the immediate and derivative way in which many contemporary textual literacies are

7. While a single day is a short period in which to memorize ten chapters of biblical text, one does occasionally see contemporary Jewish liturgical readers learn to recite multiple chapters of biblical text in the course of an hour, so it is not inconceivable.

dependent on written signs. Thus, the composers of the Mishnah and Tosefta could speak without paradox of one who "read-recites by heart" (קורא על פה), without reference to a written text (mYoma 1:3, mYoma 7:1, mSotah 7:7, mMegillah 2:1, tMegillah 2:5, bTemurah 14b). The formulators of Genesis Rabbah could imagine a situation in which one might read-recite a text before it had been written—since they forbade their audience to "read-recite [a biblical passage] from memory and write it down" (לא יקרא מפיו וכותב) (Genesis Rabbah 36:8). And the rabbis of the Babylonian Talmud did not see any contradiction in declarations that would be incomprehensible in the context of most contemporary textual literacies, such as: "The book of Esther was formulated to be read-recited but not to be written (נאמרה לקרות ולא נאמרה ליכתוב)" (bMegillah 7a). Such statements clearly equate the stability of recitation-reading and the fixity of writing. The two practices are treated as parallel, often interchangeable, and sometimes derivative phenomena. But these declarations would appear paradoxical in the context of many modern Western practices of literacy. Counterintuitively to contemporary readers, rabbinic authors did not understand recitation-reading always to *derive* from writing—but instead thought that writing could sometimes follow reading and that reading might occur quite separately from writing.

Although the formula memorized and delivered during a rabbinic recitation-reading of the Bible often reflected the written text of the Bible, a review of classical rabbinic traditions suggests that the correspondence between this recitation of a fixed formula and any actual physical text was both loose and variable. The reader might indeed read-recite exactly the same formula as that which was recorded in the written text in front of him, as in the legendary case of R. Meir who once spent Purim in a community "where they did not have a copy of the scroll of Esther written in Hebrew, so he wrote one from memory and read-recited it (כתבה מפיו וחזר וקראה)" (tMegillah 2.5). Although the spoken words and the written text in that case did indeed run in careful and exact parallel, it is important to note that R. Meir's reading was not generated by the marks on the page in front of him. For the memorized formula he read-recited in conjunction with his newly scribed text had given birth to those very marks. In this case, and in the more generic situations it parallels, the correspondence between the formula recited and that written on the page was exact *but not derivative*.[8]

8. Others have written about similar phenomena in which a written text serves as an important ritual prop but is not used as a communicative device. Consider, for instance, John Miles Foley's classic encounter with Tibetan "paper bards" who recite a memorized formula in con-

A SPOKEN SCRIPTURE   125

Any determinative relationship between the written text and the spoken formula was further obscured and loosened by classical rabbinic practices such as read-reciting a biblical passage not in conjunction with written text but instead by following the recitation-reading of another person—a mode of reading that was apparently so widespread in relation to the special psalms added to the liturgy on the Jewish festivals that it was sometimes called "reading as one reads the Hallel [the psalms read on festive occasions]" (mSotah 5:4).[9] As mSukkah 3:10 describes this practice:

> One who has a slave, or a woman, or a minor lead him in read-reciting (מקרין אותו), repeats what they say after them (עונה אחריהן מה שהן אומרין).

In such a scenario, the second "reader" is not read-reciting from a written text directly but from the oral "text" produced by another person, who in turn may (or may not) be read-reciting from a written text himself. Indeed, in many of the descriptions of this practice that we encounter in classical rabbinic sources, it seems quite likely that the reader who is leading others in their recitation of the biblical formula is himself reciting the text from memory. Thus, for instance, mBikkurim 3:7 conjures a scenario in which:

> At first, anyone who knew how to read-recite [the firstfruits passage in Deut 26:5] read-recited it and anyone who did not know how to read-recite it, they had him read-recite it after the [priests].[10] [But, as a result of this distinction, those who did not know how to read-recite the passage] refrained from bringing [the firstfruits offering]. [So] they had both those who knew how and those who did not know how read-recite after them (מקרין אותו).

It seems likely that the "reader" who was leading others in this case was himself reciting the text from memory, not only because the priest was compelled to repeat the same passage over and over again as each visitor performed the

---

junction with a blank piece of paper. John Miles Foley, "Indigenous Poems," in *Orality, Literacy, and Colonialism in Antiquity*, ed. Jonathan A. Draper (Leiden: Brill, 2004), 9–35.

9. See, also, mRosh HaShanah 4:7, mGittin 3:1, mYevamot 12:6, tPesahim 10:4, ySotah 5:4 (19d), bSukkah 38a, bYevamot 106b, bGittin 24a, and bZevahim 2b. For an alternative usage of the verb "to cause to read," see Lamentations Rabbah 1:23. For a description of this form of guided reading in other liturgical contexts, see tSotah 6:3, where the practice is called reciting as "one recites the Shema in synagogue."

10. Although the primary meaning of this passage appears to be that the offerer has not memorized the passage in question, Sifre Deuteronomy 301 suggests that some practitioners were unable to recite this short passage from memory because they were not well versed in the Hebrew language in which this passage was recited.

126   CHAPTER 4

ceremony but also for the practical reason that the priest's hands were supposed to be occupied with the ritual gestures associated with this particular recitation-reading and were thus unavailable to hold a physical text (mBikkurim 3:6). The person fulfilling his ritual obligation to read-recite a particular biblical passage (that is, the second person reciting the text) thus not only performed his own reading without reference to a written text directly but was likely taking his cues at second hand from a recitation-reading that was itself a textless performance.

In other cases, the correspondence between the written text of the Bible and the read-formula was neither derivative nor exact. A reader might look at a biblical text, for instance, and read-recite a formula that was missing from the page. As bMegillah 18b describes this process:

> If a scribe omitted letters or verses [in a biblical text], and one read-recites [the omitted verses, from memory] like a [liturgical] translator who translates [the written text into Aramaic by reciting a traditional oral formula from memory] (השמיט בה סופר אותיות או פסוקין וקראן הקורא כמתורגמן המתרגם), he has fulfilled his obligation [to read-recite the biblical passage].

In the case described here, the liturgical reader would satisfy his duty to read-recite a biblical passage by reciting the verses from memory and inserting phrases missing from the written text into their proper place in the oral recitation, just as a liturgical translator orally recites the memorized Aramaic translation of the biblical text from memory.[11] In other words, this passage informs us that a reader might read-recite words that were not written on the page.

Other traditions suggest that a reader might even adapt his recitation-reading of a text to deviate not only from what was written on the particular page in front of him but from *all* written transcripts of the biblical passage in question. Thus, a reader might omit a word or paragraph that appears in the written text of the Bible so long as he could do so imperceptibly[12]—that is,

11. This passage appears to assume the existence of a more fixed formula of Aramaic translation tradition (such as those we see described earlier in the tractate [bMegillah 3a]) rather than the more spontaneous translation practices described in earlier Palestinian traditions. On which practices, see Steven Fraade, "Rabbinic Views on the Practice of Targum, and Multilingualism in the Jewish Galilee of the Third–Sixth Centuries," in *The Galilee in Late Antiquity*, ed. Lee I. Levine (New York: The Jewish Theological Seminary of America, 1992), 253–86, especially 259ff.

12. While this practice may sound difficult to the contemporary reader, material evidence suggests that fairly extensive excerpting of this sort was regularly done in relation to the Aramaic translation that accompanied the lectionary. Michael L. Klein, *Michael Klein on the Targums, Studies in the Aramaic Interpretations of Scripture* 11 (Leiden: Brill, 2011), 190–202.

A SPOKEN SCRIPTURE   127

without interrupting the flow and integrity of the oral "text" that he generated with this creative reading. As mMegillah 4:4 declares, "How far may he skip [when read-recited from a book of the prophets]? As far as he can without the translator having to pause."[13] Other times, a reader might read-recite individual words or phrases that differed from all written transcripts of the Bible. We are familiar with this phenomenon today, of course, in the form of the traditional rabbinic list of discrepancies in certain biblical passages between the *ketiv* (כתיב) (the way the text is written) and the *kri* (קרי) (the way the passage should be read out loud). However, classical rabbinic traditions sanctioned other discrepancies that were even more striking. We learn in tMegillah 3:39, for example, that

> One should read-recite all the biblical passages written in a shameful manner as if they were written in a laudable manner (כל המקראות הכתובים לגניי קורין אותו לשבח) ... for example, wherever "he had sex with her" is written, one should read it as "he lay down with her."

In such cases, the oral formula read-recited aloud perceptibly marked its independence from the written text through a series of small deviations of both wording and meaning. All of these traditions, moreover, manifested a basic principle: the formula that was read-recited aloud in a given instance might differ quite markedly from the corresponding written document without being considered an inauthentic recitation-reading of that passage.

Sometimes a memorized biblical formula might be read-recited without immediate reference to any written text at all. The biblical passages included in the daily Shema recitations,[14] for instance, were almost always summoned from memory—and the early rabbinic authorities still conceived of the act as

13. Some early rabbinic thinkers seem to have understood this permission to omit portions of the written text to apply only to the words of the Prophets and not to the text of the Pentateuch. See, for instance, mMegillah 4:4 and yYoma 7:1 (44b). Others were apparently willing to entertain the possibility that this practice was valid with respect to all biblical works (bYoma 69b, bSotah 41a, and bMegillah 24a).

14. In the Shema recitation, practitioners read or recited three brief biblical passages (Deut 6:4–9, Deut 11:13–21, and Num 15:37–41) morning and evening as part of their private liturgical practice. These daily readings were thus not lectionaries in the traditional sense but rather a ritual repetition of the biblical passages in question that more closely resembled a form of meditation or prayer. Nevertheless, these passages do not seem to have completely lost their association with other forms of Torah reading and biblical study. As mBerakhot 1:2 states, for instance, one who recites these passages outside of the canonical hours "has not lost [all merit by doing so], [for] he is like a person who reads from the Torah."

128   CHAPTER 4

keriʾah (recitation-reading). Indeed, some early rabbinic authorities considered recitation-reading the biblical passages included in the Shema an action that need not pass through the mediation of written text at all. BSukkah 42a, for instance, suggests that a parent should teach the "recitation-reading of the Shema" to a child as soon as the child "knows how to talk"—presumably by helping the toddler to memorize a recited oral formula. According to this practice, the act of recitation-reading the Shema was first and foremost an act of speech and memory, closely tied to the ability to orally articulate words and not essentially dependent on the more developmentally advanced ability to decipher written signs. In keeping with this understanding of what it meant to read-recite these particular biblical passages, classical rabbinic traditions envision the Shema being read-recited in any number of scenarios in which an ancient practitioner would be exceedingly unlikely to have a text in hand: workers might stop to read-recite the Shema passages at the top of the tree in which they were picking fruit (mBerakhot 2:4), a man who suddenly remembered that he needed to read-recite the Shema while he was visiting a ritual immersion pool might read-recite these passages while immersed in water (mBerakhot 3:5), a person might read-recite with a shirt pulled over his head (tBerakhot 2:15), rabbis would read-recite these biblical passages while walking down a road (tBerakhot 1:2), a harvester who had taken off his clothes to work might cover his nakedness with straw and read-recite standing in the field (tBerakhot 2:14), a person might read-recite these passages in an environment so dark that one could barely distinguish between a wolf and a domestic dog (yBerakhot 1:2 [3a]), or he might read-recite while hauling a load (tBerakhot 2:7).[15]

However unlikely, these images do not appear to be mere flights of imagination. Or, at least, we encounter other classical rabbinic rulings that suggest the Shema passages were also read-recited from memory in more quotidian contexts. TBerakhot 2:5, for instance, offers practical instructions for what one should do if one is read-reciting the Shema passages from memory and accidentally skips from the first instance of the phrase "you shall write them on your doorposts" (Deut 6:9) to the verses following the second appearance of

15. See, similarly, tBerakhot 2:11, tBerakhot 2:14, tBerakhot 2:17, tBerakhot 2:20, and bBerakhot 13b. Most of these scenarios will have arisen (in imagination at least) as a result of the limited time frame allotted for reciting the Shema particularly in the morning—a period that might range from as much as three hours (mBerakhot 1:2) to as little as the few minutes preceding dawn (bBerakhot 9b), according to different opinions.

the phrase farther along in the passage (Deut 11:20)—as those who recite from memory are wont to do in situations when a text very nearly repeats itself. Indeed, the practice of read-reciting the Shema passages from memory was apparently so common in classical rabbinic circles that the generic act of reciting a text from memory came to be described in some classical rabbinic sources as "read-reciting as one read-recites the Shema" (כקורין את שמע)—which means, the rabbis explain, "reading from memory" (קורין על פיהן) (mSotah 5:4 and parallels; mTaʿanit 4:3 and parallels).

When translating the phrase *keriʾat shema* as "reciting the Shema" while rendering all other appearances of the term *keriʾah* as "reading" the Bible, modern translators and scholars imply that the phrase *keriʾat shema* represents an exceptional use of the term *keriʾah*. In other words, this translation tradition treats reciting from memory as a distinct and secondary meaning of the word *keriʾah*. As we are coming to see, however, the two meanings are actually continuous in the rabbinic lexicon. Indeed, the classical rabbinic sages themselves apparently thought of the two uses of the term as unproblematically interchangeable, since they made statements such as: "One who read-recites [the Shema] from this hour onward . . . is like one who read-recites the Torah" (הקורא [את שמע] מכאן ואילך לא הפסיד כאדם הקורא בתורה) (mBerakhot 1:2 and bBerakhot 9b).[16] To read-recite in the rabbinic context *always* meant to recite from memory—whether one did so in conjunction with a written text or without one.

The Shema passages were not, moreover, the only biblical materials that were said to be read-recited without reference to a text. Practitioners needed to be warned repeatedly not to "read-recite by heart" when reading out the biblical lectionary from the synagogue podium (see, for instance, mMegillah 2:1 and tTaʿanit 3:4 and parallels). The very existence of such a prohibition suggests that practitioners were inclined to fulfill their obligation to read-recite the lectionary by reciting it entirely from memory without making even ritual reference to the written text—and the wording of the prohibition suggests that even the rabbinic authorities who forbade this textless form of reading in liturgical contexts nevertheless recognized the act of read-reciting the biblical formula without reference to a written text as legitimate form of reading. Indeed, classical rabbinic traditions describe the rabbinic authorities themselves read-reciting a wide variety of biblical passages from memory when a text was

---

16. For an inverse analogy, see mBerakhot 2:1and bBerakhot 13a.

130 CHAPTER 4

not available—such as when walking in a funeral procession (yBerakhot 2:2 [4c]) or when visiting the fields (yAvodah Zarah 4:9 [43b]).

"Reading from memory" was not treated as a secondary or aberrant form of recitation-reading in these traditions; instead, the act of read-reciting with reference to a text is often treated as theoretically equivalent and even interchangeable with read-reciting in the absence of a written text. One set of traditions, for instance, imagines that the high priest on Yom Kippur first read-recited two biblical passages with the scroll open before him but then "rolled up the scroll of the Law, placed it on his lap, and . . . read-recited *by heart* the passage, 'On the tenth' (Num 29:7) that is in the book of Numbers" (mYoma 7:1).[17] As the sages imagined the ancient gatherings of local Temple workers that were called *ma'amadot* (standing rituals), similarly, the congregation listened to the daily Torah portion read-recited "from a scroll" at the morning and midday services but "each of them read-recited it from memory" at the afternoon service (bTa'anit 28a).[18] In such passages, recitation-reading the biblical formula from memory without reference to a written text of the Bible is a practice that is not only proudly attributed to an idealized past but is also treated as interchangeable with and equivalent to acts of recitation-reading in conjunction with a text. One might easily read in parallel to a text in the morning and read-recite from memory without a text in the afternoon. In the rabbinic vocabulary, textless recitation and recitation in conjunction with a text are equally entitled to the description "recitation-reading" since many formulators of the rabbinic tradition perceived the practice as fundamentally based in the mouths and memories of practitioners, whether or not they read-recited in the presence of a written text.

Early rabbinic descriptions of recitation-reading the biblical text thus represent the rabbinic practice of *keri'ah* not as an act through which meaning was derived from written text but as a moment in which words and meaning were brought into a (sometimes uneasy) association with written signs. Indeed, the memorized oral transcript of the Bible could be read-recited, in the rabbinic sense of that term, without reference to any written document at all. When a rabbinic Jew read-recited the Bible, according to these descriptions, he did not extract words from the written marks on the page but pulled expressions and formulas from memory, which could then be applied or correlated to the written signs in front of him.

17. See also yYoma 7:1 (44a), bYoma 70a, and bSotah 41a.
18. See also mTa'anit 4:3, tTa'anit 3:4.

Bypassing Text in Early Literacy Pedagogies:
Learning to Read as a Rabbinic Jew

It can be tempting to agree that many rabbinic authorities cultivated a radically different form of ritual reading but then all but dismiss these forms of difference as a small quirk in an otherwise largely familiar system of scholarly engagement with a textual tradition. We can gain a better sense of the extent to which many rabbinic circles cultivated a profoundly alien way of engaging with written biblical materials by looking at early rabbinic literacy education. In other words, we can begin to understand certain fundamental cultural predispositions toward text by studying the most basic mode in which many early rabbinic practitioners were taught to engage with the written text of the Bible. William Johnson has pointed out that the basic elements of Mediterranean literacy education might have been relatively uniform in late antiquity but their use and outcomes varied markedly even between relatively similar communities. As Johnson puts it, the literacy education provided to the sons of great centurions would differ from the studies provided to the son of an equestrian or senator since a "centurion's literacy" need not encompass literary literacy but instead prepared a boy "to set the password, issue formulaic order, and write brief (and, again, formulaic) letters."[19] This section, therefore, seeks to highlight certain key facets of the process of acquiring "rabbinic literacy," which would come to shape in vital ways early rabbinic modes of engaging with the written text of the Bible.

The relative paucity of early rabbinic evidence for the forms of early rabbinic literacy education might lead one to doubt that the portrait painted is accurate or complete. Yet, as Natalie B. Dohrmann has argued more generally, researchers on late antique reading cultures would do well to recognize "the rabbis as provincial exemplars and not cultural exceptions or outliers," so that we may visualize rabbinic literacy as part of "the thick web of cultural relationships built around reading and writing that includes both the imperial center and the Jewish authors."[20] The current treatment will, therefore, fill out and

19. William A. Johnson, "Learning to Read and Write," in *A Companion to Ancient Education*, ed. W. Martin Bloomer (New York: John Wiley & Sons, 2015), 146, following a comment in Horace, *Sat.* 1.71–78.

20. Natalie Dohrmann, "Jewish Books and Roman Readers: Censorship, Authorship, and the Rabbinic Library," in *Reconsidering Roman Power: Roman, Greek, Jewish, and Christian Perceptions and Reactions*, ed. Katell Berthelot (Rome: Publications de l'Ecole Française de Rome, 2020), 423.

parallel these relative sparse early rabbinic accounts of literacy pedagogy with literary and documentary evidence of similar early literacy education practices in neighboring communities—where children (including possibly the children of rabbis)[21] were taught to read in Greek, Latin, or Syriac.

Admittedly, the process of fleshing out rabbinic images of elementary education by means of parallel descriptions from Greek and Latin, or even Syriac accounts, is not without its pitfalls. Most markedly, rabbinic participation in these modes of literacy education was primarily executed in parallel or imitative educational contexts rather than being embedded within the broader streams of imperial education, as many of their early Christian counterparts were.[22] This dynamic is particularly complicated as we move into the Persian context. While a great deal of work has been done tracing connections in the *contents* of Sasanian Zoroastrian and Babylonian Jewish communal thought and ritual practice,[23] *methodological* continuities in educational practice and scholarly discourse have not always emerged so clearly. Whether this disparity reflects the complicated nature of the extant Persian evidence or authentic historical asymmetries remains unclear.[24] Yet we currently have far more evidence for pedagogical and scholastic overlap between the minority communities of Babylonian Jewish and Eastern Christian scholars, as well as their shared orientation toward Mediterranean educational traditions and practices.[25] These parallels will, therefore, constitute the mainstay of our comparison in this chapter.

21. On the debate about whether or not Libanius wrote letters to the patriarch, see Christine Shephardson, "Between Polemic and Propaganda: Evoking the Jews of Fourth-Century Antioch," *Journal of the Jesus Movement in Its Jewish Setting* 2 (2015): 160–62.

22. See, for instance, Kim Haines-Eitzen, *Guardians of Letters: Literacy, Power, and the Transmitters of Early Christian Literature* (Oxford: Oxford University Press, 2000), 53–76.

23. In addition to the voluminous oeuvre of Yaakov Elman and Shai Secunda's *The Iranian Talmud: Reading the Bavli in Its Sasanian Context* (Philadelphia: University of Pennsylvania Press, 2014), consider a sampling of recent work and the literature cited there: Carol Bakhos and Rahim Shayegan, eds., *The Talmud in Its Iranian Context*, (Tübingen: Mohr Siebeck, 2010); Geoffrey Herman and Jeffrey Rubenstein, eds., *The Aggada of the Bavli and Its Cultural World* (Atlanta: Society of Biblical Literature, 2018); Shai Secunda, *The Talmud's Red Fence: Menstrual Impurity and Difference in Babylonian Jewry and Its Sasanian Context* (Oxford: Oxford University Press, 2020), and the recent articles of Yishai Kiel.

24. For an exploration of this problem, see Shai Secunda, "The Sasanian 'Stam': Orality and the Composition of the Babylonian Rabbinic and Zoroastrian Literature," in Bakhos and Shayegan, *The Talmud*, 140–60.

25. See, for instance, Adam Becker, "The Comparative Study of "Scholasticism" in Late Antique Mesopotamia: Rabbis and East Syrians," *Association for Jewish Studies Review* 34, no. 1

A SPOKEN SCRIPTURE   133

Many Greek and Latin elites, of course, continued their education beyond these early lessons in basic literacy in a way that would ultimately render their modes of engaging with canonical texts very different from those of the rabbinic elite—many of whom continued to engage with the biblical text in the modes inculcated in their earliest literacy lessons. Nevertheless, we can begin to form a picture of geographically widespread and chronologically longstanding patterns in early reading education throughout the regions and time periods straddled by early rabbinic literature—for while by no means "ossified" (particularly at the advanced stages), "ancient education is widely recognized for its exceptional tenacity and resistance to change."[26] Tracing the shared outlines of these similar but distinct educational practices allows us to uncover and reflect upon deep-seated, but often unarticulated, background cultural assumptions about the nature of reading and writing—and their relation to canon—in the ancient and late antique Eastern Mediterranean and Persian milieus.

Read together with contemporaneous parallels, classical rabbinic accounts of early biblical education describe a pedagogical process fundamentally different from modern forms of elementary literacy education directed at producing "comprehension literacy."[27] Where many modern literacy pedagogies

---

(2010): 91–113; Daniel Boyarin, "Hellenism in Jewish Babylonian," in *The Cambridge Companion to Talmud and Jewish Literature,* ed. Charlotte Elisheva Fonrobert and Martin S. Jaffee (Cambridge: Cambridge University Press, 2007), 336–64, and *Socrates and the Fat Rabbis* (Chicago: University of Chicago Press, 2009); David Brodsky, "From Disagreement to Talmudic Discourse: Progymnasmata and the Evolution of a Rabbinic Genre," in *Rabbinic Traditions between Palestine and Babylonia,* ed. Ronit Nikolsky and Tal Ilan (Leiden: Brill, 2014), 173–231; Richard Hidary, *Rabbis and Classical Rhetoric: Sophistic Education and Oratory in the Talmud and Midrash* (Cambridge: Cambridge University Press, 2017); Richard Kalmin, *Jewish Babylonia between Persia and Roman Palestine* (Oxford: Oxford University Press, 2006), especially 61–86; Kalmin, *Migrating Tales: The Talmud's Narratives in Their Historical Context* (Berkeley: University of California Press, 2014); Michal Bar-Asher Siegal, *Early Christian Monastic Literature and the Babylonian Talmud* (Cambridge: Cambridge University Press, 2013) and *Jewish-Christian Dialogues on Scripture in Late Antiquity: Heretic Narratives of the Babylonian Talmud* (Cambridge: Cambridge University Press, 2019) and the literature cited therein.

26. Elzbieta Szabata, "Late Antiquity and the Transmission of Educational Ideals and Methods," in *A Companion to Ancient Education,* ed. Martin W. Bloomer (Hoboken, NJ: Wiley and Sons, 2015), 252–53.

27. I take as my model of modern North American reading instruction the portrait of "reading for comprehension" pedagogy described in education-theory journals such as *Theory into Practice Special Issue: New and Critical Perspectives on Reading Comprehension and Strategy Instruction* 50, no. 2 (2011). For a meta-review of this research, see Brian Street, "Literacy in Theory

134 CHAPTER 4

focus on inculcating the ability to derive information directly from written text, the form of early literacy education presupposed by classical rabbinic descriptions jumped directly from a very basic and mechanical mastery of the skill of transforming the written alphabet into spoken sound to extensive oral recitation of complex literary formulas—without many of the "intermediate" skills associated with informational reading in modern literacy pedagogies (such as the ability to decode written words and sentences for meaning).

This phenomenon is vividly satirized by Herodas, who humorously depicted the stereotypical failings of an inattentive schoolboy. The (fictional) boy's mother complains with equal vigor that her son could not recognize or reproduce the alphabet and that he recited a memorized passage from high literature (one of Aeschylus's tragedies) with poor style:

> He can't recognize the letter *a* (ἐπίσταται δ᾽ οὐδ᾽ ἄλφα συλλαβὴν γνῶναι), not even if one shouts it five times to him. His father the day before yesterday was teaching him to spell the name "Maron" and this fine scholar wrote "Simon".... And whenever his father or I ask him to recite, just as you'd ask a little child ... he strains as though through a pierced jug "Hunter Apollo" (ἐνταῦθ᾽ ὅκως νιν ἐκ τετρημένης ἠθεῖ Ἀπόλλον Ἀγρεῦ᾽ τοῦτο φημί) [a speech from Aeschylus's *Prometheus Unbound*].[28]

In this complaint, being able to recite classical literature from memory with emphasis and understanding and being able to correctly recognize and reproduce the alphabet are treated as equally basic skills. These two endeavors would be separated by years of study in an educational culture in which the study of literature is heavily mediated by decoding for comprehension. But this disgruntled mother conjures up images of an educational environment in which both tasks are something that one would assign to "a little child." Exploring the mechanics of this process reveals much about the early rabbinic conceptual relationship to reading because the early rabbinic provincial elite would frequently end their literacy education precisely at this beginning stage, which seems so counterintuitive to the modern reader. For in this system, basic competency with written text consisted in the rote ability to associate written

---

and Practice: Challenges and Debates over 50 Years," *Theory into Practice* 52, no. 1 (2013): 52–62.

28. Herodas, *Mimes, Third Mime* (Didaskalos), ll. 32–34 in *The Mimes of Herodas*, ed. J. Arbuthnot Nairn (Oxford: Clarendon, 1904), 34, here in the unique translation of Barbara Hughes Fowler, *Hellenistic Poetry: An Anthology* (Madison: University of Wisconsin Press, 1990), 238–39.

signs with spoken words, the latter being the strata of language at which meaning was thought to reside.

Learning to Translate Written Text into a Comprehensible (Spoken) Language

In both Greco-Roman and Semitic-language contexts, the first step in most formal education was to become familiar with the written alphabet and its potential combinations. In contrast to modern alphabetic education, however, the alphabetic phase of a late antique child's elementary reading education was often limited to inculcating basic phonetic decoding skills. That is, most elementary students were *not* expected to master the alphabetic word or sentence as a mode of communicative language in its own right by cultivating those facets of literacy that facilitate the process of extracting sense directly from written text, such as sight-word recognition.[29] Rather, the purpose of early literacy education in these contexts was to make the elementary student sufficiently familiar with the sounds associated with the written letters that he could transform these signs into the more "natural" mode of language furnished by the spoken word.[30] The goal of basic literacy education in this context was not direct comprehension of written language but simply to teach the student to translate written signs into comprehensible sounds—which could then, in turn, be understood as spoken language.

In a curriculum devoted largely to oral recitation and memorization of canonical works, written signs did not function as an independent visual language but took on linguistic meaning and pedagogical purpose only as they were systematically translated, syllable by syllable, into oral sounds. In order to help the contemporary reader conceptualize the difference between these

---

29. Indeed, the word unit held so little importance in Dionysius of Halicarnassus's vision of reading that he neglects to mention the unit of "words" at all in a parallel description of the process of teaching elementary reading. Dionysius of Halicarnassus, *On Literary Composition* 24, in W. Rhys Roberts, *Dionysius of Halicarnassus on Literary Composition* (London: Macmillan, 1910), 52.

30. As Cassiodorus remarks concerning writing more generally: "What happy application ... to untie the tongue by means of the fingers." Cassiodorus, *Senatoris institutitones* 1.30.1, as translated in Bruce M. Metzger, *The Text of the New Testament: Its Transmission, Corruption, and Restoration* (Oxford: Oxford University Press, 1995), 18. "In other words," as Joceyln Penny Small comments on this statement, Cassiodorus takes it as a given that "writing is meant to be spoken." Jocelyn Penny Small, *Wax Tablets of the Mind: Cognitive Studies of Memory and Literacy in Classical Antiquity* (New York: Routledge, 1997), 253n59.

two modes of reading, Penny Small cites an iconic modern homophone. First, read the following sentence silently to yourself: "It is difficult to wreck a nice beach." The message that you perceive through this form of silent reading represents the function of written text as a visual language. Now, read the sentence again slowly and aloud, trying to block out your previous understanding of the sentence. You should hear: "It is difficult to recognize speech."[31] This is the "aural" reading of this collection of written signs. In order to achieve a visual reading of the sentence, one must be able to "read by wholes" and silently reconstruct the meaning of a series of written words. If one wants to perform an aural reading of the same sentence, however, one need not be able to identify the words that make up the passage, as it is separated into visual units. On the contrary, one will perform an aural reading more smoothly if one is not aware of alternative visual renderings of the written signs—a principle that seems to have had a strong influence on the Greco-Roman literacy curriculum, as we will see in the coming pages. In a system of aural reading—like that taught in many ancient Mediterranean schools—written signs represent sounded syllables that only took on a comprehensible linguistic meaning when they were pronounced aloud in sequence to compose an oral sentence. Thus, to cite another twentieth-century analogy, alphabetic writing in this context appears to have been treated as a recording system something like modern shorthand—that is, as a technical mnemonic that represented (and was translatable into) oral language but would seldom be employed as a direct or independent form of communication.

A SMALL SELECTION OF GREEK AND LATIN EVIDENCE ON THE AT-TAINMENT OF ALPHABETIC LITERACY. Elementary Greek and Latin reading exercises, for instance, frequently cultivated aural decoding by relying on words that were challenging—or even impossible—for an elementary student to decipher at a semantic level. In some cases, such as the exercise called a χαλινός (bridle or gag), students might be given a "tongue-twister" in which "learners wrote down meaningless sequences of letters." But even regular word lists at this stage of literacy education functioned very nearly as nonsense words, since "the words included in the ancient lists are often extremely rare and thus useless for everyday life."[32] Such exercises might consist of obscure and semantically challenging words like κναξζβίχ, traditionally read by schol-

31. Small, *Wax Tablets*, 24–25.

32. Sarah Chiarini, *The So-Called Nonsense Inscriptions on Ancient Greek Vases: Between Paideia and Paidiá*, Brill Studies in Greek and Roman Epigraphy 10 (Leiden: Brill, 2018), 119.

ars as the name of an illness,[33] and φλεγμοδρώψ, whose meaning is unknown but assumed to be another medical term,[34] proper names of extreme obscurity,[35] or even true nonsense words.[36] Moreover, these categories were sometimes treated as interchangeable. In one of the school papyri catalogued by Raffaela Cribiore, a teacher at a loss to produce a complete list of bisyllabic words from *alpha* to *omega* simply fabricated a series of common nouns for the occasion (no. 100 in Criobiore, P.Gen. 2.53).[37] In the same way, another instructor composing a systematic syllabary (no. 124 in Cribiore; P.Flor. 18.6) slipped in invented names among the historical names recorded there when an appropriate example for a particular pattern failed to come to mind.[38] One teacher even poked fun at the gibberish that was given to schoolchildren to study by making up humorously outlandish definitions of the nonsense words and phrases that made up these exercises.[39] The presence of nonsense words in historical school lists emphasizes—in a way that surpasses even the use of obscure medical terminology as a primary reading exercise—that it did not "matter at this stage whether what the pupil articulates is sense or nonsense or a random mixture of the two: what matter are the mechanics of reading and sound production."[40]

The same pattern of uncomprehending aural decoding appears to have obtained as students began to decode their first sentence-length texts. Genuine sentences culled from classic literature were sometimes chosen for this exercise—just as authentic terminology and proper names were included in elementary reading lists. However, like many of the proper names and technical terms used in elementary word lists, these brief literary excerpts were specially selected for their abstruseness and difficulty of vocabulary—including, for instance, descriptions of scenery (P.Ryl. 3.545, P.Col. 8.193) and minor

33. Although William Johnson has pointed out this interpretation relies entirely on a remark in Clement. ("Learning to Read," 142).

34. Henri Marrou, *A History of Education in Antiquity*, trans. George Lamb (Madison: University of Wisconsin Press, 1982), 153.

35. Teresa Morgan, *Literate Education in Hellenistic and Roman Worlds* (Cambridge: Cambridge University Press, 1998), 104.

36. Ibid., 103.

37. Raffaella Cribiore, *Writing, Teachers, and Students in Greco-Roman Egypt* (Atlanta: Scholars Press, 1996), 43 and 197.

38. Ibid., 43 and 202.

39. One such exercise is "glossed with made-up meanings apparently intended to make fun of school practices" in a fragment attributed to Thespis (TrGF 833 fr. 4) (Cribiore, *Writing*, 40).

40. Morgan, *Literate Education*, 103.

138   CHAPTER 4

narrative asides (such as an image of Hector looking at Andromache in P.Mil Vogl. 3.120).[41] As W. Martin Bloomer puts it, "We would replicate the ancient practice if we taught children to read by setting them a piece of Shakespeare, Milton, or even Chaucer."[42] Indeed, the vital function of incomprehensibility in such verses is hinted at when Quintilian classifies obscure and difficult literary verses as χαλινοί (gags or bridles)—a pedagogical category applied elsewhere to reading drills "made up of phrases, as absurd as they were unpronounceable, each phrase containing all the twenty-four letters of the alphabet used only once [such as], βέδυ ζάψ χθών πλήκτρον σφίγξ"[43] (a text for which the potential meaning continues to be much debated but which might be most generously rendered "water, surf, earth, plectron, sphinx").[44] Ancient and late antique observers apparently agreed that a vital facet of these sentence-long reading drills was precisely that they *were* incomprehensible, even to a sophisticated reader. In all of its stages, early alphabetic literacy in this context was thus designed to facilitate fluent *rote* translation of written signs into the oral patterns that constitute comprehensible language—without the mediation of direct written communication of meaning.

A SMALL SELECTION OF EARLY JEWISH SOURCES ON THE ATTAINMENT OF ALPHABETIC LITERACY. Such semantically challenging phonetic decoding exercises have also been found on abecedaries and ostraca bearing exercises in Hebrew, despite the difficulties posed by rote decoding in a consonantal transcription system. Many surviving ancient Hebrew abecedaries are just that,[45] of course, inscriptions featuring the Hebrew alphabet with-

41. Ibid., 108–9. Perhaps students were given such obscure excerpts from the literary canon for reading practice because they were *already* familiar with the basic contours of Homeric narrative and were being intentionally presented with reading drills in which they could not draw upon this prior knowledge—just as obscure vocabulary was used in elementary wordlists so that students could not call word recognition and reading comprehension to their aid as they practiced phonetically decoding written text.

42. W. Martin Bloomer, *The School of Rome: Latin Studies and the Origins of the Liberal Education* (Berkeley: University of California Press, 2011), 131.

43. Marrou, *A History of Education*, 153.

44. Other popular examples can be found, for example, in Clement of Alexandria, *Stromata* 5.8.48–49 and in papyri 60 and 79 in Cribiore, *Writing*, 39.

45. On ancient Israelite abecedaries, see Seth Sanders, *The Invention of Hebrew* (Urbana: University of Illinois Press, 2009), 91–128, and Aaron Demsky, "The Interface of Oral and the Written Tradition in Ancient Israel: The Case of the Abecedaries," in *Origins of the Alphabet: Proceedings of the First Polis Institute Interdisciplinary Conference*, ed. Claudia Attuci and Christophe Rico (Cambridge: Cambridge Scholars Publishing, 2015), 17–48.

A SPOKEN SCRIPTURE   139

out additional writing.[46] Also in evidence among the late antique examples, however, are new kinds of alphabetical lists featuring incomprehensible and difficult terms: some medical, some proper names, and some fantastic inventions.[47] In other examples, the same standardized list of proper names in alphabetic order has been found at geographically distant sites, suggesting a more widespread educational tradition.[48] While these kinds of traces are frequently described as scribal exercises,[49] they could equally be interpreted as reading exercises similar to those described above. The limited material evidence available to us would thus suggest that some late antique Jews, at least, learned their alphabetic reading skills through pronunciation-focused and meaning-obscuring literacy exercises very similar to the Greek and Latin exercises described immediately above.[50]

At first glance, a phonetic literacy practice would seem to be hard to duplicate in Hebrew-language literacy education since an unvocalized written language necessarily leaves a certain scope of phonetic indeterminability. Yet much the same could be said of Syriac in this period, despite the earlier development of the vocalization systems in that case. Nevertheless, Syriac descriptions of early literacy education seem to follow a pattern very similar to that described in Greek and Latin sources above. In various asides about early literacy education, for instance, Mar Barhadbsabba also describes a process that moves from the alphabet to the syllabic pronunciation of names—quite difficult names, moreover, if the heavenly analogy below is taken as a fair parallel:

Just as we have the customary practice, after getting a child to read the simple letters and repeat them, we join the letters up and put together with

46. For a recent catalogue of these strictly alphabetic abecedaries, see Doron Ben-Ami and Yana Tchekhanovets, "A Greek Abecedary Fragment from the City of David," *Palestine Exploration Quarterly* 40, no. 3 (2008): 195–202.

47. Joseph Naveh, "A Medical Document or a Written Exercise? The So-Called 4Q Therapeia," *Israel Exploration Journal* 36, nos. 1–2 (1986): 52–55, and, for an alternate explanation, George J. Brooke, "4Q341: An Exercise for Spelling and for Spells?," in *Writing and Ancient Near Eastern Society: Papers in Honour of Alan R. Millard,* ed. Piotr Bienkowski, Christopher B. Mee, and Elizabeth Slater (London: T&T Clark, 2005), 271–82.

48. Catherine Hezser, *Jewish Literacy in Roman Palestine* (Tübingen: Mohr Siebeck, 2001), 85–89.

49. William Schniedewind, *Finger of the Scribe: How Scribes Learned to Write the Bible* (Oxford: Oxford University Press: 2019), 20–62.

50. This would not be surprising if Greek and Hebrew literacy were taught side by side in some circles. On which debate, see Michael Wise, *Language and Literacy in Roman Judea: A Study of the Bar Kokhba Documents* (New Haven, CT: Yale University Press, 2015), 13–22.

them names for the child to read syllable by syllable. In this way the eternal Teacher also acted: once he had got the [angels] to repeat the alphabet, then He composed with it the great name of the construction of the firmament and he read it out in their presence.[51]

Elementary instruction in Syriac syllabic reading might have required an additional step in which the teacher pronounced the word list for the student before the student tackled the words on his own, a practice something like the *praelectio* expected of a teacher of more advanced verses in the Greco-Roman context. Indeed, the parallelism might even be suggested by the respective titles of early literacy teachers in the Syriac context: the *mhagyana* (who taught basic phonetic literacy and whose title "suggests 'pronouncing syllable by syllable'")[52] and the *maqryana* (who provided lessons in the correct oral reading of biblical verses which, as we will see in the coming pages, required a *praelectio* [a *keri'ah*] of each verse which was then repeated by the students).

While descriptions of the very earliest stages of rabbinic literacy education are rare, those we have are certainly compatible with these pictures of using incomprehensible semantics as a mode of training students in oral-aural phonetic decoding. In the famous story of R. Akiva's much-delayed elementary education from Avot de Rabbi Natan, for instance, we are told that:[53]

[R. Akiva] and his son went and sat with the teachers of children. R. Akiva said to him, "Rabbi, teach me Torah." R. Akiva took hold of the top of the tablet and his son [also took hold] of the top of the tablet. [The teacher] wrote A and B for him, and he learned it. He wrote the [entire] alphabet, and he learned it. [He wrote out] Leviticus, and he learned it.

Here, again, we have a teacher moving directly from the alphabet to readings from the most technical and arcane portion of the Pentateuch. While this brief

51. As translated in Sebastian Brock, "God as Educator of Humanity: Some Voices from Syriac Tradition," in *Jewish Education from Antiquity to the Middle Ages,* ed. George J. Brookes and Renate Smithius (Leiden: Brill, 2017), 242–45.

52. Adam Becker, *Fear of God and the Beginning of Wisdom: The School of Nisibis and the Development of Monastic Culture in Late Antiquity* (Philadelphia: University of Pennsylvania Press, 2013), 88.

53. Quoted here according to the famous rendering in Avot de Rabbi Natan A 6. Although this passage is not usually cited as a witness to historical pedagogical practices, Catherine Hezser and Ivan Marcus have already suggested studying the narrative as a testimony to classical rabbinic educational practices (Hezser, *Jewish Literacy,* 76, and Ivan Marcus, *Rituals of Childhood: Jewish Acculturation in Medieval Europe* [New Haven, CT: Yale University Press, 1998], 36).

A SPOKEN SCRIPTURE 141

description does not mention names lists or similar intermediate phonetic decoding exercises that we encountered in other literary and material evidence, the (standard) use of verses from Leviticus as early reading exercises strikingly resembles the use of obscure portions of Homer (such as the ships list) for the purpose of setting the earliest readers decoding exercises they were unlikely to recognize or understand. Such a practice might also explain why small children are frequently depicted reading the books of Isaiah and Job, writings that would seem an unlikely topical choice for a young student but that do boast some of the highest rates of hapax legomena in the Hebrew Bible.[54]

In passages that describe the expected reading abilities of a Jewish "infant" (תינוק/ינוקא) in the first stages of his education, moreover, one encounters descriptions of reading skills very similar to the rote phonetic skills described in the Greek and Latin sources above—abilities that center on letter recognition and attempts to phonetically decode an alphabetic text without the aid of reading comprehension. BMenahot 29b, for instance, imagines that the average small schoolboy would be able to recognize the letter *vav* when he saw it, but would be unlikely to recognize by sight-reading the contextual absurdity of the phrase "God will be killed":

> Rami bar Tamre, the father-in-law of Rami bar Dekule, had [a text in which] the leg of the [opening letter] *vav* in "[God] killed" (ויהרג) (Exod 13:15) was cut off by a hole [and so resembled the letter *yud*]. He came before R. Zeira [to ask whether the damaged text was ritually valid for liturgical reading]. [R. Zeira] said to him, "Go and bring a young schoolboy[55] who is neither wise nor foolish [to look at the scroll]. If he reads it 'he killed' (*vayaharog*), [the scroll is still] kosher. If not, it is '[God] will be killed (*yehareg*)' and [the text is] is disqualified."

While the text states that the child in question will read the word as "he killed," this appears to mean merely that he recognizes the damaged opening letter as a *vav*, which allows the word to be read according to its original biblical meaning. The passage does not consider the possibility that the boy might produce his own alternate reading of the word but declares simply that if the child

---

54. Emil G. Hirsch, I. M. Casanowicz, Joseph Jacobs, and Max Schoessinger, "Hapax Legomena," in *The Jewish Encyclopedia* (New York: Funk & Wagnalls, 1906), 6:226–29.

55. As the word is used in bBava Batra 21a and parallels. Marcus Jastrow, *A Dictionary of the Targumim, the Talmud Babli and Yerushalmi, and the Midrashic Literature* (New York: G. P. Putnam's Sons, 1903), 581.

142 CHAPTER 4

cannot identify the *vav*, the word must then be read without the *vav* as *yehareg*. Unlike later medieval commentators on this passage, the talmudic passage itself assumes that the child in question would not be influenced in his task by reading comprehension.[56] For if one imagines the remaining text to read "God will be killed," the verse becomes positively blasphemous—thereby steering even a novice sight-reader toward the original spelling of the word.

We can find an even more vivid portrait of the rudimentary reading skills instilled in a rabbinic reading school (*beit sefer*) in the story of R. Elazar b. Arakh and the Diomset spa (bShabbat 147b).

> It is forbidden to stand in the mud of Diomset because it wearies and attenuates. . . . The waters of Diomset stole the Ten Tribes of Israel. R. Elazar b. Arakh happened upon the place, was seduced, and his lessons (תלמודיה) were uprooted because of it [i.e., he forgot what he had been taught in upper school (בית תלמוד)]. When he returned [from Diomset], he came up to read-recite the lectionary (למיקרי) from the Torah scroll. He sought to read [the verse] "*hahodesh hazeh lakhem* (החדש הזה לכם)" ["this month is to you" (Exod 12:2)], but he said, "*haheresh hayah libam* (החרש היה לבם)" ["their heart was silent"]. The rabbis requested mercy on his behalf and his lessons returned [that is, he remembered what he had learned in upper school]. As it is taught, R. Nehoray says: Be exiled to a place of Torah, and do not say that she will come after you.

In this morality tale, we encounter a portrait of a rabbi who has been stripped of the religious learning he acquired in his advanced education and is left to struggle through his communal responsibilities with only the basic skills he was taught as a child. Left with only these elementary reading skills intact, R. Elazar b. Arakh (almost) knows how to decode written signs to produce sounds, which he then translates into meaning. Faced with an unvocalized consonantal text of the Bible, R. Elazar is able to cobble together a reasonable (if inaccurate) rendering of those visual cues. Yet he does so without a great deal of facility—he mistakes *dalet* (ד) for *resh* (ר), *yud* (י) for *zayin* (ז), and *kaf* (כ) for *beit* (ב). He has not forgotten his training—these are visually similar letters that even scribes have been known to confuse when copying unfamiliar

---

56. As noted by Rashi in his commentary on this passage. As Jewish reading cultures change, later rabbinic authorities will in fact assume that their charges are able to sight-read and thus attempt to dictate how much of the surrounding context in the verse must be covered up to achieve an unbiased reading by a schoolchild. See, for instance, the various rabbinic commentaries cited in Mishnah Berurah §32:51.

A SPOKEN SCRIPTURE 143

manuscripts—but his fluency with textual cues is limited. More importantly for our purposes, perhaps, he decodes phonetically without the benefit of reading comprehension. In the context of the short biblical passage he was set, it makes little sense for God to say to Moses and Aaron, "their heart was silent," then follow with a commandment concerning the tenth day of the new month. In other words, this passage depicts an elementary school graduate in the rabbinic system as someone who possessed a tentative mode of phonetic literacy in Hebrew similar to limited hunt-and-peck literacy practices known as "craftsman literacy" among scholars of cognate communities.[57]

The mode of basic literacy described here would, of course, be markedly insufficient as a modern form of comprehension literacy. Even by the literacy standards of the late antique Mediterranean, early rabbinic traditions often describe rabbinic practitioners whose basic literacy education had left them functionally illiterate outside a narrow range of canonical religious literature.[58] And yet, the level of ability to grapple with written text described above

57. For more on "craftsman literacy" as it pertains to Jewish late antiquity, see Chris Keith, *Jesus' Literacy: Scribal Culture and the Teacher from Galilee* (London: Bloomsbury, 2011), 112–15 and the literature cited there.

58. Interestingly, these accounts suggest that even the rabbinic elite was not consistently competent at navigating written text in this period. Thus, on one end of the spectrum, one encounters (exceedingly rare) tales of rabbinic authorities who were sufficiently comfortable with written text to record brief thoughts in writing—as R. Hilfai is reported to have done in yMaʿaserot 2:4 (49d). On the other hand, classical rabbinic sources can imagine even as exalted a character as the high priest in the idealized setting of the Jerusalem Temple as someone who was not "comfortable reading" (רגיל לקרות) (mYoma 1:6) and portrays rabbinic authorities who apparently cannot sign their own name (e.g. yGittin 9:9 [50d]). While it is always possible that the sages listed here were competent to sign their names in full but actively chose to sign important documents in abbreviated forms that stretched the tolerance of rabbinic law, it is both suggestive and disconcerting to hear that major rabbinic authorities "signed with a mark" in the style of those deemed illiterate, since "those labeled illiterates in the papyri were men and women unable to append a signature in Greek to the bottom of a document." Ann Ellis Hanson, "Ancient Illiteracy," in *Literacy in the Roman World*, ed. Mary Beard, Alan K. Bowman, and Mireille Corbier (Ann Arbor: University of Michigan Press, 1991), 163. Though the inability of these sages to write would not, of course, necessarily suggest a parallel inability to read as it might in the modern United States, where reading and writing education have become so thoroughly intertwined. In the Talmudic period, as Shmuel Safrai has pointed out, the ability to write appears to have been treated as a professional skill rather than a basic component of literacy education. Shmuel Safrai, "Education and the Study of the Torah," in *The Jewish People in the First Century: Historical Geography, Political History, Social, Cultural and Religious Life and Institutions,* ed. Shmuel Safrai and Menachem Stern in cooperation with David Flusser and W. C. van Unnik (Philadelphia: Fortress, 1979), 952.

144   CHAPTER 4

would have been perfectly adequate as the basis for the next stage in the historical literacy pedagogy popular in many communities in this era and these regions.

A Student's First Encounters with Written Text

After becoming familiar with the secrets of the alphabet, an elementary student was not then required to decode written text for meaning but rather only required to correlate preformulated spoken words with the signs in a written text—once he already knew what that text was supposed to say. In this system, an elementary student was taught to read the classics of the culture by memorizing brief oral formulas from those works and matching them up with (often temporary) scraps of written text so that he could learn to associate the recited words with the written signs before him. Beyond this early stage in literacy education, the systems built on them would ultimately produce a wide range of facility with written text in different communities and individuals.[59] In rabbinic communities, however, in which practitioners seldom went on to engage with a variety of written texts as part of their communal higher education, these early literacy pedagogies appear to have been determinate in the ways that many practitioners continued to engage with the Hebrew Bible as a written text.

A SMALL SELECTION OF GREEK AND LATIN SOURCES ON A STUDENT'S FIRST ENCOUNTER WITH TEXT. To describe this step in the late antique system of literacy education can be treacherous: contemporary schools still use many of the same basic pedagogical elements, but late antique literacy education arranged these components to radically different effect as far as function and meaning. According to Greek and Latin descriptions of early literacy education, for instance, the initial step in learning to read beyond the level of phonetic decoding was for the student to gain access to a text—

---

59. Greek and Latin sources attest that over time this practice could eventually lay the foundation for a considerable facility with written text. However, many students did not progress to an advanced stage and both Greco-Roman and rabbinic sources describe readers who continued to read in this way throughout their careers—restricting their reading to literary texts that they had been orally taught. Petronius, for instance, depicts an individual who "reads a book by sight" (*librum ab oculo legit*) as someone who will be universally recognized as exceptional (*Satyricon* 75 in Gaius Petronius, *Satyricon*, ed. Michael Heseltine and W. H. D. Rouse (Cambridge, MA: Harvard University Press, 1913), 174.

A SPOKEN SCRIPTURE   145

a fact that seductively evokes images of children with their schoolbooks. And yet, where a modern school text represents a stable and semipermanent record of a complete textual excerpt that educates as the student extracts its meaning, the texts used at this stage of a late antique Mediterranean child's literacy education functioned not as a determinate guide to the student's education but as a secondary accessory to the reading process. In a way that would be alien to modern pupils, the school texts used at this stage of a child's literacy education in many late antique Mediterranean contexts were unable to function as communicative documents in their own right.

Most elementary students at this stage of their education, for instance, did not usually engage with textual excerpts of sufficient length to be comprehensible on their own. Instead, they grappled with a progressive series of very brief excerpts that passed through their hands as they studied. In one third-century reading text transcribed on a white-washed wood board, for instance, an educated hand has divided a few sentences taken from the middle of a scene in the Iliad (3.273–85) into two even briefer passages, the first section transcribed on the recto and the continuation of the passage on the verso. These minuscule excerpts were then progressively discarded as they were mastered or circulated among the students.[60] As an elementary student in the *Hermeneumata pseudo-dositheana* describes the rapid circulation of textual models through a primary school classroom: "[The teacher] asks me to read [aloud] and then I give the text to another pupil."[61] In this practice, the student does not actually encounter a piece of literature as a text but rather the passage begins to take form in the student's mind only as he masters the formulas on a series of related scraps of text. Effectively, the modern orientation of student to text has been reversed in this practice, with the late antique student's mind representing the stable literary center and the textual excerpts flowing around it. Here a text complete enough to be comprehensible exists only in the student's experience and not in the brief excerpts of written texts transcribing portions of the passage being studied.

Moderns would also perceive a reversal in the center of gravity between mind and text in the fact that many model reading texts were apparently transcribed from memory. Thus, one study text of Aristophanes (O.Bodl. 1.279) is

60. Indeed, F. G. Kenyon suggests that model texts like CM Add. MS 37516 were hung on the wall of the school room to be shared by the entire class. F. G. Kenyon, "Two Greek School Tablets," *Journal of Hellenic Studies* 29 (1909): 39.

61. As translated by Raffaella Cribiore, *Gymnastics of the Mind: Greek Education in Hellenistic and Roman Egypt* (Princeton, NJ: Princeton University Press, 2005), 15.

marked by the sorts of phonological errors that result from the imperfect transcription of a sounded formula into writing. Dental consonants were confused when the word μηθὲν was substituted for the word μηδὲν. Similarly, one double vowel was substituted for a similar one when δείξειαν was rendered δείξεεν.[62] Elsewhere in this brief fragment, the substitutions in question are the sort of unconscious syntactical adaptations that sometimes occur when one has memorized an antiquated text in which some of the words are unfamiliar. The archaic word ἀπηνέι (harsh or hard) has been replaced with a word of similar sound and meaning which would have been more familiar to a late antique speaker: ἐπαχθεῖ (heavy or burdensome).[63] In other school texts, excerpts appear to have been put to page by teachers who only partially remembered the passages in question and thus omitted phrases and segments—skipping from one remembered line to the next.[64] In a literacy pedagogy vulnerable to so much slippage, a school text did not preserve and communicate a literary tradition to a student so much as it mediated between the version of the text preserved in the mind of the teacher and the version of the text taking form in the mind of the student.

As way stations between mental texts, these transcriptions are set apart from the early educational texts that most modern scholars encountered as children inasmuch as these late antique school texts were fundamentally provisional and impermanent texts.[65] Although the written excerpts in wooden exemplars were easily erased and replaced by recoating, wooden board texts were among the most physically durable of the model texts used

62. For more examples, see Nikos Litinas, "Aristophanes on a Bank Receipt," *Zeitschrift fuer Papyrologie und Epigraphik* 141 (2002): 103.

63. Ibid., 104.

64. See, for instance, Raffaella Cribiore's analysis of catalogue entry 267 (Cribiore, *Writing*, 237).

65. For more on the concept of "impermanent text" in the Greco-Roman Mediterranean see Florence Dupont, "The Corrupt Boy and the Crowned Poet, or The Material Reality and the Symbolic Status of the Literary Book at Rome," in *Ancient Literacies: The Culture of Reading in Greece and Rome*, ed. William A. Johnson and Holt N. Parker (Oxford: Oxford University Press, 2009), 143–63; and Joseph Farrell, "The Impermanent Text in Catullus and Other Roman Poets," in *Ancient Literacies: The Culture of Reading in Greece and Rome*, ed. William A. Johnson and Holt N. Parker (Oxford: Oxford University Press, 2009), 164–85. On the use of impermanent texts in non-Mediterranean cultures, see Wendy Doniger O'Flaherty, *Other Peoples' Myths: The Cave of Echoes* (Chicago: University of Chicago Press, 1995), 57ff. Doniger compares these practices to the use of "a coded espionage message [which] would be memorized and then destroyed (eaten, perhaps—orally destroyed) before it could fall into the hands of the enemy" (57).

in elementary education. Other example texts were irrevocably marked as temporary from the outset—transcribed on the verso of ephemeral documents that had been discarded or designated for recycling. In one second-century example (P.Reinach Inv. 2089), verses i.1–8 of the Iliad have been transcribed by a teacher across the back of a papyrus administrative letter from the prefect Fl. Sulpicius Similis.[66] Nor was that an isolated case. Almost as soon as the project of cataloging such school texts got under way, Charles Oldfather observed that the "great majority" of extant literary school exercises written on papyrus were transcribed on the verso of recycled government ephemera.[67] In another example, two lines of Aristophanes (*Clouds* 974–75) have been transcribed on an even more temporary material: the back of a potsherd bank receipt.[68] And, of course, many students did not engage directly even with these model texts but with copies of these texts temporarily transcribed on a wax tablet until it was time to erase and reinscribe the tablet with the next portion of text.[69] At this stage in a student's reading education, written text was a temporary part of the process—a useful tool in the moment, perhaps, but one that played no independent or active role in preserving or communicating the contents of the child's education. Much like the subordinate role assigned to the consonantal transcript of the Bible in classical rabbinic traditions, the written excerpts from classical literature used in early Greek and Latin reading education were treated as an adjunct to the memorized oral formulas from which they were derived, and to which they would eventually return as students memorized the scripts and discarded their temporary written props.[70]

66. For a more detailed description of this document, see Andre Bataille and Paul Collart, "Papyrus d'Homere," *Aegyptus* 11, no. 2 (1931), 169–70. See, also, T. C. Skeat, "Was Papyrus Regarded as 'Cheap' or 'Expensive' in the Ancient World?," *Aegyptus* 75 (1995): 75–93.

67. C. H. Oldfather, *The Greek Literary Texts from Greco-Roman Egypt: A Study in the History of Civilization* (Madison: University of Wisconsin Press, 1923), 68.

68. O.Bodl. 1.279, as described in Litinas, "Aristophanes on a Bank Receipt," 103–5. For a brief catalogue of literary texts transcribed on ostraca for educational use see Oldfather, *Greek Literary Texts*, 63 ff. 3.

69. On the relative distribution of elementary school exercises between scrap papyrus, ostraca, and wax tablets see Lisa Maurice, *The Teacher in Ancient Rome: Magister and His World* (Lexington, KY: Lexington Books, 2013), 38–40.

70. For a theoretical reflection on temporary or "ephemeral text" as a distinct mode of writing, see Roger Chartier, *Inscription and Erasure: Literature and Written Culture from the Eleventh to the Eighteen Century* (Philadelphia: University of Pennsylvania Press, 2007), vii–45.

148   CHAPTER 4

After a student had acquired an excerpt of text, he was taught to recite it. In this process too, written text functioned as more of a prop or an aid to learning than a communicative document to be decoded: it was positioned as a way station between two oral performances. Before a student pronounced the text himself, his teacher would demonstrate to him how the text should be read—either individually as each student arrived at the passage in question or collectively as a classroom of students who moved through the same text. The latter process is the practice most frequently described in rabbinic literature, so that is the one we will explore here. In the Latin context, this practice of reciting a passage before turning to study the written text would come to be known as the *praelectio* (prereading)—ἀνάγνωσις in many Greek texts.[71] As Macrobius describes this practice in an aside in *Saturnalia* 1.24.5, "It seems to me that you still view Virgil as a boy facing a school teacher, performing our preliminary reading in a sing-song (*praelegentibus canebamus*)."[72] As Cicero likewise remarks concerning Roman education in his community, these childish memorization exercises were conducted collectively in his period in an "indispensable chant" (*carmen necessarium*).[73] And a later author such as Augustine can still sum up his youthful distaste for study by saying that his childself despised the "odious song" (*odiosa cantio*)—a vivid image conjuring the sing-song of rote elementary learning.[74] By first reciting the verses of literature to be read in the responsive sing-song that characterized elementary education in this period the teacher conveyed the sounded formula of the passage to his students in a form that would help it to take root in their memories. This exaggerated pedagogical performance allowed the student to fix some portion of the sounded formula in his memory immediately by repeating back the instructor's melodic reading line by line. Indeed, as in the parody of Herodas above, this first fragmented and stylized performance sometimes etched itself

71. Quintilian, *Institutio oratoria* 2.5 suggests that this particular practice spread from Greek-language education to Latin-language education in his own day (that is, in the first century CE).

72. Ambrosii Theodosii Macrobius, *Saturnalia* 1.24.5 in *Saturnalia*, ed. J. Willis (Stuttgart: Bibliotheca scriptorium Graecorum et Romanorum Teubneriana, 1994), 1.128. Translation my own.

73. Cicero, *De legibus* 2.59 (ed. George de Plinval [Paris: Société d'Edition les Belles Lettres, 1959], 74).

74. Augustine, *Confessions* 1.13.22 (*St. Augustine's Confession*, ed. William Watts [Cambridge: Harvard University Press, 1961], 1:42). A similar distaste for the open-mouthed collective repetition of early childhood education is expressed in Callimachus, *Epigram* 48 (*Hymns and Epigrams*, ed. Ulrich von Wilamowitz-Moellendorff [Berlin: Weidmann, 1897], 172). For more examples and a lengthy discussion of this topic, see Nicolas Horsfall, "Cultural Horizons of the 'Plebs Romana,'" *Memoirs of the American Academy in Rome* 41 (1996): 101–19.

all too firmly in the memory of the student, so that he was fated always to recite the passage in question in an awkward sing-song, straining out the verses in small droplets of spoken text "as though through a pierced jug." On a more theoretical level, these initial oral performances established the primacy of the oral formula of the canon over the transcribed text at the very beginning of a student's exposure to the work by establishing that the student could initially come to know the work only through an encounter with the oral formula. A written transcript could not speak to the student in an original and comprehensible way, however useful it might be as a secondary mnemonic in future encounters.

The slow and halting pace of the *praelectio* also allowed the student to preserve this first encounter with the sounded formula of the passage for further review by adding supplementary notations to their study texts, which anchored this additional aural information to the written signs before them. Thus, among extant Greek and Latin school texts from this period, it is not uncommon to find standard written texts transcribed by a teacher but then crudely marked in a student's hand with notations inserting additional aural information not typically included in written text in this period—such as the correct distribution of syllables within a word, word divisions, dramatic pauses, paragraphing, breathing instructions, and accents. All of the pedagogical transcripts of the Iliad described above were marked in this manner. The papyrus transcription of the Iliad i.1–8 described in the previous pages (P.Reinach Inv. 2089) was divided into series of syllables using small dots— transforming the text from a collection of written words into a record of successive sounds. Another late antique school text copied in a stylized hand on a wooden board (T.Bero inv. AM 13839; Cribiore 296)[75] is supplemented by the addition of diaereses (marks to record vocalization patterns), breathing marks, apostrophes (noting the elision of adjacent vowels), lines dividing the words, and *diplai obelismenai* (denoting the ends of verses and stanzas)— thereby converting these passages from a literary text into a detailed script for the correct use of mouth and lungs. Other school texts preserve various combinations of these techniques. These notational practices vividly illustrate the unequal roles assigned to orality and textuality in this early literacy pedagogy: as students interpolated the instructor's preliminary oral reading into the written transcript before them, the written texts of these literary works were implicitly classified as an incomplete and substandard means of communicating

---

75. In which Iliad ii.132–46 and Iliad ii.147–62 are inscribed on the recto and verso of a wooden tablet.

the contents of the canon. With the written witness transformed into a record of an oral performance, the ability to reproduce the oral formula correctly was identified as the ultimate purpose of these educational props.

EARLY RABBINIC DESCRIPTIONS OF EARLY ENCOUNTERS WITH TEXT. We do not know whether rabbinic communities infused early literacy education with as much direct access to text as Greek and Latin classes; rabbinic descriptions are unclear. However, scattered passages do suggest that some elementary schoolchildren in Hebrew-language literacy schools were taught from temporary texts. Since temporary study texts were excerpted from the Hebrew Bible (a scriptural tradition that required special handling and ritual disposal according to early rabbinic traditions), the practice was officially forbidden from an early period. But even the wording of this early prohibition raises doubts about its effectiveness in quelling the practice:

> Concerning one who writes out [the] Hallel [psalms] or the Shema [passages][76] for a small child to practice from (על תינוק להתלמד בו): even though he is not permitted to do so, [if he does, the text] is considered holy scripture for ritual purposes [literally: renders the hands unclean]. (tYadayim 2:11)

If rabbinic authorities found it necessary to institute a ruling to discourage the practice of writing out brief passages of biblical text for young children to memorize, this pedagogical method was probably sufficiently widespread in the communities within their legislative sphere to have aroused their concern. The fact they felt compelled to issue an additional decision to determine the retrospective status of such texts once they had been produced in this illicit fashion suggests that their disapproval was not entirely effective in quelling an evidently popular practice.

Novel rulings against temporary texts continue to appear in later rabbinic literature. Apparently, the practice had not been successfully stamped out, and the rabbinic authorities felt compelled to attempt to direct the practice into more amenable modes. R. Akiva is imagined to have warned, for instance, "When you teach your son, teach him from a corrected document" (bPesahim 112a).[77] Although the literal rendering of the phrase ספר מוגה might seem to be "a corrected book"—which is to say, a corrected Torah scroll—other uses of

---

76. That is, Deut 6:4–9, Deut 11:13–21, and Num 15:37–41.
77. On this vocabulary, see bKetubot 106a.

the phrase suggest that it means a shorter and more ephemeral text.[78] R. Akiva was urging those who instruct young children to do so in conjunction with carefully edited study texts rather than ad hoc (and thus inaccurate) transcriptions like the excerpt from Aristophanes casually (and incorrectly) transcribed on a bank receipt above. Rabbinic authorities also tried to discover a loophole that would render the production of temporary texts permitted. To this end, bGittin 60a rules that "one may not write a scroll for a child to learn from unless it is his intention to complete it [later]. Then it is permitted." The ruling does not appear to be a purely theoretical position, for the passage goes on to offer practical details about how one would write out such a text—and where one might temporarily break off his transcription. R. Yehudah recommends, for instance, that one must write out a passage for a child beginning at the start of a biblical book and continuing until the end of the first narrative unit—such as from the Creation story at the beginning of the book of Genesis until the story of the Flood.[79] Rulings of this sort suggest that early rabbinic authorities not only failed to curtail the use of temporary texts but were even compelled to find a way to permit the popular pedagogical method within the rabbinic legal framework.

Wax tablets—a temporary text of a biblical passage so temporary that ritual disposal and other questions need not arise—emerge as another possible solution the problem. As we saw in the famous tale of R. Akiva's belated education in Avot de Rabbi Natan, rabbinic traditions certainly describe reusable tablets inscribed with biblical verses:

> R. Akiva took hold of the top of the tablet and his son [also took hold] of the top of the tablet. [The teacher] wrote A and B for him, and he learned it. He wrote the [entire] alphabet, and he learned it. [He wrote out] Leviticus, and he learned it. He kept on learning [like this] until he had learned the entire [written] Torah. Then he went and sat before R. Eliezer and R. Yehoshua [to study the Oral Torah].

While some have demurred that this passage does not explicitly repeat the verb that would make it completely clear that Leviticus "and the entire Torah" were also transcribed on R. Akiva's schoolboy tablet,[80] this account certainly suggests strongly that the elementary school teacher pictured here wrote out

78. YKetubot 2:3 (26b), for instance, appears to use the phrase to refer to briefer scribal documents.

79. Compare yMegillah 3:1 (74a).

80. Hezser, *Literacy*, 86.

these biblical study texts from memory on the same tablet as he wrote the alphabet (just as Greek and Roman instructors were wont to do), since the mode by which R. Akiva learned his biblical verses is treated as both continuous with and similar to the process in which the teacher progressively wrote out the alphabet for him to learn on his tablet letter by letter as he mastered each one.

Whether or not most schoolchildren in rabbinic communities would have had direct access to a written text while they were learning is unclear. Early rabbinic traditions are quite clear, however, that early elementary students in these circles practiced a form of preliminary reading and repetition very similar to what is depicted in Greek and Latin sources. BBava Batra 21a suggests, for instance, that the preliminary reading performed by a "child's reading teacher" (מקרי ינוקא) determined how that child would read that verse in perpetuity:

> Rava said "Behold, if there are two children's reading teachers, one who reads fluently but is not exact and one who is exact but is not fluent, we hire the one who is fluent but not exact since in time it will all come out." R. Dimi from Nehardea said, "They place the one who is exact but not fluent, since once he perverts [their learning] he perverts [it]. As it is written, 'Yoav and all of Israel stayed in there for six months until he had cut down every male in Edom' (1 Kgs 11:16). For [Yoav] came before David and [David] said to him: 'For what reason did you do this?!' [Yoav] said to him: 'Because it is written "You will wipe out the male (*zekhar*) of Amalek" (Exod 17:14).' [David] said to him: 'But, behold, we read it "memory" (*zekher*)!' [Yoav] said to him: 'I [was taught to] read it "male."' He went to ask his teacher. He said to him: 'How should I read it?' He said to him: 'Male.' [Yoav] swung his sword to kill him. [His teacher] said to him: 'Why [are you acting like this]?!' [Yoav] said to him: 'Because it is written, "Let the one who does the work of God deceitfully be cursed [read here as: killed]" (Jer 48:10).' [His teacher] said to him, '[Why not just] abandon that man and let him be cursed?' [Yoav] said to him: 'It is written, "Cursed is one who withholds his sword from blood" (Jer 48:10).'" There are some who say that [Yoav] killed him. There are some who say he did not kill him. . . . A child's reading teacher, one who plants seeds, the slaughterer, a professional cook,[81] and a scribe are dismissed immediately and paid in lieu of notice; the prin-

---

81. Following the entry אומן in Jastrow, *Dictionary*, 27.

A SPOKEN SCRIPTURE   153

ciple is that anything in which a loss [resulting from a mistake] cannot be rectified [requires] immediate dismissal.

Just as a planter cannot easily move the seeds he has planted after they have grown, so the formulator of this remark would seem to envision the preliminary reading of a schoolteacher as implanting a mental seed that cannot be uprooted in later encounters with the text. It is an image confirmed by the case of Yoav, who well into his maturity continues to remember the pronunciation (and thus meaning) of Exodus 17:14 according to the preliminary reading of his schoolteacher.

The pedagogy of responsive reading receives more detailed description elsewhere in rabbinic literature. YMegillah 4:5 (75b),[82] for instance, suggests that the practice of reading out biblical verses to young children in a fragmented call and response was a topic of widespread ritual concern among the rabbinic authorities, who were unsure whether it was permitted to break up verses containing the name of God in this manner:

> A certain R. Shimon was the scribe-reading-teacher of Trachonitis. The citizens of the town told him to cut up his verses that their children might learn to recite (קטע בדיבירייא דקרונון בנינן). He went and asked R. Hanina [whether he should comply with their request]. He told him, "Do not listen to them even if they cut off your head!" They dismissed him from his position as scribe-reading teacher (ספרותה). After some time, he came down here. R. Shimon b. Yosinah approached him, "What did you do in that town?" And he gave him an account. [R. Hanina] said, "Why didn't you listen to them?" [R. Shimon] said, "Do we do that [that is, cut up verses]?" [R. Hanina] said, "Don't *we* cut up the biblical portion [when studying it in the academy]?" [R. Shimon] said, "But we go back and make it whole!" R. Zeira said, "If this scribe-reading teacher had been in my time, I would have appointed him as a rabbi."

Like the Alexandrian instructor described above who taught his students to recite Euripides phrase by phrase, straining out the words in small droplets, there is apparently a consensus among the townspeople in this story that small children are best taught to recite the biblical formula by having a teacher divide the verses into short phrases for his students to imitate as he recites. In other

---

82. Compare bTaʿanit 17b, bMegillah 22a, and bBerakhot 12b. For a parallel use of the term (in connection to dividing up a shofar blast), see bRosh HaShanah 27a.

words, popular practice among at least some lay practitioners under rabbinic legislative authority embraced the use of a segmented and responsive preliminary reading like that described in Greek and Latin sources as an integral part of teaching young people the biblical formula. According to yMegillah 4:5, moreover, it would seem that the average schoolteacher in classical rabbinic circles adopted the *praelectio* as a basic pedagogical tool. R. Zeira treats this particular instructor's qualms about using the technique as something that sets him apart from other schoolteachers—affiliating him instead with the more fastidious rabbinic authorities. Furthermore, by depicting this legal debate concerning the *praelectio* as a dialogue that incorporated travel between far-flung rabbinic authorities and that self-consciously spanned a variety of geographic communities, yMegillah 4:5 indicates that the practice of preliminary reading represented a legal concern in a variety of classical rabbinic communities. In other words, this passage suggests that the *praelectio* represented a sufficiently popular pedagogical method in elementary classrooms under classical rabbinic influence to elicit broad rabbinic interest in the legality and appropriateness of the method.

Other images of preliminary reading and responsive recitation in early rabbinic traditions depict a collective activity performed by the children themselves. Numerous references portray communal call-and-response recitations of the Bible as characteristic of the elementary school classroom in these circles, suggesting that a great deal of time was devoted to such responsive readings in the elementary school classrooms of rabbinic communities.[83] YSotah 5:6 (20c), for instance, describes a generic educational practice[84] in which one student leads the others in such a recitation: "Like a child who leads others in the reading of the Hallel psalms in school, they repeat after him word by word." One of the interlocutors in Leviticus Rabbah 9:3, similarly, begins a story with the casual remark, "One time, I passed by a primary school and I heard the voices of the children saying [together], 'The Torah which Moses commanded

---

83. Catherine Hezser has suggested that this preliminary reading technique was used to teach young students Mishnah (*Literacy*, 82). I would like to suggest, however, that when a classical rabbinic tradition mentions the practice of preliminary reading without specifying the contents of the exercise, the work being studied is the Bible—as it is in the passage analyzed in this paragraph.

84. That is, it seems that the practice was sufficiently widespread that the formulator of this passage could use the practice as a common point of reference when attempting to describe to a late antique rabbinic audience the way in which Moses led the people of Israel in the Song of the Sea (Exod 15:1)

A SPOKEN SCRIPTURE   155

us, the inheritance of the congregation of Jacob' (Deut 33:4)." In the context of the narrative, this description of collective recitation serves as the set up to a pointed joke that wins an argument—the practical circumstances described were too common to have distracted attention from the speaker's argumentative purpose. According to some traditions, indeed, this constant spoken refrain represented the very definition of an elementary Torah education. Thus, Genesis Rabbah 65:22 treats the collective "squeaking" of primary school children as the very essence of Jewish pedagogy. Collective chanting had become so integral to the practice of rabbinic primary education in this period that rabbinic figures could reprimand each other for asking too basic a question by associating the question with the chanting of schoolchildren saying, "You are asking me about a thing that the children say aloud every day in the schoolhouse!"[85]

As with the Greek and Latin classes described above, the general units in which students learned biblical texts appear to have been very brief. In several fictional narratives from this period, the protagonist orders the first young boy he encounters to "recite his verses"—and then uses the brief text recited as a form of divination.[86] BGittin 56a, for instance, attributes the conversion of the caesar Nero to such an encounter:

> [The emperor] sent the caesar Nero against the [Jews in Palestine]. When he arrived, he shot an arrow toward the east [and] it came and fell in Jerusalem. [He shot an arrow toward] the west [and] it came and fell in Jerusalem. [He shot an arrow in each of] the four directions [and] it came and fell in Jerusalem. [Perplexed by this phenomenon, Caesar Nero] said to a small boy, "Pronounce [literally: cut up] your verses for me (אמר ליה לינוקא פסוק לי פסוקיך)." [The boy] said to him, "And I will have my revenge on Edom at the hands of my nation Israel, etc." (Ezek 25:14). [Caesar Nero] said, "The Holy One, blessed be he, wants to destroy his house but take it

---

85. YSanhedrin 10:2 (29a).

86. See, for instance, Esther Rabbah 7:13, bGittin 68a, bHagigah 15a, bHullin 95b, and bTaʿanit 9a. BHagigah 15a-b particularly emphasizes the universality of this practice by having Elisha b. Abuya visit thirteen different schools to question the students in this manner. As Birger Gerhardsson points out, moreover, the "custom [was] widespread [also among other communities] in Antiquity of asking the schoolchild to read his pensum, and then treating it as something of an oracle—a kind of rhapsodomantia." Birger Gerhardsson, *Memory and Manuscript: Oral Tradition and Written Tradition in Rabbinic Judaism and Early Christianity* (Grand Rapids, MI: Eerdmans, 1961), 64.

out on the man [who does the deed for him]." [So] he went and ran away and converted. And R. Meir descended from him.

The plot hinges on the assumption that one might turn to any Jewish schoolboy one encounters and be assured that he will be able and willing to recite the verse or two he was studying at the moment. In this narrative, and others like it, any adult might plausibly ask any child to demonstrate his most recent educational achievement and be offered a short pithy excerpt from biblical literature. Making recitation on demand a key ingredient in a series of highly stereotyped narratives suggests that the formulators of such tales expected this educational phenomenon to be universally recognizable as a social reality among their audience—an unremarkable fact of life in classical rabbinic circles as widely recognizable as other well-worn motifs, such as kingship, war, and parenthood.

Nor does this image of a schoolboy reciting his daily verses appear to be merely a popular literary motif. Practical rabbinic legal rulings would also seem to confirm the impression that this system of memorized recitation represented a nearly universal standard in Jewish elementary education. Thus, if circumstances forced a practitioner to perform the forbidden act of entering a synagogue for nonreligious reasons (such as to get out of the rain), he was instructed to transform the visit into a purposeful religious activity by turning to the nearest child and "saying to him, 'say your [Bible] verses for me'" (bMegillah 28b). To offer this as a practical solution to a relatively common ritual problem, the formulators of bMegillah 28b and parallels must have presumed that one would virtually always have access to a Jewish child able to recite from memory the biblical verses he was studying.

While it seems clear that a responsive preliminary reading formed an integral part of elementary education in many Jewish classrooms from the classical rabbinic period, only a handful of rabbinic traditions suggest that Jewish students might also have recorded the additional oral-aural information provided by this preliminary reading by marking up study texts in a way similar to that described in the Greek and Roman sources cited immediately above.[87] The late source Soferim 3:7, for instance, questions whether one should perform a liturgical reading from biblical texts that have been "cut up"—terminology

---

87. In which notes on the correct oral performance were interpolated into the written transcript in order to preserve the oral information conveyed in the preliminary reading so that a student could learn to reproduce the oral formula without constant attention from the instructor.

A SPOKEN SCRIPTURE   157

used in other late classical rabbinic sources in connection with a young student's initial mastery of a new biblical passage:

> One does not read [the lectionary] from a [biblical] book that someone has cut up or in which he has vocalized[88] the beginnings of the verses (ספר שפסקו או שניקד ראשי פסוקים שבה). Nor does one read from one in which someone has outlined or elided the letters (גלפו או שעירב בו את האות).

Although any one of the terms used in this text might be translated in a way that does not refer to the pedagogical practices described above,[89] the fact that they appear as a series is indicative. Each of these actions was performed as part of elementary literacy education in Greek and Roman circles. As we see in Genesis Rabbah 15:9 and other rabbinic traditions, moreover, the terminology לערב את האותיות is used to refer to the elision of two like-sounding letters—as in the pairing ʿolam motzi—suggesting that the practice forbidden here consists of marking these aural elisions (or lack thereof) in the written text in some way. In light of these parallels, it seems possible that Soferim 3:7 and similar passages preserve a memory of text-marking practices in rabbinic classrooms akin to those described in Greek and Latin sources. In these rabbinic classrooms also, then, written text was treated as a way station between oral-aural transcripts.

Freeing Oneself from the Text

Exercises such as preliminary reading served a vital purpose in literacy education, of course, by allowing students to develop familiarity with written text and to correlate the literary traditions they were learning with their written iterations. In these early stages of education, however, the immediate end goal was not to create independent readers of text by weaning the students off these oral aides to reading until they could extract information directly from the

---

88. Translated here according to the variant reading שניקד ראשי פסוקים, which appears in many manuscripts and later witnesses. For more on this variant, see Joel Mueller, *Masekhet Soferim: Tractat der Schreiber* (Leipzig: Akademie der Wissenschaften in Wien, 1978), 48–49. However, the more common rendering of this phrase ("in which the beginnings of the verses have been erased [literally: uprooted]") would also represent a popular pedagogical practice in classical rabbinic circles. For as we will see in more detail below, it was not uncommon to erase or leave blank some portion of a study verse so that a student could practice filling in the missing text from memory.

89. Thus, for instance, the word "cut up" (פסקו) might be read as "cut off," "outlined" (גלף) might be read as "engraved," and "elided" (עירבו) might be read as "mixed up."

written text. Instead, the inverse appears to have been true. That is, in many cases, students were instead gradually weaned off the aide-mémoire provided by these written signs so that the memorized text stood whole and independent in their memory.

GREEK AND LATIN SOURCES ON FREEING ONESELF FROM TEXT. One technique used in Greek and Roman classrooms to wean students off of written text was to present students with progressively less and less written text as they studied a passage or lesson so that the student was forced to supply an increasing portion of the lesson from memory without cues. This principle appears to have been used at all levels of elementary education. Once a student had mastered a set of vocabulary, he might be presented with a potsherd on which the teacher had written out the first one or two letters of each word while the student was left to supply the rest.[90] A similar technique was used for students memorizing verses of Homer. On one late antique ostracon (P. Ryl. 3.545), a student has copied only the first half of some two dozen consecutive verses from the Odyssey (9.122–50), apparently so that he might tack back and forth between the memorized oral formula and a written aide-mémoire until he had mastered the passage sufficiently to do away with this mnemonic device.[91] Other examples suggest that a student might then advance to the point where he needed only a transcription of the chapter headings to cue his memorized recitation. Thus, O.Bodl. Gk. Inscr. 1506[92] includes only the beginnings of the Iliad's lines 2.483, 2.494, 2.511, and 2.517—that is, the first few words of consecutive paragraphs or logical units of thought. This outline would thus seem to represent the penultimate step in a memorization exercise like one recommended by Quintilian, in which small logical blocks of a passage were memorized independently and then strung together and practiced in the correct order until the entire passage could be recited correctly from memory (*Institutes* 11.2.27).

EARLY RABBINIC EVIDENCE OF FREEING ONESELF FROM TEXT. In the rabbinic context, likewise, the verses memorized in elementary lessons

90. See, for instance, the ostraca transcribed in Joseph Grafton Milne, "Relics of Graeco-Egyptian Schools," *Journal of Hellenic Studies* 28 (1908): 124.

91. For a detailed description and transcription of this source, see C. H. Roberts, *Theological and Literary Texts*, vol. 3, *(Nos. 457–551)* (Manchester: Sherratt and Hughes, Publishers to the Victoria University of Manchester, 1938), 193–94.

92. For a detailed description of this material, see Cribiore, *Writing*, catalogue entry 201.

A SPOKEN SCRIPTURE   159

were not a temporary by-product of the study process—but were instead understood to be a permanent acquisition for a properly acculturated Jew. In tHorayot 2:5–6,[93] R. Yehoshua is informed by gentile jailers that they held "a child from Jerusalem with beautiful eyes who is good to look at." This description, of course, holds both a promise (that the Jewish community might reclaim one of its most innocent members) and a threat (that this exceptionally beautiful child will be among the first to be sexually abused).[94] The description is thus precisely the sort of thing that a savvy jailer might say if he were hoping to raise the stakes in order to extort a large ransom for a prisoner sight unseen. R. Yehoshua therefore feels compelled to test their testimony before he enters negotiations and proceeds to verify that the child is indeed a member of his community. He does so by standing outside of the child's cell, reciting the first half of a verse from Isaiah 42:24, and waiting for the child to answer with the second half of the verse. When the child correctly completes the verse from memory, R. Yehoshua is satisfied with the child's bona fides, declares that he will not leave the boy's presence until he has redeemed him—thus protecting him from the foul end that his jailers hinted at—and the child's guards quickly collect their large ransom. Later iterations (such as bGittin 58a) transform the narrative into a story about R. Yehoshua discovering the great sage R. Yishmael b. Elisha in his youth. However, in early versions of the tale (such as tHorayot 2:5–6), the ability to recite a Bible verse of someone else's choosing from memory is treated as a feat that any Jewish schoolboy could be expected to perform—to the extent that one may tell a Jewish child from a non-Jewish child based entirely on whether or not he knows these memorized biblical formulas. Indeed, these memorized lessons run so deep that even the traumas of capture and imprisonment will not uproot them—they are considered a permanent possession of any properly educated schoolboy in Israel.

Although not discussed in detail in rabbinic sources, many of the same practices used to wean students off the written text that are attested in the Greek and Latin sources appear in several classical rabbinic rulings concerning elementary education that are difficult to explain in any other way. BShabbat 12b–13a, for instance, would seem to concern a type of document very similar to O.Bodl. Gk. Inscr. 1506 (a record of the chapter headings for a memorized passage that was being reviewed):

93. See also Lamentations Rabbah 4.4 and bGittin 58a.

94. A concern that the Tosefta discusses earlier in this passage when it warns that one must redeem a woman from captivity before a man.

[One may not read by the light of a lamp (on Shabbat).] Verily, they said, "The cantor may look [to see] where the children are reading but he does not [read himself]." You said initially, "He looks." But doesn't that mean to read? No. It means to put the heads of the sections in order (מסדר הוא ראשי פרשיותיו). [For] thus said Rabbah bar Shmuel [when he repeated this ruling], "but he puts the heads of the section in order." [So he may read the heads of the sections] but not a whole section? It was objected [that] Rabban Shimon b. Gamliel said, "The children in the [pious] house of Rabban used to order their sections and read by the light of the lamp [on Shabbat. So surely this cannot be forbidden]." [In response to this objection] let us say [either] that [this refers to] the heads of the section or [that] children are different [when it comes to the laws of Shabbat].

According to this description, schoolchildren in classic rabbinic circles concluded the week's studies of the biblical text by reviewing something referred to as the "heads of the sections" under the supervision of their instructor. Since mention of this practice is brought to bear on the question of whether it is permissible to read by lamplight on the Sabbath, the "heads of the sections" discussed in this passage must represent a written document—and, indeed, our passage describes this document as a tangible record that can be "looked at" visually. And yet, the document in question does not appear to be a transcription of a biblical passage: it is distinguished from a "section" of text that can be "read" through from start to finish by the light of a lamp. The document must be "put in order" if one is to use it as a script for a full recitation of the biblical passage—but to do so requires no more than a glancing "look" by an adult familiar with the material. I would maintain, therefore, that this passage alludes to an early rabbinic practice very similar to the Greco-Roman technique: elementary students studying a biblical passage would be gradually weaned off the visual cues provided by their study text so that, by the end of a week's unit of study, they were able to review the passage from memory with only the minimal prompting provided by the first few words of each section of text.

Other classical rabbinic traditions suggest that elementary education in these circles also made use of the other forms of textual abbreviation described above in order to aid students in their memorization of a study passage. Thus, for instance, bGittin 60a suggests two ways in which it is licit to write out a temporary biblical passage "for a schoolchild to learn from": either by "skipping" (בסירוגין) through the passage or by "using the alphabet" (באלף בית).

A SPOKEN SCRIPTURE 161

Although this tradition does not describe either of these techniques in detail, the context of the ruling (which forbids writing out biblical passages in full for a child's temporary use)[95] suggests that these techniques allowed one to make a record of a biblical passage without writing out the text in full. It seems plausible, therefore, that these phrases represent practices similar to those preserved in the Greek school texts. In the first, one transcribes the beginning half of each verse in a passage so that a student must "skip" back and forth between an incomplete written transcript and the memorized oral formula as he recites. In the second, more advanced exercise, one records only the first letter of each word in the passage (as in, P.Ryl. 3.545) so that a student is compelled to fill in the remainder of each word—and subsequent verse—from memory.

While we have no material evidence for such documents from the classical rabbinic period, biblical texts and targumic translations very similar to the ones imagined here were preserved in the Cairo Geniza, in which verses and words are abbreviated yet key vowel points and accents are marked in ways that correlated not to the formal vowel system but to their oral pronunciation.[96] From the very earliest scholarship on these fragments, scholars speculated that these abbreviated texts were written for the students to practice the correct reading—since they could be vocalized, abbreviated, excerpted without limitation.[97] For many early rabbinic practitioners who received such early literacy training, elementary reading education appears to have ended here with the successful creation of memory texts, which they could take with them into their higher education.

Concluding Remarks

Taken as a whole, these glimpse of early rabbinic literacy education describe a student's first encounters with the biblical tradition as continuous with a practitioner's mode of engaging with the biblical tradition in adult life. Neither the children nor adults described in these pages approach the biblical text as an independent communicative document from which they might acquire information. Rather, both the novice learner and the experienced liturgical reader approached the biblical text only once he *already knew what it was going*

95. See bYoma 37b quoted above.

96. For a review of these finds and the scholarship on them, see Klein, *Targums*, 97–106.

97. Michael Friedlander, "Some Fragments of the Hebrew Bible with Peculiar Abbreviations and Peculiar Signs for Vowels and Accents," *Proceedings of the Society for Biblical Archeology* 18 (1986): 93.

to say. In early childhood, a textual transcription might be literally put away or erased bit by bit. Adult practitioners are more frequently described as metaphorically discarding the written text in their engagement with the biblical tradition—so that readers must be warned not to take their eyes from the text during a liturgical reading nor dispense with textual models when copying out biblical texts. In both seminal experiences of the rabbinic encounter with written text, the memorized oral formula of the biblical text was thus treated as the more stable and familiar form of the biblical tradition for the reader. It was in the memorized oral formulas of this reading practice that meaning and transmission were ultimately thought to reside.

5

A Third Torah

ORAL TORAH, WRITTEN TORAH, AND THE EMBRACE OF A SPOKEN SCRIPTURE

IT IS DIFFICULT for a modern reader to grasp just how qualitatively different from its written counterpart the recited oral formula of the biblical text would have been for late antique practitioners. However, recent research on *piyyut* (Jewish liturgical poetry) and sounded scriptures in an early Christian tradition has begun to open doors to a richer sense of just how distinct the experience of spoken and written scripture could be. Laura Lieber's recent work, for instance, captures the myriad ways in which biblical language was made new in Palestinian Jewish circles as it was incorporated into the realms of contemporary speech and song. As she has put it in a study of Yannai and his work, "In his piyyutim, texts create texture and tradition becomes the language of innovation" as the liturgist drew "upon the familiar, canonical literary source as a kind of short-hand, employing a single, meaning-laden word or phrase in order to evoke a world of implicit meaning, both biblical-contextual and exegetical."[1] With this interweaving of contemporary voices and biblical ones, Lieber argues, "the poet or cantor . . . took a breath to breathe life into the weekly lectionary . . . audience, characters, and performer merged, history became experience."[2] As Deborah Forger has articulated this sense of animation in more literal terms, auditory-based epistemology took on material meanings in late antique contexts since "speech itself, once heard, can be a material entity

1. Laura S. Lieber, *Yannai on Genesis* (Cincinnati, OH: Hebrew Union College Press, 2010), 93, 95.

2. Laura S. Lieber, "Telling a Liturgical Tale: Storytelling in Early Jewish Liturgical Poetry," *Zeitschrift fuer Religions* 66, nos. 3–4 (2014): 225.

163

164   CHAPTER 5

and . . . sounds, and voices in particular, can be corporeally known."[3] Once human lips, tongue, and breath were engaged in spoken revelation, "through their vocalization the words enter the realm of materiality, and thus when listened to they make God capable of being corporeally known."[4] In this context, spoken scripture was alive and real to those who encounter it in a way that written scriptures absorbed through the sense of sight were not.

In the classical rabbinic context, this experiential difference between written and spoken scripture came to be theorized as a metaphysical difference. As the memorized vocal iteration of the biblical tradition increasingly became unmoored from the written text, the reading practices described in the previous chapter would not only shape the early rabbinic relationship to sacred text in the moment but would also come to have a profound impact on how rabbinic practitioners *imagined* the biblical heritage in more abstract terms. As the vocalized formula of the Hebrew Bible came to circulate independently of the written text, these two versions of the biblical tradition would come to be conceived by many as independent—sometimes even conflicting—witnesses to the scriptural revelation. Indeed, the spoken tradition of the biblical revelation would even come to be ascribed literary and ideological qualities slightly different than those attributed to the written transcript preserved in parchment scrolls, until the two iterations of the biblical tradition came to be thought of in some circles as qualitatively distinct revelations.

In this imaginary, the Sinaitic revelation was not conceived as two Torahs in the way that modern scholarship typically understands those categories.[5] That is, the products of Sinai were not imagined as a simple binary between Written Torah (scripture) and Oral Torah (rabbinic tradition). In this early rabbinic system, like some of its Second Temple predecessors,[6] the scriptural

3. Deborah Forger, "Jesus as God's Word(s): Aurality, Epistemology and Embodiment in the Gospel of John," *Journal for the Study of the New Testament* 42, no. 3 (2020): 280.

4. Ibid., 281.

5. For a recent review and critique of how the "discourse of origins in scholarship often assumes Oral Torah/Written Torah to be a solidified endpoint of an evolutionary process," see Yael Fisch, "The Origins of Oral Torah: A New Pauline Perspective," *Journal for the Study of Judaism* 51, no. 1 (March 2020): 43–66.

6. For a fascinating reconstruction of how this system might have functioned in the Second Temple and biblical periods and for a list of biblical passages that can be read as referring to the sort of bifurcation of oral and written transcripts described here, see Shaul Levin, "Hakri: Hatext hayesodi shel haTanakh," in *Hagut 'ivrit beAmerikah* (Yavneh: Brit Ivrit Olamit, 1972), especially 1.61–74. Strikingly, Yael Fisch has also identified a bifurcation of scripture itself into two scriptural Torahs in a different but more nearly contemporaneous context. She argues that, in Ro-

tradition *itself* would be bifurcated into two qualitatively distinct categories of scriptural witness to the biblical revelation, which would ultimately be designated *mikra* (the vocalized oral formula) and *masoret* (the tradition of textual inscription). With this bifurcation of the scriptural revelation itself, the binary categories of Written Torah and Oral Torah were thus mediated by a third category of Torah: an independent vocal witness to the biblical revelation that we will call Spoken Scripture.[7]

Many early rabbinic traditions, moreover, would identify this vocalized iteration of the biblical tradition with a distinct moment in the mythology of the Sinaitic revelation. For as Steven Fraade has put it, "the originary revelation at Sinai . . . is midrashically represented as an oral and aural encounter with the divine utterance prior to its textual inscription."[8] I would argue that the import of this insight here has not been fully appreciated in our collective portrait of how the biblical tradition was envisioned in the rabbinic imaginary. Many early rabbinic thinkers would treat Spoken Scripture (*mikra*) as a generational echo of this first, more authentic, biblical revelation that issued from the mouth of God—the fuller spoken scriptural revelation that was captured all too briefly in writing on the first tablets of the law before escaping its written prison to return to its natural state.[9] According to this vision of Sinai and its products, that original spoken iteration of the biblical tradition survived the destruction of the first tablets and would be passed from mouth to mouth as an intangible accompaniment to the written text—as a sort of universal soul of the biblical revelation that was linked with the written parchment bodies preserving the revelation on the second tablets, but not contained by them.

When Written and Spoken Come Undone: The Emergence of a Spoken Bible in Early Rabbinic Practice

With the memorized vocalized formula of the Bible on the tip of so many tongues, it threatened to become an independent oral literature circulating separately from the written transcript to which it was correlated. In an environ-

---

mans 3 and 10, "Paul actively generates the scripture of righteousness by deeds as written, and the scripture of righteousness by trust as spoken." (Fisch, "Origins," 58).

7. A loose translation of the Hebrew term *mikra*.

8. Steven Fraade, *Legal Fictions: Studies of Law and Narrative in the Discursive Worlds of Ancient Jewish Sectarians and Sages* (Leiden: Brill, 2011), 378.

9. For more on this imaginary, see the first chapter of this book.

166   CHAPTER 5

ment in which "reading" was performed by applying a memorized sounded formula of the biblical text to the consonantal transcript, the written text of the Bible could only function as a living document so long as members of the community carried the sounded formula in their memories.[10] It was presumed that key formulas, such as Deuteronomy 6:4–9, Deuteronomy 11:13–22, Numbers 15:37–42, and Exodus 13:1–16,[11] could be recited by many practitioners from memory with "fluency" (מיגרס גריסין) (bMegillah 18b). Indeed, some were imagined to be able to recite entire Pentateuchal lectionaries without reference to a written text.[12] Some early rabbinic practitioners are even depicted as having their memorized formula for entire prophetic books checked by their teachers in a process similar to that in which medieval Muslim students would later receive an *ijaza*[13] to transmit specific works.[14]

10. While it is impossible to hazard statistics for the rabbinic context, Hayden Pellicia has calculated that, in classical Athens, the ritual requirements of a single Dionysian festival would have left 17–22 percent of the citizen population masters of a lengthy memorized poetic repertoire—and this does not even take into consideration the many other festivals celebrated in a year. Hayden Pelliccia, "Two Points about Rhapsodes," in *Homer, the Bible, and Beyond: Literary and Religious Canons in the Ancient World*, ed. Margalit Finkelberg and Guy Stroumsa (Leiden: Brill, 2003), 101–2.

11. That is, the biblical passages included in the Shema readings, mezuzah (doorpost) scrolls, and phylacteries.

12. As the sages imagined the ancient sacrificial *ma'amadot* gatherings, for instance, the congregation listened to the daily Torah portion read "from a scroll" at the morning and midday services but "each of them read it from memory" individually at the afternoon service (mTaʿanit 4:3, tTaʿanit 3:4, bTaʿanit 28a).

13. For more on the history of this "license to transmit" and its theoretical implications, see the background discussion in Sabine Schmidtke, "Forms and Functions of 'Licenses to Transmit' (Ijazas) in 18th-Century-Iran: ʿAbd Allah al-Musawi al-Jazaʾiri al-Tustari's (1112–73/1701–59)," in *Speaking for Islam: Religious Authorities in Muslim Societies,* ed. Gudrun Kraemer and Sabine Schmidtke (Leiden: Brill, 2006), 95–127. For a comparative study of rabbinic and Muslim theories of oral transmission and the maintenance of oral-text integrity more generally, see Talya Fishman, "Guarding Oral Traditions: Within and between Cultures," in *Oral-Scribal Dimensions of Scripture, Piety, and Practice,* ed. Werner H. Kelber and Paula A. Sanders (Eugene, OR: Wipf and Stock, 2016), 49–68.

14. See, for instance, bAvodah Zarah 19a and the study of similar instances in Daniel Picus, "Ink Sea and Parchment Sky: Rabbinic Reading Practices in Late Antiquity" (*PhD* diss., Brown University, 2017), 60–66. Although as Marc Hirschman has pointed out, reading before one's teacher was not merely a rote exercise in the context of the rabbinic academy but "seems analogous to the 'expressive reading' in [more advanced] Greco-Roman education" where the first recitation "reading is followed by exegesis, and similarly in the seven examples before us in the Talmud, twice exegetical comments are made. . . . In short, this seems like an activity carried

In order for the Hebrew Bible to survive as a living archive under this dualist system of reading, a significant number of individuals would need to memorize the vocalized formula for the whole biblical canon—and thus preserve a complete oral iteration of the Bible within their memories. Such individuals had attained the status of a true Bible recitation-reader (קרא) otherwise known as a master of Spoken Scripture (בעל מקרא)—defined as one well versed in recitation-reading the Pentateuch, Prophets, and Writings (בקי לקרות בתורה ובנביאים ובכתובים) (bTaʿanit 16a).[15] Such an individual knew how "to read-recite the [entire] Torah, Prophets and Writings with precision" because he had correctly memorized the oral formula for the entire Bible (bKiddushin 49a). Although smaller communities do not always appear to have possessed a scholar who met this standard,[16] classical rabbinic traditions nevertheless depict numerous individuals "who were as fluent in the Torah as Ezra" (רגיל בתורה כעזרא)[17]—yet another expression to describe individuals

---

out also in the higher levels of education and is not just an elementary exercise." Marc Hirshman, *Stabilization of Rabbinic Culture, 100 CE–350 CE: Texts on Education and Their Late Antique Contexts* (Oxford: Oxford University Press, 2009), 72.

15. See also Sifre Deuteronomy 355, Genesis Rabbah 40:17, Leviticus Rabbah 36:2, Ecclesiastes Rabbah 6:2, bSanhedrin 101a, bTaʿanit 16a, bBerakhot 30b, bAvodah Zarah 40a, bSanhedrin 90b, bBava Batra 8a, bMegillah 28b, bEruvin 21b, bEruvin 21b, bEruvin 54b, bHagigah 14a, bBava Metzia 33b, and bBava Metzia 21b. We would also appear to find narrative descriptions of these "masters of scripture" in dialogues (such as bSanhedrin 90b and yShekalim 3:2 (47c) in which one participant in a debate can recite a series of spontaneous proof texts "from Torah, Prophets, and the Writings."

16. As Meir Bar-Ilan has demonstrated, small rural communities sometimes lacked an individual who knew the read-formula for the Prophets and Writings. See, for instance, Meir Bar-Ilan, "Illiteracy as Reflected in the Halachot concerning Reading the Scroll of Esther and Hallel," *Proceedings of the American Academy of Jewish Research* 54 (1987): 1–12 (in Hebrew); "Illiteracy in the Land of Israel in the First Centuries C.E.," in *Essays in the Social Scientific Study of Judaism and Jewish Society*, ed. S. Fishbane, S. Schoenfeld, and A. Goldschlaeger (New York: Ktav, 1992), 2:46–61; and Bar-Ilan, "Literacy among the Jews in Antiquity," *Hebrew Studies* 44 (2003), 217–22. To say that many rural communities lacked an individual who knew the literary read-formula of later biblical books does not, however, contradict studies that argue basic forms of *practical* alphabetic literary were widespread already in ancient Israel. See, for instance, Aaron Demsky, *Literacy in Ancient Israel* (Jerusalem: Mosad Bialik, 2012) (in Hebrew), and William Schniedewind, *How the Bible Became a Book: The Textualization of Ancient Israel* (Cambridge: Cambridge University Press, 2004).

17. See, for instance, Genesis Rabbah 36:26, yMegillah 4:1 (74d), and bBerakhot 4b. For more on the background of the expression "fluent in the Torah as Ezra" see chapter 1 of this monograph.

who were able to recite the entire biblical formula from memory. In practical descriptions of this phenomenon, the individual in question was often the local scribe qua elementary school teacher—someone whose primary vocation was to preserve and transmit the oral version of the text for a particular community.

This level of mastery was not limited, however, to professional memorizers—nor does the ability to recite the entire oral formula from memory appear to have been perceived as a mere techne. Such mastery is also admiringly ascribed to prominent rabbinic sages. YMegillah 4:1 (74d), for instance, attributes this ability to produce the oral formula for the entire Bible from memory not only to the famous rabbinic scribe R. Meir, but also to the nonscribal sages R. Yishmael b. Yose and R. Hiyya the Great. According to this passage, all three rabbis had purportedly memorized the oral formula of biblical text so completely that they could not only recite the entire text from memory but could even perform the more exacting task of correctly "writing down the entire formula of the biblical text from memory." Nor was the image of the master memorizer merely a hyperbolic or aspirational figure. As we will see in the coming pages, classical rabbinic traditions instituted legal rulings to govern the way that individuals who carried the Bible in their memories might engage with the biblical text—suggesting that such individuals also represented a practical reality for which Jewish law needed to account.

Many classical rabbinic traditions attest, indeed, that the oral transcript of the biblical revelation had become so thoroughly liberated from the consonantal text in early rabbinic circles that many practitioners were tempted to engage with the sounded formula of the Bible as an independent biblical witness in its own right—and to do away entirely with the putative dependence of the sounded formula on the written consonantal transcript, even in formal liturgical contexts. In the face of this possibility, early rabbinic authorities imposed legal measures to preserve at least a minimal formal correlation between the two transcripts in symbolic contexts, while apparently accepting the functional independence of the vocalized tradition as a witness to revelation in nonliturgical situations. While it was understood that individuals would inevitably "read from memory" in private or unofficial encounters, for instance, early rabbinic authorities sought to hold in check the popular temptation to recite the biblical formula from memory also in official contexts. As bTaʿanit complains, "What, may an individual now read from memory for the congregation?!" While an individual might read-recite from memory to himself, we learn elsewhere in the passage, to do as much for others in a liturgical Torah

A THIRD TORAH 169

reading is another matter entirely. For "even one as familiar with the Torah as Ezra must not pronounce it from memory and read-recite" a lectionary (yMegillah 4:1 [74d]). Classical rabbinic traditions even warn that "one who is read-reciting the lectionary from the Torah must not let his eyes wander away from the Torah" even for a moment, lest he fall into the (apparently more comfortable) practice of read-reciting the memorized formula from memory (Tanhuma Ki Tissa 34).

Yet the popular temptation to forgo reference to a written text even in public readings apparently remained so strong that rabbinic authorities were forced to retroactively invalidate such readings. Thus, "one who read-recited [the book of Esther] from memory" was declared "not to have fulfilled his ritual obligation [to read that biblical text on Purim]" (קראה על פה לא יצא ידי חובתו) (tMegillah 2:5 and yMegillah 2:1 [72d]).[18] If such rulings were deemed necessary, it suggests that some practitioners, at least, were tempted to do away entirely with the sounded biblical formula's putative dependence on the written form to which it (more or less) corresponded, even in formal liturgical settings.

It is important to note, moreover, that while such rulings sought to maintain a ritual correlation between these two transcripts of the Bible in the face of a practical unmooring, they manifest no distrust or disapprobation of the memorized tradition of the Hebrew Bible as a functional witness to the Sinaitic revelation. Nor do they express any doubts concerning the authenticity of the biblical tradition preserved in the minds of the religious authorities. For like the ironically hyperbolic declaration, "even one as familiar with Torah as Ezra may not read out the text from memory," the narrative case studies brought to "illustrate" these prohibitions emphatically maintain that practices separating the memorized formula from the consonantal transcript were not forbidden because the rabbinic authorities distrusted the recited formula or the ability of its transmitters to preserve the memorized tradition of the biblical revelation accurately. BMegillah 18b, for instance, emphasizes that R. Hananel was banned from "writing Torah scrolls without reference to a written text" even though his mastery of the memorized text was complete and perfect. Not only does the narrator assure us that R. Hananel did indeed know the entire biblical formula accurately by heart ("the words of the [entire] Torah were straight [in R. Hananel's memory]"), but the colleague who discovers R. Hananel in this illicit practice is reported to have exclaimed:

18. See, similarly, mMegillah 2:1 and bMegillah 17a.

It is indeed appropriate that the entire Torah should be written from your memory except that the sages have declared it is forbidden to write a single letter [of a biblical scroll] without reference to a written text.

The narrative formally closes the door on the practice described while simultaneously confirming the abstract principle that a well-versed rabbinic practitioner could easily preserve a true record of the biblical revelation without reference to the consonantal transcript.

Stories in which sages reconstruct or recreate the Pentateuch, such as those discussed in chapter 1, can also be read as a genre of narratives affirming human memory as a legitimate (perhaps the most legitimate) locus for preserving and transmitting the biblical tradition, despite the formal requirement to maintain written copies of the revelation. In one pithy version of a story cited elsewhere in this monograph (yMegillah 4:1 [74d]), for instance, Rabbi Hiyya declares:

I can write the entire biblical tradition (כל קרייא) for two *mina* coins. How did he do it? He purchased two *mina* worth of flax seed and sowed it, cut it, and made ropes. He caught deer [with the rope] and wrote the entire biblical formula on their hides. Rabbi heard this and announced, "Happy is the generation who has such a one in its midst."

In light of the collegial statement valorizing R. Hiyya's feat, it seems fair to interpret this vision as reflecting a broader classical rabbinic vision of the Written Torah and its status in relationship to the memorized formula. On the one hand, the formulators of this fantasy acknowledge that the "Torah had been given in writing" (as the popular rabbinic phrase put it) and should therefore continue to be put into writing for every generation. However, they simultaneously deny that the transmission of the biblical tradition in writing serves any purpose as far as communicating or preserving the biblical formula. In this story, the biblical text has been recreated from memory radically ex nihilo (stripped down to the very flax seeds needed to make the ropes with which deer hides might be obtained), but without any dire consequences that the reader can discern. The narrative thus reminds us that only the human memory preserves the memorized formula of the Bible in a full and sufficient form—with the consonantal text, and the vowels and breaths that make it pronounceable, inextricably intertwined in his mind—so that both the written text and the vocalized formula could be restored from this memorized template.

Some stories in this genre go so far as to suggest that the putative transmission of the biblical tradition in the form of a written transcript was an open legal fiction. Having forbidden the writing out of Torah scrolls from memory, for instance, Genesis Rabbah 36:8[19] immediately proceeds to relate an almost humorous narrative in which R. Meir was once permitted to transcribe a scroll of Esther from memory and then recite the memorized oral formula he had just transcribed in conjunction with this text—on the condition that he did not publicly read from the first scroll he had written out by heart but instead dutifully copied out a second scroll from that first scroll and read from the copy. For the authors of this proposal, the memorized oral formula itself was not distrusted as a witness to the biblical tradition—Rabbi Meir's memorized tradition of the text is accepted as valid in its second iteration. According to this story, it was simply necessary to reestablish a formal chain in which one written text was transcribed from another written text so that R. Meir could, in turn, establish an official correlation between a written transcript of the biblical book and the oral one. By qualifying legal references to the prohibition on reading and writing from memory with such ambiguous (and ambivalent) case studies, the formulators of these passages subtly acknowledge that there is no practical need for written transmission of the biblical tradition at all. The formal necessity for a written text is exposed by such case studies as just that—a formal requirement with no pressing practical or ideological basis.

A careful look at classical rabbinic legal rulings concerning the practice of writing the biblical text from memory similarly suggests that when the two traditions came asunder it threatened to render the written transcript a secondary, or even superfluous, witness to the biblical tradition. Many classical rabbinic traditions suggest, for instance, that the authorities were in fact compelled to suppress the practice of writing out biblical texts for liturgical use from memory—a procedure that allowed the recited formula to function as a generative text in its own right and relegated the consonantal transcript to the status of a ritual object without the power to transmit the biblical tradition. As Genesis Rabbah 36:8 and parallels continue to repeat the refrain, "even one as familiar with the Torah as Ezra may not read-recite to himself from memory and write [out the recited formula]," bMegillah 18b expands on this norm with suspicious hyperbolism, insisting that "it is forbidden to write [even] one letter that is not [copied from] a[nother] written text."

19. See also tMegillah 2:2, yMegillah 4:1 (74d), and bMegillah 18b.

As was the case for reading from memory, moreover, additional rulings suggest that the practical temptations of writing out the biblical text from memory were very real. Beyond merely issuing a blanket prohibition on reading or writing from memory, for instance, bMegillah 18b also explores the question of what legal status should be ascribed to various permutations of this practice. It asks:

> What if one organizes [the text in his mind] verse-by-verse, writes it [out one verse at a time], turns his mind [to what he is writing], and reads it out [as he writes each verse], what would be the legal status of that scenario? The rabbis must rule that such a practice would be forbidden *ab initio* since "he is [writing] from memory!"

More importantly for our purposes, perhaps, the passage goes on to clarify that even *retrospectively* such a person would not have fulfilled his ritual obligation to read in conjunction with a written copy of the biblical text—suggesting a need to clamp down on a continuing practice. The fact that such rulings were necessary suggests that the circulation of a memorized vocal formula had threatened to render the written text superfluous as a document of communication and transmission—reducing the written text to a purely ritual object that could be (re)created for liturgical purposes but that possessed no power to preserve and transmit the biblical tradition in its own right.

Linguistically, this phenomenon is manifested in a sporadic tendency throughout classical rabbinic traditions to slip into describing biblical recitation-reading using technical terminology usually reserved to describe the memorized transmission of the rabbinic Oral Torah.[20] In some such cases, the memorized formula of the Bible is simply grouped together with rabbinic oral traditions, as when R. Tarfon commands, "recite from memory for me," and his interlocutor responded with "the read-formula of the Bible, Mishnah, midrash, laws, and stories" (Avot de Rabbi Natan A 18).[21] Elsewhere, the spo-

---

20. For a recent study of the role of orality in rabbinic study practices related to the "Oral Torah," see Hirshman, *Stabilization*, 17–63.

21. Consider also passages where the equation is made by analogy, such as bMegillah 28b ("If he knows Mishnah, let him pronounce a line from the Mishnah, if he knows Bible, let him pronounce a verse from the Bible."); bBava Batra 8a ("Bring in those who possess Scripture, those who possess Mishnah, those who possess Gemara, those who possess the oral legal tradition, and those who possess the oral legendary tradition."); and bSanhedrin 101a ("[When they are visiting a tavern, let them not sing verses from the Song of Songs but], let those who are masters of Scripture busy themselves with [reciting] the Torah, Prophets, and Writings, let

A THIRD TORAH 173

ken biblical formula itself might be referred to using the terminology of rabbinic oral transmission. In most iterations of the tradition banning informational reading on Shabbat, for instance, those who recite the biblical text from memory on Shabbat are not said to be *kori'in* (reading-reciting) from memory but are referred to without qualification using the vocabulary of rabbinic oral transmission *shonin*[22]—repeating an oral tradition from memory (tShabbat 13:1, Leviticus Rabbah 15:4, Lamentations Rabbah 4:20, yShabbat 16:1 [15c]). More importantly, perhaps, classical rabbinic authors themselves noted that such elisions obscured the theoretical categories that had been established in rabbinic thought for conceptualizing the two Torahs. YMegillah 2:4 (73b), for instance, highlights the melding this pattern created between Oral Torah and the spoken formula of the Written Torah by purporting to be uncertain about the meaning of the term *shonim* when used in connection to the biblical formula:

> [There is a tradition from] Ulla of Biri by R. Elazar in the name of R. Hanina: "One who is as familiar [with the read-formula of the book of Esther] must read-recite it [in conjunction with a text] on the night [of Purim] and [may] recite it from memory (לשנותה) on the day [of Purim]." This could mean to recite the Mishnah [about the laws of Purim]. R. Abba Mari the Babylonian said, "[No, it means] to recite it means its read-formula (לשנות קרייתה) [of the book of Esther]."

The closing line makes clear that the formulators of this passage were able to recognize the authorial intent behind R. Hanina's creative use of language here—that is, his intent to convey the sense that one who has thoroughly and correctly memorized the read-formula of the book of Esther might recite this voiced formula from memory without reference to a scroll once he had performed the ritual duty of reciting the text in conjunction with one. And yet, by pointing out that one might reasonably have understood this statement to mean "recite Mishnah from memory," in keeping with the established use of the term *shonim* in the rabbinic context, the formulators of this passage also acknowledged the dangerous blurring that R. Hanina's amalgamation of these linguistic categories evoked for the contemporaneous listener. In such

---

those who are masters of Mishnah busy themselves with [reciting] the Mishnah, those who are masters of Talmud busy themselves with [reciting] the laws.").

22. The term *shonim* being usually reserved in the rabbinic lexicon for speaking about the memorized oral traditions personally transmitted from teacher to student.

a context, to use the technical terminology *shonim* to refer to the act of biblical recitation testified to a functional blurring of the line between the self-consciously oral transmission of the rabbinic Oral Torah and the vocalized manifestation of scripture. In doing so, they indirectly bear witness to the widening gap between the textual transcript of the Written Torah and its memorized vocal expression.

Other classical rabbinic traditions mark the assimilation of the vocalized biblical formula to the Oral Torah (and the corresponding increase in its divergence from the written consonantal text of the Bible) in more explicit ways.[23] In response to a story about a rabbinical student who forgot the Oral Torah because "he recited rabbinic traditions in a whisper," for instance, bEruvin 54a cites the advice of Shmuel, who opined,

> Open your mouth and read-recite scripture, open your mouth and recite rabbinic tradition, so that it will continue to exist in you and long will be your life, as it is said: "They are life to their finders and a source of healing for all flesh" (Prov 4:22). Don't read "to their finders" but "to those who put them out through their mouths."

This passage identifies both the rabbinic tradition and the read-formula of the Bible as forms of Torah tied to the mouth. Both are likewise paralleled as embodied traditions, that primarily "continue to exist in" the persons of their possessors—so tied to this corporeality, indeed, that they permeate the flesh of their preservers, healing and maintaining it. The citation of Shmuel's advice concerning the recited scriptural formula as an appropriate response to a forgetful student of rabbinic traditions highlights the transient and vulnerable nature of both, which existed primarily (if not solely) as oral traditions dependent on faulty human memory for their survival. Even these more abstract references to the phenomenon thus attest that the recited formula of the Bible frequently circulated independently from the written biblical transcript (with which it corresponded most closely in content) and was transmitted instead in conjunction with the rabbinic oral traditions that it paralleled in form and mode of transmission.

---

23. Consider, for instance, Pesikta de Rav Kahana Bahodesh hashlishi 5, which interprets the verse "two mouthed [i.e., double edged] sword" (Ps 149:6) as a reference to the "two mouths" of the Torah which need to be "worked": "the Written Torah and the Oral Torah." According to this tradition, both the Written Torah and the Oral Torah are Torahs of the Mouth (spoken and memorized traditions) which must be constantly reviewed aloud if they are to be preserved in the memory of their transmitters.

To sum up, the rabbinic practice of recitation-reading (in which a memorized sounded formula was applied to the consonantal transcript) required a vocalized transcript of the Bible to exist completely and independently in the memories of expert readers. The circulation of a continuous, memorized "vocal text" of the biblical canon in turn led some practitioners to engage these memorized formulas as an independent oral tradition rather than a facet of the consonantal text. Indeed, the tendency to treat the memorized spoken formula of the Bible as an independent work—which neither derived from nor depended on the consonantal transcript—was so strong in some circles that the rabbinic authorities were compelled to institute restrictions on liturgical recitations to prevent the use of the vocalized formula without reference to the consonantal transcript in order to maintain even a basic formal correlation between the two. Moreover, while legal rabbinic pronouncements insisted that this sounded text be treated as a facet of the consonantal transcript in liturgical contexts, narrative allusions to the circulation of these two biblical transcripts suggest that many practitioners and rabbinic authorities had nevertheless come to think of these two distinct representations of the biblical tradition as independent manifestations of the biblical revelation: a vocal record to be preserved and transmitted from generation to generation and a consonantal transcript that could serve as a ritual symbol.

The Two Bibles in Rabbinic Thought: Independent Witnesses to the Biblical Revelation

The untwining of the recited formula and the written consonantal text of the Bible in early rabbinic practices was further intensified by the fact that the contents of these two transcripts did not run entirely parallel to one another during the classical rabbinical period but diverged at the level of individual words and phrases and even, in the context of liturgical practice, at the level of paragraphs and chapters. The divergences between the contents would lead some observers to claim that biblical revelation had been fractured into two distinct (and not entirely congruent) works. Indeed, many practitioners apparently came to imagine these distinct biblical traditions not only as superficially disparate representations of the Sinaitic revelation but as independent literary works—distinguished from one another not only by subtle differences in wording but even by divergent authorial intents and distinct metaphysical qualities. Indeed, the perception that there existed two independent (and conflicting) witnesses to the biblical revelation became so strong in this period

176   CHAPTER 5

that some would argue that only one of these two transcripts could represent a true record of the Sinaitic revelation—and practitioners would begin to ask which represented the authentic manifestation of the biblical revelation. As the Babylonian Talmud would come to crystallize this instinct in a frequently repeated formulaic question: יש אם למקרא or יש אם למסורת (Is the vocalized tradition determinative or the tradition of consonantal writing)?

Deviations between the Two Transcripts

This is not the place to enter into the question of when and where the *qere* (read) and *ketiv* (written) traditions as we know them came into being.[24] Nevertheless, if we survey explicit allusions[25] to historical differences between the "read" and "written" formulas of the biblical text in classical rabbinic traditions, we can certainly say that the recited rendering of the biblical tradition and the written consonantal transcript of that work already represented two distinct versions of the biblical tradition at the time—distinguished from one another by a series of small but significant divergences in content and wording.[26] As Robert Gordis has pointed out, the most pervasive departure between the spoken and written formulas of the biblical text in the rabbinic period was the

24. A selection of earlier Second Temple examples of the phenomenon and a review of the scholarly literature on the topic can be found in Emmanuel Tov, *Textual Criticism of the Hebrew Bible* (Minneapolis, MN: Fortress, 1992), 61ff, and Tov, "The Ketiv-Qere Variations in Light of the Manuscript Finds in the Judean Desert," in *Text, Theology & Translation, Essays in Honour of Jan de Waard*, ed. S. Crisp and M. Jinbachian (Swindon: United Bible Societies, 2004), 199–207. A review of recent work on the origins of the Masoretic tradition more generally, with an emphasis on codicological studies, can be found in Gary D. Martin, *Multiple Origins: New Approaches to Hebrew Bible Textual Criticism* (Atlanta: Society of Biblical Literature Press, 2010), 79–98.

25. While rabbinic literature abounds with implicit references to read-formulas that differ from the written transcript of the Bible as we know it, it is difficult to determine precisely how much these oral renderings of the biblical text might have differed from the written version of the Bible that circulated in the early rabbinic period since no manuscript witnesses have survived. We will, therefore, consider only cases in which the rabbinic source itself explicitly uses the language of *qere* and *ketiv* or includes the formulation of the written version of the verse that circulated in that period.

26. For an alternative vision of *qere* and *ketiv* in which these two formulas are conceived not as distinct oral and written traditions but as "scripture as received" and "scripture as revised," see Michael Fishbane, "Extra-Biblical Exegesis: The Sense of Not Reading in Rabbinic Midrash," in *Return to Scripture in Judaism and Christianity: Essays in Postcritical Scriptural Interpretation*, ed. Peter Ochs (Eugene, OR: Wipf and Stock, 2008), 172–90, especially 178.

A THIRD TORAH 177

systematic replacement of the tetragrammaton in the written text with the phrase "my lord" in vocal renderings[27]—a single substitution that would alone have accounted for nearly seven thousand divergences between the written text of the Bible and the vocalized formula of the biblical text in rabbinic circles.[28]

Early rabbinic traditions also attest to a wide variety of generic practices that increased the divergence between the written and spoken iterations of the biblical tradition. Thus, early rabbinic traditions allude to words and phrases in the written text of the Bible for which euphemisms were consistently substituted in the read-formula—such as the phrase, "he revealed her nakedness," which was always to be read "he lay her down" (tMegillah 3:39). Other significant structural divergences between the liturgical read-formula and the consonantal transcript introduced in this period include the selective abridgment of books and chapters discussed in the previous chapter and the permanent omission of certain embarrassing narrative episodes from public recitations.[29] As tMegillah 3:31–40 lays out this practice:

> There are [biblical passages] which are read aloud [in public lectionaries] and translated [for the congregation], there are [biblical passages] which may be read aloud [in public lectionaries] but may not be translated [for the congregation], and there are [biblical passages] which may not be read aloud and may not be translated.

Among the episodes that might be omitted, for instance, were the list of Jerusalem's misdeeds beginning in Ezekiel 16:2 and the story of David and Batsheva. Even on the basis of these generic deviations, it becomes apparent that the vocal "text" of the Bible that circulated in the classical rabbinic context was distinguished from the written transcript of the Bible by significant distinctions in both content and wording.

---

27. For an early rabbinic reference to this practice, see mSanhedrin 10:1.

28. Robert Gordis, *The Biblical Text in the Making: A Study of the Kethib-Qere* (Philadelphia: Dropsie College Press, 1937), 30. In support of an early dating for this custom, Gordis cites Philo, *Life of Moses* 3.519, 529. See, in addition, Josephus, *Antiquities* 2.23.114.

29. See tMegillah 3:31–40 and bMegillah 25a–b for illustrative lists of such changes, though it appears that the list of euphemisms recorded in tMegillah 3:31–40 should not be read as a definitive and complete set of such omissions and replacements but rather as an exemplary list of the types of replacements that are recommended since the passage goes on to explain that all derogatory passages should be reworded in a less shameful way. In these passages, we are presented with a much-expanded version of the tradition preserved in mMegillah 4:10.

178 CHAPTER 5

Early rabbinic traditions also attest to a wide variety of more local variations that increased the divergence between the written and spoken iterations of the biblical tradition. There were certain words, for instance, that were traditionally "read but not written or written but not read"—such as the word "Euphrates" vocally interpolated into the read-formula of the verse "David defeated Hadadezer son of Rehov, the king of Tzovah, on his way to return his rule to the river [Euphrates]" (2 Sam 8:3; bNedarim 37b–38a). Other early rabbinic traditions also marked differences between "what is written" and what "we read" that do not reflect our contemporary consonantal transcripts or spoken formulas (bYoma 76b). At the same time, many of the read-formulas later recorded by the Masoretes do appear to have been employed already in this period—including the substitution of the word "courtyard" for "city" in 2 Kings 20:4 (bEruvin 26a) and the disparate renderings of Abigail's name in the written transcript and recited formula (ySanhedrin 2.4 [20b]).[30] In other cases, deviations were barely marked but simply slipped into the flow of argument quietly and unobtrusively—noted only by phrases such as קרינן or אמר קרא. YBava Batra 8:1 (16a), for example, deviates from a pattern of biblical quotations prefaced by the phrase "it is written" to state: "the read-formula informs us [the inheritance falls to] the 'nearest relative'" (Num 27:11). In this case, the formulator of this brief exegesis thought it prudent to stipulate that he was interpreting the memorized vocal formula of Numbers 27:11—which specifies that the ruling applies to the "the nearest relative" (הקרוב) in the rabbinic system—since the consonantal text of Numbers 27:11 (הקרב אליו ממשפחתו) might equally be interpreted to mean that the deceased leaves his inheritance to one who draws close to him from his family (a statement that could apply equally well to father and son in the case being debated). While bordering on the trivial in themselves, these myriad local divergences together help to sketch a picture of a broad difference between the two transcripts of the biblical tradition in this period.

Many more examples of such deviations are preserved in classical rabbinic sources because one was forced to choose one transcript over the other in order to live a biblically observant life. As the students of R. Yehudah b. Roetz complain concerning Leviticus 12:5, one might read the consonantal text as 'seventy' (shiv'im) so that a birthing mother would be impure for seventy days after giving birth to a girl child but, according to the read-formula, we pronounce the word 'two weeks' (shevu'ayim) so that she is only impure for two

---

30. For an extensive list of such changes in a single passage, see bNedarim 37b–38a.

weeks (Sifra Tazria 2:2).[31] Nor were such divergences imagined as a purely abstract problem. As bKeritot 17b explicates a particular legal debate:

> Why do they disagree? Rabbi Assi maintains that the written tradition is determinative (יש אם למסורת) and it is written "a commandment [of God]" (Lev 5:17) while Rabbi Hiyya bar Rav maintains that the vocalized tradition is determinative (יש אם למקרא) and we should read it "commandments [of God]" (Lev 5:17).[32]

In moments like these, the two biblical transcripts not only diverged but appeared to be instructing practitioners to do very different things.

How Early Rabbinic Thinkers Conceptualized This Divide

In modern practice, of course, deviations in the read-formula are recorded in nearly all printed editions of the Bible alongside the written text and therefore have come to be seen as an idiosyncratic facet of the written text itself. In the classical rabbinic period, however, these small deviations served to mark the read-formula and the written formula as perceptibly independent and not entirely congruent works. Sometimes the vocalized formula and written transcript were ascribed distinct literary projects. That is, different authorial intentions were imputed to the written text and the read-formula, as in ySanhedrin 10:2 (29a):

> [The word] "man" is in the read-formula (qere) [of 2 Sam 16:23] but not in the written transcript (ketiv) because the writings could not [bring themselves to] call [Ahitophel] a "man" [while the author of the read-formula had no such reservations].

Here the qere and the ketiv traditions are read as indicating that these two streams of transmission represent two distinct literary projects—a theoretical position that is captured by the passage in an imaginative style by ascribing different authorial intents to the anthropomorphized literary products themselves (that is, to "the writings" and the read-formula, respectively).

Other traditions describe this sense of divergence as a metaphysical gulf between the two transcripts. As bPesahim 50a comments, for instance, on the

---

31. See also bZevahim 38a and bSanhedrin 4b.
32. See similarly bMakkot 7b.

180 CHAPTER 5

divergence between the written spelling of the tetragrammaton and the spoken rendering of God's name in the recited text:

"God will be king over all the earth and his name will be one" (Zech 14:9). Is the Lord's name not one now? . . . R. Nahman bar Isaac said, "The world-to-come is not like this world; [in] this world, [his name] is written with *yud-heh* [the tetragrammaton] but it is read with *aleph-dalet* [my lord]. But in the world-to-come, it is all one. It is read with *yud-heh* [the tetragrammaton] and it is written with *yud-heh* [the tetragrammaton]."

While contemporary practitioners are so used to hearing the name of God pronounced according to the read formula (*qere*) that this divergence between the two transcripts no longer registers, the formulators of the passage cited here not only registered the disjunction but held it up as an emblem of the brokenness and imperfection in the current world. In the next world, where all is as it should be, God's name—and his revelation—will be undivided and perfect. In the current world, however, this passage opines, even God's Torah is not unified or whole but has shattered into two distinct manifestations of the biblical revelation that do not entirely cohere.

Other passages offer a glimpse of what it meant for these late antique thinkers to say that the recited formula and written transcript represented independent witnesses to the biblical revelation even when they ran in parallel to one another. The read-formula and the "written formula" were sometimes conceived, for instance, as continuous and independent biblical traditions analogous to the Bible and its Aramaic targum. One widely quoted tradition (cited here according to yMegillah 4:1[74d]),[33] for instance, declared:

["And they read in the Book of the Torah of God spelled it out and applied meaning so they understood the Bible" (Neh 8:8).] "They will read from a book," this is the spoken scripture (זה מקרא), "spelled out," this is the liturgical Aramaic translation tradition (זה תרגום), "applied meaning," this is the punctuating melody (אילו הטעמים), and "they understood," this is the written consonantal transcript (זה המסורת).

According to this vision of the Sinaitic revelation, the biblical tradition is preserved in four parallel but discrete threads: the consonantal transcript, the read-formula, the traditional melody used during liturgical Torah readings, and the Aramaic translation. The structural parallelism of the passage clarifies

33. Compare Genesis Rabbah 36:27, bMegillah 3a, and bNedarim 37b.

A THIRD TORAH 181

that the read-formula and the consonantal transcript were apparently perceived as continuous and independent works even when they ran in parallel, just as the Aramaic translation is recognizable as a continuous and independent work even when it correlates perfectly with the Hebrew Bible.

This notion was alternately expressed in the suggestion that the consonantal transcript was written in a language different from the spoken read-formula. As yMegillah 1:11 (71b) puts it:

> Only four languages are suitable for use and these are: Greek for song, Latin for battle, Syriac[34] for ululating, and Hebrew for the spoken word. And there are some who say also Assyrian [the square lettering system used in a rabbinic Bible scroll] for writing. Assyrian has a written manifestation (כתב) but it doesn't have a spoken language (לשון). Hebrew has a spoken language but it doesn't have a written manifestation. [Thus,] they chose for themselves Assyrian writing and Hebrew spoken language. . . . The Torah was given its writing (כתב) and spoken language (לשון) at the hands of Ezra.

According to this tradition, the consonantal transcript of the Bible (written in Assyrian) and the vocalized formula of the Bible (recited in Hebrew) represent parallel renderings of the biblical tradition in two complementary but quite distinct languages. More importantly, perhaps, for our purposes, the two languages in question are envisioned as fundamentally dissimilar, for one is a written language that cannot be translated into spoken words and one is a spoken language that has no written script. According to the formulator of this tradition, therefore, the consonantal transcript and the recited formula of the Bible are not two manifestations of a single literary tradition but distinct and complementary texts that can be read in parallel but never transformed from one into the other, as one might in a language that possesses both a written and a spoken manifestation.

In the classical rabbinic period, the recited transcript of the Bible and the written consonantal transcript of the biblical tradition were distinguished from one another by a myriad of small differences and even (in the context of liturgical practice) by some significant structural divergences. While many contemporary practitioners have come to see the vestiges of these divergences as an idiosyncratic facet of the written text itself, the formulators of these traditions ascribed them a very different significance. The traditions cited here

---

34. As in the word מסורס, "One who knows Syriac." Carl Brockelmann, *Lexicon Syriacum* (Eugene, OR: Wipf and Stock, 2004), 497.

appear to understand these minor divergences as superficial manifestations of a deeper divide. Some characterized the discrepancy by suggesting that different authorial intents were manifest in each of the transcripts. Others would go further and ascribe different metaphysical qualities to the vocal record of the biblical tradition and the written transcript of the Sinaitic revelation. In both cases, however, it is at this junction that a third category of Torah is born and the recited formulas of the *mikra* become an entity in their own right: a Spoken Scripture.

The Emergence of a Third Torah: What Is Spoken Scripture?

For many early rabbinic thinkers, the spoken formulas of the Bible thus constituted a work in its own right, a Spoken Scripture, if you will—with its own voice and qualities distinct from the written iteration of the biblical tradition. But where did this phenomenon fit into the early rabbinic imaginary concerning the origins and nature of Torah, which is usually described as consisting of some variation on two categories: a Written Torah (scripture) and an Oral Torah (rabbinic tradition)? If we move beyond these (emerging) categories of official thought in our readings of early rabbinic narratives about the Sinaitic revelation, a third type of revelation begins to reveal itself in the interstices. As we saw in the first chapter of this book, many classical rabbinic accounts of the revelation at Sinai placed great emphasis on the revelation of a primordial spoken scriptural revelation that preceded the inscription of the biblical text that would enter history—and it is in that moment of lost revelation that they would identify the origins of the Spoken Scripture.

A tradition preserved on bShabbat 88b,[35] for instance, draws together a series of striking and even sensual images that forcefully emphasize the spoken nature of the original Sinaitic revelation:[36]

> R. Yehoshua b. Levi said, "Why is it written, 'His cheeks are like a bed of spices' (Song 5:13)? [Because] each and every spoken word (דבר) that left the mouth of the Holy One, blessed be he, filled the whole world with [the smell of] spices." But since the first utterance filled it, how did the second

35. Compare Tanhuma (Buber) Shemot 22 and Tanhuma (Buber) Yitro 17.

36. Other traditions dwell on the physicality of God's spoken voice at Sinai in other ways. BZevahim 116a, for instance, maintains that the divine voice reverberated to all four corners of the globe.

A THIRD TORAH   183

utterance go out? The Holy One, blessed be he, would send out a wind from
his treasury [of winds] and each would pass through in order, as it is said,
"His lips are lilies dripping myrrh" (Song 5:13). Don't read "lilies"
(*shoshanim*) but rather "that which is recited by mouth" (*she-shonim*). . . .
R. Yehoshua b. Levi said, "At each and every spoken word that left the
mouth of the Holy One, blessed be he, Israel went [flying] backwards
twelve miles but the ministering angels pulled them back [to Mount Sinai],
as it is said, 'the angels of the host scattered' (Ps 68:15). Do not read 'scattered' (*yidodun*) but 'pulled' (*yedadun*)."[37]

Such images vividly assert the original spoken nature of the biblical revelation
by imagining what the physical organs and movements associated with human
speech might look like writ large in the divine mouth and lungs of God himself. The second image in this excerpt, for instance, imagines the physical experience of being caught up in the all-too-forceful breath of a divine "close
talker." It is the descriptions of taste and smell, however, that bring the embodied orality of this imagery into sharpest focus. In such images, the formulators
of this tradition not only attribute to God various organs of the human mouth
(cheek, tongue, lips); they render these organs distinctly biological by imagining what the breath of God might smell like as it picks up particles of food and
other perceptible matter when it is pushed over the divine cheeks and lips in
the process of speaking aloud. Admittedly, the biology of the divine here is far
more consistently attractive than instances of human breath usually are—carrying the scent of an ever-changing bouquet of delicious earthly scents (spices,
lilies, myrrh). The divine diet is apparently a rarified one. But even this rarified
earthiness does much to connect the voiced nature of the original biblical
revelation to the less rarified earthiness of human transmission by mouth. As
the authors of this passage pun, the scent of God's breath changes (*shonim*)
with each word to evoke the recited oral repetition (*shonim*) of the biblical
revelation. By using this language to describe the scriptural revelation at Sinai
as a spoken tradition, this passage adopts the vocabulary usually applied to the
rabbinic memorized "Oral Torah" to emphasize the orality of this scriptural
revelation. Just as this passage leverages the idea that the divine breath has a
smell to draw the audience's attention to the function of their own breath as
they repeat the spoken formulas that were produced at that original revelation.
In such descriptions of Sinai, we encounter mythic accounts of revelation that

37. That is, instead of יִדֹּדוּן (scattered, fled, or retreated) as that word appears in the context
of Ps 68:13, one should read the word as if it were vocalized יְדַדּוּן (led or pulled).

include images of a third Torah of sorts, a vocal scriptural revelation that corresponds to the Spoken Scripture circulating as a distinct iteration of the biblical revelation in some rabbinic circles.

Contemporary scholarship often treats this moment of revelation as ephemeral—a temporary reality that will ultimately be foreclosed and supplanted by revelatory inscription. As Steven Fraade has captured this sense of chronology in his work on the idea of a primordial spoken iteration of the biblical revelation,

> Striking in those rabbinic accounts of what transpired at Sinai, of what constituted *mattan torah* (the "giving of the Torah"), is not the giving or receiving of the iconic scroll or continuous written text of the Torah, but the hearing (and seeing) by the Israelites of each of God's utterances (of the ten commandments) prior to its textual inscription (in stone). . . . The Israelites are depicted not primarily as interpretive readers of a sacred written text but as interpretive *auditors* of divine utterances. Oral interpretation is mythically conceived as being in origin coincidental with oral divine revelation and *prior* to revelatory inscription.[38]

Fraade understands this primordial moment to have long-sounding echoes in the rabbinic tradition—as he puts it, "it is clear that this representation is not simply of a singular past event but of a paradigmatic and ongoing experience, whether projected back onto Sinai from rabbinic practice or forward from Sinai into the present."[39] But because it is imagined as a temporary (that is, temporally bound) aberration, this vision of a primordial spoken Torah has not garnered much widespread interest from the scholarly community.

Yet if we press a bit more on this question of temporality, the finality of the movement toward written closure becomes less clear. Without question, we encounter many images of a spoken biblical revelation in which the voiced iteration of the Sinaitic revelation receives chronological priority. At first glance, this potentiality appears to be quickly foreclosed by the inscription of these utterances into a written text. Sifre Deuteronomy 343, for instance, vividly captures this sense of closure by imagining the inscription of the tablets in a temporal sequence:

> "From this right hand a fiery law for his people" (Deut 33:2): When the word went out from the mouth (הדבור יוצא מפיו) of the Mighty One, it

38. Steven D. Fraade, "Literary Composition and Oral Performance in Early Midrashim," *Oral Tradition* 14, no. 1 (1999): 43.

39. Fraade, *Legal Fictions*, 377.

would go out by way of the Holy One's right hand to the left of Israel and around the camp of Israel [from that direction] twelve miles by twelves miles, and returned and came [back] around Israel's right side into the left hand of God. [Then] the Holy One passed it to his right hand and engraved the tablet. And [while he did so,] his voice rang through the whole world, to the very ends of the world. As it is said, "The voice of God engraves with a flame of fire" (Ps 29:7).

The temporal sequence from orality to writing in this vivid image is striking. Yet, we would do well to remember that the revelatory inscription described here is not the extant biblical text. The writing described here is not final inscription of revelation that would enter the stream of history. While the particular iteration of the tradition above does not explicitly note the broader context of this temporal move from orality to writing, parallel versions of this tradition (Mekhilta de Rabbi Yishmael Bahodesh 9 and Song of Songs Rabbah 1:2) do emphasize that this is an image of the inscription of the first tablets— that uncanny revelation that would never be bequeathed to Israel.[40] Accounts of a primordial Spoken Scripture that was foreclosed by revelatory inscription do not, therefore, depict how the biblical revelation that entered history came into existence.

These narratives participate instead in a mythology surrounding the first tablets of the law—that more perfect scriptural record of revelation lost to human history. Like the traditions about the first tablets analyzed in the first chapter, these traditions also lean heavily on the uncanny nature of the speech-writing on the first ill-fated tablets. In the version of the above tradition preserved in Mekhilta de Rabbi Yishmael Bahodesh 9, for instance, we are reminded that the lost first tablets somehow recorded a more authentic and complete record of the divine revelation inasmuch as "there was not a single utterance that left the mouth of the Mighty One that was not engraved on the tablets, as it is said, 'The voice of God engraved with flames of fire' (Ps 29: 7)." We are reminded also that the nature of the writing on the first tablets was an uncanny product nothing like human writing.[41] When Exodus records the paradoxical statement that "the entire people *saw* the voices" (Exod 20:18), Mekhilta de Rabbi Yishmael interprets this to mean that they saw "speech of fire come out of the mouth of the Mighty One and be engraved on the tablets. As it is said, 'The voice of God engraves flames of fire' (Ps 29:7)"

40. For a review of these traditions, see chapter 1.
41. For an analysis of this phenomenon, see chapter 1.

(Mekhilta de Rabbi Yishmael Yitro 9). In other words, this passage accepts the tradition (explored in chapter 1) that first tablets of the law were composed of fire and explains that the strange fiery substance of the first tablets represented a mysterious visual manifestation of an audible phenomenon: divine speech.

According to this vision of the first tablets, the original (and most authentic) instantiation of the biblical revelation in physical form was a material embodiment of divine speech. Hewing as closely as possible to the original boundless character of that speech, this lost embodiment of the biblical revelation translated these spoken communications into an ephemeral and almost intangible form of writing. In the Song of Songs Rabbah version of this tradition, indeed, the uncanniness of the original revelation derives directly from its voiced nature: "The utterance itself would engrave on its own (הדיבור עצמו היה נחקק מאליו) and while it was engraving the sound rang from one end of the world to the other" (Song of Songs Rabbah 1:2). In other words, these narratives about a primordial written scripture frequently identify that uncanny product as a more perfect—if ultimately impossible—iteration of the biblical revelation that somehow captured a spoken version of the biblical revelation in its entirety.

The Lost Revelation That Survived

In these tales of speech turned to supernatural text, the language of temporal change does not represent a finished closure—this is not a permanent move from speech to text. As we saw in the first chapter of this book, this initial paradoxical scriptural revelation inscribed on the first tablets quickly escaped from its prison of writing. When this first revelatory inscription was freed, moreover, it did not mark the end of that original revelation, according to many classical rabbinic traditions. For this primordial scriptural revelation was not said to disappear when it was liberated from the first tablets; instead, it returned to its original state. As bPesahim 87b relates: "R. Alexandri said, 'Three things returned to their source and these are: Israel [who went into exile in the land of their forebearers], Egypt's wealth [which was recaptured in war] and the writing on the Tablets.'" Or, as the Mekhilta de Rabbi Yishmael renders the tradition,[42] "The heavenly writing returned to its place, as it is said, 'your eyes alighted upon it and it was no more [for it will surely make itself wings and will fly off to the heavens]' (Prov 23:5)" (Mekhilta de Rabbi Yishmael

42. See also bPesahim 87b.

Beshalakh 1). In this version of the tradition, the survival of the first speech-writing revelation is described in geographic terms.

Other traditions suggest that this return to a heavenly existence might be better understood as a more metaphorical expression. As the Sifre Deuteronomy (Zot Habrakhah 343), for instance, explains what it means to speak of words of Torah "from heaven" in this context:

> "From his right hand a fiery law for his people" (Deut 33:2) tells us that words of Torah are homiletically compared to fire. For just as fire was given from heaven, so words of Torah were given from heaven, as it is said [regarding the fire with which God's speech was manifest], "you *saw* [this is the fire] that I *spoke* [this is the words] to you from heaven" (Exod 20:19). Just as living fire is eternal so living words of Torah are eternal."

Or, as the Song of Songs Rabbah 1:2 passage puts the case using similar language but a different metaphorical vehicle,

> Words of Torah are homiletically compared to water . . . just as living water is eternal, as it is said, "a garden fount, a well of living water" (Song 4:15) so Torah is eternal, as it is said, "they are life to those who find them" (Prov 4:22) and it is written, "[everyone who is thirsty come to the water [of Torah] come and procure and consume it [at no cost]" (Isa 55:1). Just as water is in the heavens, as it is said, "when he sends out [his] voice, waters in the heaven [will go up as clouds]" (Jer 10:13), so Torah is from the heavens, as it is said, "indeed I spoke to you from the heavens" (Exod 20:19). Just as water has many voices, as it is said, "the voice of God on the waters" (Ps 29:3), so Torah [was delivered] in many voices, as it is said, "on the third days at morning there were voices and lightening" (Exod 19:16).

In the context of such images, to say that the words on the first tablets were heavenly is not so much a comment on the locative origins of God's speech in that moment as an attempt to capture the strange nature of this original revelation that escaped: eternal, otherworldly, and unbound by the laws of physical nature.

Other traditions describe these original spoken formulas of the biblical tradition as the hidden treasure of the Torah—a truer, more valuable form of scriptural revelation, which the material written transcript obscures from view. As Midrash Tanhuma (Ha'azinu 3:3) allegorizes this position:

> When Moses went up on high [to receive the first tablets], the angels were ready to kill him. He said to them, "For the sake of these two things that

were given to me . . . you are seeking to kill me?!" When they heard that, they let him be. This can be allegorized as a great merchant who was passing through a dangerous locale. Highway robbers seized him and sought to kill him. He said to them, "For the sake of these five *mina*s that I have in my possession, you're going to kill me?!" They didn't know that he had gemstones and pearls [hidden] in his hand. So they said to each other, "What's the point of killing him? He doesn't have anything [worthwhile] with him." They let him be. But when he entered the city, he began selling priceless gemstones and pearls. The robbers said to him, "Yesterday, we captured you, and you said to us, 'I only have five *mina*s.'" But now you're taking out priceless gemstones and pearls. He replied: "Yesterday, when I said that to you, I was in danger." So, too, Moses our teacher said to the angels, "these two things with me," when he really had in his possession a great gift [hidden] in them. As it is said, "I went up to the heights [. . . and took a gift]" (Ps 68:19). Thus David said, "The Torah from your mouth [is more precious to me than thousands [of pieces of] gold and silver" (Ps 119:72). And he also said, "they are more desirable than gold [more desirable than much refined gold, sweeter than honey, sweeter than honey dripping from the cone]" (Ps 19:11). And it is said, "The utterances of God are pure utterances, [like refined silver[" (Ps 12:7).

This allegory hinges on an understanding that the written text inscribed on the stone tablets was an unattractive possession of little apparent value. By offering the angels this text, Moses is able to convince the angels to lose interest in Israel's spiritual heritage, much as the allegorical merchant was able to persuade his attackers to lose interest in his goods by displaying a few relatively useless coins. What the angels do not realize is that the Written Torah that Moses took down to Israel also included another, infinitely more valuable, component hidden from view—an inheritance that the proof texts identify as "the utterances of God's mouth." While it might be tempting to associate this hidden Torah with the rabbinic oral tradition, the refined silver of Ps 12:7 is more often associated with the biblical heritage in early rabbinic traditions and the vocabulary of dripping honey and sweetness that infuses the associated proof texts is more evocative of the early rabbinic descriptions of the early scriptural speech cited above. The hidden gem that Moses smuggled to Israel in this narrative is thus the intangible Spoken Scripture that invisibly accompanied the written text, a revelation infinitely more powerful and valuable than the visible body of the scriptural text.

As we see here, and in the sources gathered elsewhere in this book, the very first biblical revelation was described as a strange sound that one could see, a single speech act given in many voices, and an eternal revelation that would outlast the decay of this world. To say that this revelation returned to its place, then, might be best understood as a statement that this first revelation returned to its natural state as divine speech when it was freed from the tablets that precariously bound it to a written revelation. Within the early rabbinic mythology of Sinai, therefore, we do encounter images of biblical revelation that align with the notion of a Spoken Scripture. Many classical rabbinic descriptions of Sinai identify a distinctly oral moment in the biblical revelation that was temporarily captured in the first tablets of the law. Like the recited formulas of the biblical tradition, this first spoken iteration of the biblical tradition was coded as a more perfect form of scriptural revelation that was only temporarily and uneasily limited by the written word. This primordial Spoken Scripture did not disappear, moreover, when it was freed from its written form but was instead understood to have returned to exist eternally in its more natural state as a spoken echo of divine speech.

Spoken Scripture as the True Echo of Sinai

If this lost spoken echo of Sinai survived in parallel to the extant biblical text, what form did it take? Some rabbinic thinkers at least understood this lost iteration of the biblical revelation to survive in the memorized spoken formulas of the biblical tradition passed from human mouth to human mouth and read aloud during the synagogue service.

Early rabbinic traditions used a variety of metaphorical vehicles to capture this sense that a spoken biblical revelation was somehow preserved in the memorized spoken formulas of the biblical revelation passed from teacher to student. In Song of Songs Rabbah 1:2, for instance, the recited formulas of the biblical tradition are imagined almost as a physical substance passed from mouth to mouth as they are spoken:

> "Kiss me with the kisses of your mouth." . . . With each and every utterance, an angel would take the spoken utterance from the Holy One . . . and would orally kiss ["each and every member of Israel"] on the mouth (נושקו על פיו).

The phrase על פה serves here as a pun that oscillates between its literal meaning, "on the mouth," and the use of the term in rabbinic parlance, as "orally passed down."

190 CHAPTER 5

As this image is elaborated in Song of Songs Rabbah 4:11, the kiss in question is a deep one that passes the taste of that first spoken revelation from mouth to mouth as it is transmitted:

> What does the verse "honey and milk are under your tongue" (Song 4:11) mean? R. Berekhiah said, "There is no drink more disgusting than the drink that is under the tongue and you are saying, 'honey and milk are under your tongue [as a praise]?!'" ... R. Levi said, "Even one who only recites the spoken formulas of the Bible with its pleasant tunes (הקורא מקרא בענוגו ובניגונו), about him it is said, 'honey and milk are under your tongue, and the scent of your garment is like the scent of Lebanon.' As it is written: 'He approached him and kissed him and [there was] the scent of his garments' (Gen 27:27)."

Here the original spoken iteration of the biblical revelation is passed from mouth to mouth with each recitation of the memorized biblical formulas in a way that almost literally conveys a sweetness traceable back to the divine mouth at Sinai, just as in bShabbat 88b above, one who orally recites (*sheshonim*) scripture subtly partakes in the scent of lilies (*shoshanim*) that was on God's breath at Sinai.

In such traditions, hearing the vocalized formulas of the biblical revelation is imagined to generate a spoken echo in the auditor, who will in turn recite the formulas he has been taught. Hearing the biblical formulas recited thus leads the auditor to roll the formulas around on his own tongue and taste the traces of the first Sinaitic revelation. This vision would seem to explain why *hearing* a recitation of revelation is so often associated with a literal *taste* in classical rabbinic midrash. As Midrash Tanhuma (Ki Tissa 18:9), for instance, obliquely remarks:

> "Sweet dripping [of honey and milk under your tongue]" (Song 4:11). When is this? At the moment when you occupy yourself with Torah. As it says, "honey and milk under your tongue." At the moment when they stood at Mouth Sinai and said, "we will do and we will hear" (Exod 24:7)—at that moment God said to them, "milk and honey are under your tongue" (Song 4:11).

That is, a practitioner's mouth drips with the milk and honey of the first Sinaitic revelation when they read-recite the revelation that can be heard. Or as Ruth Rabbah 5:15 links the sensory experiences of sounded Torah with the sensory experience of taste:

A THIRD TORAH 191

"His heart was cheered [וייטב]" (Ruth 5:15) since he ate sweet things after the meal, which accustoms the tongue to the Torah. Or one might say because he engaged with words of Torah, as it is said, "good [טוב] to me is the Torah of your mouth [תורת פיך]" (Ps 119:72).

More than simple metaphors, such traditions depict the sounded formulas of Spoken Scripture rolling around the tongue of the hearer-reciter, imparting and partaking in a sense of taste that represents a faint trace of the sweetness that issued from the divine mouth at the moment that the first spoken iteration of the scriptural revelation was revealed.

Still other classical rabbinic traditions appear to express this idea by classifying every ritual recitation-reading of the biblical text in synagogue as a reenactment of the opening oral speech acts of Sinai. Ruth Langer and Steven Fraade have pointed out, for instance, that many rabbinic traditions equated the biblical formulas recited aloud during the lectionary with an originary vocal moment of biblical revelation at Mount Sinai.[43] Thus according to bBerakhot 45a, the congregant who read-recited the vocalized formula of the biblical tradition had taken upon himself to reenact the role of God at Mount Sinai while the congregant who recited the Aramaic translation is imagined playing the intermediary role of Moses:

> Rabbi Shimon b. Pazi [said], "Where do we learn that the translator is not permitted to raise his voice over [that of] the reader? As it is said, 'Moses would speak and God would answer him in a voice' (Exod 19:19). Saying 'in a voice' doesn't seem to teach us anything [new]. So what does saying 'in a voice' teach? [That God spoke] in the [same] voice as Moses [בקולו של משה]."

If one understands the biblical revelation to center on the conveyance of a written text, it is difficult to understand this intricate choreography of spoken words declaimed in harmony as a reenactment of the Sinaitic revelation—or even to understand the impetus for making the comparison. But if one understands the first most authentic version of the revelation to have consisted of divine speech translated into human speech, then this dual recitation of two similar but not identical iterations of revelation does indeed take on an aura

---

43. Steven Fraade, "Rabbinic Views on the Practice of Targum, and Multilingualism in the Jewish Galilee of the Third–Sixth Centuries," in *The Galilee in Late Antiquity*, ed. Lee I. Levine (New York: The Jewish Theological Seminary of America, 1992), 266, and Ruth Langer, "From Study of Scripture to a Reenactment of Sinai," *Worship* 72, no. 1 (1998): 43–67.

of reenactment. Indeed, one might even say that these later readings *participate* in this moment of Sinaitic speech in the same sense that God spoke through the "voice of Moses." That is, these moments in which the vocal formulas of the biblical tradition are publicly recited aloud were not merely conceived of as reenactments in a memorial sense but were imagined as participating in some more robust way in the continuation of that first spoken biblical revelation, which had not dissipated when the first tablets were destroyed but was being passed down from mouth to mouth through the generations.

Concluding Remarks

As modern scholars, we have almost universally reproduced in our own studies the official categories of Oral and Written Torah that began to emerge among rabbinic thinkers in the late classical rabbinic period. This binary vision has made it difficult to explain how early rabbinic thinkers could have critiqued, feared, and frequently sought to disengage from written scripture—as this book demonstrates that they did. However, a closer look at early rabbinic discussions surrounding the category of *mikra*, or Spoken Scripture, reveals that many early rabbinic thinkers would simultaneously recognize and trouble the notion of two Torahs that was emerging in classical rabbinic thought by creatively using the terminology applied in the two Torahs traditions to sketch a picture of Spoken Scripture as a third Torah hovering in the interstices between these two products of the final Sinaitic revelation. This third Torah did not destabilize the binary because it was imagined to exist both above and before it—preserving an original spoken iteration of the biblical revelation that had been given at Sinai, briefly encapsulated in the impossible product of the first tablets, but then released from this material form to pass down as the vocalized tradition that would accompany the consonantal transcript through history as an independent witness to the biblical revelation. As an alternate mode of the biblical tradition, this Spoken Scripture could be embraced as a more reliable manifestation of scriptural revelation that bypassed the limitations and dangers of circumscribing the divine will in the medium of writing—a sort of intangible biblical soul to the written Pentateuch's all-too-circumscribed scribal body. Many early rabbinic thinkers were thus untroubled by their doubts about the biblical text in part because that was not, in their conception, where the biblical revelation truly resided.

6

A Closed Book

THE TORAH SCROLL AS THE
BODY OF REVELATION

THE EARLY RABBINIC TRADITIONS gathered in the previous chapters paint a vivid picture of what it looks like when a written text ceases to "speak" as a communicative document for those who embrace it as scripture. What remains to explore is how these early rabbinic thinkers conceptualized these silent material copies of the Hebrew Bible. What exactly did they take this physical scroll to represent? How precisely did they understand this tangible manifestation of divine knowledge to function? Yet with these queries, we arrive at one of the most vexed topics in the field of biblical reception history. While the field of biblical studies more generally has been content to collapse the contents of the biblical texts with their varied material manifestations, researchers who seek to disentangle the hermeneutic facets of scripture from their artifactual manifestations[1] have found it surprisingly difficult to theorize the ways in which historical practitioners have related to tangible embodiments of their sacred texts. The Torah scroll represents one of the most stable material representations of the Bible in history and has accrued to itself a surprisingly narrow and unchanging set of ritual honorifics over the course of

---

1. Accepting Marianne Schleicher's proposal that we adopt the term "hermeneutical use of scripture" to denaturalize textual engagement with written scripture (Marianne Schleicher, "Artifactual and Hermeneutical Use of Scripture in Jewish Tradition," in *Jewish and Christian Scripture as Artifact and Canon,* ed. Craig A. Evans and H. Daniel Zacharias [London: Bloomsbury, 2011], 50) as a complement to Brian Malley's terminology for "artifactual" modes of relating to the material facets of biblical writings (Brian Malley, *How the Bible Works: An Anthropological Study of Evangelical Biblicism* [Lanham, MD: AltaMira, 2004], 41–48).

194   CHAPTER 6

centuries.[2] And yet, scholars have spent decades seeking an adequate conceptual language to capture the theoretical contours of the rabbinic relationship with the Torah scroll, without arriving at a consensus.[3]

At the heart of this ongoing struggle, it seems to me, is the extent to which the notion of an iconic text is at war with itself, at least in the early rabbinic context. Researchers in this area of early rabbinic book history have generally sought to explain the iconic or ritual power attributed to the Torah scroll as an extension of its iconic textual contents.[4] But when one looks at the early rab-

2. As David Stern as vividly shown in *The Jewish Bible: A Material History* (Seattle: University of Washington Press, 2019).

3. To cite a small selection of examples: David Ganz and Barbara Schellewald write of "clothing sacred scripture" through a "transformation and adaptation of elements that come from cult religion." David Ganz, "Clothing Sacred Scriptures: Materiality and Aesthetics in Medieval Book Religions," in *Clothing Sacred Scriptures: Book Art and Book Religion in Christian, Islamic, and Jewish Cultures,* ed. David Ganz and Barbara Schellewald (Berlin: de Gruyter, 2018), 5. Catherine Hezser and Shalom Sabar have both described the "magical" usage of Torah scrolls, pointing out that a "belief in the sacredness of the Torah seems to have sometimes led to a magical understand of the power inherent in the biblical text . . . whether in the form of Torah scrolls, mezuzot, tefillin, amulets, or tattoos on one's skin." Catherine Hezser, *Jewish Literacy in Roman Palestine* (Tübingen: Mohr Siebeck, 2001), 210–20. See also Shalom Sabar, "The Torah Scroll and Its Appurtenances as Magical Objects in Traditional Jewish Culture," *European Journal of Jewish Studies* 3, no. 1 (2009), 135–70. Following the introduction of the term by anthropologist Brian Malley, *How the Bible Works,* 40–48 and 70–72=, David Stern and Marianne Schleicher have called this the "artifactual power of the Torah Scroll," which Stern argues means that "as the Sefer Torah was used less for regular study . . . it became a ritual artifact in the synagogue service" and these "para-material elements came to endow the Sefer Torah with the status of a cult object" (Stern, *Jewish Bible,* 40). Marianne Schleicher suggests it means that "the Torah is more than just a text, it is an artifact, that is, a manipulable object that attracts personal and cultural representations" (Marianne Schleicher, "Accounts of a Dying Torah Scroll: On Jewish Handling of Sacred Texts in Need of Restoration or Disposal," in *The Death of Sacred Texts: Ritual Disposal and Renovation of Texts in World Religions,* ed. Kristina Myrvold [London: Routledge, 2010], 11). Karel van der Toorn, James Watt, and Zeev Elitzur have tried to capture this transformation by invoking different facets of the language of scripture as "icon"—arguing that, like ancient and late antique cult symbols of the divinity, the Torah came to be understood as in some sense a material "incarnation of the deity." Karel van der Toorn, *The Image and the Book: Iconic Cults, Aniconism, and the Rise of Book Religion in Israel and the Ancient Near East* (Leuven: Peeters, 1998). See also Zeev Elitzur, "Between the Textual and the Visual: Borderlines of Late Antique Book Iconicity," *Postscripts* 6 (2010): 83–99, and James Watts, *Iconic Books and Texts* (Sheffield: Equinox, 2015).

4. While scholars such as David Stern have reminded us that "the iconic features of the Torah Scroll endow it with an aura of sanctity that extended *far beyond* its status as the conveyor

A CLOSED BOOK 195

binic rituals that surrounded the biblical text with an aura of heightened supernatural power, these ritual gestures most often served to quarantine the
communicative message of that text within a ritual object that was *closed* to
interpretative scrutiny—whether literally or figuratively. In other words, the
Hebrew Bible was at its most powerful as a ritual icon in the rabbinic period
precisely when its textual facets were silenced. How then are we to understand
a sacred book that accrued supernatural power precisely when it thwarted its
own bookishness, by obscuring or hiding its sacred textual contents? At the
risk of adding yet another conceptual frame to a long list of attempts to capture
this elusive phenomenon, this chapter argues that we can begin to understand
the apparent paradox if we take seriously early rabbinic traditions that imagined the Torah scroll less as a material *object* than as a biological *body*.

In doing so, I take my cue from several scholars of South and East Asian
religion who have argued that diverse phenomena categorized in the scholarly
literature as forms of book cult are only fully elucidated when we take seriously
communal traditions that ascribe the sacred texts in question with bodily
qualities—identifying the honored book in complex but literal ways with the
body of the guru, sage, or god who gave it. In an early article in this vein, for
instance, Nikky Guninder Kaur Singh argued that Sikh practices of personal
care and relationality toward the Adi Granth (putting it to bed at night, fan-
ning the book with a whisk, approaching the text with heads covered and feet
bare, bowing before it, dressing the book daily in brocades and silks, and engaging in interpersonal consultation through bibliomancy-like reading practices) should not be dismissed as empty symbolism but recognized as embodied expressions of the tradition that "the same light, the same message, and the
same physicality was carried on from Nanak to Guru Angad and to his succes-
sor Gurus. Until the historical succession from Nanak to Angad etched in the
Tenth Guru's memory is eventually reproduced by him and he invests the
Granth with Guruship."[5] In the same way that the human line of gurus mystically partook in a shared physicality, so the textual body of the Granth is revered for participating in this shared embodiment of guruship. In some instances, a sacred book may be envisioned as embodying its divine originator

---

of a divinely inspired text" (Stern, *Jewish Bible*, 55, emphasis added), Stern and many of the
authors cited in the notes above have nevertheless imagined the ritual iconicity ascribed to the
Torah scroll to derive, ultimately, from the iconic nature of its *textual contents*.

5. Nikky-Guninder Kaur Singh, "The Body of the Gurus: Sikh Scripture from a Contemporary Feminist Perspective," *Religious Studies and Theology* 23, no. 2 (2004): 27 and 33.

in an iconic body, as a *murti* (living icon) might do.[6] But in many cases, such traditions highlight the connections between the biological sinews that bind a book and those that support the human body—between the linguistic breaths marked within its pages and those that will be breathed by human readers.[7] When practitioners are steeped in such biologically themed traditions, there is perhaps a more literal fleshy sense at play when a practitioner is said to revere "scripture as an embodied person of a Buddha" so that handling a Dharma discourse was comparable to touching a relic of the Buddha's body.[8]

If the notion is not immediately legible to us that a parchment document might partake in qualities of bodily sacrality, we would do well to remember Webb Keane's argument that functionally analogous (perhaps even identical) processes of what he calls semiotic transduction are at work transforming "from invisible to visible, from immaterial to material, and from intelligible to sensible" when divine words are rendered in material script or a spirit enters a body.[9] Given the similarities in the abstract processes believed to be work in these various transformations of divine intangibles into material realities, perhaps we should not be surprised that diverse iterations of these phenomena are often thought to converge in the instantiation of a carnal book.

In keeping with these insights drawn from cognate fields, I would maintain that we should not read the bodily imagery associated with the Torah scroll in rabbinic tradition in the weak historical sense that has typically been ascribed to the carnal book metaphor in the history of Christian (and by extension Jewish) biblical interpretation,[10] but rather in more robust terms similar those proposed by James Kearney. Kearney has argued that the notion of a carnal scripture often served historical Christian communities as a locus to explore

---

6. Joanne Punzo Waghorne, "A Birthday Party for a Sacred Text: The Gita Jayanti and the Embodiment of God as the Book and the Book as God," *Postscripts* 6 (2010): 241.

7. Vesna A. Wallace, "The Body as a Text and the Text as the Body: A View from the *Kālacakratantra*'s Perspective," in *As Long as Space Endures: Essays on the Kālacakra Tantra in Honor of H. H. The Dalai Lama*, ed. Edward A. Arnold (Ithaca, NY: Snow Lion, 2009), 183.

8. James B. Apples, "The Phrase dharmaparyāyo hastagato in Mahāyāna Buddhist Literature: Rethinking the Cult of the Book in Middle Period Indian Mahāyāna Buddhism," *Journal of the American Oriental Society* 134, no. 1 (2014): 33 and 43.

9. Webb Keane, "On Spirit Writing: Materialities of Language and the Religious Word of Transduction," *Journal of the Royal Anthropological Institute* 19, no. 1 (2013): 10, 2, and 3.

10. See Beryl Smalley, *The Study of the Bible in the Middle Ages* (South Bend, IN: University of Notre Dame Press, 1964), 1, for a classic treatment tracing the development of the metaphor that "scripture . . . like man has a body and soul. The body is the words of the sacred text, the 'letter,' and the literal meaning; the soul is the spiritual sense."

a fundamental dialectic between divine immanence and transcendence,[11] inasmuch as a sacred book written on the skin of dead animals came to serve as a symbol of the death and decay that adheres to all living things, so that the body of scripture "was both glorified and corrupt"—a daily manifestation of how divinity made immanent is simultaneously condemned to degradation and decay.[12] While this metaphor was not further enlivened in the rabbinic imaginary by the struggle to conceive an incarnate deity, elaborate systems *had* been developed in rabbinic thought and practice to deal with an analogous problem: the fact that the intangible powers of the human spirit gained agency in the world only through the constantly unraveling materiality of the human body.[13]

Nor should we be surprised by the notion that early rabbinic sages thought the problem of an all-to-material parchment revelation through the analogy of an ensouled human body. Anne Kreps, Adam Zachary Newton, and Jeffrey Tigay have recently reminded us of the extent to which "special books possessed the qualities of people"[14] in the rabbinic legal tradition so that often the

11. James Kearney, *The Incarnate Text: Imagining the Book in Reformation England* (Philadelphia: University of Pennsylvania Press, 2009), 15

12. Ibid., 17. For a full-length study of the ways in which the "logos occupied both body and book" in some strains of early Christian thought, producing a "conflation of books and people," see Anne Kreps, *The Crucified Book: Sacred Writing in the Age of Valentinus* (Philadelphia: University of Pennsylvania Press: 2022), 43 .

13. Indeed, Reuven Kimelman has argued that rabbinic literature makes the analogy between the immanence of God and the immanence of the human soul explicit. Reuven Kimelman, "The Rabbinic Theology of the Physical: blessings, body and soul, resurrection, and the covenant and election," in *Cambridge History of Judaism*, vol. 4, *The Rabbinic Period*, ed. Steven Katz (Cambridge: Cambridge University Press, 2006), 953. While Daniel Boyarin's *Carnal Israel* (Berkeley: University of California Press, 1993) firmly established that rabbinic Judaism resisted a Hellenistic antithesis between body and soul, many recent authors have sought to reconstruct more nuanced models of the fraught relationship between the tangible and intangible facets of the human subject. For a recent full-length study of the subject see Ishay Rosen-Zvi, *Body and Soul in Ancient Judaism* (Tel Aviv: Modan, 2012) (in Hebrew). For very recent contributions to the topic see Carol Newsom, "In Search of Cultural Models for Divine Spirit and Human Bodies," *Vetus Testamentum* 70, no. 1 (2020): 104–23 and the literature cited there. For the purposes of this chapter, we will accept at the very least the minimal sense of faceting or bifurcation described by Mira Balberg: "There is absolutely no denying that Mishnaic law assumes that each individual has an aspect of will, intention, and self-reflection, as well as an object-like aspect (that is, a material body) in which he or she is not different from animal and inanimate objects, and that these two aspects are not necessarily commensurate." Mira Balberg, *Purity, Body, and Self in Early Rabbinic Literature* (Berkeley: University of California Press, 2014), 50.

14. Kreps, *The Crucified Book*, 96.

concept of "persons and scrolls converge"[15]—or as Tigay puts it, a scroll acts as an "embodiment of God's presence" similar to a modern icon or an ancient idol.[16] I am simply arguing that we take this equivalency more literally and biologically than we have done to date. As Laura Lieber recently pointed out, Samaritan and Jewish liturgical poets not only dramatized and personified scripture—understanding canon as "as possessing properties of agency"[17]—but also concretized these images in ritual relations to the Torah scroll.[18] In other words, she argues that these liturgical performances personified Torah "both conceptually (how poems personify Torah) and performatively (how the physical presence of the Torah in ritual influences composition and reception)."[19]

Moreover, this literalized enmeshing of physical scripture and a personifying imaginary harmonizes with recent research about how the material world, text, and body were aligned in late antique Jewish thought. Michael Swartz has shown, for instance, that many late antique Jews approached the world itself as a form of text, inasmuch as "God embedded signs in the world that could be read by human beings with proper knowledge and consciousness."[20] While Mira Balberg has recently demonstrated specifically that early rabbinic authorities participated in late antique Mediterranean practices of bodily hermeneutics (the idea that the body "can be read like a book").[21] And, as we saw in the South and East Asian studies literature cited above, such processes are often reversible. In systems where bodies are read as books, books may also be read as bodies.

This chapter therefore argues that we should read early rabbinic practices of ritualized reverence for the Torah scroll through the logic of early rabbinic practices of human bodily sacralization. According to the elaborate systems of

15. Adam Zachary Newton, *To Make the Hands Impure: Art, Ethical Adventure, the Difficult and the Holy* (New York: Fordham University Press, 2016), 26.

16. Jeffrey H. Tigay, "The Torah Scroll and God's Presence," in *Built by Wisdom, Established by Understanding: Essays in Biblical and Near Eastern Literature in Honor of Adele Berlin*, ed. M. C. Grossman (University Park: Pennsylvania State Press, 2013), 325.

17. Laura S. Lieber, "Scripture Personified: Torah as Character in the Hymns of Marqah," *Jewish Studies Quarterly* 24, no. 3 (2017): 196.

18. Ibid., 197.

19. Ibid., 198.

20. Michael Swartz, *The Signifying Creator: Nontextual Sources of Meaning in Ancient Judaism* (New York University Press, 2012), 2.

21. Mira Balberg, "Rabbinic Authority, Medieval Rhetoric, and Body Hermeneutics in Mishnah Nega'im," *Association for Jewish Studies Review* 35, no. 2 (2011): 323–46.

practice imagined to address this challenge in rabbinic circles,[22] the human body served most powerfully as a conduit for intangible sacred forces when its orifices were closed,[23] its surfaces were clean of bodily detritus,[24] and its more animal bodily facets were covered[25]—so that its inner parts and workings were hidden from view, its fluids kept from leaking, and the constantly degrading grit of its materiality obscured from both perception and consciousness in the temporary wholeness of health and dignity.[26] As we will see in the

22. While it has been argued that archeological remains suggest nonpriestly purity practices were widespread well into the rabbinic period, (Eyal Regev, "Pure Individualism: The Idea of Non-Priestly Purity in Ancient Judaism," *Journal for the Study of Judaism* 31 [2000]: 176–202), for the sake of this chapter I will adopt the method of Mira Balberg and focus on what it meant to *imagine* or *conceptualize* Temple-based purity laws in a post-Temple world. On which, see also Ayelet Hoffman Libson, "In the Shadow of Doubt: Expertise, Knowledge, and Systematization of Rabbinic Purity Laws," *Association for Jewish Studies Review* 44, no. 1 (2020): 99–118. Moreover, it must be remembered that the rabbinic conception of human bodily sacrality and "purity" went well beyond the technicalities of biblical ritual purity—incorporating into the mental map of Temple purity many substances and categories that were of no significance in biblical laws of ritual purity, particularly questions surrounding excreted biologics such as feces and urine and problems of visibility concerning intimate nakedness. See R. R. Neis, "'Their Backs toward the Temple, and Their Faces toward the East': The Temple and Toilet Practices in Rabbinic Palestine and Babylonia," *Journal for the Study of Judaism* 43, no. 3 (2012): 328–68.

23. In saying this, I do not mean to deny Mira Balberg's more abstract reading of the early rabbinic "construction of the body as a fluid and modular entity whose boundaries are in constant flux . . . in which the body is identical to the self only insofar as the body is invested with subjectivity" (Balberg, *Purity*, 15). Rather I intend to draw attention to another, more practical aspect, of the rabbinic vision of the human body and its ability to become sacralized: the fact that the ability to become ritually pure or impure "depends upon wholeness" so that the imaginary of ritual impurity "situates the object or person in question as more complete, perfected, and consequential than objects or persons that are incapable of becoming impure" (123).

24. In this case I do not mean ritually pure so much as literally clean from feces and urine, as well as the many ritually impurifying fluids the rabbinic system inherited from biblical literature. On the incorporation of toileting practices into rabbinic systems of mental mapping concerning the Temple imaginary, see Neis, "Backs toward the Temple."

25. On the face as a particularly human facet of the human body, see R. R. Neis, "Fetus, Flesh, Food: Generating Bodies of Knowledge in Rabbinic Science," *Journal of Ancient Judaism* 10, no. 2 (2019): 181–210.

26. I intend here rabbinic traditions that imagine everyday practices of prayer or purity since vestigial priestly practices such as holiday blessings appear to have functioned according to a unique set of rules centering particularly on the visuality of the communal gaze on the priestly body. See Julia Watts Belser, "Reading Talmudic Bodies: Disability, Narrative, and the Gaze in Rabbinic Judaism," in *Disability in Judaism, Christianity, and Islam*, ed. Darla Schumm and Michael Stoltzfus (London: Palgrave Macmillan, 2011), 5–27.

coming pages, the body of revelation was likewise at the height of its super-natural powers when its material frailties were effaced by being closed in and obscured from view. Just as a rabbinic husband and wife might briefly disrobe and open their crevices to know each other (though never in the presence of sacred objects, space, or ritual),[27] so the Torah scroll was periodically un-wrapped and opened for a few moments so that its textual contents might be read out to its congregational partners. But like the inner parts of the human bodies and their biological products, it was only when the limiting materiality of the written text was contained and hidden from view that the textual vessel would become a silent conduit for a more intangible and otherworldly power. In many of the most vivid accounts of the Torah scroll and its power, the scroll thus functions less as a written communication than as a form of revelation personified—an embodied avatar of sacred knowledge and the conduit that revelation creates between the human and the divine.

Holiness and Power Do Not Derive from the Contents of the Text

As a first step toward reconceptualizing the nature of the supernatural power being ascribed to the scriptural scroll-body, we must unthink certain anachro-nistic presuppositions about *how* that the Torah scroll took on its mantle of superadded ritual power in the classical rabbinic context. In late antique rab-binic traditions, the communicative contents of scripture in and of themselves do not appear to have been conceived as conveying sacrality upon the scrolls that contain them. As we will see in more detail in the coming pages, the aura of ritual sanctity that surrounds the Torah scroll in the classical rabbinic imagi-nary was not thought to derive from the sacredness of its communicative con-tents as such.

At the most basic level, it is clear that the iconic status acquired by the Torah scroll in classical rabbinic practice was not thought to derive from the funda-mental sanctity of its sacred *message*, since even small technical deviations from the scribal ideal in the finished product were enough to dissipate the aura of sanctity that might otherwise adhere to the Torah scroll—even when the contents of the biblical message remained entirely intact. Thus, for instance, a biblical text could not be put into ritual use if one wrote the correct letter in the wrong scribal form (switching the medial and final form of the letter), if

27. See, for instance, bBerakhot 25b and yBerakhot 3:5 (6d).

the correct passage was inscribed with the wrong formatting (inscribing prose in the format for poetry or poetry in the format for prose), if the letters were not surrounded with a ritually sufficient amount of white space, if the correct lettering and formatting were inscribed in the wrong script, or if individual letters became worn or marred beyond the bounds of legibility.[28] While the communicative *message* remained intact in such cases, any deviation from the scribal writing conventions prescribed for this ritual object was enough to dissipate the heightened ritual sanctity that would otherwise have adhered to the biblical text as a ritual artifact.

Nor did the above rulings simply reflect a heightened level of scribal exactitude concerning the formatting or presentation of an iconic text. Other rabbinic rulings declare that even a model biblical text transcribed in the right script and formatting would be invalidated if it deviated in invisible ways from the parameters prescribed for Torah scroll: if it were inscribed on the wrong type of parchment,[29] written in the wrong type of black ink,[30] or bound with the wrong type of sinews.[31] The invalidation of scrolls that adhered in all visible ways to the color, shape, formatting, and lettering of a valid scroll suggests that even the most meticulous transmission of the textual message was not enough to generate the superadded aura of sanctity ascribed to the Torah scroll.

Some early rabbinic rulings, in fact, suggest that even a perfect combination of scribal conventions, ritual materials, and textual exactitude was not in itself enough to produce a Torah scroll that could function as a ritual icon. Even a perfectly executed biblical text that adhered to all scribal and ritual parameters would be rendered devoid of superadded ritual sanctity, for instance, if it were produced by the wrong type of scribe. While early rabbinic norms concerning what categories of person might represent an appropriate scribe varied,[32] it

28. See, for instance, Sifre Deuteronomy 36, yMegillah 1:9 (71d), bMenahot 30a, BShabbat 103b and parallels.

29. Whether that means the parchment from a nonkosher animal (as in the parallel case described in bShabbat 28b) or more likely a ritually invalid form of parchment preparation (as in mMegillah 2:2, yMegillah 2:2 (72d), bShabbat 79a and parallels). For a classic survey of rabbinic strictures on parchment and parchment making, see Menachem Haran, "Bible Scrolls in Eastern and Western Jewish Communities from Qumran to the High Middle Ages," *Hebrew Union College Annual* 56 (1985): 21–62.

30. MMegillah 2:2, ySotah 2:4 (18a), bMegillah 17a, bEruvin 13a, BShabbat 115b and parallels.

31. BMakkot 11a and parallels.

32. TAvodah Zarah 3:6–7, bMenahot 42b, bGittin 45b and parallels.

was accepted as a general principle that a biblical text that had been perfectly inscribed by a ritually inappropriate scribe did not acquire sanctity from its textual contents. Indeed, even a correct scribe who produced a perfect text but without the appropriate level of spiritual attention could not produce a biblical text with aura of sanctity that adhered to the Torah scroll as a ritual object.[33] Taken as a whole, such rulings suggest that even perfectly correct scriptural contents put to parchment in a text that adhered exactly to the ritually prescribed forms were not in themselves capable of creating an iconic text with a heightened level of ritual sanctity. Wherever the magic of a Torah scroll might lie according to the classical rabbinic imaginary, it was not in the textual contents.

The Most Powerful Book Is a Closed Book

Quite the contrary. When one considers early rabbinic traditions on the topic thematically, it emerges that the most ritually powerful forms of sacred writings in the classical rabbinic tradition were frequently those that had been made illegible—whether through erasure, enclosure, or some other means. In the rabbinic imaginary, the most supernaturally powerful book was an unreadable book.

The most literal instantiations of this principle appear in rabbinic reimaginings of the *sotah* ritual for a wife accused of adultery. In the biblical account of this ritual, we certainly encounter foreshadowing of the ritual power that early rabbinic traditions will ascribe to sacred texts that have been rendered illegible in some way. In the biblical account of the *sotah* ritual, the priest first orally narrates the testing oath and curse to a woman accused of adultery and receives her affirmation of understanding, then he ritually amplifies this oral act of swearing-in by writing the oath-curses on a scroll and scraping the words off into the water of testing that she is about to consume (Num 5:23). The act of writing and erasing thus already functions as a means of making the oath-ordeal ritual more efficacious or imposing in some way. How the ritual principle concerning erased writing in this biblical tradition was thought to work seems to have remained fluid, however, as late antique inheritors of this textual tradition do not appear to have agreed on precisely how the acts of writing and erasing were supposed to function in the ritual—or even what type of text was being written and erased.[34] With such an ambiguous interpretive inheritance

33. BGittin 54b and parallels.

34. Philo and Josephus, for instance, each imagine not only a different set of steps for the ritual of writing and erasing in their depictions of this biblical ritual but even envision different

A CLOSED BOOK 203

to work with, early rabbinic portrayals of the *sotah* ritual thus represent a uniquely rabbinic vision, largely unbound by practical ritual history,[35] the biblical inheritance, or any widespread late antique interpretative tradition.

In early rabbinic renderings of the *sotah* ritual, the act of writing and erasing has become a ceremony that ritualized the destruction of sacred scripture. When mSotah 2:3 imagines the priest copying out verses from the *sotah* passage in Numbers, these verses are no longer simply descriptions of ritual speech and action but have become scriptural excerpts. As mYoma 3:10 puts it, the officiating priest writes out "the biblical lectionary regarding the *sotah* (פרשת סוטה)." Nor was the language of a "biblical lectionary" apparently understood as a mere figure of speech. *Sotah* scrolls were understood to "impurify the hands"—that is, the scroll transcribed in the process of the *sotah* ritual was ruled to have the ritual status of a valid biblical scroll (ySotah 2:4 [11b]). If the ritual was aborted before the text was blotted out or if the priest continued his copying beyond the short excerpt prescribed for erasure, the scroll produced by the rabbinic *sotah* ritual required *genizah* (the passive ritual destruction to which biblical scrolls were assigned) (mSotah 3:3, tSotah 2:2, ySotah 2:4 [11b]). Later legal discussions further cement the scroll's biblical status by treating the biblical passage copied out in the *sotah* ritual as an important

---

texts being transcribed. Josephus separates the acts of writing and erasing in his ritual steps and imagines the writing in question to be limited to the name of God, which is invoked as a form of divine witness to the oral swearing in ceremony (Josephus, *Antiquities* 3.11.6 (ed. Ralph Marcus [Cambridge, MA: Harvard University Press, 1943], 272). Philo also imagines the role of writing in this ritual as a form of performative testimony that amplifies the strength of the oral warning ceremony but identifies the text as a transcription of the priest's warning (Philo, *On the Special Laws* 3.62, ed. Francis Henry Colson [Cambridge: Harvard University Press, 1958], 512). Thus, in addition to their shared tendency to downplay the ritual power attributed to erased writing, the lack of concord between these two prominent late antique renderings of the *sotah* rituals suggests that the ritual emphasis that will be placed on the act of writing and erasing in early rabbinic interpretations of this ritual should be studied as independent rabbinic developments rather than a straightforward inheritance from the biblical past.

35. I claim this with one caveat, however: classical rabbinic visions of the *sotah* ritual may have represented more than a form of exegetical imagination. Medieval sources suggest that some post–70 CE rabbinic communities may have continued to enact the *sotah* ritual in modified forms, even sometimes publicly in synagogues. See, for instance, Robert Bonfil, *History and Folklore in Medieval Jewish Chronicle: The Family Chronicle of Ahima'az ben Paltiel* (Leiden: Brill, 2009), 254–55; Lisa Grushkow, *Writing the Wayward Wife: Rabbinic Interpretations of Sotah* (Leiden: Brill, 2016), 297–300, Yuval Harari, "The Scroll of Ahima'az and Jewish Magical Culture: A Note on the Ordeal of the Adulteress," *Tarbiz* 75 (2005–2006): 185–202 (in Hebrew); Leo Mock, "The Synagogue as a Stage for Magic," *Zutot* 3 (2002): 8–14; and Michael Swartz, "Temple Ritual in Jewish Magical Literature," *Pe'amim* 85 (2000): 63–67 [in Hebrew].

precedent in debates such as whether a single biblical passage may be copied separately from a full Torah scroll (bGittin 60a). Classical rabbinic descriptions of the writing materials used in the ritual also emphasize this scripturalization of the writing in the *sotah* ritual. The *sotah* scroll may "not be written on a writing board, nor papyrus, nor *diftera* (a ritually invalid parchment)" and it "may not be written in *komos* (gum ink) nor *kankantom* (metal ink)" but may only be inscribed on a parchment scroll suitable for biblical writing in ink certified for biblical scrolls (mSotah 2:4, ySotah 2:4 (18a), bSotah 17a–b). In rabbinic accounts of the *sotah* ritual, the ritual writing to be erased had thus become a form of miniature biblical scroll.

While early rabbinic accounts of the *sotah* ritual express considerable concern about the dangers and indignities adhering to the process of erasing sacred scripture,[36] they dedicate more imaginative energy to delineating the uncanny ritual power produced by a process in which scripture is rendered illegible so that it might enter the human body. The most famous example of this imaginative energy is likely the elaborate descriptions of the variegated physical punishments that will be inflicted upon the guilty wife by the erasure waters. Indeed, many early rabbinic accounts of the *sotah* ritual imagine the dramatic height of the ritual as a moment in which the priest explains to the woman on trial the powers of the bitter waters, which will selectively roll off the "living flesh" of a clean woman but "eat into and penetrate" the spiritually "wounded flesh" of an unclean woman (tSotah 1:6, ySotah 1:7 [16d], Sifre Numbers 12). The unhappy results of this absorption are described in meticulous and almost pornographic detail in each strata of early rabbinic literature: her face will turn green or yellow, her eyes will pop out, her fingernails will fall off, her thighs will fall, and her belly will swell (mSotah 3:4, ySotah 3:4 [18c], bSotah 20b). Unlike a natural (if spiritually selective) poison, moreover, the erasure waters take lasting possession of the body that they enter so that they not only "check her now" but will wreak their havoc even if she were to newly "defile herself ten years in the future" (tSotah 2:2). But if she remains innocent of adultery, her body will be permanently transformed by the waters in (what is perceived as) a positive way so that if she naturally produced girl babies, she will now produce boy babies; if she naturally produced ugly offspring, she will now produce beautiful children; if her children were naturally dark, their siblings will now be fair; if they were naturally short, she will now produce tall

---

36. On which, see the extensive discussion in Ishay Rosen-Zvi, *The Mishnaic Sotah Ritual: Temple, Gender, and Midrash,* Supplements to the Journal for the Study of Judaism 160 (Leiden: Brill, 2012), 49–66, especially 50ff and 63ff.

children, and so forth (ySotah 3:4 [18d]). Left untouched, the scriptural passages of the *sotah* ritual need only be quietly archived along with other biblical texts that cannot be put to ritual use; but when erased, they become a potent force able to wreak radical changes for both good and ill in perpetuity.

Early rabbinic renderings of the Sotah ritual, moreover, subtly reflect upon this opposition between communicative consumption and embodied consumption. As Sarit Kattan Gribetz has pointed out, "the locus classicus for the rabbinic ban on teaching and transmitting Torah to women was embedded within the Mishnah's discussion of . . . the *sotah* ritual, in which a woman physically consumes a text in order to condemn or vindicate her body."[37] With the ironic result that the debate about whether women are permitted literary consumption of Torah is framed through an account of a woman who literally consumes a portion of the Torah, so that "a woman accused of adultery must participate in an embodied transmission of a text she is otherwise prohibited from studying or consuming."[38] Such passages thus further emphasize that the supernaturally potent Bible absorbed into a woman's body in this ritual is unreadable in multiform ways.

The early rabbinic imagination similarly depicted phylacteries and mezuzot (doorpost scrolls) as powerful forms of biblical writing made invisible. Much like the biblical passages excerpted in the *sotah* scroll, the biblical passages contained in the phylacteries and the mezuzah were ritually scripturalized in the early rabbinic imagination to the point that they were equated with the Torah scroll itself in many traditions. As mMegillah 1:8 puts it:

> There is no [difference] between Torah scrolls and phylacteries and mezuzot except that Torah scrolls may be written in any language [in addition to Hebrew square script] and phylacteries and mezuzot are only permitted to be written in square script. [But] Rabban Shimon b. Gamliel says even Torah scrolls are only allowed to be written in Greek, [so it is actually a very small difference].

As was true regarding the *sotah* scroll, rabbinic traditions speak of phylacteries and mezuzot in the formal terminology used to mark canonical scriptural writing. Like a ritually valid Torah scroll or other biblical book, phylacteries

---

37. Sarit Kattan Gribetz, "Consuming Text: Women as Recipients and Transmitters of Ancient Texts," in *Rethinking "Authority" in Late Antiquity Authorship, Law, and Transmission in Jewish and Christian Tradition*, ed. A. J. Berkovitz and Mark Letteney (London: Routledge, 2018), 181.

38. Ibid., 183.

206 CHAPTER 6

(mYadayim 3:3) and mezuzot (bShabbat 79b) are both declared to "impurify the hands"—the technical terminology used to mark writings as part of the biblical oeuvre.

While these objects retained the status of scripture in general, it was their *closedness* that seems to have uniquely defined phylacteries and mezuzot as ritual objects.[39] A phylactery that had come in contact with ritual impurity, for instance, was immersed closed in its box—on the grounds that being shut up is its essential state. As mMikva'ot 10:2 puts it,

> A mattress or leather cushion, these need water to come inside of them [during ritual immersion]. A round cushion, a ball, a [shoe or cap] last, an amulet, and a phylactery, these do not need water to flow inside of them [during ritual immersion]. This is the rule: anything for which it is not part of its nature to take things in and out, one immerses it closed [כל שאין דרכו להכניס ולהוציא טובלים סתומים].

The very inaccessibility of the biblical texts transformed them from didactic documents into a novel form of ritual power object.

Why should this be the case? In the absence of a superficially legible biblical text, the entire physical object came to take on the status and power of the Bible in continuity with its contents. Unlike a superficially analogous amulet, the unique continuity of an entire phylactery as a biblical artifact transforms even the letter *shin* embossed on the head box and the knots of the straps shaped like the letters *dalet* and *yud* into sacred letters that not only symbolize a biblical name of God Shaddai (bShabbat 62a) but actually represent a form of ritual writing with all of the restrictions attending to biblical text.[40] For in many early rabbinic traditions, it is not only the biblical texts contained *within* these objects that take on the scriptural status of a canonical object that "impurifies the hands" but also their ritual containers (mYadayim 3:3, bShabbat

---

39. And yet, this is not simply a reflection of amuletic practices in late antique Palestine—for as Megan Nutzman has demonstrated, not all amulets in this contexts were closed amulets and even amulets containing biblical text took a broader range of amuletic forms than we sometimes imagine (*Contested Cures: Identity and Ritual Healing in Roman and Late Antique Palestine* [Edinburgh: Edinburgh University Press, 2022], 15–70).

40. BShabbat 61b–62a captures the unique ritual continuity of these closed biblical objects, for example, by contrasting them with a "leather-covered amulet" which contains names "of sanctity" but does not itself become a sacred object in the same way that the physical analog of a "leather-covered tefillin" containing unreadable biblical passages will render its casing a sacred object carrying the elevated ritual status of its hidden contents.

A CLOSED BOOK 207

79b and parallels). To touch the housing of a phylactery or a mezuzah is to touch scripture. In rulings such as these, the act of enclosing a biblical text transfuses its power throughout the object that encloses it.

The act of making a biblical text illegible via enclosure appears not only to transfer its spiritual power to the resulting object but even to transform or amplify that power into a different kind of supernatural force. While books of sacred homiletic material that contained verses of biblical text had shown significant supernatural power in other contexts,[41] for instance, Rabbi Nahman would nevertheless leave such a book outside the foul and demon-filled territory of the privy for the book's own protection. Yet he would bring his phylacteries with him when he entered a privy, on the grounds that he would "be protected" in a different, and more robust, way from whatever supernatural dangers awaited him inside by the biblical texts amplified inside the phylacteries (bBerakhot 23b). It is the different quality of the supernatural power adhering to these two types of biblical verses that scholars point to when they note the powerful "apotropaic" and even magical qualities that are often ascribed to phylacteries and mezuzot in early rabbinic traditions.[42]

The apotropaic powers ascribed to these closed objects are frequently portrayed as entirely independent of the communicative message they contain, dependent instead on how the ritual object is deployed. In the Targum to Song of Songs, for instance, the people of Israel emphatically declare that "no demons can harm me" so long as their mezuzot and phylacteries are placed correctly (Targum Song of Songs 8:3). Traditions such as Mekhilta de Rabbi Yishmael Bo 11 suggest likewise that it is the ritual object itself—rather than the commandment or divine good will associated with it—that is "effective" (נוהג) against harm. As Mekhilta de Rabbi Yishmael puts it:

> Do we not learn from an *argumentum a fortiori* that if the blood of the paschal sacrifice in Egypt [protected the Israelites against the destroyer], even though it was only for an hour and it was not effective day and night and

---

41. See, for instance, Rebecca Scharbach Wollenberg, "The Dangers of Reading as We Know It: Sight Reading as a Source of Heresy in Classical Rabbinic Literature," *Journal of the American Academy of Religion* 85, no. 3 (2017): 728–29.

42. See, for instance, the review of the earlier scholarship on this connection in Yehuda B. Cohn, *Tangled Up in Text: Tefillin and the Ancient World* (Atlanta: Society of Biblical Literature Press, 2008), 3–9, and Cohn's own arguments on this matter (167–69), as well as the more recent treatment in Wojciech Kosior, "'The Name of Yahveh Is Called Upon You': Deuteronomy 28:10 and the Apotropaic Qualities of Tefillin in the Early Rabbinic Literature," *Studia Religiologica* 48, no. 2 (2015): 143–54.

208 CHAPTER 6

was not effective for all generations . . . all the more so mezuzah, which is a stronger case since it contains ten divine names that are effective day and night and for all generations—how much more so will it prevent the destroyer.

Here, the mezuzah is effective in the wordless way that the way a brushful of apotropaic blood is effective. The closest this passage comes to referencing the biblical contents of this power object is to mention the divine names contained therein—but without any reference to the message or commandment. Judah HaNasi is even famously remembered to have claimed that the protective power of the mezuzah functioned quite independently even of the people of Israel's special relationship with the divine or even consciousness of its contents—since a mezuzah could extend its supernatural protection even over a sleeping gentile (yPeʾah 1:1 [15d]).

In a similar way, a closed Torah scroll—which is to say, a scroll that has temporarily been transformed into an illegible ritual object—wielded a heightened supernatural power in the early rabbinic imaginary. Like mezuzot and phylacteries, a closed Torah scroll seems to have been imagined as a ritual object in which the biblical texts became one with the material objects that surrounded them—transforming a reading text into a solid object of a slightly different nature. Like mezuzot and phylacteries, Torah scrolls were also said to transmit their scriptural status (their ability to "defile the hands") only to those objects that enclosed them when they were shut tight—such as their mantle, wrappings, and box (tYadayim 2:12). It was as a closed object that biblical scrolls transmitted the status of scriptural sanctity to the objects that enclosed them, so that the biblical texts within came to be continuous with the materials they touched—becoming a single ritual object with a single ritual status.

This closed Torah scroll-object was often ascribed supernatural powers that an open scroll was not.[43] Certainly, scriptural verses are described as being recited on occasion for healing purposes in rabbinic communities, as they were elsewhere.[44] But it is the closed scroll-object that is more often associated in rabbinic narratives with supernatural feats, such as making entire enemy armies disappear without a trace (yTaʿanit 3:8 [66d]). Indeed, some early rabbinic sources themselves appear to mark this correlation between the power wielded by a closed scroll and its illegibility. As bSanhedrin 21b, for instance,

43. For more on magical uses of the Torah scroll in a general way, see Hezser, *Literacy*, 209ff.
44. See, for instance, bEruvin 54a.

A CLOSED BOOK 209

describes the Torah scroll that a king of Israel is instructed to write so that he may take it with him wherever he goes:

> He writes it as a sort of amulet (כמין קמיע) and ties it on his arm as it is said, "I have set God before me in all things; on account of my right arm I will not stumble" (Ps 16:8). He does not enter with it either into a bathhouse or into a privy, as it is said, "it will be with him, and he will read in it" [which means] a place that it is appropriate to read-recite [scripture] in.

In this passage, the illegibility of the Torah scroll in question is marked in multiple ways. First, the implied size of the final product suggests a form of microwriting that would make informational reading practically impossible.[45] Moreover, while Megan Nutzman has convincingly demonstrated that not all biblical amulets were closed amulets, the amount of text involved in this case could not be inscribed in any way that the entire text was legible but evokes instead images of a closed scroll, perhaps even an enclosed scroll, tied to the king's arm. These implicit images of inaccessible and illegible writing are made explicit, moreover, by the closing line of the passage. For the author cleverly subverts any suggestion that the king is supposed to study the document in question by transforming a verse about *reading* scripture into a verse about *wearing* scripture. The author of this passage thus emphasizes in myriad subtle ways that it is an illegible book that will function to protect and keep the king from "stumbling" (metaphorically and physically) as he makes his way in the world. As the author puts it, this is a tradition about the power of a Torah scroll that works "as a sort of amulet"—a subtly transformed ritual object that wields an almost magical power to smooth its wearer's way in a mode quite independent of its spiritual message.

Writing more specifically about the protective power ascribed to the Torah scroll which an Israelite king took into battle, Catherine Hezser has analogized the power imputed to the royal Torah scroll to a phenomenon described by David Cressy in seventeenth-century England.[46] To quote a slightly more extended excerpt from Cressy's work than is offered by Hezser,

---

45. I would like to thank my student, Jeremy Ray, for his study of this point.

46. Hezser, *Literacy*, 210. In this case, and others like it, Hezser argues that the rabbinic transmitters of these narratives and rulings recognized the unique "magical" qualities attributed to the Torah-scroll-as-object in such traditions but simultaneously sought to control or correct the "popular belief in the potency of Torah scrolls" that they express. This characterization of rabbinic attitudes toward scripture magic is certainly true in some cases. It seems to me, however, that many early rabbinic traditions unselfconsciously embraced the transmutation of the

[Regarding] those stories from the English civil war involving "the marvelous preservation of soldiers by Bibles in their pockets which have received the bullets." The implication in all these cases is that the power of the Bible lay not simply in its text, to be unlocked by rigorous exegesis, but rather in its ineffable holiness, its sacred magic. The Bible as an object, symbolizing and encapsulating the word of God, was believed to do duty comparable or *superior to* the Scripture as text. (emphasis added)[47]

Like the bullet-catching English Bibles above, perhaps the rabbinic Torah scroll is most effective as a talisman precisely when it, being closed, functions as a solid (and thus silent) ritual object.

Nor is the logic that a silent textual object might be more powerful than a communicative document unique to the Bible—or even scripture. Perhaps the most striking ancient example of this phenomenon is the Achaemenid Behistun inscription. This imperial inscription of royal authority was carefully inscribed in the side of a cliff only to have its commissioner, Darius, promptly destroy all means of accessing the cliff at a distance close enough to read the inscription. While (presumed) copies of this unreadable text were circulated,[48] the original remained visible but illegible—so that "the texts seem to have been intended to impress by their very existence, in an almost magical way."[49] In such cases, authoritative writing does not wield its power *despite* the fact that it is closed to scrutiny (literally or metaphorically) but rather *because* of it. Transformed from a reading text into a ritual artifact, the Torah scroll becomes an object that channels the power of the divine without dissipating that power in meaning making and exegesis.

---

closed Torah scroll into a power object, which was in continuation with the supernatural functions attributed the other kinds of illegible biblical texts explored above.

47. David Cressy, "Books as Totems in Seventeenth-Century England and New England," *The Journal of Library History* 21, no. 1 (1986): 99.

48. Seth Sanders, *From Adapa to Enoch: Scribal Culture and Religious Vision from Judea to Babylonia* (Tübingen: Mohr Siebeck, 2017), 183–86 and the literature cited there.

49. Rüdiger Schmitt, "The Bisitun Inscriptions of Darius the Great," in *Corpus Inscriptionum Iranicarum: Old Persian Texts, Inscriptions of Ancient Iran,* ed. Ruediger Schmitt (London: School of Oriental and African Studies Publications, 1991), 17. For an extended analysis of the modes of textuality promoted by this unreadable inscription, see Donald C. Polaski, "What Means These Stones: Inscription, Textuality and Power in Persia and Yehud," in *Approaching Yehud: New Approaches to the Study of the Persian Period,* ed. Jon L. Berquist (Atlanta: Society of Biblical Literature Publications, 2007), 37–41.

The Torah Scroll as the Body of Revelation

When the closed Torah scroll acted as a source of ritual power, it functioned more like the holistic mediator of a human body than a communicative document. Scholarly authors cited above have recently drawn our attention to certain forms of anthropomorphic personhood ascribed to the Torah scroll by the rabbinic imagination. I would argue that we can go further still in appreciating the extent to which many of these anthropomorphic imaginaries ascribe to the Torah scroll an almost literally biological bodily character.

A certain continuity between Torah scrolls and biological bodies is apparent at the material level in the ritual practices associated with the making, unmaking, and keeping of scrolls. As Anne Kreps has captured this notion, to say that both one who stands in the presence of a human body at the moment of death and one who watches a Torah scroll burn must tear his clothes in mourning is to suggest that "a damaged Torah scroll could 'die' . . . in similar terms to a living body."[50] Other early rabbinic rulings that equate the death of Torah scrolls and the demise of human beings take this equivalency beyond the realm of the theoretical right down to the literal skin of these two decaying bodies. The wrappings of a Torah scroll that has degraded to the point it is no longer ritually valid, for instance, may be used to wrap the dead body of a *met mitzvah* (a deceased person whose corpse has fallen on the community to buried as a religious obligation).[51] Like the human body in the rabbinic imagination, the rabbinic Torah scroll originated from "putrid" materials in a "place of filth"[52] and was permeated with the more distasteful sides of bodily materiality. With the narrowing ritual requirements for Torah scroll preparation in early rabbinic tradition, the physical materials needed to create a ritually valid Torah scroll (parchment and ink) were caustic,[53] dirty,[54] and frequently made

---

50. Kreps, "Crucified," 184–85. For an earlier contribution to this research genealogy, see Schleicher, "Dying Scroll."

51. BMegillah 26b and parallels.

52. On the human emerging from a putrid drop see the famous passage in mAvot 3:2, and on the womb as a place of filth the famous passage in bShabbat 152a and parallels.

53. The debatable metal gall inks (bEruvin 13a, bSotah 20b), for instance, were so acidic that they would eat away at not only the parchment but the writing materials themselves. See Alana S. Lee, Peter J. Mahon, and Dudley C. Creagh, "Raman Analysis of Iron Gall Inks on Parchment," *Vibrational Spectroscopy* 41, no. 2 (2006): 170–75.

54. The process of creating parchment was notoriously grisly and smelly to the point where the profession of a tanner was valid grounds for divorce (mKetubot 7:10). But even relatively

up of the detritus and effusions of biological bodies.[55] When a valid Torah scroll had been reduced to its distasteful material components by any damage sufficient to cause its ritual power to dissipate, therefore, it was treated to a cautious ritual handling modeled on the respectful disposal of a decomposing human body after its soul had left it.[56] Yet at the height of its ritual power, the Torah scroll object was also ascribed a status similar to that attributed to the most elevated form of human body—the body of a ritually valid priest in the midst of his ritual duties.[57] Like the priestly body, the Torah scroll was not only treated with deferential respect but allowed to occupy an exclusive sacred space within the sanctuary frequently associated with the mediating powers of the lost Temple in Jerusalem.[58] At both its most elevated and most degraded, the Torah scroll was approached with ritual gestures that equated it with human bodies.

A variety of early rabbinic traditions also gave these continuities a more metaphorical voice—inscribing the bodily nature of the Torah scroll into the imaginary of late antique Israel. A wide swath of early rabbinic tradition, for instance, allegorized biblical texts and their accoutrements as a very bodily human woman. When Song of Songs Rabbah 3:9–10 suggests that the Torah should be carried inside the ark like a princess is carried in a palanquin, for instance, the image bestows very specific anthropomorphic qualities on the Torah by presenting it as the body of a particular type of woman. As Tamar Kadari argues, moreover, such comparisons were often far from abstract analogies. When tYoma 2:13 allegorizes the poles of the ark pushing forward the

---

sanitary processes such as collecting and kneading soot with oil to make ink were dirty tasks (bShabbat 23a).

55. For more on the cultural and ritual significance of biologics in parchment processing, see Isaac W. Oliver, "Simon Peter Meets Simon the Tanner: The Ritual Insignificance of Tanning in Ancient Judaism," *New Testament Studies* 59, no. 1 (2013): 50–60 and the literature cited there.

56. YMo'ed Katan 3:7 83b, BBerakhot 18a, bMegillah 26b, bMo'ed Katan 26a, and parallels.

57. The now-popular analogy between the Torah scroll and the royal body does not appear to be ritually established until the Middle Ages and the first extant mention of crowning the Torah scrolls dates from the year 1000 CE. Franz Landsberger, "The Origins of the European Torah Decorations," *Hebrew Union College Annual* 24 (1952): 140.

58. See, for instance, Joan Branham, "Vicarious Sacrality: Temple Space in Ancient Synagogues," in *Ancient Synagogues: Historical Analysis and Archeological Discovery II,* ed. Dan Urman and Paul V. M. Flesher (Leiden: Brill, 1995), 319–49, and Steven D. Fraade, "Facing the Holy Ark, in Words and in Images," *Near Eastern Archeology* 82, no. 3 (2019): 156–63 and the literature cited there.

A CLOSED BOOK   213

curtain of the Holy of Holies into two protrusions with the verse, "my beloved is a bundle of myrrh between my breasts" (Song of Songs 1:13), "the verse from Song of Songs is being interpreted by the Tosefta in a very painterly and concrete way"[59] that "describes [the Torah ark's] members . . . as the limbs of a woman amidst which God rests."[60] As bMenahot 98b will later put it, "[The staves of the ark] push out and make bumps in the curtain of the Holy of Holies like two breasts of a woman."[61] In such traditions, the Torah and its accessories are being imagined in quite biological terms as the flesh-and-blood body of a human woman—concealed behind a screen, covered in cloth, protruding erotically from her clothing, and embracing her lover.

I would argue that these images painting the Torah and its paraphernalia as a female body become even more biologically explicit as they travel through the later tradition. BYoma 54a, for instance, further cements and concretizes the human referents of the erotic imagery in the Tosefta tradition quoted above when it juxtaposes that tradition with the following comment:

> R. Katina said, "When Israel came to the Temple on the holidays, they would roll back the curtain of the Holy of Holies for them and show them the cherubs [on the ark], who were intertwined in foreplay (מעורים זה בזה)[62] and would say to them 'Witness your desirability before God, which is like the desiring love of male and female!'" R. Hisda responded, "But doesn't it say, 'They shall not come to see when they pack up the [contents of] the sanctuary [lest they die]' (Num 4:20)?" And R. Yehudah said [in the name of Rav], "[This means it was prohibited to gaze on the contents of the sanctuary even] at the moment the vessels were being placed in their [traveling] cases." R. Nahman compared this in a parable to a bride who keeps herself modest from her husband so long as she is in her father's house, but once she comes to her in-laws she is not modest from her husband. [I.e., The bride-body of the ark was kept modest from the gaze of Israel during the engagement period in the desert, but her nakedness could be revealed once

---

59. Tamar Kadari, "'Within It Was Decked with Love': The Torah as Bride in Tannaitic Exegesis on Song of Songs," *Tarbiz* 71, no. 3–4 (2002): 402 (in Hebrew).

60. Ibid., 404.

61. Michael Fishbane has argued that this tradition ultimately derives from an older (and culturally broader) context of Temple fertility and sacred marriage. Michael Fishbane, *Biblical Myth and Rabbinic Myth Making* (Oxford: Oxford University Press, 2003), 175.

62. Although R.R. Neis has argued that this term could have a stronger penetrative connotation R. R. Neis, *The Sense of Sight in Rabbinic Culture: Jewish Ways of Seeing in Late Antiquity* (Cambridge: Cambridge University Press, 2013), 91n43.

the bride settled into her permanent home in the Jerusalem Temple.]
R. Hana b. R. Katina raised the objection, "[But what about] the incident
of the priest who was busy [in the Temple wood chamber and accidentally
discovered the place where the ark was hidden and died before he could
uncover it]?"[63] He said to him, "She had been divorced."

Here again, we find images of the Torah and its ark casing as an eroticized female body that can be clothed and unclothed according to her marital status.
But in this case, the metaphorical imagery is subtly made more literal by evoking the very fleshy ekphrasis of the naked cherubim engaged in loving foreplay
atop the ark at the same time as the audience is called to remember their own
human sexual activities—thereby tying the experience of human bodies more
closely still to the body of the biblical text and its accoutrements.

If we accept R. R. Neis's reading of bYoma 54b as likewise relating to the
cherubim on the ark of the covenant,[64] then the biological and sexual explicit-
ness of this crossover becomes even more vivid. For this episode closes with
the shameful exposing of the ark's metaphorical genitalia for all to see:

> Reish Lakish said, "When the gentiles entered the Temple, they saw the
> cherubim engaged in foreplay with each other. They brought them out into
> the marketplace and said, 'these Israelites, for whom those who bless them
> [are supposedly] blessed and those who curse them are [supposedly]
> cursed, they engage with such things' and immediately [everyone] deni-
> grated them, as it is said, 'those who honored her, denigrate her because
> they saw her sexual parts' (Lam 1:8)."

According to a continuous reading of the passage, this arrangement of traditions thus moves from an erotic "striptease" to a "shameful seeing of *'ervah*
(genital nakedness)."[65] In doing so, it connects the ark and its scriptural contents with the full range of human embodiment: moving from metaphors of
human biology in their most romanticized form to (what is culturally figured
as) the blunt animalism of genital exposure that strips away illusions of human
exceptionality and unveils the feminine body as both shocking and shameful
in the eyes of those who behold it.[66]

---

63. For more on this incident, see chapter 2 of this monograph.

64. As opposed to the pictorial cherubim כרובים דצורתא that are described as replacing the
sculptural cherubim of the (now lost) ark in the Second Temple, at the end of bYoma 54a.

65. Neis, *Sense of Sight*, 93.

66. And should we embrace, instead, a reading of this later narrative as referring to the ex-

A CLOSED BOOK 215

For all the seductive concreteness of such imagery, one might be tempted to dismiss the meaningfulness of even the most vivid images of biological embodiment when they are being ascribed by the rabbi to an ancient Torah enclosed in an imagined ark of the covenant situated in a long-lost Temple. As James Watt has pointed out, however, some late antique Jews and Christians appear to have identified the portable ark (ארון or תבה) used in some late antique synagogues with the ark of the covenant (ארון הברית) in the curtained shrine of the Jerusalem Temple.[67] John Chrysostom, for instance, felt compelled to rail against both Jews and their Christian visitors when he sought to refute a popular elision of Temple ark and synagogue ark:

> What kind of "ark" (κιβωτός)[68] is now among the Jews? Where the mercy seat [on the ark] is not, where there is no ark, no tablets of testimony [in the ark], no Holy of Holies [for the ark], no curtain [for the Holy of Holies], no high priest, no [Temple] incense, no burnt offerings, or any other of the accoutrements of that sacred ark of former times. For my part, it seems that this ark is no more powerful than a chest purchased from the marketplace.[69]

Reflected in complaints such as these, one glimpses a communal imaginary in which some late antique containers for Torah scrolls had become subtly superimposed with images associated with the ark of the covenant (which had remained a prominent motif in late antique art and ekphrasis). While the shapes of these late antique ritual containers varied from community to community, so often did the shapes attributed to the ark of the covenant in late antique imagery and literary imaginaries.[70] It seems eminently possible,

---

posure of cherubim pictorially depicted in the Second Temple, then the transitive power of this biological imagery comes to bear. For even revealing later images, echoes, or reproductions of this lost scripturalized cult object is enough to violate the modesty and integrity of the scriptural body.

67. James W. Watts, "From Ark of the Covenant to Torah Scroll: Ritualizing Israel's Iconic Texts," in *Ritual Innovation in the Hebrew Bible and Early Judaism*, ed. Nathan McDonald (Berlin: de Gruyter, 2016), 4ff.

68. The equivalent of תבה in as much as this is the terminology used in New Testament Greek for both Noah's ark and the ark of the covenant.

69. John Chrysostom, *Homily on John* 32.3 (P.G. 48:914). Translation my own.

70. For a survey of the possible variations, see Rachel Hachlili, "Torah Shrine and Ark in Ancient Synagogues: A Re-Evaluation," *Zeitschrift des deutschen Palästina-Vereins* 116, no. 2 (2000): 146–83; Itzhak Hamitovsky, "From 'Teva' to 'Aron': Evolution in the Character of the Holy Ark in the Mishnaic and Talmudic Periods," *Kenishta* 3 (2001): 99–128 (in He-

216 CHAPTER 6

therefore, that early rabbinic traditions about the ark of the covenant called to mind both the Temple ark and a contemporary enclosure when they spoke of the screening box of the ark as a paladin hiding the body of the princess from view; or that some would elide the curtain of the inner sanctum with that of a synagogue ark when they imagined clothing shaped to the body of a woman–Torah scroll. Although ostensibly referring to the mythical past, such traditions may well have simultaneously inscribed contemporary liturgical contexts with images that lavished a sensuous biological materiality on the community Torah scroll and its accessories.

Other strains of early rabbinic tradition ascribed a heavy freight of bodily materiality to the late antique Torah scroll in a different way. Adam Zachary Newton, for instance, has recently urged us to take seriously the anthropomorphism inherent in traditions that suggested that a scroll might "'count' as if it were another person in prayer," asking us to consider "how do persons and scrolls converge?"[71] Newton and the thinkers with whom he engages have focused on the "*axiomatic* analogy between human person and inscribed parchment" implicit in the classical legal discussions about counting a Torah scroll in a *minyan* (a prayer quorum).[72] But narrative descriptions of Torah scrolls taking part in a *minyan* are often threaded through with a distinct bodily discourse not dissimilar from the allegorical imagery cited above. In Pirke de Rabbi Eliezer 8:6, for instance, the Torah scroll serves in the *minyan* by being made to participate in the bodily postures of the quorum's human members:

> One may intercalate [the calendar] with three [people]. Rabbi Eliezer says with ten, as it is said, (Ps 82:1): "God will be established in the congregation of God." But if they fall short, one may bring a Torah scroll and unfurl it before them (פורשין אותו לפניהם). Then they are arranged into a circle and sit in order of precedence and put their faces down to the ground and unfurl their hands (פורשין את כפיהן) to their father in heaven. And the head of the academy mentions the name of God and they hear a heavenly voice that calls out and speaks in this language: "God said to Moses and Aaron saying 'this month is to you . . .'" (Exod 12:1–2). But from the iniquity of the gen-

---

brew); and Meir Bar-Ilan "The Bookcase (Ark) in Ancient Synagogues," in *Libraries and Book Collections*, ed. J. Kaplan and M. Sluhovsky (Jerusalem: Merkaz Zalman Shazar, 2006), 49–64 (in Hebrew).

71. Newton, *Impure*, 26.

72. Ibid., 26 (emphasis added). Among the sources most frequently cited in these discussions are bBerakhot 47b and yBerakhot 7:2 (53b).

A CLOSED BOOK 217

eration they might not hear anything but rather (as it if could be) the divine presence can't come to rest between them.

In this passage, the Torah scroll is transformed into a participant in the human quorum when it is made to share in the bodily postures of the participants. For just as the human participants lie flat and put out their arms (פורשין את כפיהן) to participate in this particular ritual minyan, so similarly the Torah scroll is made to lie flat (פורשין אותו) with its rolls and dowels unfurled like arms on either side in an analogous posture. Indeed, this passage highlights the resonance between the two postures by describing both the position of the human body and the position of the Torah scroll using the same vocabulary. In this passage, the scroll does not participate in the *minyan* as a human being but it does participate in the *minyan* as a body in its own right.

In other descriptive portraits of ritual gatherings, we likewise see the Torah scroll included in human quorums via the process of constituting the Torah scroll and its accessories as a body analogous to a human body. In early rabbinic accounts of the communal prayer for rain, for instance, either the Torah scroll or its ark (depending on the passage and manuscript) is made to participate in the mourning gestures of the community leaders. As the ritual is imagined in mTaʿanit 2:1–2, for example,

> What is the appointed order for fast days? They bring the ark out into the city square and place ashes on top of the Torah scroll[73] and on the head of the prince [of the Sanhedrin] and the head of the chief justice of the court, and each and every one puts ashes on his head. And the eldest from among them says before them words to inspire penitence. . . . When they stand to pray, they bring down before the ark one who is old and fluent [in prayer], who has children, and whose house is empty, so that his house might be complete in prayer.

Here, as in the intercalation *minyan* imagined above, the Torah scroll becomes a member of the ritual community when its material form is shaped to mirror the postures of the human bodies around it. When the ashes are placed on its

---

73. Here I follow Julia Watts Belser, *Power, Ethics, and Ecology in Jewish Late Antiquity: Rabbinic Responses to Drought and Disaster* (Cambridge: Cambridge University Press, 2020), 130, who points out that while the Vilna and Pesaro manuscripts have "ark" here, London, Munich 140, Munich 95, Oxford, Vatican 134, Jerusalem Yad Harav Herzog, and the Spanish printings all have "Torah scroll"—as do, I would add, Geniza fragments T-S AS 74.260, T-S AS 78.253, T-S AS 93.544, T-S F 1(1).47, and T-S Misc. 24.124.

top, the Torah scroll is thereby inducted into the small cadre of community leaders to whom the ashes are likewise applied by others.

In the Babylonian Talmud's reworking of this tradition, the bodily nature ascribed to the Torah scroll in this ritual is emphasized still further. Julia Watts Belser draws our attention, for instance, to the way in which the addition of a brief description of Rabbi Zeira's reaction to the ritual further heightens our sense of the "link between the fasting body and the Torah scroll."[74] BTaʿanit 16a tells us "R. Zeira said, 'when I saw that the sages were putting ashes on the top of the Torah scroll it made me tremble all over my whole body.'" By informing us that when "the rabbi sees them put ashes on the Torah scroll his own body begins to tremble," Belser point out, this passage emphasizes the way that "the ritual draws the Holy body into the midst of the gathered community [of bodies], bringing divine physicality into the center of the communal fast."[75]

I would argue that we can also identify an important thread of bodily discourse ascribed to the Torah scroll in this passage's elaboration on the element of shame inherent in the ritual. This is apparent in the way in which the passage heightens the shame attributed to the act of having someone else invade the bodily space of the communal leaders (and by analogy the Torah scroll) by applying ashes to their bodies for them. As bTaʿanit 15b puts it,

> If each and every person takes and places on his head [for himself, why don't] the prince [of the Sanhedrin] and the chief justice also apply it for themselves? What is the difference in this case, since another person applies it for them? R. Abba of Caesarea said, "One who is shamed by himself is not the same as someone who is shamed by others, therefore they apply it for him."

Once again, the Torah scroll comes to function as a community partner by participating in the bodily postures of the group. For with the addition of this explanation, the application of ashes to the Torah scroll is transformed, by analogy, from a mechanical necessity (since an object cannot apply ashes to itself) to a moment in which an elite body is humiliated for the sake of the people.

There is a second nexus of bodily humiliation, moreover, in the Babylonian Talmud's vision of this ritual—one that returns us to images of the Torah scroll

---

74. Belser, *Power, Ethics, and Ecology*, 131.
75. Ibid.

as an elite female body which is honored by shielding it from public view. As bTa'anit 16a elaborates on the fast day ritual,

> Why do they bring out the ark out to the public square? R. Yehoshua b. Levi said, "[As though] to say we had a modest vessel and we humiliated it with our sins."

When the concept of modesty is introduced into the ritual matrix, the act of bringing the ark out into the public square and then removing the Torah scroll from the ark for anointing with ash becomes something akin to an act of public undressing and exposure. As Julia Watts Belser has argued, "Because of communal failing and sin, the Torah has been forced out of its private dwelling place.... The verb *nitbazeh* connotes both shame and exposure, and its multivalency underscores the critical link between being seen and being shamed in this passage."[76] In this vision of the ritual, in other words, the Torah scroll is subjected to a ritual of bodily exposure and humiliation akin to that of the *sotah* (the accused wife) imagined elsewhere in early rabbinic literature. Just as that husband's shame is made manifest when his wife is removed from the privacy of her home to have her body exposed and treated in humiliating ways in the public arena, so here the community's shame is made manifest when the Torah scroll is exposed and humiliated via gestures that equate it to the human bodies around it. Thus, in bTa'anit, the Torah scroll is once again imagined to participate in the human quorum—not so much as a stable social subject (since the imagery invoked flickers back and forth between different social referents)—but as a body among other bodies.

Some Concluding Remarks

As modern scholars immersed in cultures of informational reading, it is tempting to tie the supernatural powers attributed to the Torah scroll in early rabbinic thought to the iconic message of the biblical text. And yet, early rabbinic traditions typically portray the Torah scroll as most powerful precisely when its communicative contents were inaccessible in some way. While the Torah scroll would be opened for liturgical reading in limited and highly controlled circumstances—like a scrupulously regulated rabbinic wife who undressed only for sanctioned intimacy—the Torah scroll was imagined to be at its most ritually powerful precisely when it was closed or unreadable, so that its messy

76. Ibid.

textual contents were obscured from view. Like the human body in early rabbinic logics of sacrality, the scroll-body wielded ritual power best when it was whole and covered—without open apertures leaking direct communication like uncontainable bodily fluids.

Many early rabbinic thinkers, indeed, explicitly envisioned the Torah scroll as a form of biological body. In doing so, they leveraged early rabbinic thinking about the complex nature of the ensouled human subject to grapple with a searing bifurcation they perceived in the notion of a written revelation. For just as the human subject manifested the intangible and unlimited capacities of human spirit through the limiting and constantly decomposing physicality of the human body, so written revelation referenced an intangible and multifaceted revelation of divine truth through the limiting and vulnerable materiality of insufficient written letters inscribed on constantly degrading materials. And just as the human body served most effectively as a conduit for the human subject's otherworldly facets when its material qualities were temporarily effaced so that the physical body served as a silent vessel for more intangible forces, so the Torah's scroll-body was most powerful when its limited textual chatter was silenced and its degrading material facets were temporarily hidden from view so that it could serve as silent vessel for that other more unbounded form of revelation—its embodied avatar and conduit into the human community.

CONCLUDING REMARKS

From the Third Torah to God's Monograph

WHILE IT IS OFTEN imagined that the late antique Jewish inheritors of the biblical text enthusiastically embraced that varied anthology as a perfect and harmonious blueprint for the religious life, the first half of this book confounded that portrait by exploring early rabbinic traditions in which the biblical text is described as very far from perfect and the practice of engaging with the biblical text as a blueprint for religious life is treated as positively dangerous. Chapter 1 ("A Makeshift Scripture: Tales of Biblical Loss, Reconstruction, and Forgery") analyzed a diverse body of early rabbinic traditions that imagine the biblical text as repeatedly lost, reconstructed, and remade into a makeshift approximation of the divine message. These stories were read as a form of narrative theorizing about the vulnerabilities inherent to textual transmission and the implications of that vulnerability for the prospect of preserving an authentic written revelation. The second chapter ("A Book That Kills: Rabbinic Stories about Lethal Encounters with Biblical Text") explored a genre of early rabbinic fantasy in which close encounters with the biblical text result in literal death. In these tales, rabbinic authors painted vivid literalizing portraits of the spiritual dangers thought to adhere to a written text that channels the power of the divine mind without being able to adequately represent or control that power. The third chapter ("A Neglected Text: Mistaken Readings, Bible Avoidance, and the Dangers of Reading as We Know It") explored the practical consequences of these theoretical aversions by analyzing legal limitations imposed on Bible reading in early rabbinic communities.

221

The second half of the book explored how it came to be that religious authorities who were deeply ambivalent concerning the biblical text nevertheless established the Bible as a central pillar of early Jewish religious life. Chapter 4 ("A Spoken Scripture: Unlinking the Written from the Oral in Rabbinic Practices of Bible Reading") argued that doubts about the biblical text were less pressing in early rabbinic circles because the written text had already been rendered a secondary, even superfluous, witness to the contents of the biblical revelation by a religious reading practice in which most practitioners "read" a canonical text by memorizing an oral formula that roughly corresponded to that text and ritually reciting it from memory—sometimes in physical conjunction with a written text but never drawing meaning directly from written words. The fifth chapter ("A Third Torah: Oral Torah, Written Torah, and the Embrace of a Spoken Scripture") demonstrated that many early rabbinic thinkers would come to imagine this memorized oral echo of the biblical tradition as a separate and more authentic witness to the biblical revelation that transcended the fixity, narrowness, and fragility that made the written transcript of the Pentateuch seem such an unlikely record of the divine will. This Spoken Scripture came to be imagined as a third category of revelation, somewhere between the fixed transcripts of the biblical Written Torah and the fluid traditions of the rabbinic Oral Torah. Chapter 6 ("A Closed Book: The Torah Scroll as the Body of Revelation") explored how these rabbinic thinkers came to imagine the written text of the Hebrew Bible once it had been rendered communicatively silent in communal practice. It argued that these parchment objects came to be treated less as a record of communication than a form of body that provided a material avatar for the intangible soul of Spoken Scripture.

A Remaining Question: Why Did Jewish Attitudes Toward the Bible Change?

If the modes of engaging with the Bible described in this book were, at the very least, a prominent strand within classical rabbinic approaches to the biblical text, why have they remained opaque to us for so long? I would argue that this invisibility reflects the fact that modern readers have been divided from this early Jewish approach to sacred textuality by a radical global shift in Jewish modes of engaging with sacred tradition that took place in the Middle Ages and has continued to shape Jewish approaches to the Bible ever since.

FROM THE THIRD TORAH TO GOD'S MONOGRAPH   223

In the centuries on either side of the year 1000 CE, a "veritable revolution"[1] took place in the genres and techniques with which Jews engaged the Hebrew Bible. Around the end of the first millennium of the common era, medieval Jewish thinkers from Baghdad to Troyes suddenly began producing systematic literary explanations of the written biblical text that were attentive to these ancient writings' structure, context, and linguistic form. In the scholarly literature, these new commentaries have been characterized using adaptations of the medieval terminology as alternately *peshat* commentary,[2] *zahir* and *haqiqa* exegesis,[3] or scientific reading.[4] The existence of this medieval revolution in Jewish approaches to the biblical text helps explain the way that earlier rabbinic modes of engagement with the biblical text have been obscured from view. But it also presents us with a mystery. Scholars have yet to reach a consensus about precisely how and why we see this global shift in Jewish approaches to the Bible in the Middle Ages. The shift is too marked to be coincidental but too varied to be easily explained as a single derivative phenomenon.

A profound family resemblance binds these new medieval works together—so that they are frequently analyzed as a single phenomenon. Yet there is no single feature common to these new works. Scholars writing on the Islamicate context, for instance, frequently identify the rise of single-author commentaries with a clear authorial voice as the defining feature of

1. Avraham Grossman, *The Sages of France: Their Lives, Leadership, and Works* (Jerusalem: Magnes, 1995), 457 (in Hebrew).

2. Although a definitive description of medieval usage of the *peshat* terminology continues to elude us, the most often cited definition remains that of Sarah Kamin: "*Peshat* . . . is an explanation in accordance with the text's vocabulary, syntax, context, literary form and structure in their mutual relationships. Thus, an explanation according to the method of *peshat* takes into consideration all the linguistic elements, the way they are combined and interact, while giving each element a meaning within the complete structure." Sarah Kamin, *Rashi's Exegetical Categorization in Respect to the Distinction between Peshat and Derash* (Jerusalem: Magnes, 1986), 14 (in Hebrew), as translated by the author herself in an expanded English summary of her dissertation, Sarah Kamin, "Rashi's Exegetical Categorization in Respect to the Distinction between Peshat and Derash," *Immanuel* 11 (1980): 16–17.

3. On the difference between the rabbinic category of *peshat* and the Arabic categories of *zahir* and *haqiqa*, see Raphael Dascalu, *A Philosopher of Scripture: The Exegesis and Thought of Tanhum Ha-Yerushalmi* (Leiden: Brill, 2019), 57–74 and the previous literature cited there.

4. Miriam Goldstein, "The Beginnings of the Transition from Derash to Peshat as Exemplified in Yefet Ben 'Eli's Comment on Psa. 44:24," in *Exegesis and Grammar in Medieval Karaite Texts*, ed. Geoffrey Khan (Oxford: Oxford University Press, 2003), 31.

224 CONCLUDING REMARKS

these new commentaries.[5] Yet European Jewish works in the new style often retained the structure of a "compilation" or "florilegium" well into the commentary revolution,[6] as did many Karaite[7] commentaries.[8] To cite another famous example of this inconsistency, virtually all scholars agree that the medieval commentary movement was defined in some way by its abandonment of the early rabbinic midrashic mode. Yet many of the most important contributions to this movement were replete with midrashic material.[9] This diverse medieval commentary revolution was defined less by the dissemina-

5. Ilana Sasson, "The Book of Proverbs between Saadia and Yefet," *Intellectual History of the Islamicate World* 1, no. 1–2 (2013): 161.

6. Hanna Liss, *Creating Fictional Worlds: Peshat-Exegesis and Narrativity in Rashbam's Commentary on the Torah* (Leiden: Brill, 2011), 44.

7. While Karaite and Rabbinate Judaism are often treated as entirely distinct historical religious movements, their intertwined and intertwining origins have become increasingly clear. See, for instance, Moshe Gil, "The Origins of the Karaites," in *Karaite Judaism: A Guide to Its History and Literary Sources*, ed. Meira Polliack (Leiden: Brill, 2003), 73–118, and Meira Polliack, "Rethinking Karaism between Judaism and Islam," *Association for Jewish Studies Review* 30, no. 1 (2006): 67–93; Ofra Tirosh Becker, "The Use of Rabbinic Sources in Karaite Writing," in Polliack, *Karaite Judaism*, 319–38; James T. Robinson, "Reading Other People Reading Other People's Scriptures: The Influence of Religious Polemic on Jewish Biblical Exegesis," *English Language Notes* 52, no. 2 (Fall/Winter 2012): 77–88; and Jonathan Howard, "Karaite or Rabbinate: A Hint from Menachem's *Mahberet*," *Zutot* 15, no. 1 (2018): 16–24. I am hesitant, therefore, to retrospect the historical outcomes of that exchange into this vital period—instead, treating all players simply as medieval Jews.

8. See, for instance, James T. Robinson, *The Arabic Translation and Commentary of Yefet b. 'Eli on the Book of Joshua* (Leiden: Brill, 2014), 3. For while Yefet sometimes incorporates the opinions of others by "leading the reader through his exegetical process in order to convince him that his interpretation is the correct one," "in most cases, Yefet's presentation of the opinion of other exegetes is not accompanied by commentary, except to state that his own interpretation is the correct one" so that "in this way, he allows himself to present several exegetical options without limiting himself to only one possible exegesis or taking responsibility for interpretations that may be incorrect." Meirav Nadler-Akirav, "The Literary-Historical Approach of Yefet Ben 'Eli the Karaite in His Commentary of the Book of Amos," *European Journal of Jewish Studies* 10 (2016): 172–73). Or as Meira Polliack has put it: "Yefet created a work of a summarizing nature, a 'summa' of Karaite Bible exegesis up to his time. His recourse to exegetical opinions other than his own was not only essential to his canonizing task but also formed a live reflection of the egalitarian ethos of early Karaite biblical study." Meira Polliack, "Concepts of Scripture among the Jews of the Medieval Islamic World," in *Jewish Concepts of Scripture: A Comparative Introduction* (New York: New York University Press, 2012), 95.

9. The most famous case in point is Rashi, whom Abraham Grossman estimates used midrash in approximately 75 percent of his comments. Avraham Grossman, "Studying Rashi's Jewish Worldview," in *"Zekhor Davar le-Avdekha": Essays and Studies in Memory of Dov Rappel*,

tion of particular techniques or formats than by a shared sensibility in the broadest sense.

The historical impetus for this sea change have also been difficult to identify. The dominant school to date maintains that "Jewish Bible commentary was born in the Islamic East"[10]—whether the inspiration for this emerging Jewish genre is traced to geonic adaptions of the literary techniques used in contemporaneous Qur'anic exegesis[11] or to the mediating influence of the new Karaite movement.[12] Others point out, however, that novel European Jewish commentaries from the period appear to possess their own independent genealogy deeply intertwined with the literary and religious developments in Latin Christian Europe.[13] More perplexing still, researchers have been able to document only the most tenuous historical ties between these two apparently parallel developments.[14] Thus, some point to Rashi's knowledge of the

---

ed. S. Glick (Jerusalem: Lifshitz, 2007), 288 (in Hebrew). See, also, Sarah Kamin, *Between Christians and Jews in Biblical Exegesis* (Jerusalem: Magnes, 1991), 153 (in Hebrew).

10. Daniel Frank, *Search Scripture Well: Karaite Exegetes and the Origins of the Jewish Bible Commentary in the Islamic East* (Leiden: Brill, 2004), ix.

11. See, for instance, Robert Brody, "The Geonim of Babylon as Biblical Exegetes," in *Hebrew Bible/Old Testament: The History of Its Interpretation,* vol. 1, ed. Magnes Sæbø (Göttingen: Vandenhoeck & Ruprecht, 2015), 2, and David Freidenreich, "The Use of Islamic Sources in Saadiah Gaon's 'Tafsir' of the Torah," *Jewish Quarterly Review* 93, nos. 3–4 (2003): 353–95 and the literature cited there.

12. Rina Drory, *Models and Contacts: Arabic Literature and Its Impact on Medieval Jewish Culture* (Leiden: Brill, 2000).

13. See, for instance, Robert A. Harris, "'From Religious Truth Seeking' to Reading: The Twelfth-Century Renaissance and the Emergence of Peshat and Ad Litterum as Methods of Accessing the Bible," in *The Oral and Textual in Jewish Tradition and Jewish Education,* ed. Matt Goldish, Barry Holtz, and Jonathan Cohen (Jerusalem: Magnes, 2019), 55; Hanna Liss, *Creating Fictional Worlds: Peshat Exegesis and Narrativity in the Rashbam's Commentary on the Torah* (Leiden: Brill, 2011), 39; Anna Dorofeeva, "Early Medieval Glossary Miscellanies," in *Writing the Early Medieval West* (Cambridge: Cambridge University Press, 2018), 162; and Devorah Schoenfeld, *Isaac on Jewish and Christian Altars: Polemic and Exegesis in Rashi and the Glossa Ordinaria* (New York: Fordham University Press, 2012).

14. That is to say, whether one imagines a model in which Middle Eastern Jewish traders like those mentioned in Rashi's commentary on bBerakhot 62a "might have sometimes brought with them literary sources" (Avraham Grossman, "Jewish Merchants as Cultural Agents in the High Middle Ages," in *Avnei Derekh: Essays in Jewish History Dedicated to Zvi (Kuti) Yekutiel,* ed. Immanuel Etkes, David Assaf, and Yosef Kaplan [Jerusalem: Merkaz Zalman Shazar, 2016], 95–109 [in Hebrew], 101), or whether one imagines these mercantile contacts left oral traces as in the earlier situation described in Richard C. Steiner, "Linguistic Traces of Jewish Traders from Islamic Lands in the Frankish Kingdom," *Leshonenu* 73, nos. 3–4 (2011): 347–70 (in Hebrew).

226 CONCLUDING REMARKS

grammatical theories of Menahem ibn Saruq and Dunash ben Labrat as a possible conduit from East to West[15]—while others cite possible ties between Rashi's work and the exegesis of Reuel of Byzantium[16] or the southern European works of Moshe HaDarshan.[17] Yet the extent of Rashi's familiarity with all these oeuvres and their sources remains unclear.[18] Despite concerted research on the topic, it has been challenging to provide a definitive genealogy of this new school of thought beyond broad evidence of a changing spirit of the times.

David Stern recently proposed that this emerging spirit of the times should be attributed to a technological "epiphenomenon that we might call the 'co-dexification' of Judaism,"[19] in which "codices marked a watershed moment in the history of Jewish reading and its technology"[20] that transformed the Bible from primarily "being a text known aurally to one read on a page in a codex"[21] since visual signs such as "vocalized, punctuated, and accentuated biblical texts . . . defined these codices as a book genre."[22] Yet, as with the uneven

---

15. Though Ben Saruq is never quoted directly and many of the references to both Menahem ben Saruq and Dunash ben Labrat may well have been interpolated by later authors. Ezra Zion Melammed, *Commentators on the Bible: Their Ways and Methods*, vol. 1 (Jerusalem: Magnes, 1975), 398 (in Hebrew), and Menahem Zohori, *Grammarians and Their Compositions in the Commentary of Rashi* (Jerusalem: Karmel, 1994), 189 (in Hebrew).

16. Avraham Grossman, "The Impact of Rabbi *Samuel* of Spain and Reuel of Byzantium on *Rashi's* School," *Tarbiz* 82, no. 3 (2014): 449–51 (in Hebrew); and Richard Steiner, "The 'Lemma Complement' in Hebrew Commentaries from Byzantium and Its Diffusion to Northern France and Germany," *Jewish Studies Quarterly* 18, no. 4 (2011): 367–79.

17. Hananel Mack, "I Found It in the Yesod of Rabbi Moshe Ha-Darshan: What Rashi Did and Didn't Bring from the Commentaries of Rabbi Moshe Ha-Darshan," in *Rashi: The Man and His Works*, ed. Avraham Grossman and Sarah Yafet (Jerusalem: Merkaz Zalman Shazar, 2008), 327. Though as Mack points out, as was is the case with Menahem ibn Saruq, it is not entirely clear in this case in what form Rashi received these traditions, since the evidence suggesting he saw them in writing has other possible explanations 328). Mack, "Homilist and Literalist: Rabbi Moses Hadarshan Heralds a Literal Exposition of the Bible," *Tarbiz* 81, (2013–2014): 409 (in Hebrew). For a more detailed discussion, see Mack, *Mystery of Rabbi Moshe Hadarshan* (Jerusalem: Mosad Bialik, 2010) (in Hebrew). For additional examples, see Schoenfeld, *Isaac*, 35.

18. Mordechai Z. Cohen, *The Rules of Peshat: Jewish Constructions of the Plain Sense of Scripture and the Christian and Muslim Contexts, 900–1270* (Philadelphia: University of Pennsylvania Press, 2020), 107–8.

19. David Stern, *Jewish Literary Cultures: The Ancient Period* (University Park: Pennsylvania State Press, 2015), 186.

20. Ibid., 162.

21. Ibid., 188.

22. Ibid., 164.

spread of new linguistic theories above, it is not clear that the diffusion of this media innovation preceded (or even kept pace with) the global spread of the new commentary tradition. The early developments in the new commentary movement were well on their way by the ninth century.[23] But we have quite

23. The earliest biblical commentator claimed for the new style is the ninth-century Syrian scholar Daud al-Muqammas (Sarah Stroumsa, "A Literary Genre as an Historical Document: On Saadia's Introduction to his Bible Commentaries," in *"A Word Fitly Spoken": Studies in Qur'an and Bible Exegesis,* ed. M. Bar-Asher [Jerusalem: Yad Ben-Zvi, 2007], 193–204 [in Hebrew]), followed quickly by the mid-ninth-century Persian thinker Benjamin al-Nihawendi (Robert Brody, *Sa'adyah Gaon* [Liverpool: Liverpool University Press, 2016], 58), and the late ninth-century Persian Palestinian author Daniel al-Qumisi (Geoffrey Khan, "The Role of the Karaites in the Transmission of the Hebrew Bible and Their Practice of Transcribing It into Arabic Script," *Intellectual History in the Islamicate World* 8, nos. 2–3 [2020], 239), who composed the first undisputed extant commentary to have survived the period. The genres of written biblical translations or paraphrases into Arabic composed by Jewish authors, which Ronny Vollandt argues "complemented other philological disciplines" emerging in this period, including grammars, glossaries, and commentaries, similarly appear to have been proliferating by the ninth century. Ronny Vollandt, *Arabic Versions of the Pentateuch: A Comparative Study of Jewish, Christian, and Muslim Sources* (Leiden: Brill, 2015), 74–75. We have fragmentary evidence of such translations that may date as early as the eighth century (Sagit Butbul, "Translations in Contact: Early Judaeo-Arabic and Syriac Bible Translations," in *Beyond Religious Borders: Interaction and Exchange in the Medieval Muslim World,* ed. David Freidenreich and Miriam Goldstein [Philadelphia: University of Pennsylvania Press, 2011], 60), as we do for the Judeo-Arabic genre of "questions and answers" on the biblical text (David Sklare, "Ninth-Century Judeo-Arabic Texts of Biblical Questions and Answers," in *Senses of Scripture, Treasures of Tradition: The Bible in Arabic among Jews, Christians, and Muslims,* ed. Miriam Lindgren Hjaelm [Leiden: Brill, 2017], 104–22). Likewise, while Saadiah Gaon's turn-of-the-century *Agron* (903 CE) is broadly cited as the first (semi-) extant work on biblical linguistics, the work of this very young scholar hardly marks the beginning of medieval Jewish linguistic thought but was rather part of a broader corpus of roughly contemporaneous (if not earlier) works that include the less firmly dated list of similar word forms Oklah ve-Oklah (Israel Yeivin, for instance, dates it to the ninth century, *Introduction to the Tiberian Masorah* [Jerusalem: Magnes, 1971], 130); the methodologically divergent "Risalah" of Yehudah ibn Quraish (along with his own lost dictionary) (W. Jacque Van Bekkum, "The 'Risala' of Yehuda Ibn Quraysh and Its Place in Hebrew Linguistics," *Historiographia Linguistica* 8, nos. 2–3 [1981]: 307–27); and various lost works that do not appear to have entered the rabbinic canon, such as the dictionary that Aharon Dotan pithily named "Anonymous A" (Aharon Dotan, "Beginnings of the Hebrew Dictionary: A Passage from an Early Dictionary," *Te'udah* 4 [1988]: 225 [in Hebrew]). Beyond the geographic and methodological diversity of these extant samples of late ninth- and early tenth-century linguistic thought, there is additional evidence of developing work in biblical linguistics by the ninth century in fragmentary documents, such as (1) a recently discovered palimpsest with a Greek-Hebrew glossary of difficult biblical terms written in "900 CE or earlier" (N. Tschernetska, J. Olszowy-Schlanger, and N. de Lange, "An Early Hebrew-Greek Biblical Glossary from the Cairo

228 CONCLUDING REMARKS

scant evidence for Jewish adoption of the codex form before the year 1000.[24] Indeed, research done in the last few years suggests that we find an almost

Genizah," *Revue des etudes juives* 166 [2007]: 91); (2) a list of terms of *dikduke ha-mikra* from the Cairo Geniza (first published by Nehemiah Allony in "A List of Karaite Terminology from the Eighth Century," in *Writings of the Society for Research on the Bible in Israel in Memory of Dr. Y.P. Korngreen* [Tel Aviv: Society for Research on the Bible, 1979], 324–63), which "includes Masoretic, grammatical and hermeneutical terms" that "correspond closely to the terminology and concepts of Ibn Nuh's Diqduq," and which Geoffrey Khan dates to the "early Islamic period ... when Karaism was in its embryonic stages" (Geoffrey Khan, "Medieval Karaite Tradition of Hebrew Grammar," in *Universal Art: Hebrew Grammar across Disciplines and Faiths,* ed. Nadia Vidro [Leiden: Brill, 2014], 22–23); (3) the *seder simanin* fragment which Nehemia Allony dated to "the second half of the ninth century" (Nehemiah Allony, "Seder Ha-Simanim," *Hebrew Union College Annual* 35 [1964]: 1), though Ilan Eldar has argued that it should be read together with a matching fragment, "a treatise on the *shewa,*" as a tenth-century work ("On the 'Treatise of the Shewa' and 'Order of the Signs,'" *Te'udah* 4 [1988]: 127–37 [in Hebrew]); as well as (4) tenth-century Karaite references to multiple earlier schools of linguistic thought in Jewish Persia (Geoffrey Khan, *Early Karaite Grammatical Texts* [Atlanta: Society of Biblical Literature Press, 2000], especially 9–10). Stern dates the emergence of distinct Masoretic schools to the beginning of the eighth century (*Jewish Bible,* 71). By the ninth century, then, we can say the fire of Jewish philological commentary had been firmly lit, if not yet fully ablaze.

24. These early forays into systematic biblical exegesis would, at first, seem to pose no challenge to Stern's theory as he "places the origins of the codex in Jewish culture around the beginning of the eighth century" (Stern, *Ancient Period,* 161) on the basis of the undated Geniza fragment TS 6 H9-H21, which contains the liturgical poetry of the sixth-century Palestinian poet Yosef bar R. Nissan of Neve Kiryatayim in an unusual codex of papyrus sheets featuring several remarkable codicological traits, including the fact that recently rediscovered photographs demonstrate it was bound together in a single gathering (a style widely thought to have died out in the fifth century). (Collette Sirat with contributions from Malachi Beit-Arié and Ada Yardeni, *Les papyrus en caractères hébraïques trouvés en Egypte* [Paris: Centre national de la recherche scientifique, 1985], 72–79; and Collette Sirat, *Hebrew Manuscripts of the Middle Ages,* ed. and trans. Nicholas de Lange [Cambridge: Cambridge University Press, 2002], 246). But this outlier work has only been firmly dated in the sense that its script includes elongation of letters at the end of some lines (a trait not present in Byzantine Hebrew scripts). For more on the characteristics of early medieval Hebrew scripts in Greek manuscripts, see Judith Oszowy-Schlanger, "The Hebrew Script of the Greek-Hebrew Palimpsests," in *The Jewish-Greek Tradition in Antiquity and the Byzantine Empire,* ed. James K. Aitken and James Carleton Paget (Cambridge: Cambridge University Press, 2014), 279–99. It was only introduced in Arabic manuscripts in seventh-eighth centuries, so it cannot therefore be earlier than the eighth century, though others have suggested a ninth-century date (Rebecca J. W. Jefferson, "T-S 6H9–21, the Papyrus Codex Rebound," Cambridge Library Fragment of the Month July 2009 [https://doi.org/10.17863/CAM.48228])—perhaps on the strength of the vocalization system which appears in Arabic and Manichean manuscripts from the ninth century and other Jewish manuscripts in the tenth. While the "primitive appearance" of this particular work "tends to confirm

FROM THE THIRD TORAH TO GOD'S MONOGRAPH   229

equal number of codices and texts in roll and scroll formats written with the linguistic components necessary for informational or sight reading in the ninth century—including biblical scrolls with vocalizations and translations.[25] Recent evidence also suggests that a pluriformity of formats continued to prevail even long after the codex had (belatedly) become a widely popular format for

---

the claim that the Hebrew-using circles remained attached to the older scroll format, against the general trend" in Christian Greek texts (Nicholas de Lange, *Japheth in the Tents of Shem: Greek Bible Translations in Byzantine Judaism* [Tübingen: Mohr Siebeck, 2015], 58). This suggests that the evidence for developed use of the codex in medieval Jewish circles offered by this particular document is not much earlier, if at all, than the earliest known Hebrew codex fragments from a "common Bible" (as Collette Sirat designated biblical manuscripts produced in Islamicate regions without full Masoretic notations) copied in Iran in 903/904 (Sirat, *Hebrew Manuscripts*, 46). With the paleographic consensus that the Moses ben Asher codex was copied at least a century (and possibly two centuries) later than its attributed date of 895, we are left with a scant sixteen extant codices dated to the period before 1020, including thirteen biblical manuscripts, two biblical commentaries, and an unrelated work. Nor does this dearth of codices or plurality of textual forms appear to represent a mere accident of preservation emerging from the dating of the Cairo Geniza. Only forty extant Muslim and Arabic Christian codices can be reliably dated to the ninth century (Beatrice Gruendler, *The Rise of the Arabic Book* [Cambridge, MA: Harvard University Press, 2020], 13). And these do not yet represent a single (or regionally) dominant codex form, since the wide variety of both writing materials and "mise-en-page of the early Arabic codices is striking"—suggesting perhaps a medium still in development in this new culture context (Gruendler, *Arabic Book*, 14–15).

25. From the ninth century, we find an almost equal number of texts written with the linguistic components necessary for informational or sight-reading in roll or scroll formats—including biblical texts with vocalizations and translations. These include, for instance, horizontal biblical scrolls annotated with Palestinian vocalization and accent signs, though few Masoretic notes (Yeivin, *Masorah*, 123). There are oddities such as an eighth- or "conservatively ninth"-century scroll transcribed horizontally with a doubly vocalized (with Palestinian vocalization and some Tiberian additions) Targum of Exodus on the recto (T-S 20.155) and *haftorot* lectionaries transcribed in a transverse direction (rotulus style) on the verso (Michael L. Klein, *Michael Klein on the Targums*, Studies in the Aramaic Interpretations of Scripture 11 [Leiden: Brill, 2011], 107–18). The combination of biblical text and translation is seen in another form in biblical scrolls with Babylonian vocalization and verse-by-verse Aramaic translation inline (Judith Olszowy-Schlanger, "The Anatomy of Non-Biblical Scrolls from the Cairo Geniza," in *Jewish Manuscript Cultures: New Perspectives*, ed. Irina Wandrey [Berlin: de Gruyter, 2017], 60). These biblical scrolls may well have been used for liturgical purposes as easily as study, along with the scrolls and rolls featuring original liturgical poems and other liturgy. However, there are also a variety of other extant ninth-century scrolls featuring nonbiblical works such as Hekhalot Rabbati, Avot de Rabbi Natan, various portions of the Mishnah and Babylonian Talmud and medieval-style midrash—suggesting that at this point informational reading was not firmly associated with the codex format (Olszowy-Schlanger, "Anatomy").

230 CONCLUDING REMARKS

textual transmission in tenth- and eleventh-century Jewish circles in the Middle East and North Africa.[26] The belated Jewish adoption of the codex was

26. This is true in two senses. On the one hand, Jewish biblical codices themselves came in a much wider variety of forms than Stern's account suggests. The majority of these codex forms would continue to preserve the Hebrew text in a form that would be inappropriate for independent informational reading. Thus, Ben Outhwaite follows Israel Yeivin in pointing out that "most are fragments of 'vulgar' texts, without Masorah, without accents, with many extra vowel letters and so on" (Benjamin Outhwaite, "The Tiberian Tradition in Common Bibles from the Cairo Genizah," in *Studies in Semitic Vocalization and Reading Traditions*, ed. Aaron D. Kornkohl and Geoffrey Rubenstein [Cambridge: Cambridge Semitic Languages and Cultures Open Publications, 2020], 410). Moshe Goshen-Gottstein proposed that only 15–20 percent of biblical manuscripts preserved in the Geniza could be categorized as "Masoretic codices" of a type similar to that described by Stern—and that once the vagaries of preservation are accounted for, this proportion would have been reduced to 10–15 percent or even 1 in 10 in the Middle Ages themselves, if there were "even as many as that" (Moshe Goshen-Gottstein, "Biblical Manuscripts in the United States," *Textus* 2 [1962]: 37). The next smallest category, Goshen-Gottstein argues, were private "study codices" that did not contain the Masoretic text (or even necessarily standard vocalization and spelling) but were largely readable as standalone works (38). The majority of biblical manuscripts, Goshen-Gottstein maintains, could only be categorized as "listener codices," which contained "bowdlerized" texts with varied levels of vocalization that were no more faithful to a standardized text of the Hebrew Bible than "a biblical quotation in a non-biblical text" and could be used for little more than "hearing aid" during a liturgical reading 38). More troublesome yet are the mysteriously abbreviated *serugin* manuscripts in which entire biblical sections are reduced to a series of lemmas and sporadic letters from each verse. (For a review the scholarly debate surrounding the possible purpose of these manuscripts, see Klein, *Targums*, 97–99.) Meanwhile, noncodex formats suitable for sight-reading apparently survived for a wide variety of works—including biblical ones—well into the High Middle Ages. Biblical horizontal scrolls were not universally restricted to use in liturgical recitation-reading but apparently continued to include more philological information than could be provided by a bare consonantal text, such as a recently rediscovered twelfth- or thirteenth-century Italian biblical scroll (Mauro Perani, "Il 'Rotolo di Esdra' Riscoperto A Bologna: Caratteristiche Grafiche e Scrittorie del Piu Antico e Integro Sefer Torah," in *'Ir Hefsi-Vah: Studies in Hebrew and Judaics in Honor of Guiliano Tamani*, ed. Michela Andreatta and Fabrizio Lelli [Leiden: Brill, 2019], 79–145) marked with a series of textual corrections and Masoretic *nuns* denoting an "orthographic oddity" in the corresponding line (Elvira Martin-Contreras, "The Marginal Nun in the Masora of the Cairo Codex of the Prophets: Use and Function," *Vetus Testamentum* 65 [2015]: 81–90), or that scroll featuring Aquila's translation of Kings (possibly a scroll of translated *haftorot*) that was apparently preserved in its scroll form until it was cut down for a notebook in eleventh-century Lucena (Judith Olszowy-Schlanger, "An Early Palimpsest Scroll of the Book of Kings From the Cairo Genizah," in *"From a Sacred Source": Genizah Studies in Honor of Professor Stefan C. Reif* [Leiden: Brill, 2011], 237–47). Other forms of writing physically preserved from this period include even quite exotic forms, such as an "eleventh century or earlier" Greek text

FROM THE THIRD TORAH TO GOD'S MONOGRAPH   231

certainly one of the great technological shifts in Jewish history, but it appears
to have developed in tandem with, or perhaps even followed, this broader

---

of Ecclesiastes written in Hebrew letters, which was not bound in a codex but appears to have
been gathered by sticking the sheets onto a spike (Nicholas de Lange, *Greek Jewish Texts from
the Cairo Genizah* [Tübingen: Mohr Siebeck, 1996], 71). A recent study of a sample of three
hundred tenth- to eleventh-century *rotuli* preserved in the Geniza suggests, moreover, that the
rotulus continued to be used with some regularity for "cheap books" and other works made for
a single reader (Judith Olszowy-Schlanger, "Reading in the Provinces: A Midrash on a Rotulus
from Damira, Its Materiality, Scribe, and Date," *The Courtauld*, no pagination https://courtauld.
ac.uk/research/research-resources/publications/courtauld-books-online/continuous-page-
scrolls-and-scrolling-from-papyrus-to-hypertext/2-reading-in-the-provinces-a-midrash-on-
rotulus-from-damira-its-materiality-scribe-and-date-judith-olszowy-schlanger/), not only for
rabbinic works such as the She'iltot of R. Ahai (Roni Shweka, "A She'iltot Rotulus by R.
Ephraim ben Shemarya and the Palestinian Tradition of Sefer HaShe'iltot," *Ginze qedem* 16
[2020] [in Hebrew]) or the medieval midrash Pirka de-Rabbenu ha-Kadosh (Judith Olszowy-
Schlanger, "Un rotulus du midrash *Pirqa de-Rabbenu ha-Qadosh* de la Geniza du Caire," *Annuaire
de l'École pratique des hautes études* [2012–2013]) and their study aids (Judith Olszowy-Schlanger,
"Glossary of Difficult Words in the Babylonian Talmud (Seder Mo'ed) on a Rotulus," in *Jewish
Education from Antiquity to the Middle Ages*, ed. George J. Brookes and Renate Smithius [Leiden:
Brill, 2017], 296–323), but also for various genres of biblical studies including biblical translation
and commentaries (TS Ar 1a.140), lists of biblical variants and textual difficulties known as the
Masorah (MS Bodl. Heb a 3.30) and lexigraphical works (TS AR 53.9). If these more casual
rotuli using materials of lesser quality frequently fell into the category that Miriam Frenkel has
termed "disposable writing" (Miriam Frenkel, "Book Lists from the Cairo Geniza: A Window
on the Production of Texts in the Middle Ages," *Bulletin of the SOAS* 80, no. 2 [2017]: 248),
moreover, it would not be surprising if works in this form were disproportionately reused, worn
out, or degraded beyond recognition. In addition to vertical scrolls, Judith Olszowy-Schlanger
recently identified a selection of thirty-one nonbiblical horizontal scrolls among the Geniza
fragments, many of which were rabbinic literature without any apparent liturgical connections—primarily, but not exclusively, from the transitional ninth century (Olszowy-Schlanger
"Anatomy," 49). While these numbers may seem small in comparison to the vastness of the
Geniza collection as a whole, this is an emerging area of classifications and the early results have
been significant enough that many more scholars are coming to the conclusion that even as
"Eastern communities largely adopted the codex . . . the new format coexisted with other, pre-
existing forms such as horizontal scrolls, rotuli, and pinkasim" in such a way that "the transition
from the scroll to the codex took place gradually over a long period, and during this process all
formats continued to be used" (Javier Barco, "From Scroll to Codex: Dynamics of Text Layout
Transformation in the Hebrew Bible," in *From Scroll to Scrolling: Sacred Texts, Materiality, and
Dynamic Media Cultures*, ed. Bradford A. Anderson [Berlin: de Gruyter, 2020], 93). Well into the
High Middle Ages "a fluid relationship existed between text and codex," as Sarah Pierce has put
it in *Andalusi Literary and Intellectual Tradition: The Role of Arabic in Judan Ibn Tibbon's Ethical
Will* (Bloomington: Indiana University Press, 2017), 52.

232 CONCLUDING REMARKS

bookish turn in attitudes toward the Bible.[27] Thus far, the commentary revolution remains something of a mystery.

A Speculative Explanation: Spreading the Concept of God's Monograph

I believe that the revised account of the early rabbinic relationship with the Bible offered in this book can indirectly offer us a path forward as we try to understand what happened next. We cannot attribute the medieval revolution in Jewish modes of relating to the Bible to the rise of a new book format, if what we mean by "book" is the technology of the paper codex. But what if we substituted a different definition of what we meant by "book" into this equation? Marina Rustow has recently proposed that in the Jewish Middle Ages, books proper meant texts "written in conformity with the rules of style and genre."[28] In other words, Rustow suggests that the medieval Jewish definition

---

27. Although the theory has not been proposed directly, this shift in Jewish approaches toward the biblical text could also be attributed to a technological revolution in another sense, inasmuch as we know that the spark was lit for an explosion of medieval book production in general by the arrival of paper. As Jonathan Bloom put it in his now-classic volume on the paper revolution, "The availability of paper in the Islamic lands encouraged an efflorescence of books and written culture incomparably more brilliant than was known anywhere . . . until the invention of printing with movable type in the fifteenth" (Jonathan Bloom, *Paper before Print: The History and Impact of Paper in the Islamic World* [New Haven, CT: Yale University Press, 2001], 91). Indeed, one might even suggest that rise of the new paper codex format was the technological shift that finally brought Jews to the codex form en masse. As with the codex form, however, one cannot claim, that paper was the direct instigator of the genre revolution in Jewish communities across the globe. For while codicologists such as Collette Sirat and Malachi Beit-Arié certainly affirm that "paper . . . favored the proliferation of books" in Jewish circles, paper would not really begin to be used commonly by Jews in Muslim lands until the tenth century onward (Sirat, *Hebrew Manuscripts*, 35) and would not be produced in Europe in any bulk until the thirteenth century (Sirat, *Hebrew Manuscripts,* 53), becoming the main writing material only in the mid-fourteenth century in Sephardic communities and in the mid-fifteenth century in Jewish communities in northern and central Europe (Malachi Beit-Arié, *Hebrew Codicology: Historical and Comparative Typology of Hebrew Medieval Codices* (Hamburg: Center for the Study of Manuscript Cultures, 2022), 14–15. For the dating of specific paper types and manuscripts, see Malachi Beit-Arie, *Hebrew Codicology* (Jerusalem: Israel Academy of Arts and Sciences, 1977), 26–40). Like the codex, the spread of this earlier technological revolution often lagged just behind the waves of change in Jewish biblical interpretation.

28. Marina Rustow, *The Lost Archive: Traces of a Caliphate in a Cairo Synagogue* (Princeton, NJ: Princeton University Press, 2020), 387.

of a book was roughly synonymous with the Greek category of *syngramma* (official publication):

> [Saul] Lieberman and [Gregor] Schoeler argue for the Jewish and Muslim use, respectively, of the Hellenistic distinction between the *ekdosis* or *syngramma*, the official written version of a text that was copied and disseminated in writing, and the *hypomnema*, textual material meant to circulate orally, and written down only as informal notes for strictly personal use. In Lieberman's late antique world, rabbinic literature seldom circulated as *syngrammata*. The situation is often represented as a total ban on writing down rabbinic traditions, but this is misleading. Writing down traditions for personal use—as *hypomnemata*—was perfectly fine. In Schoeler's world, Muslim scholars in pursuit of learning took notes for later study or wrote works down for oral delivery: *hypomnemata*. Books proper, as written in conformity with the rules of style and genre, were *syngrammata*.[29]

Could we say that medieval Jewish approaches to the Bible were transformed as this *concept* of the book (as an official publication defined by conformity to certain genre expectations) was increasingly embraced in Jewish circles?

I think we can. In the study of rabbinic Judaism, the Hebrew Bible has often been imagined as the lone *syngramma* in the early rabbinic library. But the current monograph has demonstrated that the text of the Hebrew Bible was not, by and large, imagined in these terms in the early rabbinic period. Instead, in a period of Jewish intellectual history dominated by *hypomnemata*, the Bible itself was often treated likewise as a form of provisional, fluid, and oralized text. With this misconception cleared away, we can argue that the medieval revolution in Jewish attitudes toward the biblical text took place as different communities began to think of the Bible as a book for the first time, in the sense that they began to conceive of the Bible as a purposeful publication written in conformity with prevailing rules of style and genre. That is, I would argue that it was not emerging technologies of the book that transformed how medieval Jews approached their written scriptures but the broader *ideologies* of writing and bookishness that were born during the paper and codex revolutions— leading medieval Jewish thinkers to see the biblical text for the first time as a book like other books.

I would like to propose, in other words, that a general global proliferation of literariness and single-authored compositions in the wake of the paper

---

29. Ibid., 387.

234 CONCLUDING REMARKS

revolution[30] began to gradually metamorphose the ways in which medieval Jews thought about the character of the Bible as a composition. Just as early rabbinic Jewry had been steeped in a literary culture dominated by *hypomnemata* and came to think of the biblical text in similar terms, as provisional written notes reflecting a more authentic oral version of this composition passed directly from the mouth of God to his followers, so medieval Jewry would come to be steeped in a culture of carefully structured single-author compositions and begin to think of the Bible as God's own divine monograph.

Which is to say, perhaps the uneven global revolution described in the previous section would be more easily explained if this commentary movement was not spread through the transfer of specific literary techniques that needed to be conveyed in detail but was instead sparked by the propagation of a novel conception of the Bible's genre. This more abstract model would go some ways toward explaining the speed with which this global revolution spread through a relatively tenuous network of international contacts. For while it has often been difficult to identify *extended* educational or intellectual connections between far-flung medieval communities, the sharing of ideas more generally has proven easier to document. In the broadening scriptural world brought about by the rise of Islam, answering basic questions about how revealed writing functioned became an increasingly intercommunal and global affair. As Ryan Szpiech has put it regarding the medieval Mediterranean, "Exegesis was always a double-valenced phenomenon that pressed against the boundaries between selfhood and otherness, community and outsider."[31] Indeed, the Islamicate world would experience a "crescendo of inter-scriptural reasoning"[32] so

30. On which, see note 27 above. The scholarly literature on the literary turn in the wake of the paper revolution is too broad to cite in full, so I will direct the reader's attention to important bookends on the medieval emergence of bookishness. For a detailed study of this emerging book culture at its font in ninth-century Baghdad, for instance, see Shawkat M. Toorawa, *Ibn Abi Tahir Tayfur and Arabic Writerly Culture: A Ninth-Century Bookman in Baghdad* (London: Routledge, 2005). For a study of the ways in which this emerging turn to the literary was manifest in the textualization of rabbinic literature as far away as Latin Europe, see Talya Fishman, *Becoming the People of the Talmud: Oral Torah as Written Tradition in Medieval Jewish Cultures* (Philadelphia: University of Pennsylvania Press, 2011).

31. Ryan Szpiech, introduction to *Medieval Exegesis and Religious Differences: Commentary, Conflict, and Community in the Premodern Mediterranean* (New York: Fordham University Press, 2015), 2.

32. Sidney Griffith, "Use and Interpretation of Scriptural Proof-Texts in Christian-Muslim Apologetic Literature in Arabic," in *Exegetical Crossroads: Understanding Scripture in Judaism,*

strong that the boundaries between communities in this realm sometime became distinctly "fuzzy."[33] Or, to put it another way, scripture was a topic that Jews, Christians, and Muslims often thought about together—if only in its broadest outlines—and new concepts of how scriptures functioned diffused through the cultural landscape beyond the well-worn paths of official educational institutions and overlaps.

If the commentary revolution was sparked by a changing *idea* of the Bible and its genre, this model would also go far toward explaining the diversity of the shapes that the final product took in each period and locale. For if we think of this notion as another permutation of Haggai Ben-Shammai's insight that the essence of the medieval commentary revolution was the "adoption of the principle that the 'Bible speaks in the language of human beings,' "[34] then the commentaries that resulted from this perspective would naturally vary by the (literary) language of the human beings in a given place and time. Or as Sarah Stroumsa has put it in another context:

> In the medieval intellectual marketplace, ideas and motifs moved from one religious or theological system to another, slightly modifying the system into which they were adopted, and, in the process, undergoing some transformation themselves. Like colored drops falling into a whirlpool, new ideas were immediately carried away by the stream, coloring the whole body of water while changing their own color in the process.[35]

In other words, what if Rashi's merchant contacts did not translate detailed technical treatises for him or teach him the complex literary conventions of their Arabic-speaking compatriots, but instead imported the *idea* that the Bible could be read as a purposeful rhetorical unit in the style of human monographs? In that case, it would be only natural for Rashi to draw on the literary models around him to implement his own vision of this novel perspective.

Christianity, and Islam in the Pre-Modern Orient, ed. Georges Tamer, Regina Grundmann, Assaad Elias Kattan, and Karl Pinggera (Berlin: de Gruyter, 2017), 73.

33. Michael Phillip Penn, *Envisioning Islam: Syriac Christians in the Early Muslim World* (Philadelphia: University of Pennsylvania Press, 2015), 182.

34. Haggai Ben-Shammai, "The Torah Spoke in the Language of Human Beings," in *To Establish the Peshat of the Bible,* ed. Sara Japhet and Eran Viezel (Jerusalem: Mosad Bialik, 2011), 60–63 (in Hebrew).

35. Sarah Stroumsa, "Whirlpool Effects and Religious Studies," in *Dynamics in the History of Religions between Asia and Europe,* ed. Volkhard Krech and Marion Steinicke (Leiden: Brill, 2012), 159.

Rashi's vision of God's monograph would not be *only* a homegrown development *or* a foreign import but would instead have a double origin. Like an Aristotelian fetus, Rashi's revolutionary commentary would be sparked by the fatherly seed of Jewish thinkers from abroad but built from local components from its European motherland.

To say that medieval Jewish exegetes read the Bible like secular literature in various ways has, of course, already been firmly established on several fronts. To cite only the smallest selection of examples: Robert Harris has argued in several venues that the approaches of twelfth-century European exegetes were so literary minded that we might say that they "essentially 'invent' the notion of literature through their contextual reading of biblical composition and their attention to what we could call its literary qualities."[36] Regarding the Middle East and North Africa, Meira Polliack has argued in numerous places that "the term *literary exegesis* seems more suitable in characterizing the unprecedented understanding of the narrative, rhetoric, stylistic, and editorial devices of biblical literature as explored by the Judaeo-Arabic exegetes."[37] Ayelet Seidler has documented how medieval Jewish poets in Spain in general, and Ibn Ezra in particular, sought to identify the literary devices of medieval Arabic and Sephardic poetry in the biblical text.[38] Hanna Liss has demonstrated the extent to which (pseudo-)Rashbam used the literary conventions of contemporary vernacular love poetry to interpret the Song of Songs like piece of secular literature, as "*the* archetype of love poetry."[39] James Robinson has shown us how Samuel ibn Tibbon could envision the Pentateuch and other biblical works as early books of philosophy.[40] My point here is simply to emphasize that a major shift, indeed perhaps the single most important innovation, in medieval Jewish approaches to the Bible across the globe in this period was the emergence of an increasingly universal notion that the biblical text should be read as a book like other books. These exegetes not only read the Bible *like* literature but *as* literature—albeit a rarified divine variety.

36. Robert A. Harris, "Twelfth-Century Biblical Exegetes and the Invention of Literature," in *The Multiple Meanings of Scripture: The Role of Exegesis in Early Christian and Medieval Culture*, ed. Ineke van't Spijker (Leiden: Brill, 2009), 312.

37. Polliack, "Concepts," 87.

38. Ayelet Seidler, "Literary Devices in the Psalms: The Commentary of Ibn Ezra Revisited," *Jewish Studies Quarterly* 22, no. 4 (2015): 379.

39. Hanna Liss, "The Commentary on the Song of Songs attributed to R. Samuel ben Meir (Rashbam)," *Medieval Jewish Studies* 1 (2007): 1.

40. James T. Robinson, *Samuel Ibn Tibbon's Commentary on Ecclesiastes: The Book of the Soul of Man* (Berlin: Mohr Siebeck, 2007), 30.

FROM THE THIRD TORAH TO GOD'S MONOGRAPH   237

Such a shift in the conception of the Bible's own genre would also explain several more facets of the new commentary movement that have not been satisfactorily accounted for in their global manifestations. While the shape of these commentaries varied widely by region and community, a handful of common features can be found threaded throughout. One of these features is the rise of a form of commentary introduction that offers an account of the purpose and structure of a biblical book. Such introductions have long been recognized among Arabic-speaking commentators.[41] This introduction form has also been long accepted as a facet of late medieval European commentary.[42] More recently, however, scholars have begun to document the emergence of more subtle versions of this introduction forms among earlier European Jewish authors.[43]

Many scholars, of course, have drawn our attention to the introduction form as an example of the ways in which biblical commentary *itself* became a single-author form.[44] But Sarah Stroumsa points out that these introductions to scriptures differed slightly from the standard Arabic literary model inasmuch as "the commentator's introduction is not meant to explain his own intention but primarily the intention of the author of the Biblical book."[45] That is, Jewish authors who prefaced their commentaries in this style often

41. See, for instance, Haggai Ben-Shammai, "Saadia's Introduction to Daniel: Prophetic Calculation of the End of Days vs. Astrological and Magical Speculation," *Aleph* 4 (2004): 11–87; Drory, *Contacts*, 118–77; and Uriel Simon, *Four Approaches to the Book of Psalms: From Saadiah Gaon to Ibn Ezra* (Albany: SUNY Press, 2012).

42. See, for instance, Sara Klein-Braslavy, "The Alexandrian Prologue Paradigm in Gersonides' Writings," *Jewish Quarterly Review* 95, no. 2 (2005): 257–89; and Eric Lawee, "Introducing Scripture: The Accessus ad auctores in Hebrew Exegetical Literature from the Thirteenth through the Fifteen Centuries," in *With Reverence for the Word: Medieval Scriptural Exegesis in Judaism, Christianity, and Islam,* ed. Jane Damen McAuliffe, Barry D. Walfish, and Joseph Ward Goerging (Oxford: Oxford University Press, 2010), 157–80.

43. See, for instance, Michel G. Distefano, *Inner-Midrashic Introductions and Their Influence on Introductions to Medieval Rabbinic Bible Commentaries* (Berlin: de Gruyter: 2009), 153–66; Robert A. Harris, "Rashi's Introductions to His Biblical Commentaries," in *Shai leSara Japhet: Studies in the Bible, Its Exegesis, and Its Language,* ed. Moshe Bar-Asher (Jerusalem: Mosad Bialik, 2007), 219–41; Ivan Marcus, "Rashi's Historiography in the Introductions to His Bible Commentaries," *Revue des etudes juives* 157 (1998): 47–55; and Michael Singer, "Restoring the Narrative: Jewish and Christian Exegesis in the Twelfth Century," in Damen, McAuliffe, Walfish, and Goerging, *With Reverence for the Word,* 70–83.

44. Drory, *Contacts*, 137.

45. Stroumsa, "Prolegomena," 137.

238   CONCLUDING REMARKS

sought less to elucidate their own exegetical approach[46] than to lay out the purpose and methods of the *biblical* book's author. Tenth-century Karaite scholar Salmon ben Yeroham, for instance, dedicates his introduction to Ecclesiastes to presenting the biblical author's intentions in the book, laying out "what Solomon . . . intended in this book" and the five foundations upon which "his book and his discourse are built."[47] In other words, many of these introductions served less to introduce the commentary itself than they did to fill in the "missing" introduction to a sacred monograph.

These supplementary introductions often attempted to rehabilitate the biblical text as a purposeful authored composition in other ways, as well. For instance, these new introductions often addressed the question of how the biblical text could be imagined to function effectively (in its newly assigned role) as a rhetorically purposeful authored composition. In some cases, these rehabilitative essays represent relatively gentle forays into the question of the biblical rhetoric and authorial purpose. In his famous query about the structure of the Torah on Genesis 1:1, for instance, Rashi grapples with the gap between the expectations set by human compositions and the compositional structure of the Pentateuch on several fronts. He famously begins his commentary, for instance, by asking why a book of divine instruction would be introduced by a long narrative portion with no legal implications:

> Rabbi Isaac said there was no need to begin the Torah before [the verse] "this month will be to you" (Exod 12:2) since that is the first commandment that Israel was given, so why begin with "in the beginning" (Gen 1:10)? So that if the nations of the world were to say to Israel, "You are robbers, since you conquered the lands of the seven nations," they can reply to them, "The whole world belongs to the Holy One, blessed be he, he created it and he can give it to whomever finds favor in his eyes. By his will it was given to them and by his will it was taken from them and given to us."

These opening comments are not simply polemical or theological asides but explicate fundamental ground rules about the literary function of the Pentateuch. While this ancient composition might easily be read as a (flawed) legal compendium,[48] Rashi explains, the Pentateuch is structured in a way that not

46. With a few notable exceptions, perhaps, such as Ibn Ezra's introduction to the Pentateuch.

47. Salmon ben Yeroham's introduction to Ecclesiastes, as translated in James T. Robinson, *Asceticism, Eschatology, Opposition to Philosophy: The Arabic Translation and Commentary of Salmon ben Yeroham on Qohelet (Ecclesiastes)* (Leiden: Brill, 2012), 169–70, 172.

48. This notion that the Pentateuch should be read as law is not, of course, a neutral pre-

FROM THE THIRD TORAH TO GOD'S MONOGRAPH   239

only conveys the laws by which Israel should live but illustrates the fundamental theological principles that underlie these norms. Rashi thus dedicates the beginning of his commentary to imagining how his readers might expect a divine composition to function and explaining (away) any deviations from the reader's literary expectations.

In other cases, these introductory remarks were not only explicit about their literary presuppositions but quite biting—straying close to accusing God of (at least appearing) to be a bad author. Saadiah Gaon, for instance, begins his commentary on the Torah with the telling comment:

> "Apples of gold in ornaments of silver is a word fitly spoken" (Prov 25:12). . . . And elsewhere in my commentary I clarified these . . . verses in context [elucidating] the nature of the phrase "fitly spoken" [with ten rules of composition]. . . . But if a man questions, saying: "If the ordering of a composition has such great importance, why don't we find [such ordering] in this book, which is to say, in the Torah? Why don't we find commandments and laws collected and ordered in sections, and divided into parts and arranged in [logical] steps? But instead we see them scattered about and isolated [from others on the topic]?" You should answer him saying: "The One Who Gave the Torah, may he be elevated and praised, did this on purpose so that those who fear him would occupy themselves and would exert great effort to carefully examine it until they held it completely in their memories and connected each declaration to those that are like it, so that they connect each point to its section and category, and by means of this their reward [for study] will be greater.[49]

In this remark, Saadiah Gaon expresses concern that anyone who knew the rules of literary composition of his own day and age would find God a very poor author. He therefore strives to explain that, despite superficial appearances to the contrary, the Pentateuch was indeed carefully crafted by its divine author. But it may not immediately appear so because the divine author did not intend to provide the reader with easy comprehension as human authors seek to do. Instead, Saadiah argues, the Pentateuch is a book that is *meant* to

---

sumption and in Rashi's context would have been polemic undertones, as Robert Harris has pointed out in "Concepts of Scriptures in the School of Rashi," in *Jewish Concepts of Scripture: A Comparative Introduction,* ed. Benjamin Sommer (New York: New York University Press, 2012), 103.

49. Moshe Zucker, *Saadya's Commentary on Genesis in Arabic and Hebrew Translation* (New York: Jewish Theological Seminary Press, 1984), 4 (in Arabic) and 166–67 (in Hebrew).

be difficult to read and comprehend so that a person might reap the heavenly rewards of his laborious reading.

Other medieval authors drew quite specifically on contemporary literary models in their rehabilitative introductions. The most well-documented case in point is probably Ibn Ezra. His introduction(s) to the Pentateuch are (in)famous for their systematic review and dismissal of previous exegetes, who he insists have fundamentally misidentified the unique genre, and thus the hermeneutic key, to the Pentateuch.[50] Uriel Simon has similarly demonstrated that Ibn Ezra's introductions to Psalms was, in many ways, dedicated to the commentator's struggle to understand the book of Psalms as a well-structured work in comparison with the *diwan*s (poetic anthologies) of his own age. For while Ibn Ezra praised the individual psalms as the height of sung poetry,[51] he devotes the all-important final "inquiry" of his introduction to the fact that it is difficult to discern any clear editorial system at work in the book of Psalms. As Ibn Ezra reads it, the highly erratic authorial attributions and superscriptions of the individual psalms are striking from this point of view, as is the fact that arrangement of poems in this collected work does not seem to follow any thematic or chronological order that Ibn Ezra can discern. This troubles Ibn Ezra because, as Uriel Simon notes, "the absence of a principle of arrangement is no commendation for an anthology of poems; this makes it hard to accept the conclusion that the Men of the Great Assembly did not do a thorough job of editing the psalms."[52] In other words, here, too, the medieval commentator is concerned that an inspired editorial committee appears to have done a poor job according to the literary standards of his day. Here again, moreover, the medieval author argues that the solution to this critical challenge lies in recognizing the true genre of the biblical book in question. For Ibn Ezra would conclude that the superscriptions in Psalms represented musical cues like the superscription in the *piyyut* anthologies of his own day, which recontextualized the book of Psalms from a poorly edited *diwan* anthology to a (more loosely organized) manual of individual liturgical compositions.[53]

The contrast between authors and editors in the preceding example brings us to another facet of the medieval commentary movement on which the

50. For a book-length study of these introductions and their attempt to thread a line in the fraught waters of previous genres, see Irene Lancaster, *Deconstructing the Bible: Abraham Ibn Ezra's Introduction to the Torah* (London: Routledge, 2003).

51. Simon, *Four Approaches*, 161.

52. Ibid., 220.

53. Ibid., 257.

emerging notion of a divine monograph might shed light. If one takes a broad survey of recent research, it emerges that virtually every commentator of the new school wrote at some level about the different hands at work in the process of producing biblical literature. To cite only a few examples: Karaites such as Yefet b. Eli introduced the concept (imported from Arabic literary studies) of a biblical *mudawwin* (composer-compiler) and devoted considerable space to documenting "the narrative and literary techniques employed by these supposed authors and editors"—which included what we would consider redactional-editorial functions, such as stringing together available material into cohesive units.[54] Byzantine Jewish authors such Reuel of Byzantium would similarly use the term סדרן to refer to such an editor, who was sometimes presented as editing a single source and at other times portrayed as "dealing with multiple, divergent sources."[55] While Andalusian authors such as Ibn Ezra would even add additional layers to this collective process, as when Ibn Ezra rallied his own extensive experience of Arabic translations[56] to make the famous suggestion that the book of Job is difficult to interpret because it was a mélange of a composition in which "Moses wrote the frame narrative and some of the headings, but translated the remainder of the book [from another language into Hebrew] . . . rather than writing it himself."[57]

---

54. Polliack, "Concepts," 95. For an extended discussion, see Meira Polliack, "Karaite Conceptions of the Biblical Narrator (Mudawwin)," in *Encyclopedia of Midrash*, vol. 1, ed. Jacob Neusner and A. J. Avery-Peck (Leiden: Brill, 2005), 350–74, and Polliack, "The Voice of the Narrator and the Voice of the Characters in the Bible Commentaries of Yefet ben 'Eli," in *Birkat Shalom: Studies in the Bible, Ancient Near Eastern Literature and Post-Biblical Judaism*, ed. Chaim Cohen (University Park: Penn State University Press, 2008), 891–916. See also, Haggai Ben-Shammai, "On the Mudawwin of the Hebrew Bible in Judaeo-Arabic Bible Exegesis," in *From Sages to Savants: Studies Presented to Avraham Grossman*, ed. Y. Hacker (Jerusalem: Magnes, 2010), 73–110 (in Hebrew); Robinson, *Yefet Ben 'Eli*, 2, 22, 29, 31, 46, 53, 82, 116, 138; Ilana Sasson, "The Mudawwin Revisited: Yefet ben Eli on the Composition of the Book of Proverbs," *Journal of Jewish Studies* 67, no. 2 (2016): 327–39; Marzena Zawanowska, "Yefet's View on the Authorship of the Pentateuch," in *The Arabic Translation and Commentary of Yefet ben 'Eli the Karaite on the Abraham Narratives*, ed. Marzena Zawanowska (Leiden: Brill, 2012), 27–57.

55. Richard C. Steiner, "A Jewish Theory of Biblical Redaction from Byzantium: Its Rabbinic Roots, Its Diffusion and Its Encounter with the Muslim Doctrine of Falsification," *Jewish Studies Internet Journal* 2 (2003): 124.

56. Eran Viezel, "Abraham Ibn Ezra's Commentary on Job 2:11: The Time and Place of Job and His Friends and the Composition of the Book of Job," *Hebrew Union College Annual* 88 (2017): 124.

57. Ibid., 126.

242 CONCLUDING REMARKS

Meanwhile, scholars of Jewish thought in Latin Christian Europe have argued that "one of the constants in northern French exegesis is the willingness of the commentators to view the biblical text as a result of human redactional activity—even as they ascribed the revelation related in that text to the Divine Author."[58] Eran Viezel argues that Rashi, for instance, "was of the opinion that some biblical books came about as the result of a two-stage process. The first stage was an extensive writing phase. The second stage . . . consisted of gathering the writings and joining them together"—sometimes at different hands.[59] Meanwhile, Mordechai Cohen argues that Rashbam similarly used the root ס.ד.ר to "connote the biblical editors who arranged the words of Qohelet."[60] And Robert Harris demonstrates that Rabbi Eliezer of Beaugency refers to a redactional editor quite separate from the prophetic authors when he made comments like that on Ezekiel 1:1 saying: "But the redactor who assembled [lit., 'wrote'] all of his words together added to what [Ezekiel] had left unclear and abbreviated."[61]

These complex medieval accounts of layered authorship and editorial activities are often read by modern scholars as something akin to contemporary "higher criticism,"[62] so that the Middle Ages stand out as a unique premodern moment when scientific observations about biblical composition were briefly acknowledged by traditional authors. Yet as we saw in the first chapter of this book, the notion that the biblical text had been (re)shaped by the forces of human history and (re)formed by human hands was already a strong thread of early rabbinic tradition. Moreover, we see many of these medieval authors directly grappling with that rabbinic inheritance in their work. Meira Polliack has demonstrated, for instance, that authors such as Ya'qub al-Qirqisani were painfully aware of the rabbinic tradition of an Ezran edition of the Bible and

58. Harris, "Biblical Exegetes," 315.

59. Eran Viezel, "The Formation of Some Biblical Books, according to Rashi," *The Journal of Theological Studies* 61, no. 1 (2010): 19.

60. Cohen, *Rule of Peshat*, 261.

61. Harris, "Biblical Exegetes," 315–16.

62. See, for instance, Robert Harris, "Awareness of Biblical Redaction among Rabbinic Exegetes of Northern France," *Shnaton for Biblical and Ancient Near Eastern Studies* 12 (2000): 289–310; Steiner, "Biblical Redaction"; Israel Ta-Shma, "Bible Criticism in Early Medieval Franco-Germany," in *The Bible in Light of Its Interpreters: Sarah Kamin Memorial Volume*, ed. Sara Japhet (Jerusalem: Magnes, 1994), 453–59; and for a survey of this trend, see Eran Viezel, "Medieval Bible Commentators on the Question of the Composition of the Bible: Research and Methodological Aspects," *Tarbiz* 84 (2015–2016): 103–58 and the sources cited there.

FROM THE THIRD TORAH TO GOD'S MONOGRAPH 243

the dangerous similarity between this tradition and Muslim *tahrif* accusations. As Qirqisani put it in his *Book of Lights and Watchtowers* (c. 937):

> They [=the Rabbinates] assert that the Torah which is in the hands of the people is not the Torah which Moses (peace be upon him) brought, but was composed by Ezra, for they say that the Torah brought by Moses perished and was lost and disappeared. This amounts to the destruction of the whole religion. Were the Muslims to learn of this, they would need nothing else with which to revile and confute us.[63]

In comments such as these, we see medieval Jewish authors struggling to come to grips with what early rabbinic traditions of layered biblical composition might mean in a world in which purposeful single authorship was taking on new meanings. I would suggest, therefore, that medieval commentators who described a process of multilayered biblical composition were not abandoning a "traditional view of God as the 'author' of the Pentateuch"[64] in favor of a novel notion that the biblical text was a human composition reflecting a divine origin. Instead, I would argue that these authors were (re)reading existing early rabbinic accounts of multilayered biblical composition in light of their own contemporary literary practices in a way that *reinstated* God as the ultimate author of this work.

While this statement makes little sense in a contemporary literary context defined by single-author texts in which the contributions of editors and other shareholders are systematically effaced, one of the most striking features of medieval Jewish literatures in both Islamicate and Christian contexts was the extent to which these works were treated as textually "open books"[65] while still retaining their claims to single authorship. As Miriam Frenkel has explained this apparent paradox in relation to the editorial work of Joseph Rosh HaSeder: "While later compilers saw themselves as 'neutral reporters' whose mission was to transmit 'information' . . . R. Joseph reflects a different approach in which the [scribal author] is committed to . . . internalizing old wisdom and reworking it into the literary language and conventions of his own

63. Meira Polliack, "Deconstructing the Dual Torah," in *Interpreting Scriptures in Judaism, Christianity, and Islam: Overlapping Inquiries,* ed. Adele Berlin and Mordechai Z. Cohen (Cambridge: Cambridge University Press, 2016), 124.

64. Polliack, "Voice," 899.

65. Israel Ta-Shma, "The Open Book in Medieval Hebrew Literature: The Problem of Authorized Editions," *Bulletin of the John Rylands University Library of Manchester* 75, no. 3 (1993): 17–24.

244 CONCLUDING REMARKS

time . . . [so that] they felt entitled to intervene in order to improve and update them."[66] Nor was his attitude toward textual growth unique. Quite the contrary. Malachi Beit-Arié has estimated that at least half of the four thousand extant medieval manuscripts were "personal, user-produced books, copied by educated persons or scholars for their own use,"[67] wherein "the scholar-copyist might intentionally interfere in the transmission, revise his exemplar, emend and reconstruct the text."[68] Or, as Israel Ta-Shma has put it, the medieval scribe functioned on a fundamental working principle of "active-aggressive adaptation."[69]

A medieval author who had come to see the Bible as a book like other books, therefore, might easily make statements about biblical authorship that would be paradoxical in our own literary milieu. Marzena Zawanowska has argued, for instance, that we can square Yefet b. Eli's technical discussions of multiple biblical authors and editors with his insistence that the entire Pentateuch was written down by Moses at God's behest if we recognize that Yefet believed that there could be more than one divinely inspired voice simultaneously at work in the biblical account[70]—for each of these writers and editors were understood to refine and perfect the biblical revelation under divine guidance.[71] As Haggai Ben-Shammai has put it, this explanation clarified the uneven nature of the biblical text by suggesting that biblical prophecy underwent two stages: "The first stage was its revelation in a message to the prophet and the second stage was the wording of these statements, their editing and development in writing for the public [by an individual who had achieved] some sort of level of prophecy."[72] By reading the earlier traditions about the compilatory nature of biblical literature through the lens of medieval book production, these commentators were both able to domesticate these ideas

66. Frenkel, "Book Lists," 251.

67. Malachi Beit-Arié, "Jewish Scribality and Its Impacts," in *Transmitting Jewish Tradition: Orality, Textuality, and Cultural Diffusion,* ed. Yaakov Elman and Israel Gershoni (New Haven, CT: Yale University Press, 2000), 230.

68. Ibid., 229–30.

69. Israel Ta-Shma, *Creativity and Tradition: Studies in Medieval Rabbinic Scholarship, Literature, and Thought* (Cambridge, MA: Harvard University Press, 2006), 80.

70. Zawanowska, "Authorship," 37.

71. For an extended discussion of how such unfolding was theorized, see Rebecca Scharbach Wollenberg, "A King and a Scribe Like Moses: The Reception of Deuteronomy 34:10 and a Rabbinic Theory of Collective Biblical Authorship," *Hebrew Union College Annual* 90 (2019): 207–24.

72. Ben-Shammai, "Mudawwin," 106.

and address their own concerns about the variegated character of the biblical text as a composition. For by claiming divine inspiration for all the human hands that had (all-too-apparently) left their mark on the biblical texts, these commentators were able to return the ultimate control and authorship of all extant biblical books to God.

It would take a monograph-length study to definitively prove the theory tentatively put forth in this conclusion. For now, it is enough to demonstrate the sorts of explanatory vistas that open for us when we are no longer constrained to explain the medieval commentary revolution as a transition from one kind of bookishness to another. Once we acknowledge the radically different nature of late antique rabbinic modes of engaging with the Bible, we can begin to recognize the sea shift in medieval Jewish attitudes toward the Bible as a product of the moment in which world Jewry truly became the people of the Book—in all senses of that phrase.

INDEX

abecediaries, 138–39

Achaemenid Behistun inscription, 210

adultery, use of biblical text in *sotah* ritual for wife accused of, 64, 67, 68–69, 202–5, 219

Aeschylus, 134

Against Heresies (Irenaeus), 31n16

Against the Christians (Porphyry), 30–31

Agron (Saadia Gaon), 227n23

Ahmed, Sara, 24–25

R. Akiva: dangerousness of biblical texts, stories of, 65, 73, 76, 77, 79, 87–93; literary pedagogies and, 140, 150–52; martyrdom of, 88–93; on unreliability of scripture, 40

Alexandrian grammarians, 102

alphabetic literacy. *See under* literacy pedagogies

amulets and amuletic practices, 194n3, 206, 209

Anonymous A, 227n23

Aphrahat, 49n51

Apostolic Constitutions, 49n51

Aquila, 230n26

Aramaic square script, 36–37

Aramaic targums. *See* targums

Aramaic transition and Ezran authorship tradition, 29, 32–39

Aristophanes, 145–46, 147

ark of the covenant: cherubim on, 214; power/dangerousness of ancient biblical material in, 81–83, 96; Temple ark conflated with, 215–16; women's body, analogy of Torah Scroll inside ark as, 212–17, 219

The Art of Reciting the Qur'an (Nelson), 11

Asian scriptures, 10–11, 195–96, 198

Assyrian/Assyrian script, 33, 36, 38, 181

Augustine of Hippo, 9, 148

Avot de Rabbi Natan, 56n63, 64n18, 140, 151, 172, 229n25

Babylonian Talmud: appearance of texts with linguistic components necessary for informational or sight-reading, 229n25; daily life, restricting bible reading in, 115n35; dangerousness of biblical texts in, 64n18, 66n24, 69n31, 69n33, 73n42, 74n44, 77, 83, 83n53, 84–96; Ezran authorship tradition and, 29, 32, 34, 36, 38, 41; Hillel in, 41–42; R. Hiyya in, 42–43; informational reading, on dangerousness of, 109n25, 110n28; literary pedagogies in, 141–43, 150, 151, 152–53, 155–56, 159–60; mistaken, faulty, and inaccurate readings in, 103–5, 106–7; on paleographic/linguistic evidence of historical variation, 39n32; on phylacteries and mezuzah texts, 206, 207; on recitation-reading (*keri'ah*), 123, 124, 125n9, 126, 127n13, 128, 129, 130n17; on *sotah* scrolls, 204; as source, 2n3; tablets of Moses, first and second versions of, 45; tablets of Moses, on first and second versions of, 46n45, 47; on Third Torah, 166, 167, 169–72, 174, 176, 177n29, 178–80, 182–83, 186, 190, 191; on Torah scrolls, 201nn28–33, 208–9, 213–14, 216n72, 218,

247

248 INDEX

Babylonian Talmud (*cont.*)
219; on triple loss and reestablishment of Torah, 40–41, 44
Bar Kokhba, 79, 81
Baruch's rewriting of Jeremiah's prophecies, 40
Beitar, downfall of, 78–81
body, Torah scroll as, 195–200, 211–20
body and soul in Jewish thought, 197n13
Book of Lights and Watchtowers (Qirqisani), 243
Buddhism, 10, 12–13, 196
burning of martyrs wrapped in Torah scrolls, 75–78, 80

Cairo Geniza, 161, 228–31nn24–26
call and response reading, 140, 148–49, 152–54
Callimachus, 148n74
canonical text, emergence of, 4, 6–8
Cassiodorus, 135n30
censorship. *See* limitations on access to written scripture
centrality of Bible to Jewish thought, 3, 19–21, 222
cherubim on ark of the covenant, 214
Christianity: access to biblical texts in middle ages and, 98–99; ark of the covenant, Temple ark conflated with, 215; carnal scripture in, 196–97; codex, adoption of, 65n22, 229n24; dangerousness of biblical texts and, 65n22, 66, 69, 71–72, 73, 74; death and dying, late antique visions of, 60; Ezran authorship tradition in, 31–32, 36; Gospel texts, concerns about Hebrew Bible used in conjunction with, 64; literacy pedagogies and, 132; medieval Jewish commentary and, 225–26, 235, 242; methodological approach to, 22; *minim* possibly identified with, 65n22, 66; Paul, on oral and written scripture, 164–65n6; reading culture and spoken scripture in, 7, 9, 10; sounded scriptures in, 163; supersessionism, 48–49, 52, 54, 56, 65n22; tab-

lets of Moses, on first and second versions of, 48–49, 52, 54, 56
Cicero, 148
Clement of Alexandria, 137n33, 138n44
Clouds (Aristophanes), 147
codex: Christian adoption of, 65n22, 229n24; ideologies of writing born with, 233; Judaism, codexification, 226–32; paper revolution and, 232n27
craftsman literacy, 143

daily life, restricting bible reading in, 112–18
dangerousness of biblical texts, 2, 17–18, 59–97; R. Akiva and, 65, 73, 76, 77, 79, 87–93; ark of the covenant, ancient biblical material in, 81–83, 96; arrest of R. Eliezer, 73–75; authority of oral tradition over written text and, 72–73; in Babylonian rabbinic tradition, 83–97; Beitar, downfall of, 78–81; betrothed daughter, biblical text compared to, 93–95; books themselves as malicious actors, 65–67; Elazar b. Dama and the snake, 69–73, 77, 82, 96; Ezekiel, book of, 83; feminine textual promiscuity/infidelity, themes of, 61–63, 64, 67, 68–69, 73–75, 93–95; to gentiles studying Torah, 93–95; R. Hanina b. Teradion, martyrdom of, 75–78, 84–89, 93; King Yannai and Elazar b. Po'irah, 95–97; in later Palestinian sources, 75–83; *minim* (sectarians/heretics), in hands of, 18, 63–68, 73–75; process of informational reading, as dangerous, 99–100, 107–12; *sotah* ritual (for wife accused of adultery), use of biblical text in, 64, 67, 68–69; in Tannaitic tradition, 63–75; as theoretical reflections, 60–61
Daniel, Ezran authorship tradition and Aramaic portions of, 32–35
Darius (king of Persia), 210
deadliness of biblical text. *See* dangerousness of biblical text
deceased body of *met mitzvah*, Torah scroll used to wrap, 211

Demonstrations (Aphrahat), 49n51
Deuteronomy Rabbah, 51n53
Dialogue with Trypho (Justin Martyr), 49n51
Didascalia, 49n51
Dionysius of Halicarnassus, 135n29
directionality of reading, 120
Divine Institutes (Lactantius), 49n51
divorce, association of second tablets of Moses with, 50–56
Dunash ben Labrat, 226

East and South Asian scriptures, 10–11, 195–96, 198
Ecclesiastes Rabbah, 48n48, 69n31, 73n42, 167n15
R. Elazar b. Arakh and the Diomset spa, 142–43
Elazar b. Dama and the snake, 69–73, 77, 82, 96
R. Elazar b. Perata, 84
Elazar b. Poʾirah, 95–97
R. Elazar the Modai, 79, 80
R. Eliezer, arrest of, 73–75
R. Eliezer of Beaugency, 242
Elisha b. Abuya, 155n86
Esther Rabbah, 155n86
"ethnography of reading," 99
Euripides, 153
Exodus Rabbah, 48n47, 50n53
Ezekiel, dangerousness of book of, 83
4 Ezra, on loss of biblical text, 29
Ezra the Scribe: Ezran authorship tradition, 17, 28, 29–39, 40, 41, 242–43; fluency in Torah attributed to, 36, 167, 169, 171

faulty, mistaken, and inaccurate readings, 103–4
females. *See* gender/sexuality
First Jewish Revolt, 80

Rabban Gamliel, 116, 117
gender/sexuality: ban on teaching/transmitting Torah to women, 205; betrothed daughter, biblical text compared to, 93–95; bodily humiliation/shame in exposure of Torah scrolls, 215, 218–19; marriage and divorce, association of second tablets of Moses with, 50–56; *sotah* ritual (for wife accused of adultery), use of biblical text in, 64, 67, 68–69, 202–5, 219; textual promiscuity/infidelity and dangerousness of biblical texts, 61–63, 64, 67, 68–69, 73–75, 93–95; Torah scroll as female body, 212–16, 219
Genesis Rabbah, 36n24, 124, 155, 157, 167n15, 167n17, 171
genizah, 117, 203
Gospel of Truth, 7
Greek and Roman reading cultures, 7, 8–9, 22–23, 132–33. *See also under* literacy pedagogies

Hadrian (Roman emperor), 79
R. Hananel, 169–70
R. Hanina, 173
R. Hanina b. Teradion, martyrdom of, 75–78, 84–89, 93
haqiqa exegesis, 223
Hekhalot Rabbati, 229n25
Hellenistic and Roman reading cultures, 7, 8–9, 22–23, 132–33. *See also under* literacy pedagogies
heretics/heresy: Elazar b. Dama and the snake, 69–73, 77; R. Eliezer, arrest of, 73–75; R. Hanina b. Teradion, martyrdom of, 76–78; *minim* (sectarians/heretics), biblical books in hands of, 18, 63–68, 73–75. *See also* Christianity
Hermeneumata pseudo-dositheana, 145
Herodas, 134, 148
R. Hilfai, 143n58
Hillel the Babylonian, 41–42
R. Hiyya, 41, 42–44, 168, 170
R. Hiyya b. Ba, 109, 110
Homer and Homeric reading, 8, 102, 138n41, 141, 145, 147, 149, 158
horizontal scrolls, 230–31n26
hypomnemata, 233, 234

Ibn Ezra, 48n47, 238n46, 240, 241
Ibn Nuh, 228n23
ibn Tibbon, Samuel, 236
icons/relics/reliquaries, sacred texts as, 12–13. *See also* Torah scrolls
ijaza, 165
Iliad. See Homer and Homeric reading
inaccurate, faulty, and mistaken readings, 103–4
informational reading: alienation of rabbinic oral scholasticism from, 108; appearance of texts with linguistic components necessary for, 229n25; dangerousness of process of, 99–100, 107–12; defined, 108, 120; liturgical performance/ritual reading versus, 3, 120; in modern literacy education, 133–34
inks used to produce Torah scrolls, 64, 201, 204, 211
Institutes (Quintilian), 158
interstitial hour, ten sacred objects created in, 46
Irenaeus of Lyons, 31, 49, 52, 54
Islam/Islamic studies, 10, 11–12, 166, 225–26, 233, 234–35, 243

Jeremiah's prophecies, Baruch's rewriting of, 40
Jerusalem, destruction of synagogues and their schools in, 80
Joseph Rosh HaSeder, 243–44
Josephus, 202–3n34
Judah HaNasi, 208
Justin Martyr, 49n51

Karaites and Karaism, 224, 228n23, 238
keri'ah. See recitation-reading
ketiv (written) tradition, 20, 127, 176, 179
killers, biblical texts as. *See* dangerousness of biblical text
King Yannai and Elazar b. Po'irah, 95–97
2 Kings, "Book of the Torah" discovered in, 35, 40
Korean *musogin*, 10

Lactantius, 49n51
Lamentations Rabbah, 40n34, 78n50, 79, 110n30, 125n9, 159n93, 173
lethality of biblical text. *See* dangerousness of biblical text
Leviticus Rabbah, 48n48, 109n27, 110n30, 154–55, 167n15, 173
Libanius, 132n21
limitations on access to written scripture, 18–19, 98–118; careful readers, modern scholarly portrait of rabbis as, 101–3; daily life, restricting bible reading in, 112–18; dangerousness of process of informational reading, 99–100, 107–12; effects/effectiveness of, 100–101; mistaken, faulty, and inaccurate readings, 100, 101–7; in "scenes of reading," 99–100; valorization of scholarship over textual fidelity, 106–7
linguistic differences between consonantal and vocal texts, 181
literacy pedagogies, 131–61
alphabetic literacy (phonetic decoding), 135–36; early Jewish sources on, 138–44; Greek and Latin evidence on, 136–38; in Syriac, 139–40; tongue-twisters, nonsense words, and obscure terms, 136–37, 138, 139, 141
differentiated from modern literacy education, 133–34
first encounters with written text, 144–57; aural notation, 149–50, 156–57; brevity, inaccuracy, and impermanence of texts used, 145–47, 150–52, 155–56; call and response reading, 140, 148–49, 152–54; early Jewish sources on, 150–57; Greek and Latin sources on, 144–50; literary inaccuracy of texts used, 145–46; memorization of oral formulas, 144; preliminary reading and responsive recitation (*praelectio*), 140, 148–49, 152–56
freeing oneself from the text, 157–58; early rabbinic evidence of, 158–61; Greek and Roman sources on, 158

Greek, Latin, Persian, and Syriac communities, using information from, 132–33
as means of accessing rabbinic modes of Bible reading, 120–21
recitation, emphasis on, 134–35
writing versus reading literacy, 143n58
liturgical performance: appearance of texts with linguistic components necessary for informational or sight-reading, 228n24; informational reading versus, 3; Pentateuchal lectionaries, ability to recite, 166; preservation of biblical tradition in, 180; recitation-reading as, 125–30; translations/translators, 126–27, 191

Macrobius, 148
"magic," Torah scrolls viewed as, 194n3, 202, 207, 208n43, 209, 210
manuscripts, papyri, Torah scrolls, and ostraca: CM Add. MS 37516, 145n60; Jerusalem Yad Harav Herzog MS of mTaʿanit, 217n73; London MS of mTaʿanit, 217n73; Moses ben Asher codex, 229n24; MS Bodl. Heb a 3.30, 145n60; MS Paris 671, 87n64; MS Schocken-Jerusalem 3654, 84n56, 85nn57–58; Munich 95, 217n73; Munich 140, 217n73; O.Bodl. 1.279, 145–46, 147n68; O.Bodl. Gk. Inscr. 1506, 158, 159; Oxford MS of mTaʿanit, 217n73; P.Ryl. 3.545, 158; P.Col. 8.193, 137; P.Flor. 18.6, 137; P.Gen. 2.53, 137; P.Mil Vogl. 3.120, 138; P.Reinach Inv. 2089, 147, 149; P.Ryl. 3.545, 137, 158, 161; T.Bero inv. AM 13839, 149; TS 6 H9-H21, 228n24; T-S 20.155, 229n25; TS Ar 1a.140, 231n26; TS Ar 53.9, 231n26; T-S AS 74.260, 217n73; T-S AS 78.253, 217n73; T-S AS 93.544, 217n73; T-S F 1(1).47, 217n73; T-S Misc. 24.124, 217n73; Vatican 134, 217n73; Vilna and Pesaro manuscripts, 217n73
Mar Barhadbsabba, 139–40
marriage and divorce, association of second tablets of Moses with, 50–56

masoret/Masoretic text, 5, 20, 104, 165, 176n24, 178, 228–30nn23–26
masters of Spoken Scripture, 167–68
maʿamadot (standing rituals), 130, 166n12
medieval commentary tradition and reading culture, 20–21, 221–45; book (syngramma versus hypomnema), reconception of Bible as, 232–45; Christianity and, 225–26, 235, 242; co-dexification of Judaism and, 226–32; genres, diversity of, 223–24, 235–36; global Jewish shift to systematic, text-based commentary, 222–25; introduction form, use of, 237–40; Islam and, 225–26, 233, 234–35, 243; literacy pedagogies and, 142n56; literature, exegetical treatment of Bible as, 236, 240; multiple authorial and editorial hands in Bible, approaches to, 240–45; origins and development, uncertainty about, 225–32; paper revolution and, 232n27; single-authored compositions, rise of, 223, 233–34, 237, 239, 243; textual openness of, 243–44
Mediterranean reading cultures, 7, 8–9, 22–23, 132–33. See also under literacy pedagogies
R. Meir, 124, 168, 171
Mekhilta, 105
Mekhilta de Rabbi Yishmael, 185–86, 207–8
memorization and recitation, reading by (keriʾah). See recitation-reading
Menahem ibn Saruq, 226
met mitzvah, 211
mezuzah texts, 106, 166n11, 194n3, 205–8
midrash: appearance of texts with linguistic components necessary for informational or sight-reading, 229n25; medieval commentaries and, 224; as source, 2n3. See also specific works
mikra, 20, 104, 122n5, 165, 182, 192, 228n23
minim (sectarians/heretics), biblical books in hands of, 18, 63–68, 73–75
minyan, 216–17

252 INDEX

Mishnah: appearance of texts with linguistic components necessary for sight-reading or informational reading, 229n25; dangerousness of biblical text in, 63, 64n18, 69, 83n52, 86; interstitial hour, on ten sacred objects created in, 46; literary pedagogies in, 142n56; on phylacteries and mezuzah texts, 205, 206; precedence over Bible reading, 114; on rabbinic literacy, 143n58; on recitation-reading (keri'ah), 124, 125–30; on Shema recitation outside of canonical hours, 127n14; on sotah scrolls, 203, 204, 205; as source, 2n3; on Third Torah, 177n27, 177n29; on Torah scrolls, 201n30, 217–18

mishneh hatorah, 32, 35
mistaken, faulty, and inaccurate readings, 103–4
Mosaic tablets. See tablets of Moses, first and second versions of
Moshe HaDarshan, 226
al-Muqammas, Daud, 227n23

R. Nahman, 207
R. Nehemiah, 113
Nero (Roman emperor), 155–56
al-Nihawendi, Benjamin, 227n23
[not] reading the bible. See written biblical text, early rabbinic relationship to

Odyssey. See Homer and Homeric reading
Oklah ve-Oklah, 227n23
ontologically textual nature of Pentateuch, 14
Oral Torah: binary reading of Written Torah and, 15–16, 164–65; dangerousness of preferring written text to, 72–73, 96; informational reading, alienation of rabbinic oral scholasticism from, 108; motives of rabbinic authorities for circumscribing Written Torah and, 59–60; targums as part of, 115n34; Third (spoken) Torah existing between Written

Torah and, 3, 19, 20, 164–65 (See also Third (spoken) Torah); triple loss and re-establishment of Torah, stories about, 41; vocabulary of, applied to Third Torah, 172–74, 183
ostraca. See manuscripts, papyri, Torah scrolls, and ostraca

paleo-Hebrew, 36, 38–39
Palestinian Talmud: daily life, restricting bible reading in, 114–15; dangerousness of biblical texts in, 69n31, 69n33, 72, 78–83, 86n61; Ezran authorship tradition in, 35, 36–38; informational reading, on dangerousness of, 107–12; literary pedagogies in, 151nn78–79, 153, 154; marriage contracts, "Palestinian formula" for, 50n53; mistaken, faulty, and inaccurate readings in, 105–6; on paleographic/linguistic evidence of historical variation, 39; on phylacteries and mezuzah texts, 208; R. Hiyya in, 43; on rabbinic literacy, 143n58; on recitation-reading (keri'ah), 123, 125n9, 127n13, 128, 130n17; on sotah scrolls, 203, 204, 205; as source, 2n3; tablets of Moses, on first and second versions of, 45, 47, 48; on Third Torah, 167n15, 168–70, 171n19, 173, 178–81; on Torah scrolls, 201nn28–30, 208, 216n72
paper revolution, 232n27, 233–34
R. Pappos b. Yehudah, 87–89
papyri. See manuscripts, papyri, Torah scrolls, and ostraca
parchment for Torah scrolls, 43, 46, 196, 201, 204, 211–12
peshat commentary, 223
Pesikta de Rav Kahana, 174n23
Petronius, 144n59
Philo of Alexandria, 177n28, 202–3n34
phonetic reading (reading out loud), 111n33, 120, 122n5
phylactery texts, 79, 80, 81, 166n11, 194n3, 205–8
physical Torah scrolls. See Torah scrolls

INDEX   253

Pirka de-Rabbenu ha-Kadosh, 231n26

Pirke de Rabbi Eliezer, 46n45, 47n46, 216–17

piyyut, 163, 240

Porphyry of Tyre, 30–31

practical literacy, 120

praelectio, 140, 148, 149, 154

priestly body, Torah scroll analogized to, 212

problem, biblical text experienced as, 2, 17–19, 221

Prometheus Unbound (Aeschylus), 134

proto-Masoretic text, emergence of, 5

purity practices in early rabbinic Judaism, 49, 199, 203, 206

qere (read) tradition, 20, 176, 179, 180

al-Qirqisani, Ya'qub, 35, 242–43

Quintilian, 138, 148n71, 158

al-Qumisi, Daniel, 227n23

Qur'an. *See* Islam/Islamic studies

rabbinic modes of Bible reading, 19, 119–62. *See also* literacy pedagogies; recitation-reading

rain, Torah scroll in communal prayer for, 217–18

Rashbam, 236, 242

(pseudo-)Rashban, 236

Rashi, 142n56, 224–25n8, 225–26, 225n14, 235–36, 238–39

reading the bible. *See* informational reading; rabbinic modes of Bible reading; written biblical text, early rabbinic relationship to

recitation-reading (*keri'ah*), 121–30; access to texts provided by, 122–23; defined, 120; lectionary readings, 129–30; as liturgical performance, 125–30; meaning applied to rather than derived from written text in, 122, 130; memorization as basis for, 119, 122; oral "text," derivation from, 125; of Shema, 127–29; as standard/common mode of rabbinic reading, 119, 121–22,

130; text [in]dependence of, 123–29; unavailability of written text, despite, 126, 128, 129–30; voiced nature of, 120, 121–22n5

relics/reliquaries/icons, sacred texts as, 12–13. *See also* Torah scrolls

restricted access. *See* limitations on access to written scripture

Reuel of Byzantium, 226, 241

"Risala" (Yehudah ibn Quraish), 227n23

ritual reading, 3, 119, 120. *See also* liturgical performance; recitation-reading

Roman and Hellenistic reading cultures, 7, 8–9, 22–23, 132–33. *See also under* literacy pedagogies

rotuli, 231n26

Ruth Rabbah, 190–91

Saadiah Gaon, 227n23, 239–40

sacrifice/slavery, association of second Mosaic tablets with, 50, 51, 56–57

Salmon ben Yeroham, 238

Samaritans: Ezra, traditions about, 30n13; personification of scripture by, 198

Saturnalia (Macrobius), 148

"scenes of reading," 99–100

scientific reading, 223

Second Temple Judaism, 5–9, 59–60, 99–100, 164, 176n24, 214n64, 215n66

sectarians. *See* heretics/heresy

semiotic transduction, 196

serugin manuscripts, 230n26

sex/sexuality. *See* gender/sexuality

Shabbat, bans on reading on, 114, 160, 173

Shaphan (in 2 Kings), 40

She'iltot of R. Ahai, 231n26

Shema, recitation-reading (*keri'ah*) of, 127–29

Rabban Shimon ben Gamliel, 80, 114, 160, 205

shonim, 173–74

shonin, 173

Sifra Behukotai, 53

Sifra Tazria, 179

254 INDEX

Sifre Deuteronomy, 40, 44, 46n45, 68, 78, 125n10, 167n15, 184–85, 187, 201n28

Sifre Numbers, 63–66, 204

Sikhism, 195–96

silent reading/reading aloud, 111n33, 120, 122n5

Sinai, revelation at: escape of original divine revelation from written form, 186–89; relationship of Third Torah to, 19–192. *See also* tablets of Moses, first and second versions of

slavery/sacrifice, association of second Mosaic tablets with, 50, 51, 56–57

smell, original divine revelation associated with, 182–83, 190

Soferim, 156–57

Song of Songs Rabbah, 41–42, 45, 185, 186, 187, 189–90

sotah ritual, 64, 67, 68–69, 202–5, 219

South and East Asian scriptures, 10–11, 195–96, 198

spoken Torah. *See* Third (spoken) Torah

supersessionism, 48–49, 52, 54, 56, 65n22

syngrammata, 233

tablets of Moses, first and second versions of, 44–57; in ark of the covenant, 82; Christian supersessionist accounts of, 48–49, 52, 54, 56; limited and deficient nature of second tablets, 48; marriage and divorce, association of second tablets with, 50–56; miraculous product, first tablet viewed as, 45–48, 185; slavery/sacrifice, association of second tablets with, 50, 51, 56–57; Third Torah and, 165, 185–86

tahrif accusations, 243

Tanhuma, 115–16, 182n35, 187–88, 190

Tannaitic tradition, dangerousness of biblical text in, 63–75. *See also under* dangerousness of biblical text

R. Tarfon, 66, 67, 172

targums: daily life, restricting bible reading in, 115–17; deviations between recited for-

mula and written text, rabbinic conceptualization of, 180–81; with linguistic components necessary for informational or sight-reading, 229n25; in literary pedagogies, 161; as part of Oral Torah, 115n34; on phylacteries and mezuzah texts, 207; tablets of Moses, on first and second versions of, 47n46; on unreliability of written scripture, 33–34, 47n46

taste, original divine revelation associated with, 190–91

tefillin. *See* phylactery texts

tetragrammaton, 177, 180

Third (spoken) Torah, 3–4, 19–20, 163–92; deviations between recited formula and written text, 176–79; emergence of, 165–75, 182; escape of original divine revelation from written form, 186–89; as independent witness to Biblical revelation, 175–82; interstices of Oral and Written Torah, existing between, 3, 19, 20, 164–65; linguistic difference from written text, 181; masters of Spoken Scripture, 167–68; preservation of original divine revelation in, 189–92; rabbinic conceptualization of differences between written text and, 179–82; recreation of written transcript from, 170–72; Sinai, relationship to revelation at, 19–192; temptation to forgo reference to written transcript, 168–70; vocabulary of Oral Torah applied to, 172–74, 183

Tibetan "paper bards," 124–25n8

Torah scrolls, 3–4, 20–21, 193–220; bodily humiliation/shame in exposure of, 215, 218–19; as body, 195–200, 211–20; burning of martyrs wrapped in, 75–78, 80; closed/silenced/illegible books as most powerful, 195, 202–10; deceased body of *met mitzvah,* used to wrap, 211; iconic or ritual power of, 194–95, 198; inappropriate scribal form/scribe invalidating, for ritual use, 200–202; inappropriate scribe invalidating, for ritual use, 201–2; inks

used to produce, 64, 201, 204, 211; as
"magic," 194n3, 202, 207, 208n43, 209,
210; message/text, sacredness not derived from, 200–202; *minyan*, serving as
member of, 216–17; parchment for, 43,
46, 196, 201, 204, 211–12; priestly body,
analogy to, 212; rain, in communal prayer
for, 217–18; scarcity of, 121; *sotah* ritual
(for wife accused of adultery), use of
biblical text in, 202–5, 219; woman, as
body of, 212–16, 219. *See also* manuscripts, papyri, Torah scrolls, and ostraca, *for specific scrolls*
Tosefta: daily life, restricting bible reading
in, 116–17; dangerousness of biblical texts
in, 63, 64n19, 65–67, 69–72, 73–75, 83n53;
Ezran authorship tradition in, 32–36; Hillel's saving of biblical text in, 41–42; literary pedagogies in, 150, 159; on recitation-
reading (*keri'ah*), 124, 128–29, 130n18; on
sotah scrolls, 203; as source, 2n3; tablets
of Moses, on first and second versions of,
50–57; on Third Torah, 169, 171n19, 172,
177; on Torah scrolls, 201n32, 208, 212–13
tractate Semahot, 75–78, 86
translations: Aquila's translation of Kings,
230n26; biblical texts combined with,
229n25; liturgical translations/transla-
tors, 126–27, 191. *See also* targums
triple loss and reestablishment of Torah,
40–44

unreliability of written scripture, 17, 26–58;
Baruch's rewriting of Jeremiah's prophecies, 40; corruption, revision attributed
to, 34–35; Ezran authorship, early Jewish
traditions about, 17, 28, 29–39, 40, 41; historical contingency of received text, early
rabbinic recognition of, 26–29; 2 Kings,
"Book of the Torah" discovered in, 35,
40; *mishneh hatorah*, 32, 35; paleo-
graphic/linguistic evidence of historical
variation and, 39; triple loss and reestablishment of Torah, rabbinic accounts of,

40–44. *See also* tablets of Moses, first and
second versions of

Vespasian (Roman emperor), 80
Virgil, 9, 148

women. *See* gender/sexuality
writing versus reading literacy, 143n58
written biblical text, early rabbinic relationship to, 1–25; binary reading of Written and Oral Torah, 15–16, 164–65; canonical text, emergence of, 4, 6–8;
centrality of Bible to Jewish thought, 3,
19–21, 222 (*See also* rabbinic modes of
Bible reading; Third (spoken) Torah;
Torah scrolls); comparative religious
studies of oralized scripture, 9–13; definition of early/classical rabbinic, 2n3;
evolving scholarly models of, 5–8; Hellenistic and Roman Mediterranean
reading cultures and, 7, 8–9, 22–23, 132–
33 (*See also under* literacy pedagogies);
medieval commentary tradition and,
20–21, 221–45 (*See also* medieval commentary tradition and reading culture);
methodology of study, 21–25; motives of
rabbinic authorities for circumscribing,
59–60; myth versus reality of, 1–4, 17,
26; problem, biblical text experienced
as, 2, 17–19, 221 (*See also* dangerousness
of biblical texts; limitations on access to
written scripture; unreliability of written scripture); rabbinic tradition, scholarly focus on, 13–17; Third (spoken)
Torah existing between Oral and Written Torah, 3, 19, 20, 164–65 (*See also*
Third (spoken) Torah)

Yannai, 163
Yefet b. 'Eli, 224n8, 244
R. Yehoshua, 105, 159
R. Yehoshua b. Levi, 109
R. Yehuda b. Roetz, 178
R. Yehudah, 151

INDEX

Yehudah ibn Quraish, 227n23
R. Yishmael, 69–73
R. Yishmael b. Elisha, 159
R. Yishmael b. Yose, 111, 168
R. Yohanan b. Nazif, 116, 117
Rabban Yohanan b. Zakkai, 50, 54

R. Yose b. Kisma, 84–89
Yosef bar R. Nissan of Neve Kiryatayim, 228n24

zahir exegesis, 223
R. Zeira, 154, 218

GPSR Authorized Representative: Easy Access System Europe - Mustamäe tee
50, 10621 Tallinn, Estonia, gpsr.requests@easproject.com

www.ingramcontent.com/pod-product-compliance
Lightning Source LLC
Jackson TN
JSHW020223080825
88971JS00004B/9